MIMEOGRAPH

Facets of the Enlightenment

Facets of the Enlightenment

Studies in English Literature and Its Contexts

by

Bertrand Harris Bronson

•

University of California Press
Berkeley and Los Angeles 1968

University of California Press
Berkeley and Los Angeles, California

Cambridge University Press
London, England

Copyright © 1968, by
The Regents of the University of California
Library of Congress Catalog Card Number: 68-56074
Printed in the United States of America

The essays collected in this volume, here listed in order of first appearance, are reprinted with the permission of the original publishers. "The Beggar's Opera," from *Studies in the Comic*, University of California Publications in English, Vol. 8 (1941). "Walking Stewart," from *Essays and Studies*, University of California Publications in English, Vol. 14 (1943). "Thomas Chatterton," from *The Age of Johnson: Essays Presented to Chauncey Brewster Tinker* (Yale University Press, 1949); to which has been added "Chattertoniana," from *Modern Language Quarterly*, XI (1950). "Some Aspects of Music and Literature in the Eighteenth Century," from *Music and Literature in England in the Seventeenth and Eighteenth Centuries*, Clark Memorial Library of the University of California at Los Angeles (1953). "The Pre-Romantic or Post-Augustan Mode," from *ELH*, Vol. 20, No. 1 (1953). "Samuel Johnson and James Boswell," from *Major British Writers*, Vol. I, ed. G. B. Harrison (copyright, 1954, © 1959, by Harcourt, Brace & World, Inc.). "Printing as an Index of Taste in Eighteenth-Century England," from the Bulletin of the New York Public Library (August-September 1958). "Personification Reconsidered," from *New Light on Dr. Johnson*, ed. F. W. Hilles (Yale University Press, 1959). "A Sense of the Past: The Percy Correspondence," from *Sewanee Review*, Vol. 67, No. 1 (copyright © 1959 by the University of the South); to which have been added excerpts from a review of *The Correspondence of Thomas Percy & George Paton* in *Philological Quarterly*, XLI (July 1962). "The True Proportions of Gay's *Acis and Galatea*," from *PMLA*, LXXX (1965). "On a Special Decorum in Gray's *Elegy*," from *From Sensibility to Romanticism: Essays Presented to Frederick A. Pottle*, eds. F. W. Hilles and H. Bloom (copyright © 1965 by Oxford University Press, Inc.). "When Was Neoclassicism?," from *Studies in Criticism and Aesthetics, 1660-1800: Essays in Honor of Samuel Holt Monk*, eds. H. Anderson and J. S. Shea (University of Minnesota Press, 1967). "Johnson's Shakespeare" first appeared as the Introduction to *Johnson on Shakespeare*, ed. A. Sherbo (Yale University Press, 1968). "Strange Relations: The Author and His Audience" first appeared as "The Writer" in *Man Versus Society in Eighteenth-Century Britain*, ed. J. L. Clifford (Cambridge University Press, 1968).

Preface

No one likely to open this book needs to be persuaded of the extraordinary appeal of the English culture in the eighteenth century. More than most historical epochs, this one excites not only interest but, beyond that, an affectionate response of a personal kind not likely to be disputed by any who have made more than a passing acquaintance with it. To be sure, it has had, and no doubt still has, enemies and hostile critics; and its friends have too often laid themselves open to censure for over-sentimentality. Nevertheless, the essays here gathered were not written to defend it, but take for granted a general enjoyment of the age; and, along with deserved disapprobation of its shortcomings, an unwillingness to disparage its virtues.

The age was, as we now recognize, extraordinarily complex; far from monolithic, and full of self-contradictions, change, and violent contrast. Its spokesmen were notably individuated, often sharply antagonistic, endowed with a high degree of articulate energy, which they cultivated assiduously in many directions, with abundant variety.

To grow even moderately familiar with activity so multifarious and diverse, with a surviving record so ample and rich, bespeaks the zealous devotion of a lifetime. Such an effort, however delightful, can never be realized. But those whose professional duty coincides with their pleasure in the same pursuit may take modest satisfaction in their piecemeal advances, and need not charge their scattered endeavors with a weight of guilt. The essays collected herein, written during three decades, are independent of one another, and do not pretend to a larger unity as parts of a sustained argument. Confined to a single century, and limited to a space set by external conditions, each addresses itself to a topic, large or small, about which the author had more than an idle curiosity, and each aims only at self-consistency in its own kind. Most of them were composed to be read on specific occasions.

This writer's serious concern with the eighteenth century began, I suppose, in the classroom, whether as student or teacher. It was his good fortune, over many years, to give a course in the Age of Johnson, and in so doing he followed his private bent by trying to encircle the required readings with a larger frame of reference than was demanded by close analysis and interpretation of the text assigned for study. This tendency led naturally to the consideration of social history, currents of thought and emotional trends, authors' backgrounds, ephemeral fashions and changing tastes; and especially to what was going on in forms of artistic expression other than literature and the literary genres. The habit of taking comparative views forces on one's attention the unevenness, relatively, in the rate of advance between the arts—how far out of step with one another they were, and how narrow and inadequate are our customary literary labels as denotative terms in a larger context. Thus are planted the seeds of a kind of impatience with the formalized, simplistic outlines of cultural history generated by our over-specialization; and, among other things, of a suspicion that in a retrospective view like ours the disappearance of the classical ideal is ordinarily put a good deal too early. Notions of this kind—if such they be—find expression in more than one of these essays, particularly the first, the fifth, and the last.

None of these papers, of course, was calculated for the classroom, though they may have been started, or found an echo, in that ambience. Some of them trace the development of a trend, some focus upon a particular author, some concentrate upon an individual work. Over all, the writer's position, I trust, is uncommitted to a *parti pris;* but is sympathetic, fundamentally, to the moral and intellectual attitude best typified, whatever the superficial contradictions, by the large humanity of Samuel Johnson: a positive and dynamic classicism.

B.H.B.

Contents

1. When Was Neoclassicism?   1
2. Who Now Reads Prior?   26
3. The True Proportions of Gay's Acis and Galatea   45
4. The Beggar's Opera   60
5. Some Aspects of Music and Literature   91
6. Personification Reconsidered   119
7. On a Special Decorum in Gray's Elegy   153
8. The Pre-Romantic or Post-Augustan Mode   159
9. A Sense of the Past: The Percy Correspondence   173
10. Thomas Chatterton   187
11. Samuel Johnson and James Boswell   210
12. Johnson's Shakespeare   241
13. Walking Stewart   266
14. Strange Relations: The Author and His Audience   298
15. Printing as an Index of Taste   326

When Was Neoclassicism?

CHAMBERS, in his provocative book *The History of Taste*, pointed out that when the greatest monuments of classic art—the Parthenon, the Athena Parthenos, and other glories of Periclean Athens—came into being, no appreciation of these master-pieces was expressed in writing. No literary evidence survives to show that the aesthetic consciousness of that golden day had reached a level more sophisticated than that of admiring "gold-and-glitter." [1] Art, to be sure, had value, but it was prized for irrelevant reasons, reasons potentially inimical to a free development of the artistic impulse. The reasons were moral, idealistic, or civil: con-cerned, that is, with useful instruction, or regulative norms, or polity. Art was always to serve some ulterior, public purpose. The artist was of little account or interest in himself but the impersonal object in view was important. Thus the name of Ictinus and his part in designing the Parthenon were only of local and immediate concern and were soon forgotten. Pericles could propose divesting the Athena Parthenos of her gold, should the city need the money. The vandalism of such an act he ignores, as he ignores the name of the sculptor, Phidias, his friend. But piety, he allows, would of course require restitution to the goddess. Likewise Herodotus, a world traveler exactly contemporary, estimates the weight of the gold he has seen and carefully inquired about, in famous temples and statues, but says nothing about the aesthetic properties—unless mere size be such—of the works he describes. Thus, for instance: "there was in this temple the figure of a man, twelve cubits high,

[1] Frank P. Chambers, *The History of Taste* (1932), pp. 273 ff.

I

entirely of solid gold." Or again, Thucydides, on any question of beauty, is equally noncommittal.

Plato, we remember, judges art as the excellence of a *copy* thrice removed from the original, and justifies it only so far as it instructs. Aristotle, in the *Poetics*, also bases the arts on imitation, and our pleasure in them in recognition—that is, of the object represented, whether actual, probable, or ideal ("such as it was or is, such as it is supposed, or such as it ought to be").[2] Led by the Sophists, eventually we approach an art appreciation loosened from the tether of pedagogy and religion, and flowing toward the Hellenistic Renaissance and the consequent Alexandrian efflorescence of patron, collector, connoisseur, antiquary, and dilettante—*id genus omne*. In due course, Rome abandons her earlier puritanic asceticism, is drawn into the Hellenistic current, and imbibes culture and corruption from the vanquished. By the time of Augustus, Rome has little more to learn, though the process continues "as streams roll down, enlarging as they flow."

Classicism, then, as a conscious theory of art, as doctrine defensible and defended, was, in the ancient world, Hellenistic, not Hellenic. May we not proceed to hazard the generalization that there can hardly be such a phenomenon as a primary, original classicism? For by the time we meet conscious formulations of aesthetic principle, it is always Neoclassicism that we confront. The doctrinal motivation is always traditional, invoking established norms, and to these the artist's individuality is subservient. Subservient, but not servile nor suppressed by them—rather, inspired—for the attitude is one of worshipful acceptance. Tradition is Law, in fullest realization of which lies the artist's supreme satisfaction. When this frame of mind has become self-conscious and deliberate, with allegiance acknowledged, we are in the presence of Neoclassicism.

Thus, the Augustan classicism of the first century B.C. was an integral part of the Hellenistic cultural renaissance: it was a neoclassical movement, consciously recreative of older and purer models. Terence remembered Menander, Catullus Sappho, Vergil Homer and Theocritus. Similarly, of course, the Italian Renaissance is a gradual recovery of the values and ideals of antiquity. Brunelleschi, Alberti, Vignola, Palladio, Lomazzo were neoclas-

[2] *Poetics* 1406b 10.

sicists in the fullest sense, votaries of ancient order and system, profound students of the Vitruvian precepts. In the following century, the learned genius of Poussin, the encyclopedic labors of Junius, and the poetical treatise of Dufresnoy led to the crystallization of the classical code by the French Academy, establishing the example of the Ancients as "one clear, unchanging, universal light." Under these auspices, English Neoclassicism is launched; and here begins *our* more particular field of inquiry.

THE ELDER of us were bred up in the critical conviction that the eighteenth century was one century we needn't worry about: we knew precisely where it stood, and what it stood for. It was fixed in its appointed place, and there it would always be when we cared to look again. We understood its values, and they bored us. The interesting thing was to see how the human spirit struggled out of that straitjacket into new life. As students of English literature, we knew that its tenets had reached their probably ultimate exemplification in the work of Pope, and that what followed in his track was only feebler and more arid imitation, while the buds of fresh romantic promise were beginning here and there to peep out timidly. That this view, or something like it, is still current is suggested by a front-page article on Christopher Smart in the *Times Literary Supplement*, entitled "Lucky Kit?" "To us," we read, "Smart seems one of the first rebels against the rational behaviour and rationalist thought which have come down like a bad debt from his century to ours." [3] One might have thought that a statute of limitation could ere now have been invoked in such a case.

However the debt may lie, certain it is that that century no longer looks so placid as formerly, whether because we have done more reading, or because events of recent decades have affected our eyesight, or because the newer telescopic lenses have altered the range of visibility and brought things into sharper focus. More seems to have been going on formerly than we had suspected. The painstaking and systematic research of our minute topographers has left seemingly few corners of the eighteenth-century terrain unscrutinized. The net result of this turning over of all such reading as was never read—well, hardly ever—has been to reveal a

[3] *Times Literary Supplement*, December 29, 1961, p. 921.

region of the most baffling complexity and self-contradiction, in which can be found almost anything we choose to seek. Wherever we pause, we are bewildered by the diversity that surrounds us: not alone in the conflict of opinion but shot through the very texture of every considerable author's or artist's work. Of even the chief spokesmen this is probably true. Pope is no exception. The difficulty of making a consistent pattern of Johnson's thinking is notorious. Yet when we look at the authoritative surveys of critical historians, such is not the impression we receive. Their momentum bears us stoutly forward, and at any point they tell us where we are, how many miles we have traveled, how far we have still to go. Best safety lies perhaps in maintaining our speed; but there might be something deceptive in this sense of undeniable progress: "The rough road then, returning in a round,/Mock'd our impatient steps, for all was fairy ground."

All the authoritative guides tell us—and we believe them, do we not?—that the road sets out from "Neoclassicism" and in due course arrives at "Romanticism," taking roughly a century to cover the distance. As we trace it, the landscape visibly alters: it grows less cultivated, more picturesque, wilder. The vegetation is ranker, the hills are higher and more precipitous; the road begins to wind, first in graceful curves (the "line of beauty"); then, adapting itself to the ruggeder country, skirting torrents overhung with jagged rock and blasted old trees, becomes ever more irregular and full of surprises. The wayfarer is at first likely to be struck with solemn awe; later, he finds himself almost breathless and gasping with fearful joy; and at last, in self-surrender, now with streaming eyes, now with shouts of apolaustic abandon, identifies himself with the spirit of what he beholds—or rather, perhaps, identifies what he beholds with his own exalted and pathetic state.

But we have been snatched aloft on the wings of metaphor. Let us decline from the resulting over-simplification and try to regain our composure. And first, returning to Neoclassicism, let us acknowledge that, if regarded as a distinct phase of Art, separate in time and visible effects, in England it never really existed. Or, if it ever took palpable shape, that was only in the pages of certain bloodless theorists, whose formulations, when themselves regarded as efforts of the imagination or works of art, are the sole extant examples of its whole-hearted enforcement. Conceptually, it exists as a theoretical terminus that was not and could not be reached in practice, a *reductio ad absurdum* of valid and defensible ideals.

We observed that Classicism, wherever it achieves self-consciousness, in works of art or in underlying doctrine, is always retrospective and therefore essentially neoclassical. Now we have declared that in actual fact a truly neoclassical work of art, as the term is usually employed, was never created in England. The solution of this apparent contradiction is that for practical purposes the troublesome term Neoclassicism is otiose and expendable. It pretends to a distinction without a difference, for the difference is only in degree, not in kind; while the instances of it are hypothetical. The simple term Classicism, then, with occasional inflections, will answer all our needs, and the tautological *neo-* may be dismissed unlamented.

We know pretty clearly what we mean by Classicism, and therefore need not be over-elaborate in definition. Briefly to recapitulate: Man, being endowed with ratiocination, has as his birthright the key to proper conduct. What he does ought to be in conformity with the best use of the faculty that so far as he can tell distinguishes him from all other living things. If he so employs it, he may arrive at reasonable inferences about his relation to the universe, and his limitations; about his responsibilities and obligations to himself and to society—"Placed on this isthmus of a middle state." He ought thereby to be led to the recognition of those ideals of truth, morality, order, harmony, which he shares with his fellow man.

In Art, the classical ideals follow from these premises. All the arts—the nobler ones especially—imitate nature, in the sense that they search for a norm, or an ideal, that shall perfectly fulfill and express the natural capabilities or potentialities of the entities, or class of entities, represented: not for the worse but for the essentially typical, or for the better. Analysis has ranked the categories and genres from high to low, has differentiated their characteristic excellences and shown their special objectives. It has noted the appeal of simplicity, the charm of variety within perspicuous unity, the desirability of balance and proportion. And it has discerned a large number of proprieties great and small which can be drawn up and codified at will under the general head of

Decorum. The latter are what provide the Dick Minims with their chief exercise and they are, to be sure, the readiest subjects for discussion and debate.

From the ancient classical world we have by a miracle of good fortune inherited a body of literature in many kinds, a large amount of sculpture and sufficient remains of architecture to serve as enduring models of such shining merit that they can hardly be surpassed. They establish the moral and rationally ideal bases of art, teach virtue, and provide inexhaustible illustration of aesthetic beauty and truth . . . So much may suffice by way of summary.

WHATEVER date may be chosen to mark the beginning of the new age of classicism, in England the emotional state of the last decades of the seventeenth century, like the political situation, is in equilibrium highly precarious. Everywhere the dominant impression is one of instability and insecurity, of which the Stuarts in their brilliant undependability are almost the paradigm. A music characteristically of poignant, nostalgic sweetness, frequent change of tempo, brevity of movement. An architecture eclectic and experimental in its major examples, inclining to the theatrical and grandiloquent. A poetry incapable of broad definition, containing Milton, Butler, Marvell, the pyrrhonism of Rochester, the sweep of Dryden: in over-all summary uncommitted and capable of anything from the sublime to the obscene. Classic control is an ideal then but seldom exemplified and, in a society standing in need of the strong purgatives of Swift's satire, most often perceptible only through a screen of negative images. On the heels of the brittle artificiality of Restoration comedy, and subsiding from the stratosphere of Dryden's heroic drama, the tumultuous rant of Nat Lee, the passionate distresses of Southerne, and the pathos of Otway, the last decade of the century sees the rise of sentimental comedy and the stage is committed to the new era with irresistible parting tenderness, tears of welcome, abundance of fine feeling and flown phrasing. "'Tis well an old age is out, And time to begin a new." The air is heavy with *un*restrained emotion. John Dennis, the foremost dramatic critic of the new decade, and no contemptible judge when all is said, puts Otway next to Euripides for "a

Faculty in touching the softer Passion"[4]—a rating which will be repeated when, much later, Joseph Warton exalts him among "sublime and pathetic poets."[5]

Sublimity is constantly in the thought of Dennis and his contemporaries, made vividly aware of Longinus by Boileau. With consequent editions, translations, and commentaries arriving post with post, Longinus in the front of the eighteenth century is a name to conjure with, in the defense of irregular genius and unbounded Nature. The critics invoke him with a fervor not often accorded the tame Quintilian, who "the justest rules and clearest method joined." The six lines devoted to Longinus in that handbook of Augustan orthodoxy, Pope's *Essay*, are a timely corrective of too rigid notions of that school:

> Thee, bold Longinus! all the Nine inspire,
> And bless their Critic with a Poet's *Fire*.
> An *ardent* Judge, who *zealous* in his trust,
> With *warmth* gives sentence, yet is always just;
> Whose own example strengthens all his laws;
> And is himself that great Sublime he draws.
>
> (ll. 675–680)

Pegasus spurns the common track, takes a nearer way, and all his end at once attains. Here Pope cites an interesting analogy:

> In prospects [i.e., natural scenery] thus,
>   some objects please our eyes,
> Which out of nature's common order rise,
> The shapeless rock, or hanging precipice.
> Great Wits sometimes may gloriously offend,
> And rise to faults *true* Critics dare not mend.
>
> (ll. 156–160)[6]

A quarter of a century earlier, Dennis, crossing the Alps, called Longinus to mind. Walking, he says, "upon the very brink . . . of Destruction," he was moved to introspection:

---

[4] "Remarks upon Mr. Pope's Translation of Homer" (1717), *Critical Works*, ed. Edward Niles Hooker (1943), II, 121.

[5] Joseph Warton, *An Essay on the Genius and Writings of Pope* (1756), I, dedication. Otway was demoted in later editions.

[6] Ed. Warburton, 1744. Earlier editions place the last couplet at ll. 152–153; Warburton returned to that order in 1764.

. . . all this produc'd . . . in me . . . a delightful Horrour, a terrible
Joy, and at the same time, that I was infinitely pleas'd, I trembled . . .
Then we may well say of her [Nature] what some affirm of great Wits,
that her careless, irregular and boldest Strokes are most admirable. For
the Alpes are works which she seems to have design'd, and executed
too in Fury. Yet she moves us less, where she studies to please us more.[7]

This passage, penned in the very year when Pope was born, and
published in 1693, must surely have lain in the poet's mind, to
produce the same comparison between "great wits" and wild Nature at the opportune moment. But the coincidence failed to
sweeten the personal relations of the two men.

Along with frank emotional outbursts, preoccupation with the
appearance of Nature is one of the traditional signals, as all know
who gladly teach and all who docilely learn, of the rising tide of
Romanticism. Yet here at the outset of the century, in the very
Citadel of the Rules, we observe these full-fledged extravagancies.
Loving description of a gentler Nature fills early pages of Pope,
in the 1704 half of *Windsor Forest,* in the *Pastorals*—recall the
extremes of empathetic trees and blushing flowers: these springing
under the footfall of beauty, those crowding into a shade. Pathetic
tenderness, heightening to overwhelming passion, suffuses the
Elegy and the amazing *Eloisa to Abelard.* And later, of course,
praise of Nature and of God in Nature finds supreme expression
in the first Epistle of the *Essay on Man.* Already, however, by
the date of the latter, Thomson had published the most extended
paean to Nature in all her moods that his century, or probably any
century, was to see in verse. But, as we shall increasingly observe,
it is significant of a trend that, as the years passed, Thomson tried
to intellectualize his spontaneous overflow of powerful emotion by
injecting more and more sociological, philosophic, politico-eco-
nomic, and other filler: "untuning the sky," to borrow a phrase
from an elder poet, by cerebration.

DURING THESE same decades external Nature was receiving tribute
in other art forms as well as in poetry. By this time, a great tonal
poet, Handel, had written work that both in quantity and quality
sets him high among those artists of all time who have made Nature
an important part of their subject matter. I do not speak meta-

[7] *Miscellanies in Verse and Prose* (1693), ed. Edward Niles Hooker, II, 380–381.

phorically but with literal truth. To illustrate, an example may be cited, convenient because brief and universally familiar, though all but unrecognized in such a connection. In the opera *Serse*, there is an aria mistakenly called the "Largo from *Xerxes*," or more popularly, "Handel's Largo." As we know, Handel was a dramatic composer, which means that his creative imagination went hand in hand with textual idea. This is not to say that the process of translating consisted of choosing particular notes to represent named objects—though, in its place, he did not disdain particular imitation of that kind. His genius, however, lay in finding musical equivalents for moods, emotions, scenes coming to him in verbal form. Thus, in the aria mentioned, he is calling up the musical image of a tree: a tree which has grown with the seasons, in the favoring sun and air, and has put forth spreading branches that provide a cool, rustling delight in which to respire and be thankful, "Annihilating all that's made/To a green thought in a green shade." The verbal statement is perfectly explicit about this:

Recitative: Fair, soft, leafy branches of my belovèd sycamore, for you may fate shine brightly. Let thunder, lightning, and storm never outrage your precious peace, nor desecrate you with violence.

Larghetto (not *Largo*): Never gave tree a dearer, sweeter, more lovely shade. (Ombra mai fù di vegetabile cara ed amabile soave più.)

The world, of course, has taken that larghetto to its heart for a talisman against mischance in all weathers. But when we return to the stated literal meaning, could (we ask) that total experience, sensuous, sensible, spiritual, be more satisfyingly evoked?

Nature in Handel's music is a topic large enough for extended study. *L'Allegro ed Il Penseroso*, for example, contains abundant responses, from the obvious sound effects of the chirping cricket, the fluting bird song, the ringing round of the merry bells, and the "bellman's drowsy charm," to the subtle impressionism of the "whisp'ring winds soon lull[ing] asleep" in a D-minor cadence hushed with twilight, and the rising moon evoked by a voice-line that climbs slowly for an octave and a half. Our total sense of the work, to quote Winton Dean, "is not a matter of pictorial embellishment, but of a creative sympathy transfusing the entire score, a sympathy with English life and the English scene which is perhaps the profoundest tribute Handel ever paid to the land of his

adoption."[8] But on the larger subject of Handel's intense suscep-
tibility to nature's more permanent features, Dean declares, with
a just disregard of irrelevant temporal considerations: "There is
something Wordsworthian in Handel's view of nature, and a
strong element of Hellenic pantheism; a consciousness of the
immanence of some superhuman power, aloof yet omnipresent,
is often combined with a sense of mystery and awe."[9]

To understand Handel's music as description inevitably requires
a little concentrated study. Our contemporary notions of the true
and proper functions of music are so opposite to the traditions
out of which his art grew that at first it seems almost belittling
to suggest that he intended his compositions to be understood so
literally. But it will not do to ignore the fact, or to laugh off the
theory behind it as the midsummer madness of an era now happily
outgrown. The problems of imitation in the arts are basic to all
classical theory and practice. It is especially important for us to
realize that the kind of imitation involved in Handel's work is not a
mere invitation to free subjective reverie on the listener's part, the
uncontrolled Träumerei, beginning anywhere, to which the latter-
day concert-goer is all too prone. If we wish to converse in this
tongue, we must learn it. Simply to follow it at all, we have to
know its scope and purpose.

The musicians of that period believed that music could and
should be a kind of sound-language, precise in the expression of
ideas, emotional states, conceptions. But they always started from
verbal language, and built an accompanying system of tonal equivalents. Motion swift or slow, rough or even, unbroken or interrupted, was easy enough, given the verbal clue; so too were onomatopoetic concepts, ideas of sound or sound-producing agents,
water, wind, animal noises—as exemplified, for instance, in Vivaldi's
Seasons. Place relations like high or low, near or far, found ready
musical equivalents—again if words confirmed them. Handel's
contemporary and boyhood friend, Johann Mattheson, who developed this language with extreme elaboration (1739), made a useful
classification.[10] He divided the "figures" or loci topici into two
sorts, loci notationis and loci descriptionis. The first were the ab-

[8] Winton Dean, Handel's Dramatic Oratorios and Masques (1959), p. 320.
[9] Ibid., p. 63.
[10] Johann Mattheson, Der volkommene Capellmeister (1739).

stract technical devices of music, like inversion, repetition, imitation in its compositional sense. The second were the devices with nonmusical implication, emblematic in meaning, allegorical, metaphorical, of pictorial similitude. In practice, of course, the two kinds were mutually collaborative and consubstantial. The metaphysical and ethical significance of Music had not yet faded from memory. Music had once been next to Divinity in importance because on earth it was the image of celestial order, harmony, and proportion: the Higher mathematics, in fact, with a capital H. It *must* therefore have intellectual meaning, and there ought to be no unbridgeable gap between the physical and metaphysical in music. To give it ideational significance and coherency was not merely right but almost an obligation. As Bukofzer admirably stated the case: "Music reached out from the audible into the inaudible world; it extended without a break from the world of the senses into that of the mind and intellect . . . Audible form and inaudible order were not mutually exclusive or opposed concepts . . . but complementary aspects of one and the same experience: the unity of sensual and intellectual understanding."[11] *Die Affektenlehre*, then, was not the quaint, Shandean aberration it is commonly reported to be. It strove to bring a little more of the unknown within the bounds of the knowable; to introduce evidences of order at the frontiers of rational experience. It became absurd only when it was pushed to extremes—as happened also to rules vainly imposed on other forms of aesthetic expression.

One of its benefits was to describe and objectify emotions in such a way that our private feelings could be shared—identified, experienced, and made generally available in a recognizable musical shape. This, I take it, is the implulse behind all allegory, The process of personifying the passions in *descriptio*, by means of rhythm, tonality, modes, and keys with an established significance, renders music continually allegorical and thereby intellectually viable. This is the rationale of Handel's music, and, basically, it embodies a profoundly classical ideal. Let us not be intimidated by the term Baroque, which in music is a neologism of perhaps mainly negative utility. So universal a man as Handel will not be contained in a narrow room, and we must be wary of trying to impound him. But one thing is certain: it is not for being a revolutionary that he

[11] Manfred Bukofzer, *Music in the Baroque Era* (1947), p. 369.

was exalted in his own century. Nor, on the contrary, when in the days of Mannheim and Vienna the classical forms of that great musical age were reaching perfection, was it for being reactionary that Handel's towering genius was arriving at full recognition. From the middle of the century on, whatever school was in the ascendant in England, his fame never ceased.

To emphasize Handel's firm classic alignment is not to do him any injustice. Apart from external nature, the themes that seldom fail to strike fire in his imagination, from *Acis and Galatea* and *Esther* to the very end, were drawn from two sources, the Old Testament and Greek myth. His chief formal innovation lay in the use he made in the oratorios—but not the operas—of the chorus, where his debt is to Greek tragedy via Racine's imitative handling of it. In him appears a similar deployment of choral participation on two levels: that is, both within and above the dramatic action. The chorus concentrates the issues and sums them up; and they rise in and out of that involvement and not as a moral tag superimposed from without. This important insight I owe again to Winton Dean. "With Handel," Dean declares, "as with the Greeks, the force of such pronouncements varies in proportion with their dramatic motivation. The central themes of *Saul, Belshazzar, Hercules,* and *Jephtha,* round which the whole plot revolves, are envy, *hubris,* sexual jealousy, and submission to destiny—all favorite subjects of the Greeks—and it is no accident that those works are conspicuous both for the grandeur of their choruses and for the overriding unity of their style. Handel in this temper reminds us again and again of Aeschylus." [12]

WITHOUT leaving problems of imitation, and still pursuing the classical ideals, we may shift now to the subject of landscape gardening, wherein the mid-century is seen to have defined its sympathies and characterized itself in especially typical fashion. Not the least characteristic fact here is the confluence of contradictory impulses that blur the purpose and direction of changes taking place. Are we watching the gradual repossession of England by Nature with the approach of the Romantic Age, or is the motivation behind this movement quite another thing? Which, it may be asked, is the more romantic, in the deepest sense, the appeal to the

[12] Dean, *Handel's Dramatic Oratorios and Masques,* p. 41.

eye or the appeal to the mind which "creates, transcending these,/ Far other worlds and other seas?"

Several kinds of imitation are involved here, of which we may distinguish two or three in what may have been the order of their emergence. Under the guidance of Sir William Temple, who led away from the stiff, geometrical garden patterns in vogue at the end of the seventeenth century, with their radiating or parallel straight walks, clipped hedges, trees shaped in balls, cones, pyramids symmetrically balanced, the century opened with a strong impulse toward the "Sharawadgi," the supposed sophistication of oriental irregularity. Pevsner has shown the political overtones of English "liberty" in this movement. Shaftesbury's declared approbation of the "horrid graces of the wilderness" indicates British restiveness under too strict control, and also reflects anti-Gallic sentiment in opposition to the rule of Lenôtre.[13] The English Constitution was a *natural* growth, was it not?

This tendency soon broadened and blended with Augustan ideas of classical attitudes toward Nature. The great Roman poets were all poets of nature, assuming the pastoral frame of mind, reveling in country philosophizing, cultivating the natural delights of their rural retreats. The mood was inherited from the Hellenistic development of natural parks and gardens, associated with the Muses and philosophical discussion, and carried on in the Sicilian pastoral tradition and its Alexandrian sequel. Country life in the sumptuous villas of the later Roman nobles, statesmen, generals, not to mention emperors, had much of what the English landed gentry emulated in their great estates; and similar attitudes toward the natural scene seem to have been generated in both worlds.

Even before William Kent came the experiments of Vanbrugh and Bridgman at Castle Howard, Blenheim, and Stowe in romantic gardening. H. F. Clark observes:

The triumph of the irregular occurred during the rise of Palladianism in architecture. Both were derived from classical sources filtered through the work of Italian Renaissance scholarship . . . Irregular gardens were as classical and correct as the buildings of the Burlington group . . . [Sir Henry Wotton's precept that] "as fabrics should be regular, so gardens should be irregular," was a truth which classical

[13] Nikolaus Pevsner, "The Genesis of the Picturesque," *The Architectural Review* (November 1944); also the same author's *The Englishness of English Art* (1956), p. 156.

authority was found to have practiced . . . [This, it was asserted,] was
"the method laid down by Virgil in his second *Georgic*." Addison,
whose vogue as a leader of taste was enormous, brought the weight
of his authority to the side of change by claiming that his own taste
was Pindaric, that in his garden it was difficult to distinguish between
the garden and the wilderness.[14]

Chiswick Park, begun after Burlington's first visit to Italy, was
one of the first of the new irregular gardens, in which, it appears,
Pope himself had a hand along with Bridgman. Kent continued it,
and Pope theorized the work in his Epistle to Burlington.

Nothing is clearer than that these designers painted primarily
to the mind's eye, and aimed at presenting to the observer temporal
vistas. "What an advantage," exclaims Shenstone,

must some Italian seats derive from the circumstance of being situate
on ground mentioned in the classicks! And, even in England, wherever
a park or garden happens to have been the scene of any event in history,
one would surely avail one's self of that circumstance, to make it more
interesting to the imagination. Mottoes should allude to it, columns, &c.
record it; verses moralize upon it.[15]

Like the poets with their bejeweled incrustations of literary quotation, they enriched the scene by setting up as many echoes as
possible, by every variety of associational device that might stimulate the imagination and excite emotion. Urns and obelisks, statues
and temples evoked the classical nostalgia on three levels: through
the recollection of actual classical scenes; through such scenes
idealized in the idyllic canvases of Poussin and Claude; and by
recalling images and sentiments from the ancient poets with whose
work so much of their literary experience was impregnated. This
art, then, was an imitative art not only in a pictorial sense but also in
its close kinship to literature.

The art of music and the art of gardening are alike in the fact
that specific meaning in both must be introduced from another
medium. Music, we have seen, expresses ideas by developing a
metaphorical language that must depend on verbal assistance for
correct interpretation of any but the most rudimentary conceptions. But modes and keys acquire independent meaning from
repetitional use; and conventional rhythms, meters, and musical

[14] H. F. Clark, *The English Landscape Garden* (1948), pp. 12–13.
[15] William Shenstone, "Unconnected Thoughts on Gardening" in *Works* (1768
ed.) II, 113.

figures will convey an accepted sense without the help of inter-mediaries. Obviously, we must have been tutored in order to understand: it is not enough to be sensitive to musical impressions. Similarly, now, gardening developed its own *Affektenlehre*. The language of flowers has always been a very arbitrary one that had to be memorized; but the toughness and durability of oaks, the dark foliage of yews, the cadent habit of willows, have supplied an obvious symbolism that by association is generally known and acknowledged.

It may be that in some parts of the Orient the language of vegetation has been pursued to such a degree of cerebral sophistication that complex ideas can be formulated by its means alone. If so, it would of course presume in the recipients equal study, knowledge of conventions, and fastidious discrimination in their use. Among the English, poets have been the earliest interpreters and moralizers of natural phenomena. Topographical poetry was already in vogue by the time the landscape artists began to elaborate the extrasensory content of nature in their pictorial compositions. "So," writes Dyer in "Grongar Hill,"

> So we mistake the future's face,
> Ey'd thro' hope's deluding glass,
> As yon summits soft and fair,
> Clad in colours of the air,
> Which, to those who journey near,
> Barren, brown, and rough appear . . .
> Thus is nature's vesture wrought
> To instruct our wand'ring thought.
>
> (ll. 121–126, 99–100)

The landscape designers determined to make equally certain, by the employment of adventitious means, by architecture, sculpture, inscriptional mottoes, artful scenic punctuation,[16] and control of point of view, that the significance of their statements should be rightly understood. Indeed, it sometimes seems as though they resent the pulse of life and would fix the scene in a single moment of time, like the garden in Chaucer's dream, where the sun was always temperate and never set, and change of seasons was unknown. "To see one's urns, obelisks, and waterfalls laid open," Shenstone reflects, "the nakedness of our beloved mistresses, the

---

[16] The neat word is A. R. Humphreys's in *William Shenstone* (1937), p. 100.

Naiads and the Dryads, exposed by that ruffian Winter to universal observation: is a severity scarcely to be supported by the help of blazing hearths, chearful companions, and a bottle of the most grateful burgundy."[17]

But, as the decades passed, purposes were clarified, subtler meaning was directed to a wider "literate" public, and taste altered. Imitation grew more sophisticated and in a sense more philosophical. The classical idea of what nature herself intended in an imperfect realization of purpose in any given local effort, struggling with intractable elements, became the overriding concern. The genius of place held the secret, and it was the duty of the artist to consult this genius and liberate it into perfect expression. The art, however, lay in ridding it of local idiosyncrasy and domestic encumbrances, which were like bad personal habits, the uncouth awkwardness of village speech, dress, or manners. It was a generalized, ideal beauty that was sought, the perfect classical statement that did not imply stereotyped repetition or dull platitude but became a fresh and living realization of universal truth. "Great thoughts," Johnson said, "are always general."

To reconstitute the face of nature in this way was to compose three-dimensional paintings not from devotion to the charms of nature but according to an intellectual conception as classical as the modeling of antique sculpture. Truth to an ideal beauty, essentialized from a myriad of imperfectly beautiful particulars, was the object here as there: to be real but not realistic, natural but not naturalistic—"the artifice of eternity," the mind's embodiment. "Objects," Shenstone wrote, "should indeed be less calculated to strike the immediate eye, than the judgment or well-formed imagination." To be sure, there are natural proprieties, rules derived from Nature's own practice, "discovered, not devised." "The eye should always look rather down upon water." "The side-trees in vistas should be so circumstanced as to afford a probability that they grew by nature." "Hedges, appearing as such, are universally bad." "All trees" (that is, species of them) "have a character analogous to that of men . . . A large, branching, aged oak is perhaps the most venerable of all inanimate objects."[18]

[17] Shenstone, "Unconnected Thoughts," II, 121.
[18] *Ibid., passim.*

It must be apparent, then, that what we have been tracing is not the development of a more and more romantic love of an external Nature uncontaminated by the hand of man; but rather a more and more subtly refined Art, working with natural phenomena as its plastic elements, on the same classical principles that had been operative in literary art, sculpture, architecture, and were now coming to new and vigorous life in English painting, and, soon after, in the classical revival in France. How, then, is it permissible to use this art of landscape gardening as proof of the continual progress toward Romanticism? Brown's notorious "capabilities" were basically a classical theory—a point too seldom acknowledged.

So far as concerns the cult of the Picturesque, it may be fair to say that it is the belated psychologizing stepchild of the much earlier cult of irregularity, via the theories of Burke at the mid-century and concerned to rationalize, not to retreat into, wilderness. It set up "savage" Rosa, who had not lacked earlier admirers—note Walpole's outburst, going over the Alps with Gray in 1739: "Precipices, mountains, torrents, wolves, rumblings, Salvator Rosa!"[19]—on a higher pedestal than Claude, partly in conscious protest against a late classicism that it felt had become too pure. The asymmetry of the older Baroque tradition, continued on the Continent in the Rococo, no doubt also helped to familiarize sensitive spirits with these "Gothic" tastes.

THE CONNECTION between the landscape gardener's and the painter's point of view was patent to all. Shenstone pronounced: "Landskip [which he distinguishes from 'prospects,' or distant views] should contain variety enough to form a picture upon canvas; and this is no bad test, as I think the landskip painter is the gardiner's best designer. The eye requires a sort of balance here; but not so as to encroach upon probable nature."[20] But there was as yet no school of English landscape painters to provide models, and of course Shenstone was looking toward Italy. Not until the seventh decade, when Richard Wilson translated the English scene into classical terms, was the need supplied. Hitherto, no painter of the English natural scene had appeared who could hold a candle to Claude or the Poussins. And, in fact, when we look for classicism of

[19] Horace Walpole to Richard West, September 28, 1739.
[20] Shenstone, "Unconnected Thoughts," II, 115.

any sort among *early* eighteenth-century British painters, it is very hard to find. The sequence of names, Holbein, Van Dyck, Lely, Kneller, covers in symbolic outline much of the earlier history of British art. Against this long tradition of foreign lawgivers, and the current snobbery of the Connoisseurs, Hogarth fought with every weapon he could find or invent. He managed to loosen the soil for a British planting. He was no traditionalist and neither by precept nor practice did his influence tell in the direction of Classicism. It was not, however, ancient art he was tilting against but snobbery and pseudo-connoisseurs.[21] But neither would anyone be likely to attach a Romantic label to him. Although he was a theorist, he was by temperament an improviser more interested in facts than in formulas. His masterpieces, e.g., Captain Coram's portrait, his Mrs. Salter, the sketches of the Shrimp Girl, and his Servants, do not set up for "ideal nature," though the Coram has been called one of the great original landmarks of British portraiture.

Ellis Waterhouse dates the beginning of the classical age in British painting precisely at 1760, with the accession of George III and the first public exhibition of the newly incorporated Society of Artists. [22] To this exhibition Reynolds contributed his "Duchess of Hamilton as Venus." The following year Hogarth sent his ill-starred "Sigismonda"; in 1764, Benjamin West entered his first classical history picture. But matters were already getting out of hand because the rules were so permissive that anything sent in was eligible to be shown—even paper cutouts; and the Academy was inaugurated in 1768 to introduce some needful measures to control rights of entry.

Thenceforward, after the establishment of the Royal Academy, throughout Reynolds's presidency, in spite of shortcomings and backslidings, the principles of the Grand Style predominated. During the decade of the seventies, Reynolds made his most determined effort to emulate the old Renaissance masters. This was also the time of his greatest influence. From the late seventies through the early eighties, Barry was doing his big work ("Progress of Human Culture") for the Royal Society of Arts, the logical

[21] J. T. A. Burke, "Classical Aspect of Hogarth's Theory of Art" in *England and the Mediterranean Tradition* (1945).

[22] Ellis K. Waterhouse, *Painting in Britain, 1530–1790*, Pelican History of Art (1953), p. 157.

fulfillment, if not the triumph, of the doctrine. The history picture, in full panoply and classical costume, stood up for the main, and West, with crown patronage, Gavin Hamilton, Copley, Opie, Northcote, and Reynolds as well, strove to realize the ideal. But other winds were blowing, and the mesmerism of Raphael and Michelangelo lost compulsion with the passing years. By 1790, the history piece had been, if not declassicized, then refurbished in modern guise, and "ideal nature" in the Grand Style, though still a noble ideal, no longer compelled assent—at least in England.

None the less, with the presidential addresses of Reynolds, we are given the *first* great *literary* statement of the classical ideal in painting. Professor Bate goes even further, declaring that "Reynolds' *Discourses* comprise perhaps the most representative single embodiment in English of eighteenth-century aesthetic principles."[23] The *Discourses* were delivered over a very long span—from January 1769 to December 1790—and were first published complete in 1794. They had a cumulative power; and it is beyond contradiction that eighteenth-century classical *doctrine* reaches its climactic formulations in the last decades of the age.

As for Reynolds's own enormous achievement on canvas, it is very difficult to confine. "Damn him," exclaimed Gainsborough in grudging acknowledgment, "how various he is!" At the end of his life, Reynolds simply and regretfully confessed that Michelangelo's example had been too lofty for imitation: "I have taken another course, one more suited to my abilities, and to the taste of the times in which I live." [24] Nevertheless, this clear and uplifted spirit, this "very great man," as Johnson justly called him, did incontrovertibly succeed, without violating the bond of individual portraiture, in typifying and idealizing for all time a class, a portion of society, a way of life, in dozens of his numberless subjects. In the abundant best of his canvases, we seem to have been shown, not merely so many named personages, but a great deal of the age in which they lived. In a subtle way, he reconciled the individual portrait to the generalized, ideal history piece, a marriage most fully exemplified in his monumental *Family of the Duke of Marlborough*, but demonstrated as well in many of his more informal works.

[23] Walter Jackson Bate, *From Classic to Romantic* (1946), Chapter III, § 6, p. 79.
[24] Conclusion of the Fifteenth Discourse, December 10, 1790.

If there were stirrings against the classical teaching of Reynolds in the art of painting, the doctrine was hardly questioned when applied to sculpture. Reynolds devoted his Tenth Discourse to this subject. In it he rebukes all attempts to include elements of the picturesque, or such pictorial effects as flying drapery or wind-swept hair, or contrasts of light and shade, or imbalance, as a child against a full-size figure, or a stooping figure as companion to an upright one. The delight of sculpture, he declares, is an intellectual delight in the contemplation of perfect beauty, in which the physical pleasure has little part. This art only partly represents nature. "Sculpture," Reynolds pronounces, "is formal, regular, and austere; disdains all familiar objects, as incompatible with its dignity, and is an enemy to every species of affectation. . . . In short, whatever partakes of fancy or caprice, or goes under the denomination of Picturesque . . . is incompatible with that sobriety and gravity which is peculiarly the characteristic of this art." [25]

It is plain that the work of the previous generation of sculptors, even the great Roubillac in his funerary monuments, would not have been approved by Reynolds, because their work was semi-dramatic, and aimed to make a theatrical statement. But the new members of the Royal Academy, Nollekens, Flaxman, Banks, and Bacon, received the doctrine *con amore*. Nollekens persisted, after his years in Rome, in modeling even Johnson without benefit of wig, evoking (it is said) Johnson's growling protest: "Though a man may for convenience wear a cap in his own chamber, he ought not [in a bust] to look as if he had taken physic." Flaxman's work is filled with the distillation of eighteenth-century ideas of "the just designs of Greece." [26] He worked in Rome 1787–1790. Bacon's statue of Johnson, in St. Paul's, in toga and cropped head, perfectly fulfills Reynolds's notion of "ideal nature." Indeed, Katherine Esdaile, the historian of British sculpture, is filled with indignation at the lamentable triumph achieved by classicism over the native tradition of good homely realism. It is certain that in this art, if naturalism means the tendency toward Romantic indi-

[25] Conclusion of the Tenth Discourse, December 11, 1780.
[26] An offshoot of this impulse is to be observed in the sudden flood of Homeric illustration after 1750, reaching its classical climax about 1790. See Dora Wiebenson, "Subjects from Homer's Iliad in Neoclassical Art," *Art Bulletin*, XLVI (March 1964), 23–37.

vidualism, the last two decades of the eighteenth century were a palpable retrogression from its arrival.

A kindred spirit is visible in architecture. The Burlingtonian tradition, carried past 1750 by Isaac Ware, James Paine, and Sir Robert Taylor, was reinvigorated, reoriented, and archaeologized, in part through the excitement over Pompeii at the mid-century, and by investigation all the way from Paestum, Sicily, Athens, as far eastward as Palmyra. The fifties were a decade of strenuous field work by both English and French in Greek and Roman antiquities. Soufflot and Leroy, the Comte de Caylus, Stuart and Revett, William Chambers, Winckelmann, Clérisseau, were some of the best known, and Piranesi, who published three sets of Roman engravings by 1754—not to mention the official volumes on Herculaneum beginning to appear in 1757. Robert Adam's first tour lasted from 1753 to 1758. He filled notebook after notebook with archaeological studies. His brother James followed his example in 1760. James Stuart's and Nicholas Revett's *Antiquities of Athens*, published in 1762, was based on their investigations of the previous decade. Lord Anson's London house, in the Greek style, was the first conspicuous result. Between the two stricter modes, the Palladian and Athenian, falls the revolutionary Adam work, more various, freer, but classical in inspiration, and enormously successful, influential, and fashionable. Fiske Kimball, in fact, our most painstaking authority on the Rococo, credits Adam's vogue with being responsible for the demise of that style even in France, its originator.[27] Sir William Chambers likewise throws his weight solidly behind the classical tradition (apart from sowing his wild oats in Chinese gardens); so did the Woods of Bath; and even James Wyatt, although flirting occasionally with the Gothic, began and continued throughout his career with classically designed buildings. Fashions in architecture are not easily overturned. But the Adam brothers were thoroughgoing, and did really change the look of things. And their regulation, of course, affected all the interior appointments, from carpet to ceiling, wall decoration, furniture, and lighting. Wedgwood, who belongs to the same decades, with his Etruscan and classical pottery adorned with charming antique luting modeled by Flaxman, fitted in beautifully here. Moreover, thanks to the practical improvements of Caslon

[27] Fiske Kimball, *The Creation of the Rococo* (1943), pp. 207 ff.

in type-founding, and the fanatical perfectionism of Baskerville in the middle decades, fine printing was moving on a parallel course. Along with the extreme beauty and refinement of his Roman type, Baskerville was learning how to manipulate the white space on his page, until his Latin titles sprang out three-dimensional, like antique urns and pedestals standing in the open air, bearing classical inscriptions. His example was not lost on his immediate successors, and in the hands of the Foulis brothers, of Bensley, and Bulmer—with the aid of such designers as Wilson, Fry, the Martins, and Figgins—printing became more classically splendid right to the end of the century. It would be hard to conceive of any piece of furniture more thoroughly at home in the library of an Adam house than some of the magnificent quartos and folios that were published in the years when those great houses were built or remodeled: Syon, Osterly, Kedleston, Kenwood, Luton Hoo, Mellerstain, Newby Hall, and many another. Appropriately, some of the most sumptuous volumes were works of the line of architects already named, Burlingtonians and Classicists both: Campbell's *Vitruvius Britannicus*, Burlington's *Fabbriche Antiche*, Chambers's *Treatise*, Stuart's and Revett's *Antiquities of Athens*, Robert Adam's *Ruins of Diocletian's Palace* and the Adam brothers' *Works in Architecture* are only a few of the most distinguished. They had, moreover, an international circulation and international influence.

If, in summarizing our impressions of the latter decades of the century we recall that Goldsmith then showed in his two great essays in decasyllabic couplets how freshly the Augustan music could be reembodied in the hands of a master of that tradition; if we add to Reynolds's *Discourses* Johnson's *Lives of the Poets* (1779–1781): we shall be in no danger of attributing to Classicism an early demise. If we set beside these masterpieces Gibbon's magnificent elegiac monument to ancient Rome (1776–1787), a supreme embodiment of the Augustan spirit—an epic, as Lewis Curtis demonstrates, reared to celebrate Wisdom and Moral Virtue guiding Power, and warning against surrender;[28] and if, moreover, we remember Burke's nobly conservative defense of the principle

[28] "Gibbon's Paradise Lost" in *The Age of Johnson: Essays Presented to Chauncey Brewster Tinker*, ed. F. W. Hilles (1949), pp. 73 ff.

of continuity and tradition: we shall not imagine that the Classical Age dwindled or died from anemia and decay. Classicism is a faith, and, being a faith, therefore never fully realized but demanding constant effort from its devotees to attain the values it essentially embodies: the humane ideals of rational truth, moral virtue, order, and beauty expressive of these goods. The community of artists and thinkers with whom we are here concerned, whatever their individual variance, ardently professed and diligently sustained these convictions in art and in life. Burke's *Letter to a Noble Lord* (1796) is not the least splendid expression of that spirit, and George Sherburn's sentence upon it is finely appropriate: "The echo from Virgil may serve to remind us that Burke's art came from the ancients, and that with the figured and fervent mood of his last works eighteenth-century prose goes out in a blaze of noble artifice." [29]

IN STUDYING the past, we have grown so habituated to our progressive way of anticipating the future in its earliest premonitory signs that we seldom allow a moment's reflection to the oversimplification and really gross distortion of the historical truth of any actual moment of the past which this practice entails. To the people who are living in it, the present seldom looks like the future. Very few have the leisure for prophecy—except of calamity—or the power of disinterested observation and detachment. The present is always a confused muddle of conflicting values and doubtful issues, and the battle never ceases.

Much earlier, I quoted a dubious couplet: "The rough road then, returning in a round,/Mock'd our impatient steps, for all was fairy ground." It would not be surprising if no one recognized the lines, which intrinsically are hardly memorable. They are part of Johnson's crafty demonstration that in Pope's celebrated onomatopoetic description of the labors of Sisyphus—

> With many a weary step, and many a groan,
> Up a high hill he heaves a huge round stone;
> The huge round stone, resulting with a bound,
> Thunders impetuous down, and smoaks along the ground.

[29] George Sherburn, "The Restoration and Eighteenth Century" in *A Literary History of England*, ed. Albert Baugh (1948), p. 1094.

—"the mind governs the ear and the sounds are estimated by their meaning." [30] They do not make very good sense; but I intended to impose on them a kind of symbolic sense, to suggest that the looks of the road and the speed of the passage were highly subjective matters, largely dependent upon—or at least radically affected by —the purpose and preoccupations of the passenger. I have wished in this paper to spend an hour looking at the eighteenth century as if it were a spatial rather than a temporal panorama. For a while I was tempted to take as my title, "From Romantic to Classic," thinking thereby to point the moral in a ready and easy way. The pretty paradox seemed to provide a sort of compass or a means of escape from the bewildering complexities wherein I was stumbling. And indeed it was a help, though insufficient, by its inherent magnetic property of lifting by attraction one sort of matter from the indiscriminate mass.

But, in the end, it had to be rejected because the truth is that, as historians, we are not obliged to travel the road either in one direction or in the other. Both ends of the panorama are equally open to our elevated, timeless vision. A topographical map does not itself move: it lies open to inspection. It is not like Rabelais's Island of Odes, "où les chemins cheminent, comme animaux." Its roads, on the contrary, stay exactly where they are laid down.

It is worthwhile, I think, and corrective of the distortions arising from our obsession with interpretation *ex post facto,* to try to look at an Age in the richness of its complexities and contradictions. If we did not know—or if we could awhile forget—that the Age of Romanticism followed on the heels of the Age of Enlightenment, should we not quite naturally be seeing the eighteenth century in quite another than the customary view: as in fact a period when the spirit of Classicism steadily *refined* its values, grew increasingly *assured* in its declaration of them, and never knew better their true and vital meaning and importance than when on the verge of losing them?

> This thou perceiv'st, which makes thy love more strong,
> To love that well which thou must leave ere long.

Hence, I have been concerned to call to mind the emotional ferment, the resistance to rule, the communion with external

---

[30] Johnson, Life of Pope, paragraph 332 (*Lives of the Poets,* ed. G. Birkbeck Hill [1905], III, 231).

nature, all those signs and signals of "Romanticism" that complicate the *opening* of the Age of Reason; next, the irregular and disconcertingly rhythmless horizon line where at unpredictable intervals the different arts thrust up their temporal peaks; and, toward the close of the century, the passion for order, the lofty vision of a timeless beauty, the powerful affirmations of faith in man's ability to define and by strenuous effort to approximate it by the rational use of his human endowment, his shared inheritance, native and natural: the persistent and lasting devotion to the Classical Ideal.

On Choosing Fit Subjects for Verse;
or, Who Now Reads Prior?

PRIOR. Good day, Mr. Johnson. Fancy meeting you here!

JOHNSON. I know not, Sir, whether I am to take your exclamation as an affront or a sign of humility. Whatever your intention, I may remind you that our jails have generally had a common court, open to both debtors and felons.

PRIOR. Your analogy, Mr. Johnson, provides no very comfortable alternatives. And if I choose the one, where does that leave you?

JOHNSON. Nay, Sir, it is within every man's power to refrain from felonious acts. But in a deeper sense, Mr. Prior, to be in debt is the unhappy condition from which none is ever exempt.

PRIOR. Indeed, Mr. Johnson, deep or shallow, I have every reason to agree with you. I have run the gamut of indebtedness both in a public and in a private capacity.

JOHNSON. Why, Sir, I recall something of your mortifications as Her Majesty's servant. Howbeit, I am sure your facility in French did not suffer by the enforced delay, and for this I envy you. Depend upon it, a man does not like to be *reduced* to Latin when French is the *parole* of the company.

PRIOR. You are pleasant, Sir; and I forgive the harmless complacency. Let me suggest "elevated" as the more accurate verb.

JOHNSON. Very well; but, when I spoke of obligations, I was thinking not so much of debts financial or social as of the obligation to improve all the opportunities of Good which are afforded us. In particular, for reasons not hidden from your percipience, of

26

the best use of our literary talents. The value of your diligence in the service of two sovereigns I put beyond question, Mr. Secretary *and* Mr. Ambassador, and I respect—indeed, I honor you—not only for your public spirit and skill but also for the sang-froid and good-humor with which you bore your reverses.

PRIOR. You credit me, I fear, with more sang-froid than I possessed. But I detect an unspoken reservation in your compliments. No doubt, you mean to suggest that in poetry I might have endeavored to better purpose. You have allowed me the name but when it comes to praise, am I too sensitive in feeling that you are not overgenerous? At least, I can plead that my contemporaries thought better of my writings than you appear to do, and since, by time's whirligig, your—"Life," do you call it?—of Prior is more frequently read over than my own verses, it has come to pass that your opinion is of exaggerated importance to my fame.

JOHNSON. Why, Sir, thus it is. But, ironic though the case be, I doubt that I am to apologize, since I wrote only what I believed.

PRIOR. And still believe.

JOHNSON. Since you press me, your Excellency, you cannot resent a candid reply. It is true that I had not read *all* your poetical pieces, but the tree is neither better nor worse for an additional crab or two: the relish is the same.

PRIOR. Yet, Sir, have you not formerly remarked that a tree which could produce many crabs was better than one that produced only a few?

JOHNSON. Perhaps, Sir, I may: and, if you care to rest your reputation upon multiplicity, I would not diminish it by a single crab . . . But, bating your private relaxations, where I cannot follow you, my esteem for you is such that if you care to discuss the points wherein I may have done you wrong, my attention is at your disposal. But is not the heart of the matter, Sir, that you never found your subject? You have tried all styles, and your variety won you readers of many tastes, from grave to gay: but did it not also argue an incertain Muse, and an inability to find a level and a matter truly congenial to your temperament and talents?

PRIOR. It is hard, Sir, if variety must be a synonym for insecurity. A young poet will naturally practise the skills he sees to be in high estimation. When I began to essay, Cowley's name was still powerful, as you know. If I could not rise to his pitch of Pindaric sub-

limity, it was no unworthy object to emulate his example and seek
to excel in a kind that such numbers were attempting. The note,
however, was overstrained for my generation: we did not *discount*
sublimity, but on most occasions preferred to talk "like folks of
this world."

JOHNSON. Would that you had done so on all! So late as the
King's birthday in 1690, as I recall, "Apollo turn'd the Mistick
Book" to read Albion's future; and ten years later, Janus was
"casting" his "elder look" at the records of ages past—since William himself was no doubt too pressed to ply his book. And even
after Ramillies, as I have heretofore complained, in troop Mars and
Bellona, Jupiter's Eagle, Cadmus with his teeth, and Brute and the
tale of Troynovante: *id genus omne*, easy, vulgar, and—not to
mince the matter—disgusting.

PRIOR. Mr. Lexicographer, why not toss in the rest of your
apparatus of disparagement: "cold and lifeless," "puerile and unaffecting," "despicable"? Panegyric is not a comfortable mode for
moderns in any circumstances, whatever the reason. Perhaps our
Pyrrhonists have rendered us too skeptical of human nature. The
loftier the intended tribute, the harder it is to sustain the note of
conviction.

JOHNSON. Sir, conviction is not the root of the trouble. In
lapidary inscriptions a man is not upon oath. In the forms of
civility no man looks for entire sincerity. The praise of excellence
is due, therefore, not to what is deeply felt but to the happiest
expression of an attitude assumed. But triteness is tedious in any
case, and only a schoolboy can be pleased by redundancy of
repetition.

PRIOR. I believe you, Sir. You have yourself been a formidable
practitioner of one branch of the art of panegyric, if only from
ambush: no one who recognized you supposed you truly meant
what you said.

JOHNSON. You must be referring to vicarious dedicatory addresses. There, I must acknowledge a private delight in the attempt
to clothe imagined sentiments in stately robes. Since I was not
speaking for myself, I could give full attention to propriety of
expression, without fretting about what I felt *in propria persona*.

PRIOR. There is another element of first importance in this sort
of writing, Mr. Johnson: namely, the occasion thereof. Though

you may not have traced me in it, I have given close attention to the problems of the *genre*. Of these, the foremost is surely that of its ephemeral nature. A birthday, a coronation, or a victory is not likely to hold the public attention long after the event. When once the bell of panegyric has been struck, its reverberations must inevitably diminish with each successive moment, until time has stilled the vibrations forever. Although great verse can prolong the process, it can never recall the initial impact of the stroke, and the eulogist must be content to let his triumph die into history. What artificial preservative can be found, think you, to revive the garland of praise or make it blossom in the dust?

JOHNSON. None, Sir, none. Everything has its day. And I have wondered not only why the race of verse-men in your aera was so assiduous in attempting to bestow immortality on that which its own nature forbids to expect longevity, but also why the poets of my generation, who in the last war have had such incitements to similar effort, have been content to see England's glorious achievements entrusted to the Gazetteer.

PRIOR. Perhaps *our* ill success taught them humility. The difficulties are certainly very great. But I am gratified to recollect your allowance that my burlesque of Boileau's "Ode on Namur" has, if I may quote you, "such airiness and levity as will always procure it readers." To be sure, "airiness" and "levity" are epithets not often accorded a victory-ode. And I am sure you apprehend that I was already seeking ways, if not to untune the spheres, yet to lower the pitch of panegyric to less dizzying heights, where a mortal may breathe, without at the same time debasing the achievement of my countrymen. Admittedly, M. Boileau played into my hands by his own ballad-quatrains and by providing the scheme. And I could borrow the panoply of his classic splendor while I mocked it . . . Not a perfect solution, perhaps; and virtue could not so inoculate the old stock but that I aspired to the grand flight again in the *Carmen Seculare*, "with Pindar's rage without his fire," and stumbling after Horace and Virgil. I grant it was audacious but the cosmic sweep of William's fame deserved a lofty tribute. I strove, by employing classical analogies and judicious comparisons with antiquity, to keep the King's achievements on an exalted but still human level; and by the use of heroic verse intermixed with occasional short lines I tried to combine dignity with agreeable variety. Dibben's Latin translation at least testifies to a contemporary success; and if you found it unendurable, I may appeal to the revolutions of taste and put today to your *Irene* the question you ask of my *Ode*: "Who can be supposed to have laboured through it?"

JOHNSON. A palpable hit, Mr. Secretary, but no very cogent argument for superior excellence. Dryden's slighter rhymes for his "Secular Masque" of the same year are likely to outlast your tip-toe'd grandeur.

PRIOR. But when I came to celebrate Blenheim, Mr. Johnson, I was more of your mind and earnestly tried to hit a style of panegyric that would snaffle Pegasus and enable me to pace the solid earth. To quote your favorite author, I "soberly did mount an arm-gaunt steed." Though you may not applaud the result, yet you must approve the attempt. Pray, indulge me in a modest satisfaction over the strategy of my Epistle. Pretending to look at the event with the eyes of Boileau, a poet condemned to turn out nothing but odes to victory, I could sympathize with the awkwardness of his being faced with an overwhelming defeat:

> Some Daemon envying France mis-led the Fight:
> And Mars mistook, tho' Louis order'd right.

The staggering proportions of the French losses: how could they be described? Thus, say:

> Push'd thro' the Danube to the Shoars of Styx
> Squadrons eighteen, Battalions twenty-six . . .

But, protests Boileau,

> is it thus You English Bards compose?
> With Runick Lays thus tag insipid Prose?
> And when you should your Heroes Deeds rehearse,
> Give us a Commissary's List in Verse?

> Why Faith, Despréaux, there's Sense in what you say:
> I told you where my Difficulty lay:
> So vast, so numerous were great Blenheim's Spoils,
> They scorn the Bounds of Verse, and mock the Muse's Toils . . .
> What Poet would essay . . .
> [To] make Arithmetic and Epic meet;
> And Newton's Thoughts in Dryden's Stile repeat?

From this vantage-point, all I need do is suggest what the genius of Boileau could do in my circumstances, and go on to sketch the

possibilities of such a Paean: with Anna, sovereign from the Thames
to the Danube, seated in Windsor attended by the gods of War
and Love, by Thames, his brethren across the Channel, the tritons
and river-nymphs, Marlborough and St. George and Victoria. You
conceive, Sir, that this is a way of declining the gambit and, while
pointing to the great idea, acknowledging myself unequal to filling
it out. Credit me, my dear Sir, with judgment and restraint. Indeed,
I felt the force of your objections to English Pindar ere you were
born, and I foreknew Mr. Addison's sentiments in his pleasant
Edict against the mythological strain, which I am sure you remember, since you studied him to so good effect; and which I have
good reason to remember, because it anticipated an affair in which
you allow me to have played an influential, though a troublesome,
part. My friend Adrian Drift, here, whom you formerly consulted
about me, will doubtless be able to quote the entire proclamation.
Cannot you, Drift?

DRIFT. Yes, your Excellency, if you wish me to. It is in the five
hundred three and twentieth *Spectator:*

Whereas the Time of a General Peace is, in all Appearance, drawing
near; being informed that there are several ingenious Persons who
intend to shew their Talents on so happy an Occasion, and being
willing, as much as in me lies, to prevent that Effusion of Nonsense,
which we have good Cause to apprehend; I do hereby strictly require
every Person, who shall write on this Subject, to remember that he is
a Christian, and not to sacrifice his Catechism to his Poetry. In order
to it, I do expect of him in the first Place, to make his own Poem,
without depending upon Phoebus for any part of it, or calling out for
Aid upon any one of the Muses by Name. I do likeways positively
forbid the sending of Mercury with any particular Message or Dispatch
relating to the Peace, and shall by no means suffer Minerva to take
upon her the Shape of any Plenipotentiary concerned in this Great
Work. I do further declare, that I shall not allow the Destinies to
have had an Hand in the Deaths of the several Thousands who have
been slain in the late War, being of Opinion that all such Deaths may
be very well accounted for by the Christian System of Powder and
Ball. I do therefore strictly forbid the Fates to cut the Thread of
Man's Life upon any Pretence whatsoever, unless it be for the sake
of the Rhime. And whereas I have good Reason to fear, that Neptune
will have a great deal of Business on his Hands, in several Poems which
we may now suppose are upon the Anvil, I do also prohibit his
Appearance, unless it be done in Metaphor, Simile, or any very short
Allusion, and that even here he be not permitted to enter, but with

great Caution and Circumspection. I desire that the same Rule may
be extended to his whole Fraternity of Heathen Gods, it being my
Design to condemn every Poem to the Flames in which Jupiter
thunders, or exercises any other Act of Authority which does not
belong to him: In short, I expect that no Pagan Agent shall be introduced, or any Fact related which a Man cannot give Credit to with
a good Conscience.

PRIOR. Thank you, Drift: your memory indeed is impeccable.
You will probably not recall, Mr. Johnson, that I ended the Blenheim poem with these lines:

> Nor want just Subject for victorious Strains,
> While Marlboro's Arm Eternal Laurel gains;
> And where old Spencer sung, a new Eliza reigns.

When the occasion for another Ode to the Queen arrived with
the Ramillies Campaign, I was struck with the idea of celebrating
the Victory in a style resembling that of Spenser himself, borrowing the great strokes of Horace's famous Ode, the fourth of the
fourth Book. You were very severe with the result, calling the
stanzas tedious in their massed uniformity, the diction neither
ancient nor modern, the figures puerile and despicable, and the
total piece cold and lifeless. I will not attempt to refute your
strictures. I would only ask you to observe that I was seeking
another way to evade the unnaturalness of our speech when raised
to the height of sublimity. We lack not the power to rise to heights
of imagination but, save in Milton and our older poets, especially
Spenser, have not found an utterance with sufficient majesty to
sustain our flights. If, so to put it, I might translate my poem into
a less familiar diction, unhackneyed by common employments, I
hoped to elude the familiar embarrassment and achieve a medium
congenial to the ancient grandeur of conception and ceremonial
pomp. But I found it more difficult than I had expected.

JOHNSON. Mr. Prior, it is but too plain that you found it impossible. Every reader will assent to your own expressed disclaimer
in the fourth stanza, which I happen to recall:

> Me all too mean for such a Task I weet.

DRIFT. Sir, allow me to protest that you are unjust to the point
of stark insensibility. How admirably he has transfused into his
Ode the *Impetuous Heat* of *Horace,* and all the Graces of *Spenser's*

Diction, must be obvious to every judicious Reader . . . And the
Column he erects at the End of his Poem, to the Honour of his
Mistress and her Commanders (in the last eight stanzas), will out-
last the stateliest Monument of Brass or Marble.

JOHNSON. Sir, if you mean to be serious, I must reply that your
loyalty to your master is only surpassed by your lack of critical
discernment.

PRIOR. Come, Gentlemen, there is no occasion for such heat. I
have already conceded the justice of your charge, Mr. Johnson, in
lines which compare us poets to a squirrel in a rolling cage:

> The foolish Creature thinks he climbs:
> But here or there, turn Wood or Wire,
> He never gets two Inches higher . . .
> In noble Songs, and lofty Odes . . .
> [We] tread on Stars, and talk with Gods . . .
> Brought back, how fast soe'er [we] go:
> Always aspiring; always low.

Fortunately for all of us, retrospectively, the advent of His Han-
overian Majesty removed the challenge of rising to great occasions,
and thereafter I quitted the peaks of Parnassus. Let us accordingly
descend to the more agreeable level of what you are pleased to
dub my "amorous effusions." But here again, I find, you take
exception.

JOHNSON. Why, yes, Sir, I do. Nature and Passion seldom mo-
tivate your love-songs, which have the coldness of Cowley without
his wit. Your classical allusions are redolent of the college lamp;
and your Cloe has little reason to be moved by pedantry so remote
and unaffecting.

PRIOR. Dear Sir, you quite mistake. With Cloe I had (forgive
me!) a *prior* understanding. There was no need of verses to bring
us together. Did you, if I may ask, attain *your* object by addressing
your Tetty in verse? Or did you save your poetry for more formal
and distant relationships?

JOHNSON. Why, then, Sir, were you forever writing verses to
Cloe?

PRIOR. Mr. Johnson, I find I must invite you to dive a little
deeper into human nature. My verses to Cloe were more to be
*over*heard than to be received as incitements to love. Does the bee
offer back the honey to the flower? . . . Moreover, Sir, you had in

Mrs. Thrale a learned lady who could appreciate your Latin odes, and in your day in fact a circle of literary ladies. Intellect in ladies was, I admit, less important to me, and I doubt that Cloe or Jinny or Lisetta knew more Latin than did Chaucer's Pertelote. Probably I came closer than usual to speaking out in "A Better Answer to Cloe Jealous"—a poem for which I suspect you have a liking; but how little I counted on familiarity with lettered learning is hinted in one line of it:

The God of us Verse-men:—You know, Child, the Sun.

And you will also recall my sage advice in another poem which concludes:

Be to her Virtues very kind:
Be to her Faults a little blind:
Let all her Ways be unconfin'd:
And clap your Padlock—on her Mind.

JOHNSON. Then, Sir, it appears that I was not far from the truth in saying that your love-verses have neither gallantry nor tenderness.

PRIOR. Nay, Mr. Johnson, the very poem already named provides *a better answer*. You force me to quote my own verses in self-defense:

What I speak, my fair Cloe, and what I write, shews
The Diff'rence there is betwixt Nature and Art:
I court others in Verse; but I love Thee in Prose:
And They have my Whimsies; but Thou hast my Heart ...

JOHNSON. But, Sir, you have just now said that your verses were not addressed to Cloe but to the audience.

PRIOR. Very true: a paradox, is it not? And, moreover, I was writing *verse* when I declared:

I court others in Verse; but I love Thee in Prose.

Two negatives make a positive, Mr. Johnson. My verses, as I told you, were to be overheard. But was it not clear to Cloe that there was prose to follow? And was there no gallantry nor tenderness in the next stanza:

So when I am weary'd with wand'ring all Day,
To Thee my Delight in the Evening I come:
No Matter what Beauties I saw in my Way,
They were but my Visits; but Thou art my Home.

JOHNSON. I know not, Sir, that you have extricated yourself from this paradox, as you call it. But surely, a pedantic lover might have avoided the labefactation of grammar in the final stanza:

> For Thou art a Girl as much brighter than *Her*,
>   As He was a Poet sublimer than *Me*.

PRIOR. I am flattered that you remember it, though I hoped you might. But this is the plague of writing for two publics at once—or a public and a private. I do not recall that Cloe taxed me with the grammatical lapse.

JOHNSON. And what have you to say, Sir, in defense of "Henry and Emma," the greatest of all your amorous essays? Do you deny that Emma's example, who resolves to follow an outlawed murderer wherever fear and guilt shall drive him, deserves no imitation; and that the experiment by which Henry tries the lady's constancy is such as must end either in infamy to her, or in disappointment to himself?

PRIOR. Nay, Mr. Johnson, I will not be held answerable for the morals of a piece three hundred years old, which has given pleasure to many generations of lovers before I took it in hand. If you are impervious to romance, I cannot help it.

JOHNSON. Why, Sir, I will not disparage a passion which never to have known is not to have lived. But what has passion to do with a dull and tiresome dialogue, wherein every point is seized upon that may serve to delay the conclusion, until a man is ready to hang himself for impatience? Where the original spends two lines on dress, you spend twenty. Where we read, in the ancient version,

> As cut your hair up by your ear,
>   Your kirtle by the knee,

you give us a whole anatomy of Fashion:

> No longer shall thy comely Tresses break
> In flowing Ringlets on thy snowy Neck;
> Or sit behind thy Head, an ample Round,
> In graceful Breeds with various Ribbon bound:
> No longer shall the Boddice, aptly lac'd,
> From thy full Bosome to thy slender Waste,
> That Air and Harmony of Shape express,
> Fine by Degrees, and beautifully less:

> Nor shall thy lower Garments artful Pleat,
> From thy fair Side dependent to thy Feet,
> Arm their chaste Beauties with a modest Pride,
> And double ev'ry Charm they seek to hide.—

PRIOR. Hold, Sir: you did not know the beauties I had in contemplation.

JOHNSON. Had I done so, I might have unveiled them with less reluctance and greater despatch. No, Sir, I give it up. If there is nothing to say, let us not fill the vacuity with stuff from a milliner's shop, or people Old England with Patagons!

PRIOR. If you think my lighter verses cold, Sir, at least you ought to allow them decency. The strategy of my immediate predecessors in love-poetry, as you must have observed, was to reason the lady out of her virtue by ingenious argument; to provide her with the specious pretence of being overcome by the superior strength of masculine intellect, not natural inclination. My lyrics are innocent of these iniquities, at least.

JOHNSON. Sir, I believe you are right. No lady was ever seduced by verses of yours; though how far matters may have proceeded before you had leisure to compose, I know not. "Calm of mind, all passion spent" is more your temper and moment of composition. Your best things proceed *in* company, *with* company, in a domestic setting. Whom were you addressing in one of your happier pieces, which begins,

> As Cloe came into the Room t'other Day?

PRIOR. You, Sir; I was addressing you. But if Cloe read it, was it not gallant enough to have pleased her?

JOHNSON. There, Sir, I confess you have me. Perhaps, on a nearer view, in a polite society there can no longer be love-poems *à deux*, in closet conference, or summer house. But we still prefer the affectation of intimacy, and a pretense that the lovers are unaware of being observed.

PRIOR. Trust me, Sir, on this point we are in accord. My difficulty was that I could find no fit subjects for verse at that pitch. Or, to alter the figure slightly, at that distance my whispering would not carry to an onlooker. Yet I too was impelled to bring my poetic oblations to a divinity that—we agree—makes life endurable. You were too near the truth when you called these offerings "the dull exercises of a skilful versifier resolved at all adventures to write something about Cloe, and trying to be amorous by dint of study."

JOHNSON. Sir, this is nobly conceded.

PRIOR. But, Mr. Johnson, were you not from time to time open to the same charge? Is it even certain that in your verses, "To Miss Hickman playing on the Spinet," you did not follow mine, "To the Countess of Exeter, Playing on the Lute," in the final turn you gave your compliment?

JOHNSON. It is long since I have thought of it. I do not remember.

PRIOR. I will revive your memory. You conclude thus:

> When old Timotheus struck the vocal String,
> Ambitious Fury fir'd the Grecian King:
> Unbounded Projects lab'ring in his Mind,
> He pants for room, in one poor World confin'd.
> Thus wak'd to rage by Musick's dreadfull Pow'r,
> He bids the Sword destroy, the Flame devour.
> Had Stella's gentle touches mov'd the Lyre,
> Soon had the Monarch felt a nobler fire,
> No more delighted with destructive War,
> Ambitious only now to please the Fair,
> Resign'd his Thirst of Empire to her Charms,
> And found a Thousand Worlds in Stella's Arms.

Mine go as follows:

> To burning Rome when frantick Nero play'd,
> Viewing that Face, no more he had survey'd
> The raging Flames; but struck with strange Surprize,
> Confest them less than those of Anna's Eyes:
> But, had he heard thy Lute, He soon had found
> His Rage eluded, and his Crime atton'd:
> Thine, like Amphion's Hand, had wak'd the Stone,
> And from Destruction call'd the rising Town:
> Malice to Musick had been forc'd to yield;
> Nor could he Burn so fast, as Thou cou'dst Build.

JOHNSON. I know not, Sir, whether I remembered your piece or no. I will only say that for its elegance it deserves to be remembered.

PRIOR. Be careful, Mr. Johnson, or we shall commence friends; and that, I fear, would be of much greater advantage to me than to you.

JOHNSON. Nay, Sir, such a compliment from you is worth much. Perhaps no man, unless it were Chaucer, has by his personal example held the dignity of Poetry higher in the world of State Affairs than yourself.

PRIOR. Your words do me honor, especially in that they allow me to hope that the labor spent on my more philosophical and thoughtful works was not entirely vain.

JOHNSON. Indeed, Sir, it was not. I suppose you to refer more particularly to your *Alma* and your *Solomon*, which together fill no small part of your great volume, and of which the *Solomon* especially contains many shining passages, many of polished elegance, many of splendid dignity, that rise even to sublimity when occasion calls. I have said in print how far from deserving to be neglected the work is, in my opinion. You had before you the noblest models, from Holy Writ and Antiquity; and, if your heroic numbers do not attain to their level, you have only fallen short where no one else has succeeded. If you have fallen short, yet you are far from having failed; and your readers will often come upon passages to which they may recur for instruction and delight: passages from which the poet may learn to write, and the philosopher to reason. When I composed *The Vanity of Human Wishes*, I was not unmindful that you had preceded me in your imitation of Juvenal on old age, in your last book; and on the argument of your whole discourse, that, as you phrase it, "the Pleasures of Life do not compensate the Miseries," I, like every thoughtful man, have often pondered, and more than once in speech and writing have confessed its truth. To this my poem and my *Rasselas* are witnesses.

PRIOR. You were right, Sir, in surmising that I set store by the *Solomon*, and hoped for credit from posterity in its merit. You allow that it deserves not to be neglected. But we both know that it *has* been neglected. It would have been better for my peace of mind had I not been persuaded by my Lords Harley and Bathurst to unlock my Scritoire, and instead had left it as a legacy to be divulged after my coffin was nailed.

JOHNSON. Perhaps, Sir, you might have spared yourself some ephemeral chagrin by withholding it. But you must consider that you enjoyed the acclaim of friendly judges, whose praise meant more than that of the general—at least for the time; and that, having locked it up nine years already, you were not to be considered precipitate in soliciting the approval of the living, whatever course the problematical judgment of posterity might take. That Pope, moreover, was your immediate beneficiary in his *Essay on Man* is of itself ample justification and glory. Besides, Sir, I am afraid the truth is that no man is much regarded by the rest of the world. If it be true, as your great Preceptor teaches, that all is vanity, the utmost which we can reasonably hope—or fear—is to fill a vacant hour with prattle, and be forgotten.

PRIOR. Considering our present circumstances, Mr. Johnson, I had hardly expected to be reminded of this truth. But if, under sufferance, we may revert to literary criticism, is it strictly accurate or fair of you to give, as a sufficient explanation of the tediousness of my poem that "the reader is only to learn what [Solomon] thought, and to be told that he thought wrong?" or that "the event of every experiment is foreseen, and therefore the process is not much regarded?" I would ask you whether the questions Solomon puts to the Rabbins in the first book are not questions which the visible universe itself puts to any thinking man almost from the dawn of thought; or whether, indeed, throughout the whole course of the poem, the hero of it does not contrive to think justly, however his conduct lapses from rectitude under the stress of successive disappointments, and whatever his ultimate bafflement?

JOHNSON. Upon consideration, Sir, I cannot deny that your objection to the force of my explanation is well founded, and that my remarks were too facile. But whatever the explanation, the fact remains that the work is tedious, and that the power of tediousness propagates itself. He that is weary the first hour is more weary the second. By your own admission, Solomon's queries to his Rabbins require no superior wisdom to conceive, but are obnoxious to the most vagrant attention; and since, *ex hypothesi*, they are unanswerable, I question whether, after two centuries and a half, your admirable poem will continue to find readers, unless among those upon whom sits the incubus of duty, or a bulimic curiosity.

PRIOR. You have expressed yourself with such finality upon the poem, Mr. Johnson, that I feel as if I had attended upon the dividing of my own child. I will not risk the sacrifice of *Alma* to your reconsideration.

JOHNSON. *Alma*, Sir, has had many admirers, I will not say undeservedly. Its spangles of wit make a fine show, and if it had a perspicuous plan it might have earned a lasting place in our poetic annals. It may be that you mistook your genius in not going in for witty satire. There is, thanks to the sin of Adam, a tartness in satire that keeps it flavorsome long after panegyric has grown insipid.

PRIOR. For turning aside from it I gave my reasons in "Heads for a Treatise on Learning." In my time, and for one with his fortune to seek, it was too dangerous. My two chief attempts, the "Satyr on the modern Translators" and "Satyr on the Poets," I thought it wiser to suppress, and never acknowledged. However agreeable for the time to its writers and encouragers, Satire in the long run does neither party good, considering the uncertainty of fortune's spinning wheel. In any case, having much business of another sort, I could never have forged a two-handed engine like Mr. Dryden's, or a rapier like Mr. Pope's.

JOHNSON. That you would have acquitted yourself with credit, as you did in all else, I do not doubt. Yet perhaps you chose the wiser part. In the many kinds that you did practise, however, there is one that strikes me as especially noteworthy, as it is especially rare. I mean the short Tale, in the art of which, to my mind, you have seldom been equalled in our tongue, and seldom perhaps in any other.

PRIOR. I confess that I am surprised by your commendation, though the more obliged; for I should have supposed that their moral tone might offend you.

JOHNSON. To be sure, they are not unblemished; and it is to be regretted that for that reason they are unsuitable for a lady's dressing-table, and not much to be commended to the young. But the art of telling is the great merit, and this you have in preeminent degree.

PRIOR. From your naming only four Tales, Sir, I suppose you discriminate rather sharply between related kinds. A dozen and a half of my pieces, I suppose, might be mistaken for tales. I perceive why things like "The Conversation," which relates to me, and "Cupid and Ganymede," or "Mercury and Cupid," or "The Dove," which relate to Cloe, should be ruled out; and why "To a Young Gentleman in Love," which by its title remonstrates with an infatuated youngster, should be considered too personal, although I have called them tales. Also, I suppose, "Erle Robert's Mice," by the same token, since, without mentioning the Chaucerian language, the identity of the persons is as transparent as gauze. But there are others.

JOHNSON. You must consider, Sir, that the definition turns upon nice distinctions. In Lilliput, refinements are important that would be overlooked in Brobdingnag. We are to differentiate between the Compliment, the Epistle, the Dialogue, the Character, the Fable, and the Tale. Compliments you have already excepted. Epistles, to which our old acquaintance Swift was much given, may have an element of narrative in them, whether for illustration or interest biographical or immediately personal. But because of their personal address, these I should also extrude, as you likewise have consented to do. "The English Padlock" might be a shining instance of dialogue but that the homiletic note is overstressed and the interchange one-sided. "The Turtle and Sparrow" is another dialogue that largely excludes narrative interest. Your "Chameleon" and "Epitaph on John and Joan" are notable examples of the Character, in the best sense of the term. "Merry Andrew" is hardly more than aphoristic anecdote. "The Thief and the Cordelier," to be sure, tells a story; but its ballad-form and galloping measure are too indecorous for our aim; and the same is true of "Down-Hall," which again is autobiographical besides. "Truth and Falsehood," otherwise acceptable, and which you have denominated a "tale," is pure fable, with allegorical agents, and a narrative scarcely particular otherwise than as it gains point from the personification. . . . No, Sir, I think we must limit your tales to those I named at the beginning: "Hans Carvel," "The Ladle," "Paulo Purganti," and "Protogenes and Apelles." You may rest your claims upon those. And I think it worth considering, whether at another time in England's history it would have been possible for any man, of what genius soever, to have written pieces of this *peculiar* felicity. Certainly, in epochs earlier than your own, they do not exist. Chaucer, perhaps, in his merrier tales, shows the combination of qualities requisite—humor, sophistication, wit, and sociability; but he required a larger canvas, a stir and bustle of the whole community. The Elizabethans have nothing to compare: nothing of the elegance, nothing of the sharpness of edge, the civility, of your vignettes. Your seventeenth-century forebears dreamed not of such things: your note was not in their gamut. Sir, when they were light-hearted they would not often take pains. And when they were serious, they were sober and un-social. Meditation, not tales, was their concern; and when it turned outward, it was toward an intimate companion, not a company.

But, sir, did you not have a further advantage? Did you not know your circle of readers, their turn of thought, their prejudices, their manners, their habit of speech, as no poet since has known his audience? A small, homogeneous, literate society was the indis-pensable condition for such a precarious and delicate balance as you contrived to sustain in these tales. Their familiarity can take every-thing for granted; their sprightliness is sure of response; they are easy with the sort of ease that is not given, but merely shared. They are careful only to keep the pitch, to use the expected word, to keep the numbers smooth, to be civil and comfortable, without *appearance* of care. As thus:

> But when no very great Affair
> Excited her peculiar Care;
> She without fail was wak'd at Ten;
> Drank Chocolate, then slept again:
> At Twelve She rose; with much ado
> Her Cloaths were huddl'd on by Two:
> Then; Does my Lady Dine at home?
> Yes sure;—but is the Colonel come?
> Next, how to spend the Afternoon,
> And not come home again too soon; . . .
> A Turn in Summer to Hyde-Park,
> When it grew tolerably Dark.

You and I, Mr. Prior, have watched the social scene disintegrate by degrees; and even in my day I know not that it would have been possible to write with such an air of effortless fluency. When *my* contemporaries attempted a tale, they flew off, like Hall-Stevenson, into slap-dash Pindarics, or, like Crabbe, they marched in sedate heroics. Not that I mean to derogate your achievement by a particle. No one else, I believe, could equal it even in your own day, unless once Swift, in his "Baucis and Philemon." Gay tried it and failed. And I cannot call to mind a comparable success in later times, except from that surprising young Scot, Robert Burns, in his "Tam o' Shanter."

As I observed just now, it is a pity that three of your masterpieces in this kind are stained with improprieties that cannot but hinder their fame. I fear that in consequence four or five of your shortest and happiest trifles may outlast all the rest. But I cast my vote for your "Protogenes and Apelles" as the most unexceptionably superior example of your skill: a felicitous mingling of ancient and modern images.

PRIOR. So, sir, I am to rest my expectations of future remembrance on this slender basis: a handful of dubious tales and trifles. I had hoped that I had built a solider claim.

JOHNSON. Why, Sir, man is seldom willing to let fall the opinion of his own dignity. But in the ever-increasing multiplicity of claims for present notice, which of us all can expect celebrity of the kind that levies a tax on the future expenditure of time? a tax that later generations may acknowledge or deny at will? If the day should ever arrive when the pleasure and profit of reading our English authors shall be placed on a parity with the ancients, and be made a duty in our schools, do you suppose that your major writings would become required reading, or that the masters of that distant time will flog their snivelling charges for not being able to recite:

> Now, Solomon, rememb'ring Who thou art,
> Act thro' thy remnant Life the decent Part?

PRIOR. They might do worse, Mr. Johnson, if Letters continue on their present course. I confess I cherish the timid hope that, instead of seeming worse in a couple of centuries, my poems may actually improve with age, and even appear worthy to be collected and annotated like classics, by learned dons, under the aegis of a University Press.

JOHNSON. An innocent fancy, my dear Sir, and one with which, since confession is now the mode, I too have sometimes humored my my imagination. But, in our soberer moments we may both be consoled with the knowledge that if we are disappointed of our hopes, yet we have made an effort for distinction, and that a little more than nothing is as much as can be expected from a being who, with respect to the multitudes about him, and before him, and behind him, is himself little more than nothing.

The True Proportions of
Gay's Acis and Galatea

THE MASQUE, or serenata, or pastoral opera, *Acis and Galatea*—in eighteenth-century printings it was indifferently categorized—has been not so much neglected as quite ignored by the biographers and critics of John Gay. In its entirety, words and music, it is a masterpiece, and the reasons for its lying unregarded, except by historians of music, deserve to be scrutinized because they signalize a recurrent failing on the part of those who write on the arts, when a work exists simultaneously in more than one medium. Only lately, in truth, has criticism begun to cope with Shakespeare himself as drama existent in and for living embodiment on a physical stage and nowhere else, not even in the mind of Coleridge. (Theatrical criticism is by habit only piecemeal commentary on separate productions.) Similarly, to set small matters beside great ones, only of late has the ballad of tradition begun to be considered as *song* and not as a literary or pseudo-literary *genre*, sufficient and self-sustaining in its text alone. And the bardic tradition of the Ugo-Slavs is teaching us much about the Homeric epics of which former generations were unaware. Signs, in fact, are here and there beginning to appear of an unwillingness to rest content with the one-dimensional conception of arts which are only half-fulfilled until they are realized in two dimensions or more. A drawing of a sculpture is not enough; a sculpture of an action is not enough; pantomime does not suffice the spoken scene;

the verbal text of a musical *scena* will not satisfy. Nor can any of these be adequately criticized on a basis of missing dimensions.

There is, however, a special professional myosis that overtakes literary critics in the presence of a text of any length deliberately contrived for union with music. By the very practice of their craft sensitive judges of poetry are unfitted for a just estimate of the merits of such a text. It is not simply that they continue, as they do, to evaluate on the same *level* of poetic excellence as usual, but that they insist on the same *kind* of superiority as that required for words alone. Such a procedure is necessarily mistaken, because by the nature of the case *other* standards are requisite. It is easy to illustrate the difference. *Lycidas,* for example, carries within it its own sufficient orchestration. Any music added to it could do no more than blunt the richness of its harmonies, and dull the effect of what it conveys in and of itself. On the other hand, applying the same verbal rule, critics have been unanimous in deploring Nahum Tate's text of *Dido and Æneas.* But has anyone ever gone away unsatisfied from a valid rendition of Dido's "lament" in Purcell's embodiment of it? Is it even possible to conceive a more profoundly moving statement of poignant farewell than Dido's last words so expressed? But the transcendent majesty of this passage has required for its realization the unhurrying repetitions of word and phrase which are only latent in the text supplied to the composer. So supreme and perfectly matched a statement of tragic emotion in words and music does not argue any deficiency on the one side or on the other. The text is there for the composer, not to change but to fulfill: to express, and to magnify to the measure of its inherent capability. But when the literary critic sits down without the composer to read the bare libretto, it is as if he were trying to read a microfilm with the naked eye. Small wonder that without special advantages he can see nothing great. The critical myopia is well seen in the brief comment allowed to Gay's *Acis and Galatea* by the only historian of Pastoral Drama in England: "It is not . . . pure or finished pastoral. The operatic touch is upon it, and the banality of operatic recitative."[1] What? a pastoral opera with operatic touches? Fie upon it! it will discredit our mystery!

[1] Jeanette Marks, *English Pastoral Drama* (1908), p. 83.

Even by a recent critic very sympathetic to Gay, *Acis and Galatea* has been instanced as an example of "the *false* idealizations of the debased pastoral."[2] Now, Gay was an acute and sensitive judge of style and diction, as the diverse felicity of his work amply demonstrates. We are perhaps overfamiliar with the features of the pastoral scene and possibly, like Johnson, "disgusted." Quite a full vocabulary for it could be compiled from Pope's *Pastorals* alone. Here are examples: the terms for large natural appearances, *mountains, rocks, plains*, and *vales*. The aspects of water, *stream, flood*, or *fountain*. The movements of air, *gales, zephyrs* gentle, soft, or cool. The vegetation, in *groves, shades, bowers, vine*, and *spray*. The painted glories of the *vernal* or *verdant* season. The *quires* of birds, *warbling* or *murmuring*. The *nymphs bathing* in *crystal fountains;* the *swains* shepherding their *flocks* and *herds*. It is with full awareness that Gay employs all these terms in his masque. For with equal deliberation elsewhere he banishes them when he chooses a different end. His "alphabetical catalogue of names, plants, flowers, fruits, birds, beasts, insects, and other material things," appended to *The Shepherd's Week*, has a humorous but also a critical purpose: "Calf, Capon, Carr, Cat, . . . Chalk, Churn, Cock, Corns, Cur, Cyder" and so on. So, whilst in *Acis and Galatea* we have:

> The Flocks shall leave the Mountains,
>   The Woods the Turtle-Dove,
> The Nymphs forsake the Fountains,
>   Ere I forsake my love,

we find its counterpart in "Wednesday; or, The Dumps":

> Sooner shall cats disport in waters clear,
> And speckled mackrels graze the meadows fair,
> Sooner shall scriech-owls bask in sunny day,
> And the slow ass on trees, like squirrels, play,
> Sooner shall snails on insect pinions rove,
> Than I forget my shepherd's wonted love.

There is no quicker way to get a vivid impression of Gay's sensitiveness and tact than to read half a dozen of the mythico-pastoral masques that were being turned out by his contemporaries in the first two decades of the century. The pitfalls that beset

[2] Sven M. Armens, *John Gay Social Critic* (1954), p. 3.

one who cannot dance on this tightrope are obvious to all but those who have tried and tried again. For example, in Cibber's *Venus and Adonis*, 1716, Adonis, *solus*, opens with a song:

> How pleasant is ranging the fields,
> > When we mount with our hounds in the morning!
> > When we hollow,
> > And follow
> The scent ever burning!
> > (*Venus descends from her Chariot*)
> But soft! What nymph is this,
> Whose gaudy form and dress
> Seem rather of a court
> Than of the rural sport?

Or again, unless he seem not shepherd enough to serve as instance, we might quote Sir Trusty, in Addison's *Rosamond*:

> How unhappy is he
> That is ty'd to a she,
> And fam'd for his wit and his beauty!
> > For of us pretty fellows
> > Our wives are so jealous
> They ne'er have enough of our duty.
> But ha! my limbs begin to quiver,
> I glow, I burn, I freeze, I shiver;
> > Whence rises this convulsive strife?
> > I smell a shrew!
> > My fears are true,
> > I see my wife.

Or, with scarcely the excuse of comic relief, there is the dialogue of the plotters in Theobald's *Decius and Paulina*:

SIMO.	Say, *Ida*, does the pious Fraud succeed?
IDA.	Peace, Fool, I would thou wert not here,
	That Face does too much Business wear.
SIMO.	I stand corrected, and to shew
	I value your Advice, I'll go.

But this is beyond the pastoral pale. Close at hand stands Congreve's opera, *Semele*, 1706, with a song for the heroine containing these lines (incidentally, not used by Handel, but in the text received for setting by John Eccles):

> I love and am lov'd, yet more I desire;
> > Ah, how foolish a Thing is Fruition!
> As one Passion cools, some other takes Fire,
> > And I'm still in a longing Condition.

Or take the same author's masque of *The Judgment of Paris*, 1701, for setting which to music no less than four prizes were awarded to four composers, including Eccles and the younger Purcell. The piece contains a deal of machinery and spectacle. Each of the goddesses descends in turn, dismounts from her car, displays her charms and offers bribes. With all three beauties together confronting him, Paris, like Macheath subsequently, grows confused, and sings:

> Apart let me view then each heav'nly fair,
> For three at a time there's no mortal can bear;
> And since a gay robe an ill shape may disguise,
> When each is undrest,
> I'll judge of the best,
> For 'tis not a face that must carry the prize.

But it is too easy to multiply examples of gross impropriety. Directly to the point for comparison with Gay is Motteux's libretto, dated 1701, of *Acis and Galatea*, written for music by Eccles. He adds to the usual company a rustic couple, Roger and Joan, for cheap laughter; makes Galatea act the coquette, playing her lovers off against each other; lets Acis profess infidelity; and brings matters to a happy conclusion with a marriage between the titular characters. The tone of the piece is suggested in an earlier scene, while Polyphemus is expecting to win the nymph. Acis taunts him, in Galatea's presence, to this effect if he marry her:

> I'll hug her, I'll love her, I'll bless her, I'll kiss her,
> 'Till a pair of huge Horns
> Thy broad Forehead adorns.

The present point is that Gay, gifted with a playful wit and more alive than most to the vulnerabilities of the pastoral *genre*, seldom or never makes a false step in his operatic masque; while the rest, however distinguished in other kinds of work—Addison, Aston, Cibber, Congreve, Motteux, Theobald—repeatedly fall headlong. The only possible exception is John Hughes, who happened incidentally to be a good musician as well as a poet.

THERE IS a pervasive suavity about this masque of Gay's: a delicacy and finesse, a propriety akin to Virgil's but without the ulterior glance, the looking before and after: with more of the substance of Ovid's narrative than any other borrowing, yet with-

out his overripeness; with much of the apparent simplicity, emotional directness, and closeness to the natural roots that characterize Theocritus; and with a refined humorous perception especially visible in the treatment of Polyphemus. In Theocritus, this
character is something of a country clown, at once boastful and
self-abasing, clumsy, vain, ridiculous, justly proud of his posses-
sions, his thousand cattle, his milk and cheese and fruits, of his
skill in piping; but aware too of his handicaps, insecure of his power
to charm, and fearsome even when most appealing. Ovid, on the
contrary, makes him repulsive, bloodthirsty, grotesque, tremen-
dous and terrible, a malevolent phenomenon tamed momentarily.
He has none of the bumbling, puppy-like way of Theocritus'
monster. With his pinetrunk for staff and his pipe of a hundred
reeds, he is gigantic. His rages are those of Ætna: the mountains
and waves "feel" his piping, and he will certainly overwhelm anything that opposes him. Gay has blended the two, softened the
revulsion, kept the awkward appeal of his gentler moods, humanized his ludicrous violence while preserving the menace of his
presence. He is a natural force, spontaneous, immediate, uncontrol-
ledly impulsive, dangerous: but yet allied to the Sicilian scene, like
the earthquake or volcanic eruption. As a person of the drama, he
is much the most fully realized.

Full realization of character is not, of course, the object of this
kind of writing, and indeed could only defeat it. Enough substance
to justify our sympathy or antipathy, without affronts to legitimate
expectation, is all we require. Much more deeply significant than
his innate tact, due emphasis, and unforced appeal, is the fact that
Gay has known how to endow his figures with a kind of meta-
phoric universality, so that they generate sympathetic vibrations
and overtones, and thereby subtly engage the elemental depths
of human feeling and experience. This is a largesse rarely to be
met in the convention-riden Arcadian scene.

In his thirty-sixth *Rambler*, Johnson asserts that "there is scarcely
any species of poetry that has allured more readers, or excited more
writers, than the pastoral." But, on the contrary, it seems to be true
that, from Johnson onward for the last two hundred years at least,
there is scarcely any species of poetry that has increasingly repelled
more readers than the classical, true, and unaffected pastoral. Of
all *genres*, it is most opaque to the modern ironic temper and sen-

sibility, and in fact in the present century is almost impervious to sympathy, unless by an imaginative effort so determined as to be self-defeating, or by perverse misinterpretation.

It is, therefore, of all things welcome if we can call up for an *explication de texte* one who can teach us how to read such a document in the spirit in which we may suppose it was intended to be received, when

> Omne tulit punctum qui miscuit utile dulci,
> Lectorem delectando pariterque monendo.

In the present case, fortunately, we can appeal to a guide exactly contemporary with the poet, possessed of unexcelled tact and understanding, of sympathy natural and unforced, an interpretive genius of the highest order, who can take us, phrase by phrase, through the whole work—a happy relief, surely, from historians who appear literally to abominate their subject as "the very nadir of English drama,"[3] or guides for whom the term Pastoral is but a pair of bifocal spectacles through which to view their own ambiguous preoccupations. Our particular guide, of course, is Gay's collaborator and interpreter, of whom Gay had once written:

> There Hendel strikes the strings, the melting strain,
> Transports the soul, and thrills through ev'ry vein.[4]

Handel's manuscript of *Acis and Galatea*, in its original autograph, shows that the work was written (and probably first performed) as a single uninterrupted sequence, not broken into three acts as printed in 1732. This is of first importance at one crucial point, as will be seen; and after that point no logical opportunity for a break occurs. Gay opens with a chorus of shepherds and shepherdesses which, as the work progresses, plays a functional and increasingly dramatic rôle. Its text at the outset looks quite banal, and the reason for this needs to be understood. Much of Gay's text is in the imperative mood, full of hortatory exclamation and invocation. The literal reader is repelled when he finds a deal of exhortation to so little action, and topics proposed without much discussion. But these are not intended to stand unsupported. What Gay does in his first twelve lines is to display the simple raw colors of the pastoral palette. It is the composer's business to mix and

---

[3] Marks, *English Pastoral Drama*, p. ix.
[4] John Gay, *Trivia*, Bk. II, ll. 497–498.

blend them, to dispose and musically to organize, to select and exhibit, to isolate, emphasize, recall, and reveal: to paint, in other words, with the colors provided. The first chorus is exactly what is needed by the composer for establishing a mood of country gaiety. The first couplet is stated in square harmony, so that the words are all distinct:

> O the Pleasure of the Plains,
> Happy Nymphs, and happy Swains . . .

But they are not heard thus. They issue in a burst of delight: "O! the pleasure of the plains!" Then a vocal pause, and then "the pleasure!" and again a pause; then "the pleasure! O the pleasure of the plains!" The second line is now uttered and we begin to learn what is meant by *happy*. The voices, dividing, toss the word back and forth, varying a staccato háp-pý, on a repeated eighth, with a legato ha-a-a-a-áp-py, with four sixteenths and an eighth on the first syllable; so that we get echoes of merriment and bounding feet in the crossing hap-py, hap-py, ha-a-a-a-ap-py many times repeated. The voices rejoin, and again scatter; unite on a threefold repetition, in unison, of "free and gay"; scatter again on "dance and sport," with bursts of unfettered laughter in the staccato explosives on the vowels—actually ha! ha! and ho! ho! injected into the middle of those two prolonged monosyllables, *dance* and *sport*.

With the change of metre at line five, Gay introduces a reflective sentiment, and in miniature recapitulates the change of seasons:

> For us the Winters rain,
>   For us the Summers shine,
> Spring swells for us the Grain,
>   And Autumn bleeds the Vine.

Gay is always aware of the demand of the *aria da capo* for a slight emotional deflection at the change of key, and has made obvious provision for it here. Handel follows this lead and gives the lines to a solo voice in the relative minor. This is repeated by the chorus, whereupon we are brought back again to "the pleasure of the plains."

Galatea now enters on a recitative of longing, which she follows with an air of which the text is:

Hush, ye pretty warbling Quire,
Your thrilling Strains
Awake my Pains,
And kindle soft Desire.
Cease your Song, and take your Flight;
Bring back my Acis to my Sight.

To the composer—but perhaps not to the critic—the first word, "Hush!" implies precedent sound; implies bird-song. Hence, Handel leads off with a long ritornello in which the birds flood the grove with their delicious warbling—sopranino recorder and violins in thirds—until Galatea stills them, momentarily, with her single word. They resume for another two bars, when again she cries, more pleadingly, "Hush, ye pretty warbling Quire!" In a moment they recommence, and again she silences them, continuing with mutual response, and then, in plaintive phrases with lingering imitation, herself floating, bird-like, down again into the repeated first section of the *da capo*.

Gay's strategy in character portrayal is itself Handelian: generally speaking, to represent a single state of mind in each aria, so that by the sum of these successive personifications of emotion the whole character becomes known. Needless to say, the music is expected to seize and project the particular emotional phase of being; and our conviction about the character relies upon the clarity of its musical expression. Thus, the impatient, uncertain anxiety of the searching lover appears melodically in the short, separated phrases of Acis, first aria: "Where shall I seek/the charming Fair?" and later. . . . "Where?"/"Where?"/"Where,—whére shall I" etc.; and with greater intensity at the change of key: "O te-e-ell me, tell me if you saw my Dear." At this point; Damon tries to stay him with a word of warning, prophetic in retrospect. But Galatea is at once discovered, and Acis sings the charming song of objectified passion which is one of the chief *literary* beauties in the work:

Love in her Eyes sits playing
And sheds delicious Death—

phrases so happily English that they quite gravel the German translator of the libretto

Liebe sitzt gaukelnd ihr im Aug'
Und strahlet tödtliche Lust.

More noteworthy is the pretty contrast between this truly courtly lyric and the parallel to come, equally delectable in its own natural comparisons, of Polyphemus, summoning his rustic muse in praise of sweet Galatea's beauty and his love. "O ruddier than the Cherry" is the homely Gay of *The Shepherd's Week*, with an added tunefulness.

Acis' praise is met by the simple and tender delight in reunion of Galatea's "As when the Dove," for which Handel has found the perfect musical enbodiment; and the two move into a duet of sheer joy, expressive of moments when words do not count, for the glad heart transfigures even the poorest of them.

Immediately, without preparation and according to the original intention without pause, there follows the first stunning, dramatic stroke of the opera. With the last exuberant "happy, happy, happy we" of the lovers, the Chorus, magnified now to the proportions of Greek tragedy, suddenly enters on notes of doom:

> Wretched Lovers, Fate has past
> This sad Decree, no Joy shall last;
> Wretched Lovers, quit your Dream.

As well it might, the shock of this abrupt counterstroke stirred Handel's creative imagination to its depths, and he responded with some of the greatest pages he ever wrote. It is impossible to overstate the effect of the plangent waves, overlapping, chromatic, of the ever-recurring words, "Wretched Lovers, quit your Dream." The lovers' lot has suddenly become the lot of us all from the world's beginning, realized with Virgilian compassion and oceanic compass. The imminent peril is soon defined as the monster Polypheme; but the earlier phrases continue without cessation, and well over us, as if the particular shape of Fate—monster or erupting mountain or invisible worm—did not so much matter, 'tis enough, 'twill serve.

To be sure, Polyphemus *is* gigantic, and at his tread

> The Mountain nods, the Forest shakes,
> The Waves run frighted to the Shores.

He can roar, too; but it is not so much his terrible aspect as his ludicrous human qualities that Gay chooses to emphasize. We cannot hate him: he is not naturally malevolent. But, though he has his gentle side, he is short on second thoughts and acts on impulse.

Patience is not his virtue. The chief need is not to antagonize or get in his way.

Gay gives the cue in his first six words: "I rage, I melt, I burn." Handel teaches us how they should be read. *Rage* is sung on an ascending octave, *furioso*, in sixteenths with ornaments. "I rage" is then repeated, tonic to major third; again, third to fifth; but when we look for another repetition, fifth to octave, languishing thoughts arrest the monster and he drops back to the third on the words, "I melt," sung *adagio* for just half a bar! Instantly the furioso mood reanimates him; but he melts again into "soft enchanting accents" before his comically repetitive aria, "O ruddier than the Cherry, O sweeter than the Berry." Handel enhances the fun by assigning the accompaniment of "an hundred Reeds of decent growth To make a Pipe for [his] capacious Mouth" to the smallest, highest recorder. After further efforts to persuade the nymph, in a remarkably attractive recitative like a half-fledged air, Polyphemus, rejected by Galatea with open loathing, bursts suddenly into a superbly vigorous denunciation of subservience in love: marvelously cross-rhythmed, straining to break out of metrical fetters in sheer exasperation.

(Damon's air which follows, however ingratiating, seems rather unnecessary here and out of place; and in fact it was written by John Hughes to be inserted, after the rest was set. It is this song, "Would you gain the tender creature?" and not "Love in her Eyes sits playing," as the Faber edition incorrectly notes,[5] that is to be found in Hughes's collected Poems, 1735.)

Acis is now in his turn enraged by Polyphemus' "hideous Love" and adds a new dimension to his character in the martial determination of his next aria, "Love sounds the Alarm, and Fear is a-flying" —significantly in C major, a key used only here and in "Happy We." Damon does what he can to calm him, with the sage sentiments of "plaisirs d'amour": "Consider, fond Shepherd, how fleeting's the Pleasure." Galatea adds her entreaties against rashness and doubt of her remaining steadfast. She and Acis now commence a duet exchanging vows of eternal love; to which is added, in supreme irony, while the lovers' assurances heighten in tender urgency, a third voice, Polyphemus' exclamations of wrath upon seeing the two together. As they sing their last lines,

[5] *The Poetical Works of John Gay*, ed. G. C. Faber (1926), p. 426 n.

No Sleep to Toil so easing,
As these dear Smiles to me,

his imprecations culminate in the indignant "Presumptuous Acis,
die!" while he hurls the rock that crushes his envied rival. In the
eight following bars of recitative, Acis expires with a cry for help
and a prayer, *adagissimo e piano*, fading into silence in a chromatic
descent on basses and violins *senza cembalo*, reminding of Purcell
and intensely poignant. In fact, everything from the duet and trio
to the final note of the opera belongs to the world's great music.
So much the libretto allowed, or better, awakened in the composer's mind.

The succeeding chorus, "Mourn all ye Muses," in five-part
harmony, is a dirge of extreme beauty. The varying emphasis given
to Gay's four lines is revealing. The first line, "Mourn all ye Muses,
weep all ye Swains," is sung but once.[6] After a two-bar vocal pause,
filled by soprano strings and oboes, the second line, "Tune, tune
your Reeds to doleful Strains," is sung and immediately repeated.
Neither of these lines is used again. But, as we should have foreseen,
the third and fourth lines,

Groans, Cries, and Howlings, fill the neighb'ring Shore;
Ah! the gentle Acis is no more,

evoke a rich and elaborate response. The flexible treatment of the
words is masterly, and deserves close examination in the score itself:
it defies summary description.

What follows is as surprising as anything in the opera—a stroke
of sheer collaborative genius. On paper, it looks only like an alter-
nation of Galatea's complaint, with admonition by the Chorus not
to grieve. It commences with a heavenly long cantilena by the oboe
supported only by cello and continuo, full of quiet sadness, *pia-
nissimo ed adagio*. One bar ahead of the conclusion of this meditation, Galatea enters with words for the same thought: "Must I my
Acis still bemoan?" The notes are immediately repeated by the
oboe before she continues, phrasing with exquisite musical sensibility the brutal outrage of Acis' *extermination*, "Inglorious crush'd
beneath that Stone." This line is repeated but quite transformed by
the altered notes: the first time falling from octave to fifth, the

---

[6] The *ed. prin.* reads, "Mourn all the Muses, weep all the Swains." Probably
the printer mistook *ye* for the common symbol of *the*.

second time descending to the tonic, then rising with indignant protest to the octave on the word "crush'd," which is prolonged in an undulating sob. As she reaches the last word of the phrase, "Stone," the Chorus suddenly breaks in with the single word, "Cease!" The silence that follows is not complete only because Galatea's voice sustains the word "stone" for four bars on a single note. She has neither heard nor heeded; and through the held note they twice repeat the remonstrance, "Cease, Galatea, cease to grieve." Oblivious of interruption, she reiterates her protest. At the word "crush'd" the Chorus insistently breaks in again, and then twice more, with intermittent pauses, while she continues her lament, impervious to comfort, on a long descending scale of a whole octave. The Chorus, urgently reasonable, pleads, "Bewail not whom you can't relieve"; and as they pause she again lifts her voice to the octave, while they once more urge, "Bewail not," etc. She now adds a new line, solo: "Must the lovely charming Youth Die for his Constancy and Truth?" On the last word they again beseech, "Cease, Galatea, cease to grieve." She exclaims, "Die!" and they continue the same entreaty several times in altered tones, each pause filled with her single word of despair, followed then by the whole line, "Die for his Constancy and Truth!"

Now they urge, "Call forth thy Pow'r, employ thy Art, The Goddess soon can heal the Smart." At this point she at last attends and asks, solo, "Say, what Comfort can I find, For dark Despair o'er-clouds my Mind." From here to the end, in square harmony, they press their proposed solution, in short insistent phrases: to give Acis immortality by changing him to a stream that will continue ever to glide through the beloved landscape. It may be simple but surely not unmeaning coincidence that the closing bars of this wonderful episode anticipate with identical notes, though in a different metre, the ritornello that opens "He shall feed his Flock like a Shepherd," in *Messiah*, unimagined as yet for another twenty-some years.

(I suspect that there is a disarrangement in the text immediately following. In the 1732—*editio princeps*—printing, Galatea's recitative is:

> 'Tis done, thus I exert my Pow'r Divine,
> Be thou immortal, tho' thou art not mine.

Halfway through the following aria, but in the 1764, not 1732, text, occur the lines:

> Rock, thy hollow Womb disclose!
> The bubbling Fountain, lo! it flows.

These lines are absent from the earlier text altogether, but they occur in the Handel score, and there is in the music a place for them where 1764 prints them. Logically, however, they belong *before* " 'Tis done!" And in musical logic as well, because the liquid thirds and dotted rhythm of the *larghetto* begin immediately after the recitative, in the long leisurely ritornello before the aria; and it is much too late to produce the bubbling fountain where it now appears, after it has been flowing already for twenty-five bars. Gay would naturally write the four lines in the order now suggested; while Handel, wanting a brief dramatic diversion in the music, may probably have transposed the lines to accommodate it, feeling that the shift would not be noticed—as indeed appears to have proven fact to this day. Handel's order found a place in 1764, printed probably, as other indications also suggest, from the score; while the lines stricken from Gay's text where they properly belong were not, when the text was originally printed, reintroduced at the later, and inappropriate, place.)

What, to conclude, can be said of this final aria of Galatea's, "Heart, thou Seat of soft Delight," save that, as Winton Dean observes, "It is one of the most sublime things Handel ever wrote?"[7] Perfectly consoling and heart-searchingly tender, as if re-consigning Acis—and all dead lovers—to the elements out of which they drew their original being: back into nature, in their "large recompense."

> Now Lycidas, the shepherds weep no more;
> Henceforth thou art the genius of the—

not *shore* but *plain.* The final chorus, words and music, is a perfect blend of recollective tribute with returning life:

> Galatea, dry thy Tears,
> Acis now a God appears . . .
> Hail, thou gentle murm'ring Stream,
> Shepherds' Pleasure, Muses' Theme,
> Through the Plain still joy to rove,
> Murm'ring still thy gentle Love.

[7] Winton Dean, *Handel's Dramatic Oratorios and Masques* (1959), p. 166.

In the version of the opera printed in 1764, there is a stage-setting, as follows:

A rural prospect, diversified with rocks, groves, and a river. Acis and Galatea seated by a fountain. Chorus of nymphs and shepherds, distributed about the landscape, and Polyphemus discovered sitting upon a mountain.

As it happens, this a sufficiently accurate description of a Sicilian landscape painted by Nicolas Poussin, entitled "Landscape with Polyphemus," of which there is more than one copy. The canvas may or may not have provided a model for the setting; but it stirs one's imagination. One dreams of an ideal performance of this opera, with no visible actors, but glorious voices, a perfect orchestra, and a cinema screen, upon which are thrown in continuous succession by a roving camera, in shifting perspective, appropriate detail after detail from the classical landscapes, figures, rocks, trees, and streams, of Poussin's pictures.

But even without Poussin, it is my conviction that, after due attention, we must recognize *Acis and Galatea* as one of the greatest works in the English pastoral tradition. If it be objected that Handel wrote it, I answer, Not without John Gay! But let me reiterate in conclusion the point with which I began. I am not asserting that by itself Gay's libretto is one of the greatest pastoral poems in English. I do say that Gay provided Handel with an almost ideal pastoral libretto; and that together they created a supreme masterpiece in that *genre*. It can only be truly apprehended *as a pastoral opera*, words and music inseparably united. This indivisibility, while it accounts for the critics' neglect, is the very proof of the achievement.

The Beggar's Opera

A CCORDING TO thrice-told report (a "most sweet robe of dur-
ance"), we owe it to Jonathan Swift's belief that a "Newgate
pastoral" would make an "odd, pretty sort of thing" that *The
Beggar's Opera* came into being. A more appropriate parentage
could hardly be invented: the work is just what ought to have
resulted from the impregnation of John Gay's somewhat feminine
mind by the robust ironic intelligence of the Dean. That the union
was brilliantly successful we do not need to be reminded. The
play "was received with greater applause than was ever known. . . .
The ladies carried about with them the favourite songs of it in
fans, and houses were furnished with it in screens." For two hundred years and more it has given unceasing delight.

Reasons for this extraordinary success are not immediately apparent in the fable itself. A rascally thieftaker and receiver of
stolen goods discovers that his daughter is married to a highwayman. Deliberation convinces him that he stands to win more by
the reward for the highwayman's death than by what the latter
may bring him if allowed to go free. Knowing that his son-in-law
is promiscuously fond of women, he bribes two jades to put the
man off his guard while constables rush in and arrest him. The
highwayman is lodged in Newgate, but promptly gains his liberty
through the Keeper's daughter, another sweetheart. Soon after
escape, he is again betrayed by his fatal weakness, again confined,
and condemned at once to be hanged. His last hours are disturbed
by the wrangling of his two chief loves, the thieftaker's and the
gaoler's daughters, both of whom get admittance to his cell. Their

importunity reconciles him to the idea of dying, and his resolution is confirmed by the appearance of four more "wives," each with a child. At this point, in order that the piece may not end unhappily, a reprieve is cried, and the play closes with a general dance.

On the face of it, there is nothing in this farcical plot—or no-plot —to bespeak consideration. How could such a scarecrow have been filled with vitality enough to last two centuries and to show every promise—if the world endure so long—of lasting for another, besides producing a numerous progeny, from *The Village Opera* of Charles Johnson to the Savoy Operas of Gilbert and Sullivan? Out of what textiles have the garments been woven that so miraculously cover this tawdry frame, and what is the magic that has kept them fresh?

It is not a facile formula that will account for such a wonder. From how many and what various fields Gay collected his elements, the careful investigations of several scholars in recent years have taught us.[1] French *Comédie en vaudevilles*, realistic Elizabethan comedy, the Italian tradition of Harlequin and Columbine, recent operatic fashions with both Italian features and elements of the English masque, contemporary news sheets and popular song—all these and more supplied Gay with the simples which his own genius enabled him to compound with such extraordinary felicity.

After so much patient research on *The Beggar's Opera*, it may well seem that the squirrel's granary is full and the harvest done. We must not be ambitious now to add anything considerable in the way of information to what scholarship has already amassed. Coming after those who have "led away the corn," we ought to be satisfied if, gleaning here and there, we may "find an ear of any goodly word that they have left." One or two aspects of the subject do await fuller illustration. But, in addition, reading the play in the light of all that is known about it, we may still feel that its continued popularity poses questions that invite further scrutiny of its pages. Exploring once again the familiar configurations of character and scene, and meditating upon the way in which they exfoliate or, like concentric rings in water, are forced outward by some inner generative impulse into wider and wider areas, can we not press closer than heretofore toward the secret of their vitality?

[1] See especially W. E. Schultz, *Gay's Beggar's Opera: Its Contents, History and Influence* (1923), and E. M. Gagey, *Ballad Opera* (1937).

May we not, in considering afresh the appeals that evoked response
when the play was young, as well as those which are still potent,
sharpen our perception of its peculiar qualities, and, in so doing,
enrich our understanding of the ways of the comic spirit? The
effort is surely worth the cost.

BEFORE PASSING to broader considerations of enduring value, our
attention may reasonably be engaged by certain matters which
were of importance to the play's first audiences but which now
are generally overlooked or ignored. Without any pretense to an
exhaustive summary of the findings of scholarship, we may at
once note a few of the reasons why *The Beggar's Opera* should
have captured the favor of its immediate public. We know that
its political implications made part of its appeal. An audience that
could interpret Addison's *Cato* as a tract for the times was not
slow to catch the allusion to Walpole in a catalogue of thieves
which included "*Robin* of *Bagshot,* alias *Gorgon,* alias *Bluff Bob,*
alias *Carbuncle,* alias *Bob Booty.*" The First Minister's methods
of political bribery, his success in amassing a private fortune, were
easily read into an account of the tricks of gangsters. A recent
quarrel with Townshend was perceived in the Peachum-Lockit
dispute. Walpole's personal habits were understood in the remark,
"He spends his life among women"; and Macheath's passion for
the whole sex would have been interpreted in the same way even
if Gay had not pointed it in that direction by transparent insinu-
ation.

Then, too, the habitual Philistinism of the British attitude toward
certain forms of art found cheap support in the gibes against the
absurdities of opera. Gay asks to be forgiven for not making his
own opera throughout unnatural, like those in vogue. He has
omitted Recitative, he declares, but he has introduced all the
favorite operatic similes: "the *Swallow,* the *Moth,* the *Bee,* the
Ship, the *Flower*"; and in his avoidance of catastrophe he has followed good operatic tradition: "for you must allow, that in this
kind of Drama, 'tis no matter how absurdly things are brought
about," and an Opera "must end happily."

A matter not so frequently adverted to is the debt of *The Beggar's Opera* to D'Urfey's *Pills to Purge Melancholy* for some of
its immediate popularity. D'Urfey's collection, in its third, six-

volume, edition, had but recently appeared. It had gathered a vast
quantity of songs from current and late Restoration plays, from
single sheets and printed broadside ballads, incidentally including
at least two-thirds of the sixty-nine tunes which Gay used in *The
Beggar's Opera*. The *Pills* were familiar to most of the male part,
at least, of Gay's audience. A large majority of the tunes he chose
were associated with amorous words, and not infrequently Gay
kept phrases, refrain lines or half lines, or followed the earlier
verbal patterns, for his new lyrics. There is no doubt that he thus
won the amused attention of all whose tastes had made them
familiar with the originals. In the printed text of the play, the titles
alone of many of the airs would suggest the content of the songs:
"O Jenny, O Jenny, where hast thou been"; "Thomas, I cannot";
"When once I lay with another man's wife," and so on. He makes
use of Congreve's familiar and wittily naughty song, "A Soldier
and a Sailor," and keeps a line of the refrain of the catchy but
obscene "Tom Tinker's my true-love": "This way, and that way,
and which way I will." Similar play is made with the phrase "what
I dare not name" in Mrs. Peachum's "If Love the virgin's heart
invade," and, in other songs, with "Pretty Poll," "Over the hills
and far away," and "How d'you do again." One of the best-loved
songs in the play, Macheath's "If the heart of a man is deprest
with Cares," is closely modeled on its original, a song in *The
Modern Prophets*, the first stanza of which is as follows:

> Would you have a young Virgin of fifteen Years,
> You must tickle her Fancy with sweets and dears,
> Ever toying, and playing, and sweetly, sweetly,
> Sing a Love Sonnet, and charm her Ears:
>   Wittily, prettily talk her down,
>   Chase her, and praise her, if fair or brown,
>   Sooth her, and smooth her,
>   And teaze her, and please her,
> And touch but her Smicket, and all's your own.

A good deal subtler is the transformation of D'Urfey's song in
The Country Wake, called "The Mouse Trap." D'Urfey bewails
the hampering effect of marriage on a man's liberty. In contrast
to the carefree frolics of bachelor days, he describes the married
state in terms like the following:

> We're just like a Mouse in a Trap,
>   Or Vermin caught in a Gin:
> We Sweat and Fret, and try to Escape,
>   And Curse the sad Hour we came in.
>
> This was the worst Plague could ensue,
>   I'm Mew'd in a smoky House;
> I us'd to Tope a Bottle or two,
>   But now 'tis small Beer with my Spouse.

Remembrance of these words gives additional piquancy to Mrs. Peachum's praise of marriage. Only *after* a woman is married, she declares, does she win her freedom. Maidens are like unminted gold, with no currency: but

> A Wife's like a Guinea in Gold,
>   Stampt with the Name of her Spouse;
>   Now here, now there; is bought, or is sold;
>   And is current in every House.

There is a similar reversal, but in the opposite direction, in Polly's song, "Virgins are like the fair Flower." The words in *Dioclesian*, set to Purcell's exquisite melody, conclude as follows:

> In fair Aurelia's Arms, leáve me expiring,
>   To be Imbalm'd with the sweets of her Breath;
> To the last moment I'll still be desiring;
>   Never had Hero so glorious a Death.

Keeping this image in mind, listen to Polly's comment on the cropping of the fair flower.

> But, when once pluck'd, 'tis no longer alluring,
>   To *Covent-Garden* 'tis sent (as yet sweet,)
> There fades, and shrinks, and grows past all enduring,
>   Rots, stinks, and dies, and is trod under feet.

For the tune of "Our Polly is a sad Slut," no less than six sets of words, for the most part high-spirited and indecent, are to be found in D'Urfey's *Pills*. In all of them the idea of women "flinging themselves away" is not far to seek, so that the knowing ear would find a large allowance. Gay has not followed any of the six closely; the talk of Polly's fashionable apparel comes nearest to a song of a fashion called "The Button'd Smock," in which occur the ensuing lines:

> For some will have the out-side fine,
> To make the braver show;
> But she will have her *Holland* Smock
> That's Button'd down below.

For a number of his other lyrics Gay has taken hints from the subject matter of the original songs. Macheath's disillusioned comment on the power of money, "If you at an Office solicit your Due," is based on two songs of worldly advice to the same tune in D'Urfey: "Advice to the Ladies" ("Ladies of *London*, both Wealthy and Fair") and "Advice to the Beaus" ("All Jolly Rakehells that Sup at the *Rose*"). "Come, Sweet Lass" begins with an identical line. With the substitution of "Polly" for "Shepherd," Polly's "When my Hero in Court appears" ends with the original four-line refrain:

> And alás poór Shépherd,
> Alack and a welladay;
> Before I was in Love,
> Oh every month was *May*.

Macheath's "But Valour the stronger grows, The stronger Liquor we're drinking" is set to the ancient drinking song of "Old Simon the King":

> For drinking will make a man Quaff,
> Quaffing will make a man Sing;
> Singing will make a man Laugh,
> And laughing long life doth bring.

That universal favorite, "Fill ev'ry Glass," derives from a curious drinking song in D'Urfey celebrating Marlborough, Eugene, and d'Auverquerque, the words in French but accompanied with an English version. The song begins, "Que chacun remplisse son verre"; or, according to the D'Urfey translation, "Fill ev'ry glass"; its last stanza is particularly in the mood of Gay:

> Si nous a[i]mions autant la Gloire
> Que boire nous serions des Heros;
> Car parmi les verres [et] le[s] Pots,
> Nous sommes seurs [*sic*] de la victoire.

Lucy's confession to her father, "When young at the Bar," is a rare example of debasement by Gay or his original. Little remains of the charm of Purcell's song in *The Fairy Queen*, except subject and inviolably lovely melody, to which the words had been these:

> If Love's a sweet Passion, why does it Torment?
> If a bitter, oh tell me! whence comes my content;
> Since I suffer with Pleasure, why should I complain,
> Or grieve at my Fate, when I know 'tis in vain?
> Yet so pleasing the Pain is, so soft is the Dart,
> That at once it both wounds me, and tickles my Heart.

This song, incidentally, had gained a well-deserved popularity by the turn of the century. It appears on broadsides as well as in D'Urfey, and its title stands above many another ballad to designate the tune to which the new words should be sung.

Having brought his hero as it were to the foot of the gallows, Gay cast about for some piece of music that would rise to the needs of this important occasion. He found just what he wanted in Lewis Ramondon's "Hymn upon the Execution of two Criminals," a dirge in three-two time with appropriately lugubrious words, which may be seen in D'Urfey's final volume of the *Pills*. Its introductory stanzas will sufficiently display its character:

> All you that must take a leap in the Dark,
> Pity the Fate of *Lawson* and *Clark;*
> Cheated by Hope, by Mercy amus'd,
> Betray'd by the sinful ways we us'd:
> Cropp'd in our Prime of Strength and Youth,
> Who can but weep at so sad a Truth;
>   *Cropp'd in our Prime*, &c.
>
> Once we thought 'twould never be Night,
> But now alass 'twill never be light;
> Heavenly mercy shine on our Souls,
> Death draws near, hark, *Sepúlchres* Bell Toles:
> Nature is stronger in Youth than in Age,
> Grant us thy Spirit Lord Grief to asswage.
>   [*Grant us thy Spirit*, &c.]

These melancholy measures Gay divided for a grand trio between his three principals, Macheath, Polly, and Lucy, not neglecting the admirable hint of St. Sepulchre's bell for operatic effect: "But hark!" sings Macheath, "I hear the Toll of the Bell." Whereupon they all echo in chorus, "Tol de rol lol!"

In the course of the opera Gay has introduced among the arias sundry duettos in the proper contemporary operatic manner, to vary the entertainment and underline the burlesque. Polly and her mother share one, Polly and Macheath three, and Polly and Lucy another three. There is likewise due use of a chorus at several points, and, for an echo of operatic ballet, three dances are introduced, including Macheath's cotillion of ladies and the grotesque dance of prisoners in chains. Thus most of the musical elements of real opera are used by Gay, in his fashion. To introduce recitative he would have had to employ the services of a composer. What he does, instead, is to suggest a parody of recitative in Macheath's meditations in the condemned hold. The Ladies, as the Beggar announces in the Introduction, always reckon a Prison Scene "charmingly pathetick"; and in this affecting passage it would not do to allow his hero to express himself in ordinary fashion. Here Gay constructs a medley, linking phrases out of nine familiar melodies (including one from Purcell's *Bonduca*, Farinel's *Ground*, Carey's *Sally*, the popular "Why are mine Eyes still flowing," and *Chevy Chase* and other ballad tunes) and rising to *Greensleeves* by way of closing aria. The fun of this sequence was considerably lessened in the late Hammersmith production (otherwise admirable) by the omission of more than half the excerpts. The omissions unfortunately resulted also in obscuring Gay's equating of his hero's courage with the amount of liquor he contained at the moment. Macheath tugs at the bottle after nearly every phrase. Raising his spirits with a brimmer, he boldly chants (to Purcell's air of "Britons, strike home"),

> Since I must swing,—I scorn, I scorn to wince or whine;

but his next words are,

> But now again my Spirits sink,

and he promptly endeavors to "raise them high with wine." After another phrase or two, he turns to brandy for further assistance. Thus he ascends by degrees to his ironic aria (omitted at Hammersmith):

> Since Laws were made for ev'ry Degree,
> To curb Vice in others, as well as me,
> I wonder we han't better Company,
> Upon *Tyburn* Tree!

But the effect soon wears off: "O Leave me to Thought!" he entreats Polly and Lucy in the trio which follows:

> I fear! I doubt!
> I tremble! I droop!—See, my Courage is out,
>   [*Turns up the empty Bottle.*
> POLLY.   No token of Love?
> MACHEATH.   See, my Courage is out.
>   [*Turns up the empty Pot.*

The whole scene is treated as the most extravagant burlesque, and it is time to pursue the hint which Gay has dropped earlier about pathetic prison scenes, and inquire whether anything in particular lies behind the burlesque here.

Considering the amount of minute investigation accorded *The Beggar's Opera*, one wonders that no student appears to have examined the contemporary operas of Handel, Buononcini, and Ariosti, to learn whether general parody anywhere becomes specific. For if the search has been made, the results of it, whether positive or negative, have nowhere been announced in print. Schultz, indeed, has noted Sir John Hawkins' observation, that "possibly Macheath's appearance in Newgate fetters might be supposed to ridicule the prison scene in *Coriolanus*, performed a few years before." [2] But Hawkins flouted the notion generally of burlesque in Gay's play, and Schultz did not—or could not—verify his suggestion here. F. W. Bateson, in a 1934 edition of *The Beggar's Opera*, converted "possibly" into "probably" and amplified the note: "a hit probably at the prison scene in Attilio Ariosti's opera, *Caius Marius Coriolanus*, produced in 1723." A glance at Burney's History supplies the fuller reference and the date. *Marcius* has been miscopied *Marius*; but the fact is irrelevant, for the opera was doubtless known simply as Coriolano. Suggestion of any specific parody in this direction thus rests where Hawkins left it in 1776.

Schultz has caught one other allusion in the Beggar's preliminary statement: "I have observ'd such a nice Impartiality to our two Ladies, that it is impossible for either of them to take Offence." "This," Schultz observes, "seems to have no bearing on Polly and

[2] Schultz, *Gay's Beggar's Opera*, p. 143.

Lucy"; and he continues with the correct explanation, though vaguely expressed: "it is clearly a reference to the quarrel between two rival singers, Cuzzoni and Faustina, in 1727, over the leading part in an Italian opera." Now this quarrel was the most notorious event in the annals of the operatic stage during the two years preceding the appearance of Gay's work. Faustina Bordoni was imported in the spring of 1726 at the fabulous salary of £2500. Cuzzoni, already established, was receiving £2000. Cuzzoni, in spite of what Burney calls her "native warble" and "a perfect shake," was dumpy and singularly unattractive in personality. Faustina seems to have been an appealing creature, and pleasing to the eye, as well as the possessor of an equally miraculous voice. Fashionable London at once took sides. Lampoons were published on both parts in the papers, and the friends of the two singers met in the theater to hiss their enemies off the stage in turn, until the universal clamor broke up the performance. Matters came to a hysterical climax when, in a performance of Buononcini's *Astyanax*, in the spring of 1727, the rivals actually resorted to mutual scratching and hair pulling on the stage. Nobody could possibly have remained ignorant of this notorious dispute. Gay's allusion to it goes much beyond an introductory reference. The rivalry of Polly and Lucy, in this view, takes on added comic significance:

LUCY. If you are determin'd, Madam, to raise a Disturbance in the Prison, I shall be oblig'd to send for the Turnkey to show you the Door. I am sorry, Madam, you force me to be so ill-bred.

POLLY. Give me leave to tell you, Madam: These forward Airs don't become you in the least, Madam . . .

[Then a song:]

LUCY.   Why how now, Madam Flirt?
                     If you thus must chatter;
                 And are for flinging Dirt,
                     Let's try who best can spatter;
                         Madam *Flirt!*

POLLY.   Why how now, saucy Jade;
                     Sure the Wench is tipsy;
                 How can you see me made   [*To him.*
                     The Scoff of such a Gipsy?
                         Saucy Jade!   [*To her.*

In this song, the monosyllable *Dirt* occupies a running passage nearly three bars long, in true bravura style, and in strong contrast to the usual note-for-syllable habit of the settings. The quarrel subsequently works toward a fateful climax. "I could murder that impudent happy Strumpet," cries Lucy; and she proceeds to make the attempt. In a speech which is the exact counterpart in English of contemporary Italian operatic recitative, she declares: "Jealousy, Rage, Love and Fear are at once tearing me to pieces. How am I weather-beaten, and shatter'd with distresses!" This launches her naturally upon her next aria, built on the figure of the Ship ("I'm like a Skiff on the Ocean tost"), and rising to its climax:

> Revenge, Revenge, Revenge,
> Shall appease my restless Sprite.

In the right operatic tradition, she has prepared a poison draught against Polly's arrival; and, dropping to speech again, she says:

I have the Rats-bane ready.—I run no Risque; for I can lay her Death upon the Ginn [this of Cuzzoni!].—But say, I were to be hang'd—I never could be hang'd for any thing that would give me greater Comfort, than the poysoning that Slut.

Polly enters, and there is pretense of a reconciliation, Lucy recommending—pleasantly enough, in the light of her intentions—a "quieting Draught." "I wish," she says pointedly, "I wish all our Quarrels might have so comfortable a Reconciliation"—a patent allusion to matter outside the play.

But Faustina and Cuzzoni will take us yet further. When Faustina arrived early in 1726, the very first task which Handel set himself was to write an opera in which both stars could sing, and in which neither could claim that the other's role was better than her own. The job seems to have taken him nearly a month! and a handsome piece of work it was, in which the arias were shaped as by the hand of an expert *couturier* to display the special excellences of each voice. The recitatives were evenly divided, and the duets so artfully contrived that now Faustina and now Cuzzoni had the foremost part. Each lady had as well a duet with the leading man. The opera was *Alessandro*. It opened on May 5, and proved so popular that, instead of the usual twice, it was performed thrice a week for the rest of the season. The plot is very largely taken up with the rivalry of Rossane and Lisaura for the love of Alessandro, who, outwardly at least, vacillates deplorably between them, inclining to the nearer, and not fixing upon Rossane until the last possible moment. "How happy could [he] be with either, Were t'other dear charmer away!" Throughout the three[3] acts of the opera, the ladies consequently live upon the rack, singing all the while of their pains and doubts and jealousy. "How sweet love would be," sings Lisaura, "were it not for jealousy with its icy poison." There is no close parody in *The Beggar's Opera* of any particular scene in *Alessandro*, but a kind of condensed parody occurs here and there of broader vistas. Thus, in *Alessandro*, there is a scene in which the hero comes back from martial exploits to his two loves. Alessandro greets Rossane with a loving embrace, and is well received, whilst Lisaura watches with inward rage. Then he turns to Lisaura with the words: "Delightful Lisaura, no less gladly do I return to thee." Thereupon, Rossane starts away in jealous wrath. Alessandro follows her, and Lisaura exclaims that she cannot longer endure this unworthy treatment: "More unstable is this inconstant one than the wave, more easily set in motion than a leaf." So in balder fashion do Polly and Lucy bid for Macheath's notice:

POLLY. Hither, dear Husband, turn your Eyes.
LUCY.   Bestow one glance to cheer me.
POLLY. Think with that Look, thy *Polly* dyes.
LUCY.   O shun me not—but hear me.
POLLY. 'Tis *Polly* sues.
LUCY.   —'Tis *Lucy* speaks.
POLLY.   Is thus true Love requited?
LUCY.   My Heart is bursting.
POLLY.   —Mine too breaks.
LUCY.   Must I
POLLY.   —Must I be slighted?

Again, in the third act of Handel's opera, the women meet by themselves to take stock of the situation. "Let us leave jealousy, deceit, and trickery, fair Lisaura," says Rossane; "let us both equally love the conqueror of the world, and let Alessandro's

<hr>

[3] Schultz credits Gay with breaking the five-act theatrical tradition. "Gay's three acts," he declares, "among the very first to stand alone, furnished a pleasing contrast to the five acts of the majority of comedies; and . . . exerted a real influence, if we may judge by later work . . . [which took up] the battle for a shorter dramatic scale" (*ibid.*, p. 281). But Gay was merely following the established operatic tradition in this matter.

heart fall to her who shall have the better hap in true loving constancy." "In vain you try to put me down with your fine boasting," replies Lisaura; "as for me, I would imitate the fair flower which turns toward the sun's brightness, and finds solace in admiring his beauty. Yet I differ in that I long for what consumes me, whilst the flower only follows that which gives it life." Similarly, Gay's ladies meet to discuss their mutual unhappiness. "Ah, *Polly! Polly!*" cries Lucy; " 'tis I am the unhappy Wife; and he loves you as if you were only his Mistress." "Sure, Madam," Polly answers, "you cannot think me so happy as to be the Object of your Jealousy.—A Man is always afraid of a Woman who loves him too well—so that I must expect to be neglected and avoided." "Then," says Lucy, "our Cases, my dear *Polly*, are exactly alike. Both of us indeed have been too fond." Rossane, however, has premonitions of felicity, and in a brilliant aria she describes her feelings in images comparable to those in which Lucy earlier expresses Polly's good fortune. While like the rudderless skiff, cries Lucy, "I lye rolling and tossing all Night, That *Polly* lyes sporting on Seas of Delight!" "Si nella calma azurro," sings Rossane, "brilla il mar, se splende il sole, e i rai fan tremolar tranquilla l'onda."

All this makes something of an Alexander out of Macheath, and indeed the two heroes have significant traits in common. Both have attained their greatest successes in the same manner—by force of arms—and both tower above their associates in magnanimity. The parallel is hinted by Swift in a letter to Gay. "I wish," Swift writes, "Macheath, when he was going to be hanged, had imitated Alexander the Great when he was dying. I would have had his fellow-rogues desire his commands about a successor, and he to answer, Let it be the most worthy, etc." (March 28, 1728). But Alexander's death was not in the opera. What was in the opera was Alessandro's passion for the sex, and his reluctance to say no to a pretty face. He comes upon the sleeping Rossane and thinks to obtain a kiss. But Lisaura is on the watch and promptly comes forward. When Alessandro perceives her, "Come," he says, "beautiful Lisaura, and console the distresses of a sorrowful heart." Rossane awakes at that moment, but feigns continued slumber. Mockingly, Lisaura repeats the words she has just heard him use to her rival: "Let me kiss you, lovely rubies"; and departs with disdain. Alessandro turns back to Rossane for solace of his pains. She in turn picks up the words he has just addressed to Lisaura, pointing them against him with scorn: "Proud eyes beloved, let me no longer languish,"—and mockingly abandons him. "What honor," he exclaims ironically, "is given to the world's conqueror! Alexander made a mock by two stubborn women!" So, at a great remove, sings Macheath:

> One wife is too much for most husbands to hear,
> But two at a time there's no mortal can bear.
> This way, and that way, and which way I will,
> What would comfort the one, t'other wife would take ill.

Until someone can make a careful examination of the whole file of Italian operas that were produced in London before 1728, it will not be possible to draw up an exact account of Gay's use of them. The operas of Ariosti and Buononcini have not been accessible to the present writer, but a cursory inspection of Handel's operas alone is enough to reveal a good many interesting parallels. Thus, in several of them the poisoned cup appears. *Flavio* (1723) has a scene of quarreling fathers. *Ottone* (1723) has a pirate, a daring, resourceful, wild fellow, who might almost have given hints for Macheath. *Ottone* was very popular, its phrases, according to Burney, passing current among musical people almost as the *bons mots* of a wit circulate in society. In *Giulio Cesare* (1724) there is a scene in a seraglio in which the tyrant Ptolemy gets into a genial frame, forgets his mistrust, and lays aside his sword, whereupon, at a sign from Cornelia, Sextus rushes in and attempts to stab him. In outline, this is close to the capture of Macheath.

Hawkins may have had a special reason for suggesting *Coriolano* as the original of the prison scene in *The Beggar's Opera*. But he could have pointed equally to several of Handel's operas for prison scenes that the ladies might have considered "charmingly pathetick." *Silla* (1714) has an affecting one; *Tamerlano* (1724), a fine and popular opera, of which the favorite songs were separately published by Walsh, has another, involving a cup of poison. *Radamisto*, in the opera of that name (1720), is condemned to death by the tyrant Tiridate. Zenobia, Radamisto's love, is given the choice of marrying Tiridate or of carrying death to her lover.

She enters the prison with the poisoned bowl and, as she approaches Radamisto, tries to drink it herself. Unable to move because of his shackles, he can do nothing to prevent her. But the cup is dashed to the ground by Tiridate, who enters just in time. A nearly identical scene is worked out in *Floridante* (1721)—sufficient testimony to its theatrical appeal. *Rodelinda* (1725) contains an equally telling prison scene, which has recently been favorably compared (by Hugo Leichtentritt) to the famous one in Beethoven's *Fidelio*, with which, indeed, it has striking features of resemblance. *Alessandro* itself has a prison scene, though one not so affecting as the preceding; and, speaking generally, there is hardly an opera in which someone does not suffer duress for a time, and later make his escape by force or stratagem.

Of all the operas mentioned, *Floridante* seems most likely to have contributed elements to *The Beggar's Opera*, not only in the prison scene, but also in two noteworthy parting scenes between the hero and his love. Floridante, meditating in his dungeon, displays fine courage without any of the fortifying draughts which Macheath found so necessary under similar circumstances. Chained to a pillar, he sings defiantly: "These shackles and this horror cause no fear in my breast. My torment is welcome to me." He greets as his deliverer the cup of death which his love comes to bring him. "Oh cara soave morte!" he cries to Elmira: "oh troppo a te crudele, troppo pietoso a me, fiero tiranno! candida man, lascia ch'io stempri in baci su te il cor mio! tu dolce puoi far morte." Polly and Lucy only wish that they might suffer in Macheath's place; but Elmira attempts to exhibit "l'ultima prova d'un amor fedele" by drinking the poison herself, in this intensely dramatic and memorable scene.

The parting between Polly and Macheath at the end of Act I is obviously patterned on the fervent protestations and lingering farewells of high romance. "Is there any Power, any Force," asks Macheath, "that could tear me from thee?" And they sing together the well-known duet, "Were I laid on *Greenland's* Coast—Were I sold on *Indian* Soil." "But oh!" says Polly, "we must part." And she sings the plaintive "O what Pain it is to part!" concluding, with perhaps a little admixture of Juliet: "One Kiss and then—one Kiss —begone—farewell . . . A few Weeks, perhaps, may reconcile us all . . . MACHEATH. Must I then go? POLLY. And will not Absence change your Love? . . . O how I fear!—How I tremble." And they sing a final song as they part, "looking back at each other with fondness; he at one Door, she at the other." With all this it is interesting to compare the conclusion of Act I of *Floridante*:

FLORIDANTE. Ch'io parta? ELMIRA. Ch'io ti perda? Anima mia! In van l'invidia rea lo spera. FL. In vano me'l prefigge il destin, se non m'uccide. Solo partir? ELM. Sola restar? FL. Lasciarti? ELM. Più non vederti? Oh Dei! Non so. FL. Non vo'. ELM. Troppo amo. FL. Troppo adoro. Ahi! che a pensarlo sol, sento che moro.

Elmira then sings an aria, not about Greenland's coast, but to the following similar effect: "I shall sooner see the stars plunge into the sea than abandon my dear love. Thou art my life, my fate." To this, Floridante replies in similarly impassioned style, and a little later both join in a duet which prettily rings the changes on the same theme:

FL.	Ah mia cara, se tu resti,
	infelice a morte io vo.
ELM.	Ah mio caro, se tu parti,
FL.	se tu resti,
ELM.	se tu parti,
FL.	infelice a morte io vo.
ELM.	per l'affanno io morirò.
ELM.	Altra spene
FL.	altro bene
ELM.	senza te, cor mio, non ho.
FL.	senza te, cor mio, non ho.

If this was not the scene which Gay had in mind, it will, under submission, do well enough.

It does not appear to have been Gay's method to paraphrase the actual songs or scenes of his originals. Rather, he re-created, so that while many of the images reappear so sharply that we cannot doubt a reminiscence, yet it is hard to convince ourselves that a specific passage is the unquestionable original of one in Gay. For example, is or is not Lucy's "I'm like a skiff on the ocean tossed, Now high now low with each billow borne" indebted to the air of Berenice in *Scipione?*—

Com' onda incalza altr' onda,
pena sù pena abbonda,
sommersa al fin è l'alma in mar d'affano.

In general, all Gay's similes except the ones which are obviously ludicrous, like the housewife's rat, may be suspected of operatic parentage. The following parallel, however, seems to be more than fortuitous. Polly, toward the end of Act II, has a song—set, it is amusing to note, to an air by Sandoni, Cuzzoni's own husband —which reads as follows:

> Thus when the Swallow, seeking Prey,
>   Within the Sash is closely pent,
> His Consort, with bemoaning Lay,
>   Without sits pining for th' Event.
> Her chatt'ring Lovers all around her skim;
> She heeds them not (poor Bird!) her Soul's with him.

In the opera *Scipione*, produced a year and a half before *The Beggar's Opera*, Berenice, a prisoner of war, is followed by her lover, who sings this aria:

> Lamentando mi corro a volo,
> qual colombo che solo,
> và cercando la sua diletta
> involata dal casciator;
> E poi misero innamorato
> prigionero le resta stato;
> mà la gabbia pur lo alletta,
> perchè restaci col suo amor.

It may be objected that we have been assuming a rather intimate acquaintance on Gay's part with the particulars of Italian opera. Not more intimate, in my opinion, than the probabilities warrant. That Gay was himself musical admits of no dispute. All his life he wrote ballads and lyrics to be sung, and from first to last his works display a wide familiarity with popular song. (That Pepusch, as Burney suggests, selected the tunes for *The Beggar's Opera* and *Polly* is pure nonsense, not worth a moment's consideration. If the internal evidence of the lyrics did not disprove the suggestion, the list of popular songs at the end of Gay's *Shepherd's Week*, 1714, would by itself be enough to resolve any doubts.) He himself is known to have played the flute. He moved in a fashionable set that would as a matter of course have interested itself in opera, just as people of fashion today, whether or not they love music, attend the opera for social reasons. But Gay had a better reason, for he was even professionally connected with it. He wrote the libretto of *Acis and Galatea*, which, in 1719 or 1720, Handel set to music that puts this work among the composer's masterpieces. There is little probability that Gay intended a serious attack upon Italian opera, and he may even have been somewhat appalled at the amount of damage caused by his play. For his ridicule does not go beyond poking affectionate fun at conventions which, like most conventions objectively regarded, have their ludicrous side. Handel had the sense to see this truth, and there is no evidence that *The Beggar's Opera* ever caused a rift between the two men. Years before *Acis and Galatea*, Handel had set a lyric for Gay's early play, *The What D'Ye Call It*. (Gay used the tune again in his opera.) And in 1732, after *The Beggar's Opera* and *Polly* had done their worst, Handel returned to *Acis and Galatea* in order to rework it. Intrinsically, there is nothing in *The Beggar's Opera* which even approaches significant criticism of serious opera; and Professor Dent,[4] in contrast to most who have written on the subject, has sound sense on his side when he declares: "The Italian opera was killed, not so much by the fact that *The Beggar's Opera* made its conventions ridiculous (for its conventions could at that time have been ridiculous only to quite unmusical people), as by the incontestable attraction of the new work itself." [5] Everything considered, *The Beggar's Opera* may more properly be regarded as a testimonial to the strength of opera's appeal to John Gay's imagination than as a deliberate attempt to ridicule it out of existence.

Further evidence of Gay's serious musical taste lies closer at hand. So much has been made of the popular character of the melodies in *The Beggar's Opera* that it will probably surprise most readers to learn that nearly a third of the airs employed are by known composers; for none, I believe, of the editions of the play, nor of its songs, takes the trouble to point out the fact, although students have traced nearly every one of the tunes to earlier sources. We have hardly noticed how amply Gay laid under contribution the most reputable composers of his age. Purcell leads

[4] E. J. Dent, *Händel* (1934), p. 77.
[5] Neither, though the point is hardly worth defending, does Gay's epigrammatic motto for *Muzio Scaevola* sound like the word of a man who despised the class to which this work belonged:

> Who here blames words, or verses, songs, or singers,
> Like *Mutius Scaevola* will burn his fingers.

the list, in number as in excellence. But Handel follows him close; and among other composers who make an appearance are Bououoncini, Sandoni, Akeroyde, Leveridge, and Eccles. Nevertheless, Gay had a sure ear for a good tune, whether or not it bore the distinction of a famous name; and it cannot be said that the anonymous airs which he selected are noticeably inferior, as a class, to the others.

WHAT HAS neither been forgotten nor ignored is the poet's ability to devise excellent lyrics for his tunes. In approaching this aspect of the play, we move at once from the ephemeral causes of its popularity to grounds which have permanent validity. Gay's easy grace, his power of being witty whilst remaining fluent and singable, have never been touched unless by poets who have written with a tune in mind. Even Burns—who did so write—though his emotional range was much wider and deeper, seldom hit the level of Gay's succinct wit in song, but generally resorted to ampler forms for his most pungent expression. In mere singing quality, few English lyric poets have surpassed Gay at any time since Elizabethan days, and probably none save Burns since his own day. Everyone has his own favorites in *The Beggar's Opera*, and it is almost an impertinence to single out for quotation things so familiar and beloved. But Gay's special flavor, his ironic wit, his perfect sense of how to match a tune with words, are brilliantly displayed in Macheath's sardonic meditation upon experience:

> Man may escape from Rope and Gun;
>   Nay, some have out-liv'd the Doctor's Pill;
> Who takes a Woman must be undone,
>   That Basilisk is sure to kill.
> The Fly that sips Treacle is lost in the Sweets,
>   So he that tastes Woman, Woman, Woman,
> He that tastes Woman, Ruin meets.

More typical, perhaps, of Gay's performance is the Gilbertian verve and speed of the following:

> If you at an Office solicit your Due,
>   And would not have Matters neglected;
> You must quicken the Clerk with the Perquisite too,
>   To do what his Duty directed.

Or would you the Frowns of a Lady prevent,
She too has this palpable Failing,
The Perquisite softens her into Consent;
That Reason with all is prevailing.

In quite another category stand the lines of the cotillion in Act II—a silvery Augustan echo of the golden chime of the Renaissance:

Let us drink and sport to-day,
Ours is not to-morrow.
Love with Youth flies swift away,
Age is nought but Sorrow.
Dance and sing,
Time's on the Wing,
Life never knóws the return of Spring.
CHORUS. Let us drink &c.

The note of that stanza, though it exactly expresses the nostalgic quality of much of Purcell's music, is very rare in Gay's work.

The scrupulous ear that so nicely adjusted the phrases of the lyrics has exerted the same felicitous control over the dialogue. Not enough praise has been accorded to Gay's prose. The wit of his epigrams, to be sure, has received applause. But the perspicuous timing of his cadences, even in passages devoid of epigrammatic pointing, is worthy of careful study. He never taxes the ear. The ease and polish of his phrases is perfectly calculated for oral delivery. It is self-conscious, but not insistent; and it has just the right amount of emphasis to gratify the listener. Take for example a passage which eschews the advantages of aphorism, the quarrel of Peachum and Lockit—a delightful and conscious parody[6] of the familiar scene between Brutus and Cassius in *Julius Caesar*, as well as a fling at the differences between the brothers-in-law, Walpole and Townshend:

PEACHUM. Here's poor *Ned Clincher's* Name, I see. Sure, Brother *Lockit*, there was a little unfair Proceeding in *Ned's* case: for he told me in the Condemn'd Hold, that for Value receiv'd, you had promis'd him a Session or two longer without Molestation.

LOCKIT. Mr. *Peachum*—this is the first time my Honour was ever call'd in Question.

PEACHUM. Business is at an end—if once we act dishonourably.

[6] See Swift to Gay, March 28, 1728: "I did not understand that the scene of Lockit and Peachum's quarrel was an imitation of one between Brutus and Cassius, till I was told it."

LOCKIT. Who accuses me?

PEACHUM. You are warm, Brother.

LOCKIT. He that attacks my Honour, attacks my Livelihood.—And this Usage—Sir—is not to be borne.

PEACHUM. Since you provoke me to speak—I must tell you too, that Mrs. *Coaxer* charges you with defrauding her of her Information-Money, for the apprehending of curl-pated *Hugh*. Indeed, indeed, Brother, we must punctually pay our Spies, or we shall have no Information.

LOCKIT. Is this Language to me, Sirrah,—who have sav'd you from the Gallows, Sirrah!

[*Collaring each other.*

PEACHUM. If I am hang'd, it shall be for ridding the World of an arrant Rascal.

LOCKIT. This Hand shall do the Office of the Halter you deserve, and throttle you—you Dog;—

PEACHUM. Brother, Brother—We are both in the Wrong—We shall be both Losers in the Dispute—for you know we have it in our Power to hang each other. You should not be so passionate.

LOCKIT. Nor you so provoking.

PEACHUM. 'Tis our mutual Interest; 'tis for the Interest of the World we should agree. If I said any thing, Brother, to the Prejudice of your Character, I ask pardon.

LOCKIT. Brother *Peachum*—I can forgive as well as resent.—Give me your Hand. Suspicion does not become a Friend.

PEACHUM. I only meant to give you Occasion to justify yourself.

When he heightens the dialogue by the addition of epigrammatic statement, Gay comes very near the level of Congreve himself. What he lacks of the Congrevean brilliance, he compensates for by never giving more at a time than ordinary attention will sustain without conscious effort. He seldom allows himself Congreve's length of phrase. It is illuminating to compare the pace of the two:

FAINALL. You are a gallant man, Mirabell; and though you may have cruelty enough not to satisfy a lady's longing, you have too much generosity not to be tender to her honour. Yet you speak with an indifference which seems to be affected, and confesses you are conscious of a negligence.

MIRABELL. You pursue the argument with a distrust that seems to be unaffected, and confesses you are conscious of a concern for which the lady is more indebted to you than is your wife.

Gay's tempo is more rapid: his cadences beach themselves much sooner, with an impact that is less impressive to watch, but more immediately felt:

PEACHUM. Dear Wife, be a little pacified. Don't let your Passion run away with your Senses. *Polly*, I grant you hath done a rash thing.

MRS. PEACHUM. If she had had only an Intrigue with the Fellow, why the very best Families have excus'd and huddled up a Frailty of that sort. 'Tis Marriage, Husband, that makes it a blemish.

PEACHUM. But Money, Wife, is the true Fuller's Earth for Reputations, there is not a Spot or a Stain but what it can take out. A rich Rogue now-a-days is fit Company for any Gentleman; and the World, my Dear, hath not such a Contempt for Roguery as you imagine.

For the most part, Gay's epigrams do not bear lifting out of their contexts so well as do Congreve's; but Congreve would have found it difficult to better the aphorism of Macheath:

Do all we can, Women will believe us; for they look upon a Promise as an Excuse for following their own Inclinations.

Gay has invented for us a vivid group of people, with an appeal that is hard to resist. They are so delightful, and, in the discrepancy between their reprehensible ends and the self-righteousness with which they pursue them, so ludicrous that we may miss the richer significance of the satire in our mere spontaneous enjoyment. The matter is treated with so light a hand that we incline to ignore its serious implications. It is important, therefore, to remind ourselves of the actual weight of these persons, for without this solid underpinning Gay could hardly have made his play carry the considerable cargo of its deeper meaning—could hardly have made it a social commentary which, for all its surface playfulness, fulfills some of the profoundest ends of comedy.

Each of the leading characters is a positive force. Let us hold in abeyance for the moment our amused perception of their real worth, while they parade before us in the favoring light of their own self-regard. Peachum is a man of responsibility who has constantly to make decisions affecting the welfare and the lives of many people. He has to weigh the importance of particular cases, adjudicate conflicting claims, and issue commands. And his orders are not lightly disobeyed. His wife has a proper sense of her husband's importance in their world, and of her own position. She shares his counsels, but respects his authority and does not abuse her privilege. Her solicitude for her family's reputation is keen, her maternal sense is well developed. She does not lightly give way to emotion, but, on a sufficient occasion, her passions are impressive. Polly is neither feather-brained nor impulsive, but basically prudent and steady. She accepts, and respects, her parents' values, and her single point of difference with them is rationally grounded though admittedly in significant accord with her inclinations. Filch, the servant, recognizes that his own interests are identified with his masters', and is accordingly trusted and accepted almost as one of the family. He is a boy of the brightest parts, quick and apt, ready to give his best efforts to the discharge of his varied responsibilities. Lockit is another, but lesser, Peachum, with a philosophy equally well developed though not quite so fully uttered, and with a visible satisfaction in the power he wields. His daughter Lucy is a Salvator Rosa set over against the Claude of Polly. In her tempestuous nature we can trace Ercles' vein:

> The raging rocks
> And shivering shocks
> Shall break the locks
> Of prison gates.

She has a streak of tenderness, but in anger she is terrible and dangerous. She is crafty and determined in pursuit of revenge, and does not flinch from the possible consequences. As for Macheath, his sang-froid, dash, and prodigality of purse and person make him a favorite with both sexes. He is not easily cast down, and he knows that there are things worse than death in the human lot. Hazlitt calls him "one of God Almighty's gentlemen." His gallantry and good breeding rise, declares Hazlitt, "from impulse, not from rule; not from the trammels of education, but from a soul generous, courageous, good-natured, aspiring, amourous. The class of the character is very difficult to hit. It is something between gusto and slang, like port-wine and brandy mixed." [7]

None of these persons appears to be suffering from a sense of inferiority. Their words give proper dignity to their ideas, and their conduct proceeds in accordance with principles to which they have given a good deal of thought. Without in the least minimizing the pleasure of their company, one may assert that, with the possible exception of Polly, they all have a better opinion

[7] *On the English Stage*, July 27, 1816, quoted by Schultz, *Gay's Beggar's Opera*, p. 274.

of themselves than we do. For we are not taken in: we know them for the immoral rogues that they are. They are the most immediate objects of Gay's satire. However loftily they bear themselves, the human reality of their lives is sordid and contemptible. Remembering the dreariness of many of the products of "realism" in later days, we may well be grateful for an occasional example of the mock heroic, which subjects to the purposes of humor the matter generally reserved for "realistic" treatment. The flair for this inverted kind of burlesque has, for reasons which might elsewhere be significantly pursued, been all but lost in our time. It is enough to note here that, in our recognition of Gay's burlesquing of the high-flown manners and sentiments of operatic romance, we ought not to lose sight of the fact that he is simultaneously ridiculing a low society by decking them in all this borrowed finery. For burlesque has a two-edged blade, though both edges need not be equally sharp. "Had the Play remain'd, as I at first intended," says Gay in the person of the Beggar, with glancing irony, "it would have carried a most excellent Moral. 'Twould have shown that the lower Sort of People have their Vices in a degree as well as the Rich: And that they are punish'd for them."

The characters in the play are aware of our low opinion of them, and stand on the defensive against us. Offspring of corruption as they are, feeding on sin and death, what are their bulwarks, that so magnificently shore up their self-respect?

It is not by maintaining that the bases of our criticism are unsound that they are able to repel our attack. Truth and falsehood, good and evil, right and wrong are for them fundamentally the same as they are for us. Peachum, for example, accepts the conventional morality, and can even afford to make gestures of kindliness when they do not interfere with more important considerations. He delights "to let Women scape." "Make haste to Newgate, Boy," he commands Filch, "and let my Friends know what I intend; for I love to make them easy one way or other." And Filch, in the orotund fashion of sentimental drama, replies, "I'll away, for 'tis a Pleasure to be the Messenger of Comfort to Friends in Affliction." Neither Filch nor Mrs. Peachum is a stranger to feelings of gratitude and good will. Peachum, moreover, is above petty animosities. When Polly recoils from the idea of having Macheath impeached, protesting that her blood freezes at the thought of murdering her husband, Peachum replies:

Fye, *Polly!* What hath Murder to do in the Affair? Since the thing sooner or later must happen, I dare say, the Captain himself would like that we should get the Reward for his Death sooner than a Stranger. Why, *Polly*, the Captain knows, that as 'tis his Employment to rob, so 'tis ours to take Robbers, every Man in his Business. So that there is no Malice in the Case.

Clearly, these are no devils. Evil is not their good.

Rather, they stand us off by admitting the justice of our cause and then diverting our attack all along the line to their betters. Gay himself is easily deflected and we follow him in full cry. Here we reach the second degree of his satire, and it is on this level that the main attack is launched. People in the honorable walks of life—men of great business, ladies of fashion, lawyers, courtiers, statesmen—it is these who come in for the hottest fire. "Murder," declares Peachum, "is as fashionable a Crime as a Man can be guilty of. . . . No Gentleman is ever look'd upon the worse for killing a Man in his own Defence." If Macheath cannot do well at the gaming tables, the fault lies in his education: "The Man that proposes to get Money by Play should have the Education of a fine Gentleman, and be train'd up to it from his Youth." "Really," replies Mrs. Peachum to her husband, "I am sorry upon *Polly's* Account the Captain hath not more Discretion. What business hath he to keep Company with Lords and Gentlemen? he should leave them to prey upon one another." Society is a casino. Both sexes play; and since the only purpose that motivates their play is the desire of gain, it follows that very few persons are above sharp practice. "Most Ladies take a delight in cheating, when they can do it with Safety," declares Mrs. Trapes. Gamesters are the vilest of Mechanics, but "many of the Quality are of the Profession," and they have admittance to the politest circles. "I wonder," remarks Matt of the Mint, "I wonder *we* are not more respected."

> Thus Gamesters united in Friendship are found,
> Though they know that their Industry all is a Cheat;
> They flock to their Prey at the Dice-Box's Sound,
> And join to promote one another's Deceit.

But if by mishap
They fail of a Chap,
To keep in their Hands, they each other entrap.
Like Pikes, lank with Hunger, who miss of their Ends,
They bite their Companions, and prey on their Friends.

Money will do anything in this fashionable world. Ladies marry
in hopes of soon being widows with a jointure. When Polly announces that she has married for love, her mother is horrified:
"Love him! I thought the Girl had been better bred." And to
marry a highwayman: "Why, thou foolish Jade, thou wilt be as
ill us'd, and as much neglected, as if thou hadst married a Lord!"
But Polly herself knows—at least in her own opinion—"as well
as any of the fine Ladies how to make the most of my self and of
my Man too."

No love is lost in those exalted spheres. And even friendship
proceeds merely upon the foot of interest. "Those that act otherwise are their own Bubbles." Promises are plentiful, but a court
friend was never known to give anything else. Quite the contrary:
"In one respect," says Peachum, "our Employment may be reckon'd
dishonest, because, like great Statesmen, we encourage those who
betray their Friends." But again: "Can it be expected that we
should hang our Acquaintance for nothing, when our Betters will
hardly save theirs without being paid for it?" And think of the
legal profession. Robbery may be common elsewhere, but beside
the wholesale robbery of the law it is nothing at all. "Gold from
Law can take out the Sting," but, on the other side,

It ever was decreed, Sir,
If Lawyer's Hand is fee'd, Sir,
He steals your whole Estate.

It appears, then, that if the Newgate people are culpable, they
are merely imitating their betters, who must be charged with
equal blame. But grant so much, and we must grant more. The
criminals press their advantage by suggesting that guilt is propor-
tional to the amount of harm done, which in turn depends on the
degree of power to execute it. There is no question where the
power resides. The statesman may think his "trade" as honest as
Peachum's, but logic will say him no. Thinking of our own days,
we shall have little heart to contradict logic. Then, sings Macheath
unanswerably:

Since Laws were made for ev'ry Degree,
To curb Vice in others, as well as me,
I wonder we han't better Company,
     Upon *Tyburn* Tree!

But Gold from Law can take out the Sting;
And if rich Men like us were to swing,
'Twould thin the Land, such Numbers to string
     Upon *Tyburn* Tree!

Moreover, Macheath and his gang have one more shaft to shoot, for what it is worth. They can set an example of loyalty and generosity and honor among themselves. "Who is there here," cries Nimming Ned, "that would not dye for his Friend?" "Who is there here," adds Harry Padington, "that would betray him for his Interest?" "Show me a Gang of Courtiers," says Matt of the Mint, "that can say as much." Macheath prides himself upon being a man of his word and no court friend. "We, Gentlemen," he declares, "have still Honour enough to break through the Corruptions of the World.—And while I can serve you, you may command me."

Here the defense rests its case. The ground has been occupied before, and will be again. The abuse of power, the chasm between profession and practice in high place, the constant defeat of principles by wealth, the oppression of desert born a beggar, "the spurns that patient merit of the unworthy takes," the immorality and selfishness of privileged society—all these themes are the stock-in-trade of satirists, familiar to our ears as household words. This is the habitual level of Swift, whose way is to show how much more reprehensible those are whom the world admires than those whom the world despises.

But Gay's satire does not stop at this point. There are hints in *The Beggar's Opera* of a more revolutionary doctrine. If we really believe in truth and justice and the general welfare, doubtless we should all be glad to see temporary violations of these principles set right. We should welcome, should we not, a fairer distribution of this world's goods, juster apportionment of the right to life, liberty, and the pursuit of happiness? But do we not, on the contrary, resist by all the means in our power any attempts at readjustment? Are not Macheath and his fellows more active laborers for the general good than we? We adopt the principles but obstruct their realization. The Newgate gentry adopt them and work for the cause:

BEN BUDGE. We are for a just Partition of the World, for every Man hath a Right to enjoy Life.

MATT OF THE MINT. We retrench the Superfluities of Mankind. The World is avaritious, and I hate Avarice. A covetous fellow, like a Jack-daw, steals what he was never made to enjoy, for the sake of hiding it. These are the Robbers of Mankind, for Money was made for the Free-hearted and Generous.

Who, then, are the true friends of man? Are they not the so-called enemies of society? Is it possible to be actively a friend of mankind without being a revolutionary? The established order is radically iniquitous: how can we defend the *status quo* and remain true to the principles to which we profess allegiance?

Thus it becomes clear that *The Beggar's Opera*, half a century before Figaro burst upon the world, foreshadowed in significant ways the point of view which Beaumarchais was to develop with such devastating results.[8] That the political and social implications of the earlier work did not explode with equal violence is in large measure due, of course, to the different temper of society at the time. But equally it is due to the broader base of Gay's satire. Figaro, besides being the spokesman of democratic defiance against rank and privilege, is basically the wholesome representative of those conventional virtues that popular sentiment judged worthy of perpetuation. He is therefore a revolutionary symbol to which generous souls could pay sympathetic homage.

There is no comparable figure in the earlier play. For the Newgate knaves, however they may color their actions, are only masquerading. When their conduct is scrutinized, it is obvious that self-interest is at the bottom of everything they do. It is shot through with bad faith and disloyalty even to their own class. Jealousy and suspicion are the rule here as elsewhere. In the end,

[8] "Mais il y a un jour où se remassent dans une explosion unique tous les sentiments de toute nature, moraux, politique, sociaux, que l'oeuvre des philosophes avait développés dans les coeurs, joie de vivre, avidité de jouir, intense excitation de l'intelligence, hains et mépris du présent, des abus, des traditions, espoir et besoin d'*autre chose*: ce jour de folie intellectuelle où toute la société de l'ancien régime applaudit aux idées dont elle va périr, c'est la première représentation du *Mariage de Figaro* (27 avril 1784)."—Lanson, *Hist. de la Litt. Française*, p. 807.

Macheath is forced to draw the inevitable conclusion from his experience: "That *Jemmy Twitcher* should peach me, I own sur-priz'd me!—'Tis a plain Proof that the World is all alike, and that even our Gang can no more trust one another than other People."

The world is all alike! That is the final lesson of Gay's satire. We laughed at the obvious reversal of accepted values which runs through the play. We laughed to hear Black Moll's industry commended, knowing that that industry was actively expended upon thievery and playing the whore. Laziness is a vice, and it was refreshing to see sloth in the performance of crime meet with its due punishment. But, *mutatis mutandis*, were we not laughing at ourselves? As Peachum told his wife, "The World, my Dear, hath not such a Contempt for Roguery as you imagine." We are all cheats, paying lip service to one set of principles and motivated in actual truth by another. Every man presents to the world an idealized dream picture as his authentic and veracious self-portrait. The institutions of society, which we pretend are so solidly established, rest on a fiction that has no external actuality. The ideals we profess are impossible to live by in this world, for they are undermined both from within and without. Private interest seldom coincides with public good, and private interest has the controlling hand, whether in the political, the social, the commercial, or the sexual sphere. Of this truth we are reminded in the play. "Now, *Peachum*," soliloquizes Lockit, "you and I, like honest Tradesmen, are to have a fair Tryal which of us two can over-reach the other." "All men," reflects Mrs. Peachum, "are thieves in love, and like a woman the better for being another's property." "Of all Animals of Prey," says Lockit, again, "Man is the only sociable one. Every one of us preys upon his Neighbour, and yet we herd together." "Well, Polly," sighs Mrs. Peachum, "as far as one Woman can forgive another, I forgive thee." The opposition of class against class, youth against age, sex against sex, individual against individual, is both inevitable and involuntary. We are predatory by the mere physiological premises of our common humanity. Under the conditions of existence, idealism is a merely relative term. "Oh, gentlemen," cried Hotspur before he died,

> the time of life is short;
> To spend that shortness basely were too long
> If life did ride upon a dial's point,
> Still ending at the arrival of an hour.

The irony is that, paying homage all our lives to these principles, it would hardly be possible to point to a single hour in which we lived in entire accordance with them. This is the doom of man, and each of us postures as if it were reversed for him, condemning others for what he excuses in himself, and generally playing such fantastic tricks before high heaven as are enough to make immortals laugh themselves to death. Fixed in this dance of plastic circumstance, we persist in declaring that we are the captains of our souls. Existence itself is the ultimate irony.

To go on breathing in the utter vacuum of this realization is impossible, and most of us are able to enter it only at rare moments. Acceptance of the pessimistic view may generate reactions which are diametrical opposites. The picture may be seen as comedy, or it may be seen as tragedy. To the romantic vision, speaking generally, it will appear tragic; to the classical, comic. The romantic attitude, being chiefly concerned with the individual ego, finds this spectacle of a divided self all but intolerable, and, to restore inner consistency, may take refuge in the Byronic pose. If I cannot be true to the ideals I profess, let me overturn those ideals and set up others that will be valid, and in accordance with the facts of my existence. "Evil, be thou my good!" Thus, in solitary grandeur, the diabolist may enjoy the luxury of integrity. For man in society, however, such an escape is hardly possible. The eighteenth century was not an age of solitaries; its characteristic orientations concerned man as a social being. It took little pleasure in exploring the orbit of the lonely soul through infinite space; it derived strength and assurance from solidarity. The contradictions of life become once again endurable when shared with one's brother men, and it is possible to be objective in contemplating the universal lot. Thus the age of Gay tended to see the irony of existence as fundamentally comic. For Swift, indeed, who had to watch the comedy through eighteenth-century eyes but with the passionate emotions and gigantic ego of a romantic, the spectacle turned bitter. Gay's good-humored view of it, as seen in *The Beggar's Opera*, is essentially characteristic both of his age and of himself. It was Gay who devised for his own epitaph the well-known lines:

Life is a jest; and all things show it.
I thought so once; but now I know it.

Some Aspects of Music and Literature

T HIS IS the century which Leichtentritt, in his comprehensive
survey, *Music, History, and Ideas,* accounts preeminently a musical age: that is, an age which found its supreme and most characteristic expression in music. Of no earlier age in the world's history, he
declares, can this be said. Whether in architecture, sculpture,
painting, poetry, or philosophy, the earlier past can produce monuments of the very first magnitude, unsurpassed by anything in
the last 250 years. But with the advent of Bach and Handel, music
reached a towering height which was the undeniable climax of
its history of the previous 2000 years and relative to which, in their
own march of achievement, there were no comparable peaks at
this time in the other arts.

WHICHEVER way we turn, while we trace the cultural topography of eighteenth-century England—its ideological or artistic
hills and vales and water-courses—we are within sound of music.
Are we following the antiquarian and historical impulse? There
are for evidence the Three Choirs Festivals, begun in 1724 (and
still continuing); the Academy of Ancient Music, established
1725/1726; the Madrigal Society, formed about 1741; the Ancient
Concerts, founded in 1776. There are the two ambitious and important Histories of Music, by Hawkins and Burney. There are
the ample compendia of earlier cathedral music, anthems and
motets, gathered by Greene and Boyce and Arnold. Are we
observing the powerful and strengthening interest in the earlier
poetry? With it go the abundant fresh settings of Elizabethan

and seventeenth-century lyrics. There is the Shakespearean revival, of which Arne's and Boyce's settings and incidental pieces
are only the most successful musical manifestation among many
attractive things. And still more impressively there stretches the
long line of varied and magnificent settings by Handel of great
English texts: the Bible, Milton, and Dryden foremost among
them.

It is in keeping with an age that thought Man the proper study
of mankind that its major emphasis (and accomplishment) in
music should be dramatic and, in a broad sense, social. As, in
material things, the achievement of the century was not cathe-
drals but dwelling-houses and what went into them and round
them, so its characteristic musical expression was Song, the matching of words and notes in varying degrees of complexity and
employed in all kinds of social ways. Along with the uses of song
in the theater—in opera, ballad-opera, "musical entertainment,"
and play—go the concerts in the pleasure-gardens, an endless opportunity for the development of talent in the smaller forms, and
for the enjoyment of music in a socially informal and *al fresco*
setting. Dozens of composers from excellent to indifferent, scores
of singers, and absolute shoals of light lyrics were launched at
these concerts; the verbal product being gathered and printed
from time to time, with or without music, in book and pamphlet
form; and the individual songs appearing by thousands on engraved
single sheets. Warwick Wroth's vivid work, *The London Pleasure
Gardens of the Eighteenth Century*, contains many details of this
musical fare, and is doubtless familiarly known. Frank Kidson's
and Alfred Moffat's admirably selected and edited *Minstrelsy of
England* and *Songs of the Georgian Period* contain several hundred
of the songs and you will remember the delightfully printed *Songs
of the Gardens*, edited by Peter Warlock for the Nonesuch Press,
and containing among its two dozen songs pieces by Worgan, De-
fesch, Festing, Boyce, the two Arnes, and James Hook.

Neither should we forget those other outlets for social music
on the semi-professional level, the convivial clubs that were formed
for the practice of catches, canons, and glees. Some of these were
long-lived: the Noblemen's and Gentlemen's Catch Club, founded
in 1761, and still in existence (though but a babe to the Hibernian
Catch Club of Dublin, the oldest musical society in Europe, es-

tablished about 1680 and still alive); the Glee Club, begun 1787; the Concentores Sodales, and doubtless many another, like Goldsmith's Club of Choice Spirits. The best of them, as is well known, offered annual prizes for compositions in these popular forms, and the bulk of their work is to say the least imposing. Thomas Warren, Secretary of the Catch Club, edited thirty-two volumes of their pieces. Samuel Webbe published nine volumes, James Sibbald four, J. Bland twenty or more volumes of Gentlemen's and Ladies' collections (separately!). *The Apollonian Harmony* of about 1790 has six volumes; Horsley's *Vocal Harmony* contains nine. In addition there are many similar collections of pieces by individual composers—Hayes, Webbe, Callcott, Cooke, J. Stafford Smith, and others.

But on the amateur and popular levels the appetite for song was fed by a constant supply of song-books from beginning to end of the century. Noteworthy at the outset were the successively larger editions of D'Urfey's *Songs Compleat, Pleasant, and Divertive*, better known as *Pills to Purge Melancholy*, culminating in the six-volume collection of 1719–1720. This work may be regarded as almost a national collection of the popular song of that era. It includes favorite pieces by known composers, but in the main it comprises the floating melodies of the second half of the seventeenth century—such things as were familiar and readily available for use with a new topical song or a comic or rowdy ballad or lampoon on politics or fashion—"filthy tunes," as Falstaff called such melodies. The distinction between folksong and popular song had not yet been conceived, and might have been still harder to draw in that day, because popular music was so much more truly of the people and so much closer to folk-music then than later. But there was a difference, D'Urfey's tunes often displaying citified, or at least suburban, tricks of modulation, and other self-consciousness less visible in the comparable and contemporary dance-collections of the Playfords. The miscellaneous character of the *Pills* must be emphasized, however, as well as the free and folk-like way in which D'Urfey pushed his tunes around to accommodate them to the words. The Scottish collections of the same date, Ramsay's *Musick for the Tea-Table Miscellany* and Thomson's *Orpheus Caledonius*, were, as we should expect, more folkish; but the closely subsequent English collections, such as Walsh's and Watts' *Musical Miscellany* in six volumes, cater to a much more sophisticated taste. The long file of ballad-operas in their printed form are of course in themselves little anthologies of popular melody.

Several of the collections of the mid-century display their social character to the eye as well as to the ear. Bickham's *Musical Entertainer*, now a great rarity, offers an engraved scene with each song, 200 in all, and sometimes of considerable historical interest, like those picturing Vauxhall. Another of the same type, but still larger, is *Clio and Euterpe*, 1762, full of pleasant vignettes. In those years, also, pocket-size volumes of words alone were testifying to the passion for song. Some of them were surprisingly full: the three collections called respectively *The Linnet*, *The Thrush*, and *The Robin* together contain nearly 2000 lyrics, of which the tunes were presumed to be familiar to the purchaser. Toward the end of the century come Ritson's three-volume collection of *English Songs*, his two-volume collection of *Scotish Songs*, and his *Ancient Songs*; and, as fitting counterbalance to D'Urfey at the beginning, the national anthology of Scots song named *The Scots Musical Museum*, again in six volumes. This collection, as is well remembered, is the work for which Burns wrote so many of his deathless songs and for which also he preserved many a lovely folk-tune.

Of most of the collections named, profane love was the commonest theme. But we must not ignore the comparable flood of songs of sacred love current during the second half of the century among the "People called Methodists." Of these Charles Wesley wrote the words of perhaps 7000, to be sung to simple and familiar tunes, many of them probably taken from the great ocean of folk-music. It is on account of this outburst that George Sampson in a fine Warton Lecture recently called the Eighteenth Century "The Century of Divine Songs"; and although the phenomenon has been generally neglected in histories of literature and of music, it is obviously of great significance. There are increasing signs that the stature of Charles Wesley as a poet, at least, is gradually becoming recognized.

Throughout these decades, but particularly after 1740, the theorists in aesthetics were busy debating the relations and analogies between music and the other arts, and the specific capabilities and functions of music. Critics like Avison, Brown, Beattie, Webb, and Sir William Jones produced a series of essays that, while they hardly keep abreast of current musical practice, at least offer descriptions of the baroque, and partially organize the attitudes and ideas underlying it. Their treatises have been briefly but competently surveyed by Herbert Schueller.[1] He points out that their discussions mainly revolve about the problems of imitation in music, a subject with a long history, but able still to generate heat; and I shall ask you to spend a little time in considering certain aspects of it, more especially as they bear on the interconnections of music and literature.

WE ARE aware that the theory of imitation extends far beyond a single province, and that, not without appeals to the authority of Aristotle, the doctrine was widely held in the eighteenth century that all arts are imitative. For the sake of a suggestive parallel with music, not I hope too far-fetched, we may begin with landscape gardening. This art, so typical of the period, could also be regarded as an art of imitation. For it imitated nature: not by leaving nature alone, but by divining the *meaning* latent in natural phenomena and creatively assisting its quasi-pictorial realization. That meaning, as the century saw it, included, and was incomplete without, references to human life and thought, which added temporal dimensions—remembrance of things past, ideas of antiquity and of classic art, sentiments of mortality and divine hope—to the spatial dimensions that met the eye. Hence the importance of ruins, statues, grottoes, church spires, urns and inscriptions, in Shenstone's conception of the art. These were not merely, as Humphreys so neatly writes, "the punctuation marks in the grammar of natural meaning." Such allusions helped to give definite communicable significance to landscape. The parallel here with music is worth a moment's attention. In both arts the media are possessed of immediate sensuous appeal and rightly managed carry their own inherent patterned validity. But that explicit ideational content which the century demanded of its artifacts has to be borrowed or imported from without. They lend themselves very readily to associations, and in due course with repetitional use a language begins to develop, capable of subtler and subtler refinements of meaning, until (conceivably) the point is reached where the natural or the musical element can state its precisely shaded intention symbolically, with-

[1] *The Musical Quarterly* (October 1948).

out the presence of the interpretative device. Whether the Orientals ever developed the art of landscape to such a degree of ingenuity I do not know, but we all know the "meaning" of a yew-tree or an oak—if not of a flower in a crannied wall. And we have lately learned that Bach habitually wrote for instruments with an extra-musical implication in mind.

In some sort, of course, the art of the landscape gardeners had already been adumbrated by the landscape poets, selecting and composing the significant items of the natural scene and supplying a meaning:

> See, on the mountain's southern side,
> Where the prospect opens wide,
> Where the evening gilds the tide,
> How close and small the hedges lie!
> What streaks of meadows cross the eye!
> A step methinks may pass the stream,
> So little distant dangers seem;
> So we mistake the future's face,
> Ey'd thro' hope's deluding glass;
> As yon summits soft and fair
> Clad in colours of the air,
> Which, to those who journey near,
> Barren, brown, and rough appear;
> Still we tread the same coarse way:
> The present's still a cloudy day . . .
> Thus is nature's vesture wrought
> To instruct our wand'ring thought.

Later generations of nature poets were to drop the explicit gloss (though perhaps not so often as anti-classicists suppose), and it might at first be guessed that they had moved on to that foreseen stage where the natural detail carries a current meaning, like coin of the realm. But the fact is otherwise; for what these later poets are pursuing is not a common but a private meaning. They have a tryst with a secret love, into whose eyes they look for their own image, and who seems to answer their every mood. Autobiography is their métier; they sing themselves. Our present affair, however, is not with novelties of feeling but with conventions of expression—and more particularly with musical conventions.

In so far as music communicates extra-musical meaning, it, like verbal languages, is a system of aural signs to which in certain contexts particular significance has been attached and which can be combined in a great many meaningful ways. Such a language must depend upon an agreement at least approximate among its users as to sense and modes of employment. In the main, these will be matters of arbitrary convention, like the meaning of words and phrases and the logic of grammar, which have to be painfully learned. The assertion might at first seem to contradict the notion of music as an imitative art; but we shall soon have to discriminate between kinds of imitation. On the primary level, music is of course capable of rudimentary mimicry of certain physical phenomena: sounds animal and human, sounds of water and wind and thunder, sounds of motion. Sounds, the theorists agreed, can be loud or soft, high or low; motions can be continuous or interrupted, even or uneven, swift or slow. Music can reproduce these activities in elementary fashion, and *may* be so understood. But according to 'Hermes' Harris and the Encyclopedists, sound and motion pretty largely comprise the proper limits of musical imitation.

On this basic level, it is interesting to compare Johnson's remarks on Pope's dictum, "The sound must seem an echo to the sense." "This notion of representative metre," writes Johnson,

and the desire of discovering frequent adaptations of the sound to the sense, have produced, in my opinion, many wild conceits and imaginary beauties. All that can furnish this representation are the sounds of the words considered singly, and the time in which they are pronounced. Every language has some words framed to exhibit the noises which they express, as *thump, rattle, growl, hiss.* These, however, are but few, and the poet cannot make them more, nor can they be of any use but when sound is to be mentioned . . . The fancied resemblances, I fear, arise sometimes merely from the ambiguity of words; there is supposed to be some relation between a *soft* line and a *soft* couch, or between *hard* syllables and *hard* fortune.

Motion, however, may be in some sort exemplified; and yet it may be suspected that even in such resemblances the mind often governs the ear, and the sounds are estimated by their meanings. . . . Beauties of this kind are commonly fancied; and when real are technical and nugatory, not to be rejected and not to be solicited.

It will be noticed that Johnson puts poetical imitation exactly where the theorists put musical imitation, with the same limitations to sound and motion. He touches, moreover, on false re-

semblances arising from the heedless crossing of literal with figurative meanings. By analogy, the point raises consideration of one
of the most notorious and widespread kinds of musical imitation.
The commonest example is the picturing of high and low by sudden steep ascents and descents in the notes that carry or accompany
the words. Baroque composers were far indeed from following
Johnson's advice to treat such effects as fortuitous. So long ago as
1597, Thomas Morley had written:

> If the subject be light, you must cause your music to go in motions
> which carry with them a celerity or quickness of time . . . ; if it be
> lamentable, the note must go in slow and heavy motions . . . More-
> over, you must have a care that when your matter signifieth ascend-
> ing, high heaven and such like, you make your music ascend: and . . .
> where your ditty speaks of descending, lowness, depth, hell and other
> such, you must make your music descend. For as it will be thought a
> great absurdity to talk of heaven and point downward to the earth:
> so it will be counted great incongruity if a musician upon the words
> *He ascended into heaven* should cause his music to descend.

To be sure, "high" and "low" in music are figurative expressions,
but the metaphor in post-classical times seems by the Western
world to have been universally understood, and it requires some
effort to think it away. In fact, any discussion of music finds it
indispensable. But, once having accepted the convention of an
"up" and a "down" among musical tones, we can of course extend the figurative analogies at will. Bach uses the device of dropping to the lower bass to suggest Adam's "fall"; and also to indicate
night, and darkness, and hell. Handel, in the Cecilia Ode, writes
Dryden's phrase, "depth of pains and height of passion" as E to
A above, to A at the octave, and back to E, the octave leap coming
on the word *height*—and such was no doubt Dryden's intention.
Other instances occur at the line, "What passion cannot Music
raise and quell," and again at "wond'ring, on their faces fell To
worship."

We are already far enough from the physical correspondences
with which we began, and we had best try to see what is happen-
ing. Two points are clear. The first is that we should get nowhere
in grasping the full intention without the words. In order for the
sound to seem an echo to the sense, we must start with the sense.
The second point is that we are forced to perform a ratiocinative

rather than an intuitive act. There is no need to object to this necessity. It is proper to an honest echo to start from the sense, and it
seems a bit perverse of Johnson to complain because he cannot have
it the other way round. After all, Pope said "seem," not "be."
When Johnson says that "in such resemblances the mind often governs the ear, and the sounds are estimated by their meaning," he
is objecting to an axiom. But I must beware of putting more weight
on an echo than an echo will bear, and I return to the baroque
tonal language.

WE SHALL waive for the present any discussion of the question,
Whether music *ought* to express any but musical ideas, and agree
that for some of the very greatest masters it has in fact done so.
It should be profitable to look a little more closely at some of the
means employed to that end. For this language is surely related to
some of the profoundest and most characteristic elements of the
eighteenth-century temper. To keep within bounds, let us draw
most of our illustrations from a single masterpiece, Handel's setting of Dryden's *Song for St. Cecilia's Day*, for Soprano and Tenor,
Chorus, and Orchestra. Dryden's poem belongs to the year 1687.
Handel's work was written and performed in 1739, in an atmosphere of national excitement over the war with Spain, which gave
topical significance to the third stanza.

   The prevailing tonality of the work is D major, and the spirit
of it, over all, is one of confidence and power and trust. The choice
of key is of course by no means haphazard. This particular tonality
is selected, not because Handel has thought of some musical themes
that promise to lie comfortably in the key of D major, but
because the dominant mood of Dryden's Ode *means* D major. The
tonality could have preceded the formulation of a single phrase
of the music in Handel's imagination. Why D major has this significance is not easy to tell, but it is not by Handelian fiat that it
does so. Handel is following a tradition that has its origin in mists
of cosmological theory—involving the music of the spheres, planetary influences, the attributes divine and human and affective that
were believed to inhere severally in each of the ancient modes.
Some of the aura surrounding the medieval modes floated over to
influence the baroque feeling for keys. Primarily, however, it is
less a matter of feeling than of received doctrine. It has nothing

to do with private impressions or sensibilities—as a hyper-sensitive modern with absolute pitch will see the color of old rose when he hears C-sharp minor. On the contrary: this is objective, in that it is determined by the intellect rather than by the sense. It is not a meaning originally inherent in the key, but one that was put there by cogitation. It belongs to the *idea* of the key rather than to the sense-impression—inevitably so, in an era when pitches were inconstant, and when mean temperament had yet to be firmly established. But by Handel's day the intellectual significance of the keys was sufficiently fixed to enable an emotional meaning to associate itself with the idea. So every fresh authoritative use of a particular tonality within the range of its accepted definitions could serve to confirm and refine and enrich the knowing experience of that tonality.

The tonality established also serves a structural purpose. In the present work, Handel departs from it several times, not in the way of occasional modulations to avoid monotony—though that, too, he does—but in order to change the subject or take up another case. Because Dryden's poem is artfully contrived with provision for musical effects, the tonal architecture is by implication relatively fixed, and this fact, like the designing a house for an owner who knows exactly what he wants, raises special problems in musical tact and logic. Dryden's third, fourth, fifth, and sixth stanzas are deliberately disconnected, describing various passions and the evocative power of several instruments. Handel, besides heightening these contrasts, must give the series a semblance of cohesion, and the sequence of chosen tonalities will be an important aid. Contrast alone in music will not suffice as an organizing principle. If we consider that the pace of the Ode when read is about fifteen times faster than that of Handel's musical utterance, we can realize the much greater need in the latter to establish an underlying unity and to clarify relationships between the parts. Most of this work of tonal, as well as metrical, articulation is naturally brought into sharpest focus at the ends and beginnings of adjacent movements. During these moments we become aware of the subtle way in which two keys can reveal their kinship in the very act of asserting their difference.

Handel begins the Ode with an orchestral overture composed of three short, sharply contrasted movements. The first is *larghetto*, and employs a figure breath-taking in its suggestion of controlled power, a muscular crouch and spring from dominant up to tonic, tonic to third, tonic to fifth, tonic to octave, and back to the starting-point—each return to the tonic being emphasized by an appoggiatura or turn that seems to establish the foothold more securely. Halfway, the tonality shifts from D major to A major, from which at the end it launches into a fugal *allegro* in D major again. The vigorous drive of this second movement is then quieted into a minuet, and we are ready for the voices. Nothing up to this point is able *by itself* to suggest any extra-musical ideas; and, in fact, all three of these movements are found again in the Fifth Concerto Grosso as the opening and closing parts of that work, which belongs to the same year.

Over sustained chords the tenor announces the first lines of the Ode, recitative: "From harmony, from heav'nly harmony This universal frame began." And then, to a tonality dark and continually shifting, no sooner defined than defying definition, come the words, "When Nature underneath a heap Of jarring atoms lay." The orchestra, we begin to notice, is running changes on broken diminished triads, until it occurs to us that here is a continual succession of the most avoided, "most dangerous" interval in music, the dreaded tritone, the "diabolus in musica." "Fa, sol, la, mi" hums Edmund in *Lear*, and we know at once that he is plotting deviltry; and here are mi's contra fa's thick as leaves in Vallombrosa. The churning, yeasty but unassertive, figure continues while the lines are repeated, the melodic line at "could not heave her head" making a futile effort to rise and falling back dejected. Then, imperceptibly, the tonality clears to A major on the words, "The tuneful voice was heard from high," and the voice, unaccompanied, rings out three times on the cry, "Arise," with an interjected trumpet-like echo from the orchestra. Now, suddenly, there is a wild burst of life among the strings, on a disjunctive but energetic figure, as of particles striking together and rebounding chaotically and violently. This ceases, after two bars, as suddenly as it began; and the voice, on a melodic line that arches like a bow, announces,

> Then cold, and hot, and moist, and dry
> In order to their stations leap;

and suddenly again, with the same furious energy, the divided orchestra tosses a leaping figure in sixteenth-notes from one side to the other. We take it at first for more chaos, until we notice what the alternating choirs of high and low had concealed, that the leaping figures are entering at every beat on a perfectly regular and controlled descending scale. After two bars, the chaos returns, to be silenced by the voice repeating its declaration. Thereupon, chaos once more breaks in, but after a bar and a half falls into order as before on the leaping downward scale sequence, and after brief gestures of rebellion at the repeated words, "And music's pow'r obey," the movement is brought to an end with the same demonstration of orderly control:

> Those opposed eyes,
> Which, like the meteors of a troubled heaven,
> Did lately meet in the intestine shock
> And furious close of civil butchery,
> Shall now, in mutual well-beseeming ranks,
> March all one way.

One would surely have thought that so startlingly dramatic a *tour de force* as this would have been acclaimed on every hand. That it has escaped overt notice is proof how far out of the habit we have grown of scrutinizing this music for a kind of meaning which has latterly come to seem almost illegitimate, but which to the makers of it was indigenous to their conceptions. In his *Music in the Baroque Era*, Bukofzer has put the essential point with admirable force (p. 369):

Music reached out from the audible into the inaudible world, it extended without a break from the world of the senses into that of the mind and intellect . . . We must recognize the speculative approach as one of the fundamentals of baroque music and baroque art in general without either exaggerating or belittling its importance. If abstract thoughts could be enhanced through poetic form, as we see in the philosophical poetry of the baroque era, then by the same token concrete works of art could be enhanced through abstract thought. Audible form and inaudible order were not mutually exclusive or opposed concepts, as they are today, but complementary aspects of one and the same experience: the unity of sensual and intellectual understanding.

Handel saves the rest of Dryden's first stanza—appropriately in view of the recapitulative content—for separate treatment by full chorus and orchestra. The orchestra opens with a syncopated theme of driving, purposeful energy. Incidentally, we may remark that Handel knows better than anyone how to use syncopation to suggest eager, anticipatory impatience. With him it never suggests reluctance to go forward or an inclination to walk on the grass. The difference between his use of it and that of some later exponents is the difference between receiving a succession of electric shocks and brushing against India rubber. Handel here keeps his orchestra pressing vigorously ahead; but he spaces out the vocal parts in broad sustained tones, except at the line, "Through all the compass of the notes it ran," where he runs divisions up and down the scale, an octave at a time for the voices and two or more in the strings. The movement ends with unflagging energy, and still in D major. Now is introduced the first structural shift of tonality. Handel with stanza two moves into G major, a key for him of calm confidence, of sunlight and security. The vocal statement is anticipated by a long cantilena for 'cello. The whole movement, which carries all of stanza two, is more of a hymn of praise and thanksgiving for "celestial sound" than of awe for music's power. It is a gently floating, sometimes soaring, meditative *andante* for soprano, in 3/4 time: a long moment of repose in a work full of excitement.

The stanza that follows returns to D major. It makes an obvious bid, with rather obvious effects, for popular applause. The trumpet has rather less solo work than one might have expected, though that is possibly because the instrument has a way of making itself felt as soloist, whatever else is going on. The drums also have less to do than we anticipate. The treatment of the tenor's line, "With shrill notes of anger and mortal alarms," is noteworthy: three descents from A major dominant to tonic on the same pentachord, with a concluding roulade on the last syllable; and above, a true trumpet call—not thematic—on successive triplets at the fifth, octave, and tonic. The movement reaches its climax with repeated cries of "Hark!" and "Charge!" over a drum-roll. The whole stanza is then repeated in compressed form by the full chorus and orchestra.

Handel finds it intolerable to obey Dryden's instructions and pass at once from all this martial excitement to the "soft complaining flute"—an effect which Dryden, aiming only at a striking contrast, did not wish to shun. The reason may lie in the fact that while reading the verses we are mainly conscious of the contrast alone, while in music the order of the contrast becomes much more important. To move from the "big" emotion of war directly into the "little" emotion of hopeless love strikes us as anticlimactic. At least, one may suspect that had the order been reversed there would have been no difficulty. Dryden's trumpet and drum might have been shifted except for the fact that his flute, violin, and organ form an ascending sequence from earthly to heavenly, and so to the day of judgment and the dissolution of the "universal frame." There is thus no other suitable place for stanza three, and Handel respects the given order. He solves the difficulty, at least in part, by inserting an instrumental march in the same key, thereby bringing the martial fever under public, if still martial, control, and at the same time separating the antipathetic stanzas three and four. Even so, were there to be a break in performance, this would be the moment for it—that is to say, after the March.

For the flute stanza, Handel drops to the relative minor, B minor —the second extended shift of tonality in the work. This one, like the first, is a leisurely *andante* in 3/4. It is marked by imitative dialogue between the flute and the soprano, the voice assuming an impersonal, instrumental quality, with ornamental trills. Above lute-like "warbling" in the bass accompaniment the word "warbling" is itself extended over six bars of vocalization.

At the violin stanza, there is another change of key, this time to A major. The reasons appear to be intellectual rather than descriptive or impressionistic, and indeed this movement is one of the least pictorial of all. Leichtentritt tells us that in his operas Handel is likely to employ G minor when depicting "passionate outbursts of jealous fury."[2] And elsewhere, he uses A major for amorous delight. What motivates the present brilliant and spirited *allegro*, which seems on its face to exhibit no distress commensurate with the anguished words?

It seems clear that the reasons are partly strategic. To follow the pathetic *andante* portraying love-melancholy with another equally poignant minor movement would be ill-advised. No doubt Handel could invigorate the music sufficiently to differentiate the love-madness from the love-sadness. But G minor following upon

[2] *The Musical Quarterly* (April 1935).

the heels of B minor obviously would not do in any case: the clash of tonal systems precluded it. E minor would be possible but its connotations were also elegiac. Now, there is no reason why jealous pangs and fury should not be brightly and boldly articulated, and a major key is therefore both permissible and indicated by the context. Because of its tuning, the violin's two most congenial and brightest keys are D major and A major, and of these A major is the more brilliant. This was the moment of all moments in the work for the violin to be displayed. It was not yet time to return to D major, which Handel would need again for his big concluding chorus, and which in any case belonged especially to the trumpet.

Why did Dryden use the term "sharp" in characterizing the violins? If they were sharp in one sense, they were out of tune; and if they were sharp in another, were they not unpleasant in tonal quality? It seems likely that the epithet was due to recent events. When Charles came back from France, he came with a special liking for violins which he insisted should play for his pleasure on most festive occasions and even in church. They had a noticeably brighter tone than the viols, and began everywhere to displace the old-fashioned instruments. One who had the sound of the viols in his ears from childhood would be likely to think the new-fangled violins (only then being brought by N. Amati to their classical perfection of form and tone) too bright by half, however fashionable they might be at Court. The change was familiar to everyone in Dryden's generation; and no doubt it was the impact of this recent shift in tonal fashion that lay behind his choice of the term "sharp" to describe the violin timbre, which made them suitable to express jealous pangs and height of passion.

Handel's way of depicting these emotions is entirely symbolic rather than expressive in the modern sense. We have to learn from the words what the intention is, and then listen through the mind's ear. Apart from a conspicuously recurring figure of ascending chromatic notes (which conventionally indicate anguish), the intensity is signified by long ladder-like passages in sixteenths, all in the violin part except for two elaborate roulades on the accented syllable of "desperation," each three bars long. The texture of this movement is not very different from what one finds in a typical allegro in one of the violin sonatas. It is pure baroque, and as such makes more of a demand today on the listener's enlightened sympathy than any other part of the work. There is a very similar and familiar treatment of Rage in the *Messiah* ("Why do the nations") and in Polyphemus' recitative in *Acis and Galatea*.

The *larghetto* which follows, in praise of the "sacred organ," is a hymn of the most ethereal loveliness, certainly the aesthetic climax of the Ode. For the first time the organ plays its compelling role, in perfect accord with the words. The movement carries Handel's special stamp of grave, lofty serenity, which the world identifies with the *larghetto* from *Xerxes*. As in the other two slow movements for soprano, the metre is again 3/4, with repeated chords on the second and third beat of each bar. The shift of tonality from the preceding movement is thrillingly dramatic, like being lifted to a purer air. F major is the established key for ideas of pastoral and contemplative happiness, and remained so throughout the century. Leichtentritt reminds us that Beethoven wrote his Pastoral Symphony and "Spring" sonata in this key. For Handel it clearly also carried religious connotations, and was pastoral in a double sense. It is not an accident that at the words, "Notes inspiring holy love, Notes that wing their heav'nly ways," we are reminded of the nearly identical musical phrase in the *Messiah*, "He shall feed his flock." There is a momentary disturbance of the mood of rapt contemplation in two bars occurring after the voice has finished: a reference to F minor, like a wisp of cloud crossing the sun, and vanishing.

This divine movement is followed by a short and rhythmically vigorous one in the same tonality, *all a hornpipe;* and that by eight bars, *largo*, of recitative in A minor. The work then returns to D major for the final chorus, laid out on massive chorale-like lines, the soprano solo alternating with the full choir of voices and strings. At "the last and dreadful hour," the tonality shifts to D minor, and with "this crumbling pageant" goes into a succession of alien keys, ending on A major. The soprano now enters alone, in D major, rising to high A with the announcement, "The trumpet shall be heard on high," and holding the high note for four bars while the trumpet climbs in partial imitation up to the same note, a second trumpet then joining on a fanfare below, supported by the whole orchestra and chorus. The last two lines are treated first canonically by chorus and strings, then in concert with the whole orchestra; and the work is finished.

WE NEED not labor any longer the importance of tonality in this world, except to emphasize that it was a component of a *current* musical language and, as such, neither had to establish its significance independently in the individual work, nor was limited to a personal meaning elaborated by a single composer. It was rooted in general agreement, and had the strength of common consent. But it was only one element in this language. Bukofzer tells us that Andreas Herbst, a mid-seventeenth-century theorist, distinguishes *verba* and *res*, words and things. The *things* meant are states of being, emotional states, like sadness, as distinct from verbal notions or ideas. The *res* are connected with specific tonalities, as we see in Handel's practice. But the translation of ideas or *verba* into music is more complicated. Ideas were classified as *Motus et Locorum:* words of motion and place; nouns, verbs; and adverbs of time. To correspond with these, musical tropes were devised. The system was enlarged and developed by Johannes Mattheson, the close friend of Handel's youth. Music, he says, is sound-speech (*Klangrede*) and declares: "It is the ultimate aim of music, by means of the naked tones and their rhythm, to excite all passions as successfully as the best orator." The purely technical side of music must be understood and employed, but "Descriptio" is the surest and most essential means. The *Affekten*, the Passions, have to be "beschrieben oder gemalet," described or painted.

"Great thoughts," wrote Johnson, "are always general." The fundamental urge of the new classicism was to discover Law, to get beyond the private to the common significance, to escape from the prison of particulars to the freedom of the general, to the realm of great thoughts that embrace man and his place in the universe. Baroque music is but one manifestation of this far-reaching ambition, but it is, I think, a rather neglected one in this view. It was in order to give music a meaning as broad and general as philosophy or literature that the baroque language was developed. The ruling postulates and habits of thought of the age find significant expression here as elsewhere, and instructive analogies and correlations with the literary arts can be discovered.

Fundamental agreement as to ends gives rise to analogous conventions among means. Perhaps we can push our exploration of one or two of these conventions a little farther on the less technical side.

Because men wished to understand and rationalize human existence, they needed to objectify the emotional life; and the doctrine known as *Affektenlehre* is a major effort to get the passions out where men can look at them. It is a form of personification, and thus perforce has radical connections with earlier allegorical impulses and with the dominant forms of medieval and renaissance art. The urge to allegory had of course by no means died out in the eighteenth century. The widespread love of personification in the poetry of the age is a notorious manifestation of it; and the allegorical fable in the periodical essays is another. It sometimes appears where we least expect it. One might trace a line through the morality plays back to the medieval literature of personified debate, to the *Roman de la Rose* and beyond, if one were to look for the antecedents of the following paragraph in *Tom Jones* (Bk. VI, ch. 13):

Black George having received the purse [intended by Sophia for Tom], set forward towards the alehouse; but in the way a thought occurred to him, whether he should not detain this money likewise. His conscience, however, immediately started at this suggestion, and began to upbraid him with ingratitude to his benefactor. To this his avarice answered, That his conscience should have considered the matter before, when he deprived poor Jones of his £500. That having quietly acquiesced in what was of so much greater importance, it was absurd, if not downright hypocrisy, to affect any qualms at this trifle. In return to which, Conscience, like a good lawyer, attempted to distinguish between an absolute breach of trust, as here, where the goods were delivered, and a bare concealment of what was found, as in the former case. Avarice presently treated this with ridicule, called it a distinction without a difference, and absolutely insisted that when once all pretensions of honour and virtue were given up in any one instance, there was no precedent for resorting to them upon a second occasion. In short, poor Conscience had certainly been defeated in the argument, had not Fear stept in to her assistance, and very strenuously urged that the real distinction between the two actions, did not lie in the different degrees of honour but of safety: for that the secreting the £500 was a matter of very little hazard; whereas the detaining the sixteen guineas was liable to the utmost danger of discovery. By this friendly aid of Fear, Conscience obtained a complete victory in the mind of Black George, and, after making him a few compliments on his honesty, forced him to deliver the money to Jones.

From his general censure of Fielding, Johnson should have excepted this good-humored dissection of a limed soul, which conforms so closely to Imlac's prescription. It would be too painful to stretch so perfect a confection upon the rack of pedagogical demonstration, but I cannot resist remarking that it is the allegorical machine that has here turned Black George into Everyman. This strikes me as a shining example of benefits forgot by later times— benefits derived from the skillful use of personification, or what I once only half-playfully called the "Abstractive Correlative."

Turning back now to music, we may inquire how the same intention was fulfilled in that medium. How does Handel personify? The process is naturally best seen in his operas, and in this connection I should like to cite a few sentences from Leichtentritt (*Music, History, and Ideas*, p. 150), who gives much more authority to the answer than I could possibly do. "In Handel's manner of psychological analysis and characterization," he writes,

the systematic, rationalistic spirit of the age is reflected. A character in a Handel opera is expressed musically by the sum of the arias given to him. Each aria reveals a different characteristic. Thus, for instance, in the opera *Alceste*, the heroine, Alcestis, expresses in her [six] arias the various sentiments agitating her in such a manner as to reveal to the listener her individual character . . . presenting every emotion in isolation, unmixed, pure, and leaving it to the listener to form an impression of [the] character as a whole. [In Handel's dramatic music] the contest of emotions *in abstracto*, rather than the acting characters, is the central point of interest.

If this be true—and one's own experience confirms it—one can easily perceive how closely analogous in this province of his art is Handel's technique to that of the allegorist in verse or prose. It impersonalizes personality by giving the facets of the individual emotional life separate and independent embodiment. The "passions" are objectified in a series of personifications, and thereby we approach "general and transcendental truths, divested of the minuter discriminations, exhibited in their abstracted and invariable state." Thus Handel can write—to appropriate the rest of Johnson's statement—"as the interpreter of nature, and the legislator of man-

kind . . . presiding over the thoughts and manners of future generations, as a being superior to time and place."

Even in the Ode, matters are conducted, although (because of
Dryden's libretto) more arbitrarily, according to the same rationalistic ordonnance. Here the passions are represented as absolutes,
disconnected or at least separable from men. We may compare
the even clearer cases of Alexander's Feast and Collins' Ode, *The
Passions*. One wonders, parenthetically, whether some lingering
vestiges of this ancient mythology survived as genuine belief into
the eighteenth century, to give a sense of helpless irresponsibility
to persons, whether actual or imagined, in the throes of some
emotional seizure. It would go far to explain the actions of Tom
Jones in a crisis, or Boswell's fatalistic submission to his fits of
Hypochondria, if it were so. Dryden, subscribing for poetic reasons
to the ancient doctrine, depicts music's power to raise and subdue
any passion at will, like what is delivered of Orpheus. There is a
double personification here: the passions are personified, and the
musical instruments that serve to rouse them have an autonomous
life. This last is a poetical fancy that, so far as I know, has nothing
to do with the *Affektenlehre* with which we have been concerned.
The theorists were indeed very sceptical about the powers of
instruments by themselves to paint the passions meaningfully, unless
where words had already given a clue. That particular instruments
had associations or affinities with particular moods was not denied;
but the potential range of allusion was ordinarily too wide to be
of much use. The drum, yes; the sacred organ, yes. The flute and
the lute are arbitrary, and the violin is so, too. The trumpet, even
in the Ode itself, has very divergent connotations, first as the
inciter to battle, and then as the "tuba mirum spargens sonum Per
sepulcra regionum." But the essential importance of words in the
theory of the passions is reflected in the text of the Ode by being
made instrumental to the climax—at least if I understand the climax
correctly. For it is when "vocal breath" is added to Cecilia's playing
that the angels become confused. (I suppose it is possible to interpret "vocal breath" as the perfecting of the instrument itself
by adding a *vox humana* stop.) Thus, it is the marriage of "perfect
music unto noble words" that produces the highest, richest musical
achievement. There are profound causes for the post-classical, last-
minute emergence of pure instrumental music in Western history,

to its present position of dominant importance. Never before, probably, has caviar been served as the main course.

We have, of course, not even scratched the surface in describing the intellectual complexities of this baroque language of music. The four levels of meaning in medieval explication are relatively simple, compared to some of Bach's convolutions of significance. The curious may consult Manfred Bukofzer's illuminating essay, "Allegory in Baroque Music" (from which I have drawn facts and illustrations), for a demonstration of five different allegories simultaneously appearing in a single cantata by Bach—not one of which would be perceptible to the untutored listener at a performance.

IT IS LITERALLY shocking to turn from a complexity such as this, involving art and mind and heart in total devotion, to the products of the popular musical genius—the vulgar music in the best sense. There are, of course, scores of levels—the cliffs of Helicon are terraced—from those who, as Burns puts it, "never drank the Muses' stank" upward to where there is an uneasy awareness of what is still above. When, in the famous song in *Semele* ("Where'er you walk"), Handel subjects the monosyllable "shade" to melismatic treatment, with two rests interrupting its flow, he is describing the spreading umbrage, not unbroken, of the animated trees. When, in Polly's complaint of the "saucy jade" her rival, she sings to Macheath, "How can you see me *made* the scoff of such a gipsy?," treating the monosyllable "made" in nearly identical fashion, we realize what kind of sense the average "sensible" person would probably make out of such artifice. No doubt, also, the common-sense view had many defenders who happened not to set down their judgment in writing.

One of those who did so—a very distinguished one—had clear reasons for his opinion, and a practised pen. This was John Wesley, who published a pamphlet entitled "Thoughts on the Power of Music." To him, the hint of intellectual appeals in music was at best ridiculous, at worst sinful. His distinctions did not stop half way. It is, he holds, within the power of melody "to raise various passions in the human mind." But harmony, "namely, a contrast of various notes, opposite to and blended with each other," appeals not to the emotions but to the intellect. "What," he writes, "has counterpoint to do with the passions? It is applied to the ear, to the imagination, or internal sense. It no more affects the passions than the judgment." As for instrumental music, "artificial sounds without any words at all," what use does it serve? It has nothing to do with the passions, with the judgment, with reason, or common sense: "All these are utterly excluded by delicate unmeaning sounds." Polyphony? "Appointing different words to be sung by different persons at the same time . . . is glaringly, undeniably contrary to common-sense." Nevertheless, "this astonishing jargon has found a place even in the worship of God. It runs through (O pity! O shame!) the greatest part of even our Church Music! It is found even in the finest of our Anthems and in the most solemn parts of our public worship. Let any impartial, any unprejudiced persons say whether there can be a more direct mocking of God." [3] Doubtless, Wesley approved of the caveat in one of his brother's hymns:

> Still let us on our guard be found,
> And watch against the power of sound
> With sacred jealousy,
> Lest haply sense should damp our zeal,
> And music's charms bewitch and steal
> Our hearts away from Thee.

Nevertheless, John Wesley had every right to consider himself a music-lover. It was owing originally to him that music became an essential element in the Methodist worship. He insisted on the importance of congregational singing; determined what kind of music should be sung; and gave instruction as to when and how it should be sung. He stood for no whining and droning, but ordered his followers to sing out with wholehearted, open-mouthed fervor, and at a good pace. He selected tunes for his own and his brother's hymns, and he assembled and edited a number of hymn-books before the definitive collection of 1780, which has been the heart of all subsequent Methodist hymnals. Musical talent ran in the family, and rose to genius in a later generation.

It is difficult to recover an accurate idea of early Methodist hymnody. In this country, Methodist tune-books dating before 1800 appear to be virtually non-existent. For our information,

[3] See Fred Luke Wiseman, "John Wesley as a Musician," in *Wesley Studies by Various Writers* (1903), pp. 156–160.

therefore, we must rely on one or two very brief recent studies and on indirect contemporary testimony. James T. Lightwood has identified the contents of the earliest collection, the so-called "Foundery Tune-Book," of 1738. It contained forty-two tunes, of which a third were English, a third were German, and the rest mostly of unknown origin. The German tunes came mostly from Freylinghausen's and Jacobi's song-books of 1705 and 1722, and reflect the profound influence of the Moravians on Wesley. They are mostly chorales. The English sources are miscellaneous and go back as far as Day's and Parker's psalm-books of the 1560's. A few are by known composers: Tallis, Gibbons, Croft, and two or three others, including—rather surprisingly—Handel, whose march in *Richard II* is here adapted and named "Jericho." The authoritative psalm-books are rather lightly drawn upon by Wesley, who was quite willing to reach out in secular directions for a good tune.

The 1742 collection was somewhat larger, and that of 1761, "Select Hymns with Tunes Annext, designed chiefly for the use of the People called Methodists," contains 102 tunes and 133 hymns. Included is Wesley's Grounds of Vocal Music. The hymns are arranged according to metrical pattern. They include most of the 1742 collection, and sixteen tunes written for the Methodists by J. F. Lampe, rather more florid than the others. Nearly half the collection is in triple time; nearly a third in a minor key. The last line or half-line of the hymns frequently repeats as a sort of refrain, and there are four "Hallelujah" refrains; but none of the so-called "Old Methodist Tunes" appears in this book. For a clue we turn elsewhere.

In the autumn of 1766, an attack of the gout took Horace Walpole to Bath, whence he wrote to Chute, on the 10th of October:

My health advances faster than my amusements. However, I have been at one opera, Mr. Wesley's. They have boys and girls with charming voices, that sing hymns, in parts, to Scotch ballad tunes; but indeed so long, that one would think they were already in eternity, and knew how much time they had before them.

This passage raises questions: Did Wesley, who himself preached on that particular day, approve or merely tolerate the part-singing? Was it canonic, like the "fuguing-tunes" of early American worship, or only SATB harmony? This was the Countess of Huntingdon's chapel, where things were done with more refinement than elsewhere; and Walpole adds in the same letter that he is "glad to see that luxury is creeping in among them before persecution," so the music may not have been typical. But what are we to understand by "Scotch ballad tunes"? In Wesley's own hymnals, so far as I can discover, there are no tunes that would be likely to be taken as Scottish folksong, though a few of those from unknown sources appear to have Welsh affiliations. On the other hand, we now know, thanks largely to George Pullen Jackson's researches, that the very stuff out of which the so-called "white spirituals" were made throughout the last century, in New England and the Southeast, was British traditional folk-music, including a large infusion of Scottish tunes in gapped scales. Baptists and Methodists were the chief disseminators of these songs, and of course the latter have within recent memory always enjoyed a reputation for lyrical enterprise in their worship. A likely inference is that long before the days of Moody and Sankey, and even before the days of Lowell Mason, the Methodists were employing a great many folk-tunes that never got into their hymnals and were never perhaps officially sanctioned. With Wesley's single-minded love of melody, and with his all-powerful approval, Methodism was a singing faith; and the traditional tunes would be the ones that his congregations would have known and loved from childhood. If perhaps he himself would have preferred more discrimination in choosing, his lay-preachers certainly would be hospitable to the use of the people's own music; and Wesley, seeing that it was innocent and apt for the work of God, would not be likely to stop it. There is a familiar story that Charles Wesley, interrupted in his preaching by some rowdy sailors singing "Nancy Dawson," compounded with them by declaring that he liked their tune well, and promising to supply them the next day with some better words to it. In any case, anyone who poured out hymns at Charles Wesley's rate of speed would always be bankrupt of fresh tunes, and would welcome them from every quarter. There must have been a natural reluctance to use the same tune again and again, always with a new text; and once a favorite tune and text had become closely united, they would not easily be divorced. The official tune-books were certainly insufficient for the thousands of hymns that Charles Wesley wrote.

Thus it must have happened that Methodism became one of

the main disseminating agents of popular melody. At the same time, even on the higher levels there was a growing revulsion from the complexities of the baroque to simpler forms, in every kind of music, vocal or instrumental. The tendency toward the plain, the uncomplicated, the popular, was part of the spirit of the age, and was manifest on the Continent as well as in England. In Germany, for example, Leichtentritt can declare (*Music, History, and Ideas*, p. 163), with the exhaustive work of Max Friedlaender to support the statement: "The hundreds of song melodies written at this time . . . seem almost primitive in their bare harmony, their intentional lack of all artistic complication. Nevertheless, it was out of their artless style that Schubert's incomparable songs grew in the course of time." The seeds had been sown, and interest in popular balladry and songs was springing up everywhere, to lead to Herder and the brothers Grimm, to Percy, Ritson, Scott, and Jamieson. It was, if not inevitable, at least beautifully appropriate that at this historical moment, and no other, Robert Burns should make his appearance.

Burns was one of the few poets who never, or seldom, wrote a lyric without a tune in mind to which it was to go. The consequence of this fact is, of course, that the metrical conditions of his composition were settled in advance. He had no freedom to innovate or to alter the stanzaic pattern during the course of the song; and, if he made any dramatic shift in the tone from one stanza to another, it was almost certain, he could rest assured, to be neutralized in its effect by having to conform to the normative musical statement. For any variety, he would have to rely on the refrain, which to make its due impact would have to be a full-length *burden*—that is, of equivalent length with the stanza proper. Or, if the tune had no such element, it would be less monotonous if it were a double-strain tune, accommodating two quatrains in a single full statement. In another view, these two cases are identical: quatrain plus *burden* equals two-strain tune. Although I have not taken a thorough census, I think it will be found that a large majority of Burns's songs conform to the double pattern, and fill out an eight-phrase tune or its equivalent. The texts that are printed in quatrains must be checked by the tunes themselves unless the number of stanzas is odd; and sometimes the odd stanza will prove to be a *burden* that is intended to be sung after each regular stanza.

Indeed, to leaf through the texts of his songs is to realize that they are nearly unthinkable without their tunes. Their verbal patterns, their repeated lines, the frequent incidence of "O" at the end of lines, the undodgeable refrains or choruses: these all presume a musical reference. Let two examples chosen at random stand for all:

> Landlady, count the lawin
> The day is near the dawin,
> Ye're a' blind drunk, boys,
> And I'm but jolly fou.
> Hey tutti, taiti,
> How tutti, taiti—
> Wha's fou now?

And this:

> My love she's but a lassie yet;
> My love she's but a lassie yet;
> We'll let her stand a year or twa,
> She'll no be half sae saucy yet.
> I rue the day I sought her, O;
> I rue the day I sought her, O;
> Wha gets her needs na say she's woo'd,
> But he may say he's bought her, O!

This is as much as to say that in sober truth we owe the existence of Burns's lyrics to Scottish folk-music and Burns's familiarity with it. And of course the debt does not stop there. His texts are themselves so interwoven with traditional matter that the more we know of his antecedents, the less sure we become that his part in the most spontaneous and best-loved songs is more than a cleaning-up of the clarty, a filling in of the forgotten, and a civilizing of the ramgunshock—forbye the putting a wheen smeddum in the smeerless.

By its very nature, the folk-tune is better suited to pure lyric than to narrative. The folk-tune is always beginning again, at an unchanging pace, at the same emotional pitch, in unvarying statement. It takes kindly to a series of parallel expressions of an emotion—a single emotion, whether joy or sadness, love or grief— where the element of story is withheld. Narrative asks naturally to vary the pace, to change the pitch, to introduce delays or suspensions or surprises, but always to be going on and never repeating. The effectiveness of the folk-ballad—when it is effective—

depends partly on the tension that arises from this opposition, the musical form exerting a steadying and controlling power over the extravagant text. But it was to be expected that sooner or later, as music became less objective and more impressionistic, there would be an attempt to make the musical vehicle reflect more intimately the changes of meaning and mood in the text—in the smaller forms as in the larger. The solution was not completely attained until the nineteenth-century art song came into being. One answer of the eighteenth century to this problem was the *glee*, which employed a varied succession of short subjects, each one being brought to a cadential pause before the next was taken up. One is tempted to call the glee the poor musician's madrigal; but it took a good musician to write a good glee. Yet another answer, closer to the folk level, is offered by Burns in his so-called "cantata," "The Jolly Beggars." Here the connecting narrative tissue is called "recitative," probably without any expectation of its being actually sung; while musical variety is attained by the introduction of a series of songs, each independent of the others and sung by a different personality.

Burns had of course no way of making the details of his text conform to the details of his musical medium. There is, for example, nothing in the music to which he set his sardonic "Merry hae I been teethin' a heckle" that can bring out or truly express the sense of his words:

> Bitter in dule I licket my winnin's
> O' marryin' Bess to gie her a slave.
> Blest be the hour she cool'd in her linens,
> And blythe be the bird that sings on her grave.

Yet there is often a chameleon quality about these Scottish tunes that makes them notably adaptable to different uses. The same air will be mischievous and spirited or pathetic, according to the speed and mood in which it is sung. A good example is "Hey tutti taiti," which we have already noticed as the drinking song, "Landlady count the lawin," and which Burns made world-famous by his words, "Scots wha hae," and to which, later, Lady Nairne wrote her tender "Land of the Leal." The adaptability appears to be especially Scottish, and I suspect that part of the cause lies in the gapped scales so frequently appearing in the music of that country, so uncommon in English folk-music. These are natural bridges from mode to mode; and each pentatonic scale has latent reference to three heptatonic and two hexatonic scales, every one with its own special character and feeling.

BY WAY OF conclusion, looking back over the century, we can I think distinguish two phenomena of greatest significance for the vital interconnections of music and literature. The first culminates in the first half, the second in the latter half, of the century. The first is the strenuous and almost successful effort to evolve a language that could convey general and abstract truths with a high degree of objectivity, by means of the mutually interpretative support of which words and tones were capable: a conventional language that, rather than pursuing novelties, relied, as did all classical diction at its best, upon using the accepted modes of expression with deepened awareness, refined sensitivity and precision. The second phenomenon is the part, the multifarious and far-reaching part, played by popular song in transition from classicism to individualism. The influence of Percy's *Reliques* on the theory and practice of the elder romantic poets has long been acknowledged; but the inseparable role of humble melody in conditioning the formal and stylistic habits of the ballad and of all popular lyric has, I think, been imperfectly recognized. Here, too, but from the opposite direction, a common and universal language is being evolved, not by the cerebration of an aristocratic tradition, but by the gradual and unconscious sifting out of those graces and subtleties that could not be immediately seized and retained by the unforced memory of the people as a whole. Burns's best-loved songs speak to the mind and heart of our common humanity; and it was only, it would seem, by descending to rest for a historical moment "flat on the nether springs" that a new cycle could be begun on a radically different principle, the exploration of individualism.

Personification Reconsidered

PROBABLY no page of criticism in the English language is better known than that in which Dr. Johnson dispatches *Lycidas* to the limbo of failures of which the little life is feebly sustained by the reputation of their authors. Let us briefly recall the grounds of that notorious verdict. They are as follows. The poem affects a personal grief in terms which belie the fact. Taken literally, lines like "We drove afield . . . batt'ning our flocks" are merely untrue, and therefore arouse, and ought to arouse, no answering sympathy. Taken allegorically, "the true meaning is so uncertain and remote that it is never sought, because it cannot be known when it is found." The poem is filled with second-hand invention in the exhausted pastoral tradition, loaded with classical allusions "such as a College easily supplies," and indecently—not to say impiously—mingled with the sacred truths of Christianity. "Where there is leisure for fiction there is little grief . . . He who thus grieves will excite no sympathy; he who thus praises will confer no honour."

A word of explanation is in order about this essay on Personification. When it was published in 1959, it had the unpleasant air of deliberately ignoring important scholarly work that had appeared in the previous decade. The neglect was unavoidable. The essay was printed as originally written in the Autumn of 1946, unchanged because the author, in the short interval between acceptance and appearance, had neither time nor opportunity to reconsider and revise. An abridged form of portions of the essay, long since published in ELH in September 1947, had been prepared for delivery at a meeting in December 1946. Unused portions of the original were subsequently borrowed for a review article a decade later. After this, it was not anticipated that in its original form the essay would be required. But until now, it has been a misdated event in a chronological series of essays on this subject.

It is this last pair of assertions to which we should particularly attend.

Admittedly, Milton's professed grief over his personal loss in the death of Edward King fails to stir much pity. We cannot and do not meet Johnson's objection with a contradiction. Rather, we tax him with obtuseness for not perceiving, or not acknowledging, that Milton's sincerity is vindicated on other, and subtler, grounds. Yet, after we have pointed out how wrong, because irrelevant, Johnson was, his objection, on its own terms, still stands: personal grief for a friend has no foothold here; and Edward King's human merits are not in this place exalted.

It is worthy of remark that Johnson's objections to *Lycidas* are further produced and illustrated in reverse by his own elegy on the death of Dr. Levet. That poem is a positive restatement and demonstration of his negative criticism of the great monody. Moreover, the contrast between the two poems is in the highest degree illuminating. With no "leisure for fiction"—no time for telling "of rough satyrs and fauns with cloven heel"—Johnson here sets himself squarely to the task of "conferring honour" by his lines, and expects, if successful, to excite sympathy from our common humanity. To achieve these ends, he first utters a general truth about the transitory nature of human pleasures, and then goes on to show where in general, and why, Levet will be especially missed. Without exaggerating Levet's knowledge, Johnson illustrates his fidelity in well-doing, in terms that must command universal assent to the man's merit. The reader's response is simply: "How admirable a being! how natural to lament his loss!" The formal contrast between this poem and *Lycidas* is perfect: the one an expression of deep personal loss, but stated in language so general that we merely infer the private grief as a natural part of the common experience; the other a medley of general themes miraculously blended under the guise of private grief, a "melodious tear" bewailing "a learned Friend unfortunatly drown'd in . . . 1637," a grief asserted literally and figuratively, but non-existent, or present only as a gently pervasive melancholy. In the one poem, pretence; in the other, reserve: artful pretence of a personal loss; and actual private grief masked in general statement.

The latter formula, of particular emotion conveyed in generalities, was powerfully evocative and convincing to Johnson's age, whilst the other was, for him at least, a mockery. If, apart from the unimaginable beauty of the verse, we of to-day prefer the Miltonic and find the Johnsonian statement relatively cold, the fact has far-reaching causes and implications. The major difficulty—for our own time, at any rate—of eighteenth-century poetry is here epitomized.

To predict that the uninformed reader, confronted for the first time by Johnson's poem in an anthology, will be but mildly impressed requires no great hardihood to-day. And the reason is already evident: Johnson has been at pains to put his particulars in the most general form. His success is registered in stanzas like the following:

> No summons mock'd by chill delay,
>   No petty gain disdain'd by pride,
> The modest wants of every day
> The toil of every day supplied.

To the modern reader, this of all forms of statement is the least tolerable. Esoteric obscurity, utter unintelligibility, were far to be preferred: and under personal agony (another's), our heads are bloody, but unbowed. But this, this is too removed from breathing reality. Give us the quickening particular, and let us for ourselves perceive within it the class.

In the face of so alien a mode, the instructor resorts to biographical annotation. He reads from Boswell; he explains the mutual dependence, the mutual respect, which subsisted between Johnson and Levet for a third of a century; he points out Johnson's freedom from snobbery in praising so justly, so nobly, so uncondescendingly his pensioner, the uneducated, inarticulate fellow who had picked up all he knew of medicine from waiting in a tavern frequented by doctors. Thus enlightened, our average reader softens to the poem: gradually his prejudices disappear, and he even likes it very much. He may reach the point—many have—where, from emotion, only with difficulty can he read the poem aloud.

What is the meaning of this little parable? Not, we suspect, that the eighteenth-century style has reached its mark; but rather that that style has been circumvented, been counteracted by having the receiving mind supplied with the facts which reduce all those generals to particulars. The actual focus of the mind's attention has subtly shifted to the vital and undeniably moving relationship that gave rise to the poem, and the poem itself now but serves as the door to recollection. It is doubtful if many readers to-day get beyond this point to a genuine and unforced enjoyment of the generalized style for its own sake.

The situation is curious. It is a truism that the eighteenth century was fond of abstractions, but we do not stop to realize what this truly means. What it usually means is that since, on the whole, to-day abstractions fail to move us, the aesthetic response of the eighteenth century, nourished on such things, must therefore have been relatively thin. This attitude is all but universal in critical writing from Wordsworth's time to our own. See, for example, how it underlies the position of even so sympathetic a critic as Thomas Quayle, writing of poetic style in the eighteenth century:

> In its groping after the "grand style," as reflected in a deliberate avoidance of accidental and superficial "particularities," and in its insistence on generalized or abstract forms, eighteenth century poetry, or at least the "neo-classical" portion of it, reflected its inability to achieve that intensity of imaginative conception which is the supreme need of all art.[1]

Now, so interpreted, the truism, or at least its corollary, may not be true at all—in fact, is almost demonstrably false. No inference, surely, is more unforced than this: that if eighteenth-century poets labored long and hard to raise their immediate personal experiences and emotions to the most general statement, they did so because their keenest aesthetic delight lay in that direction. They were neither humanly incurious of, nor emotionally insensitive to, particulars, as almost any page of Boswell will prove; but personal statement gained force, conviction, vaster horizons, when lifted to the plateau of the general consensus. Force, conviction, and vaster horizons do not weaken effects for those who experience them. We work to-day in an opposite direction: we are, roughly speaking, insensitive to the *emotional* appeal of a general statement. This insensitivity, I suspect, is our characteristic weakness—meaning by *us* all who have been vitally affected by the intellectual drift of the last hundred and fifty years toward Egocentricity. Impartially

[1] Thomas Quayle, *Poetic Diction* (1924), p. 13.

considered, however, *under*valuation of the general statement has no more valid claim to be taken as an absolute in aesthetic judgement than has *over*valuation.

It may be objected that such undervaluation on our part has not been proved. Now it is next to impossible to be aware of one's own under- or over-evaluations—or those of one's own time—because these are precisely level with the sensibilities of ourselves or our age, and therefore fully experienced as valid: just as young persons are more alive than their elders to certain ideas and images, which come to them with emotional overtones to which at their years they are naturally peculiarly susceptible. We can never be truly aware of our over- or under-valuations until we have outgrown them, whether as individuals or as an age.

At any rate, waiving for the present any final judgement in the matter, the fact of an enormous "shift of sensibility" (Frederick Pottle's useful phrase) in the area under discussion is beyond dispute. We have moved from a taste for the abstract—which (in other than aesthetic fields) is often supposed a mark of maturity—to a preference for the concrete. The fact permeates all our judgements and makes it very difficult for us to meet the eighteenth cntury on its own ground, to experience aesthetic satisfactions comparable to theirs. Our responses all tend to show, so to put it, a negative displacement. With regard to poetry like that of Johnson, we are in a position analogous to Johnson's with regard to *Lycidas,* in that the basic sensitivity to an alien mode of expression is lacking to us as to him. It may be guessed that one day the pendulum will swing back. Meanwhile, it is a capital duty of criticism to be aware of this parallax, and to try by imaginative sympathy and understanding to allow for and correct the ever-present displacement. Nowhere, perhaps, is the necessity more acute than in the field of eighteenth-century personification; and to a consideration of that problem we may now address our attention.

PERSONIFICATION, as it relates to poetry, is one portion of the total field of metaphor. It is impossible to discover any valid distinction in kind between personification and metaphor in general, and it follows that critical acceptance or approval of metaphor entails similar acceptance of personification, as a metaphorical species. Metaphor is everywhere acknowledged as the core of poetic statement. Contemporary critics, as it happens, are intensively engaged in examining the nature and functions of metaphor; and this fact should indicate, among other possibilities, that the present age is acutely sensitive to metaphor. So, with varying emphasis, was the age of the Romantic poets and critics, Coleridge, Wordsworth, Hazlitt.

Now, whilst Coleridge taught us more perhaps than anyone else, before or since, about the nature of poetic language and the working of poetic imagination, most of what the Romantics had to say about personification was unfavourable. They inveighed against it, and although their greatest spokesmen made clear by qualifications that the warnings were directed primarily against its abuse, the negative injunction has generally been taken in the widest sense, and the critical rule been everywhere solemnly deferred to and reinforced.

It is therefore worth pausing to insist upon the radical inseparability of personification from other kinds of metaphor. All, of course, rest on submerged similes. The blood kinship becomes self-evident, however, if we set examples side by side. Here is Blake's description of the Charity-school children:

> O what a multitude they seem'd, these flowers of London town!

Conversely, Herrick addresses violets in this manner:

> Welcome, Maids of Honour,
>   You doe bring
>   In the Spring;
> And wait upon her . . .
>
> Yet though thus respected,
>   By and by
>   Ye doe lie,
> Poore Girles, neglected.

Once again, Herrick writes:

> There's not a *budding* Boy, or Girle, this day,
> But is got up, and gone to bring in May.

It is obvious that the first two figures are basically identical, the same equation being implicit in each. In the one it is "Children equal Flowers"; in the other, "Flowers (violets) equal Children (girls)." In the third example, the propriety of the epithet, *budding*, is dependent upon the same proposition. We may call the first a case of metonymy, the third a metaphorical descriptive adjective, and reserve the name personification for the second alone; but it is obvious that these distinctions are merely technical and superficial. Nor, fundamentally, does it matter whether the analogy be conveyed by means of noun, verb, adverb, or adjective. We may complete the present series by setting the budding boys and girls over against a *weeping* willow, where the name implies a forgotten but not obliterated personification.

If we turn to abstractions, the same process is evident: for examples, Marvell's "vegetable love"; Cleopatra's

> For his bounty,
> There was no winter in't; an autumn 'twas,
> That grew the more by reaping;

Rückert's

> Du bist die Ruh,
> Der Friede mild,
> Die Sehnsucht du,
> Und was sie stillt;

Vaughan's

> If thou canst get but thither,
> There growes the flowre of peace,
> The Rose that cannot wither;

Collins'

> Spring, with dewy Fingers cold,
> Returns to deck their hallow'd Mold.

And when we speak of a "coming-out party," we make use of an abstract concept which doubtless contains embedded in it the radical image of springtime budding—of a flower "newly springing," as Jeremy Taylor would say, "from the clefts of its hood."

In view of these vital interconnections, we need, when confronted by the Romantics' hostility to personification, to take some critical bearings. Are we to go on believing that metaphor is necessary and wholesome, but that personification, a portion of metaphor, is a slow poison, of which, they say, the eighteenth-century poets eventually died? It will be best to return to the laboratory and review our analyses in the hope of surer guidance. Some indulgence must be craved for so academic—not to say pedantic—an exercise. But without it, I fear, we cannot profitably proceed.

The threshold of personification is not by any means easy to fix. Initial distinguishing marks, in English, are indications of sex and active (as opposed to passive) qualifying, whether by noun-appositive, adjective, verb, or adverb. Apostrophe is one of the commonest and simplest ways of marking the intention. It will be generally agreed that personification ought to be perceptible through the ear as well as through the eye; and this raises the question of capitalization, which cannot be disposed of in an easy phrase.

Coleridge ran afoul of Gray's lines,

> In gallant trim the gilded vessel goes,
> Youth at the prow and pleasure at the helm,

on the ground that "it depended wholly on the compositor's putting, or not putting, a small capital . . . whether the words should be personifications, or mere abstractions." [2] It is certainly difficult to deduce from eighteenth-century practice any consistent principles of capitalization; but a few observations may be hazarded on this subject. In the first place, up to at least the middle of the century, in the more carefully and elegantly printed books, it was a widespread convention to capitalize *all* nouns.[3] Moreover, while this practice of capitalization remained a general habit, there was obviously no compulsion upon the reader to think personification whenever he saw a capital. Now, Gray's own MS of the first draft of his *Elegy* proves that he was in the habit of capitalizing *every*

---

[2] *Biographia Literaria*, ch. 1.

[3] Where this custom was consistently observed, it made possible refinements in meaning which later were lost to view. Thus, for example, in the first edition of Parnell's *A Night-Piece on Death*, where almost without exception the nouns are capitalized, occur the lines:

> . . . think, as softly-sad you tread
> Above the venerable Dead,
> Time was, like thee they Life possest,
> And Time shall be, that thou shalt Rest.

Here the capitalization of *Rest* proves that word a noun, and the whole couplet is knit together with a parallelism—"they formerly possessed life, thou shalt possess rest"—which gives an antithetical force to the thought, lost (I believe) in every later printing.

noun. In this respect there is an utter lack of correspondence between his MSS and the earliest and most authoritative printed texts. It follows that he was indifferent to the capitalization of his poems, and left the matter entirely to his printer. His own sense of personification, therefore, was quite independent of typographical distinction: so that the reader is at liberty to import just so much of a sense of personification as he feels appropriate to the particular case, and neither more nor less. When Gray wrote:

> Let not Ambition mock their useful toil,
> Their rustic joys and destiny obscure:
> Nor Grandeur hear with a disdainful smile
> The short and simple annals of the poor,

he capitalized Toil, Joys, Destiny, Smile, Annals, and Poor, as well as Ambition and Grandeur; but the edition of 1768, by reducing all but the last two to lower case, puts for us an entirely misleading and disproportionate emphasis on the personifications, one which there is no evidence to show that Gray intended. But even this later text, could we read it, as Gray did, with a capitalizing habit of mind, would not obtrude its personifications upon us as it does to-day.[4] The personifications are there to be sure in any typographical dress, but they were not intended to clamor for attention. Coleridge's objection, therefore, is doubly answered: first, Gray does not base his personifications on a typographical device; and, second, it matters not at all to Gray whether Coleridge or another decide to take the words as personifications, or as "mere abstractions." Why not Personifabstractions? Let the reader determine the proportions to suit his taste. Must we have always thwacking full-bodied personifications? In the Realms of Gold, has an edict gone forth to slay all but the most robust inhabitants? Surely, no. It is time, after a hundred and fifty years, to try anew to make a few simple distinctions between sorts of personification.

First, then, I shall distinguish between two main classes, object-personification and abstract-personification. The conferring of primary human attributes upon an object or objects inanimate, or

---

[4] It is perhaps worth remark that our disregard of the capitals which commence every line of conventionally printed verse is a current analogy for the state of mind here desiderated. The German convention is of course another. By Coleridge's day, the older capitalizing habit had been all but universally abandoned in printing.

animate but non-human, constitutes the first class. For example, Wordsworth's "Earth fills her lap with pleasures of her own." An older convention would also include here invocation of the dead or the absent, as Wordsworth's "Milton, thou shouldst be living at this hour!" The other main class, the abstract-personification, may be exemplified by Wordsworth's

> Truth fails not; but her outward forms that bear
> The longest date do melt like frosty rime, &c.

Now, each of these classes can be legitimately divided into two sorts which, it appears to me, are genuinely distinct in kind, apart from the degree to which they may be elaborated. Differences of degree[5] I forbear to categorize, as being impossible to sustain except in the most obvious instances. The difference in kind which I seek to establish holds equally for object- and abstract-personification. It is a difference which I shall discriminate by the terms *non-restrictive* and *restrictive*. I have in mind the distinction between a personification which imposes no particular image, apart from what may be felt by the reader as inherent in the personified concept, and a particularizing, or restrictive, characterization—the arbitrary bestowal of an image or pictorial figure upon the concept, which acts as a limitation controlling our imaginative freedom. A few examples will, I trust, clarify the distinction.

When Wordsworth writes, "The river glideth at his own sweet will," he is personifying in such a way as to allow us to continue to see the river as a river. This is a non-restrictive object-personification. Another is "Fair Star of evening . . . on the horizon's brink Thou hangest, stooping" etc. Another is the same poet's coy Primrose of the Rock:

> So blooms this lonely Plant, nor dreads
> Her annual funeral.

Or, once more,

> The moon doth with delight
> Look round her when the heavens are bare.

[5] For example, Dr. Hugh Blair's "The first is, when some of the properties or qualities of living creatures are ascribed to inanimate objects; the second, when those inanimate objects are introduced as acting like such as have life; and the third, when they are represented, either as speaking to us, or as listening to what we say to them." *Lectures on Rhetoric,* lecture XVI (1813), I, 377.

Similarly, a non-restrictive *abstract*-personification is Wordsworth's Nature, in "Three years she grew":

> Then Nature said, "A lovelier flower" ...
> "This child I to myself will take.
> Myself will to my darling be
> Both law and impulse" ...
> Thus Nature spake—the work was done.

Or, again, his abstraction Immortality, in the *Ode:*

> Thou, over whom thy Immortality
> Broods like the day ...
> A presence which is not to be put by.

Now, when, on the contrary, Wordsworth particularizes his characterization of Earth in the following fashion:

> even with something of a mother's mind ...
> The homely nurse doth all she can
> To make her foster-child ...
> Forget the glories he hath known ...

he is making a restrictive object-personification. Similarly, when he addresses Duty as "Stern Daughter of the Voice of God," and continues:

> thou dost wear
> The Godhead's most benignant grace;
> Nor know we anything so fair
> As is the smile upon thy face,—

he asks us to picture the abstraction in a special form; and this is an example of restrictive abstract-personification.

Within these four types, I believe all instances of personification can be comprised—and it is a peculiar pleasure to be able to find illustrations of all the four in Wordsworth. Whilst it would, of course, be easy to continue subdividing and refining, these broad divisions are possibly sufficient. Since they are not determined according to degree of intensity or of elaboration, they allow for the utmost variety in these latter respects, and are comparatively objective.

I am anxious not to becloud these clear and, as I believe, unforced distinctions with qualifications and debatable borderline cases. But it would be less than candid not to acknowledge that

the different kinds may be found in combination, and sometimes
shading into one another. If we bear in mind that the non-restrictive
figure characterizes *within* the normal field of the concept, whilst
the restrictive tends to characterize *outside* that field, we can
usually agree on a particular case. Thus, when Thomson conjures
up a "bright patrol" of virtues, among which are "Courage composed and keen" and "sound Temperance, healthful in heart and
look," we have little hesitation in calling them non-restrictive, for
the epithets merely reinforce the sense of the abstract, and may
therefore be said to lie within its proper sphere of definition. But
when Milton writes "speckl'd Vanity," he is characterizing beyond
the normal or intrinsic range of definition, and is thus creating a
restrictive personification. Again, when Thomson introduces "Activity untired, with copious life informed, and all awake," we may
confidently classify the figure as non-restrictive; but there might be
doubt about "rough Industry," or "white Peace," or "undaunted
Truth." One may venture the guess that the personifications most
likely to give offence will generally be found, not among the bare
personified abstractions like Gray's "Youth at the prow, and
Pleasure at the helm," which every reader may take at his own
pictorial level, but among the non-restrictive abstracts which have
been elaborated with the semblance, but not the substance, of
restrictive characterization.[6] These are usually flabby figures that

---

[6] It is, however, to be acknowledged that restrictive personifications, carried to
an extreme, have their own peculiar odor of over-ripeness. Léon Morel noted an
instance in Congreve's Ode *On Mrs Arabella Hunt, Singing*, of which one is
tempted to remark, Ripeness is all:

> And lo! Silence himself is here.
> Methinks I see the Midnight God appear,
>   In all his downy pomp arrayed,
>   Behold the rev'rend shade:
>   An ancient sigh he sits upon,
> Whose memory of sound is long since gone,
> And purposely annihilated for his throne.
> Beneath, two soft transparent clouds do meet,
> In which he seems to sink his softer feet.
> A melancholy thought, condensed to air,
>   Stol'n from a lover in despair,
>   Like a thin mantle, serves to wrap
> In fluid folds his visionary shape.
> A wreath of darkness round his head he wears,
> Where curling mists supply the want of hairs,
> While the still vapours, which from poppies rise,
> Bedew his hoary face, and lull his eyes.

have to be energized—if they can be—by the reader's own unaided effort; and they are probably responsible for much of the special insipidity of dilution which permeates too great a proportion of second- and third-rate eighteenth-century verse. For offensive example, the following pseudo-restrictive figure of Thomson may stand preeminent:

> While in the radiant front, superior shines
> That first paternal virtue, public Zeal;
> Who throws o'er all an equal wide survey,
> And, ever musing on the common weal,
> Still labours glorious with some great design.

Yet another sort of elaboration, blindly stumbling between restrictive and non-restrictive object-personification, is exemplified by the passage immediately following the one just quoted. When Thomson proceeds, "Low walks the sun," the personification is evident, and the verb lends a restrictive force; but when he adds, "and broadens by degrees," the figure of a walker is withdrawn in favor of a more literal delineation; yet the verb is sufficiently neutral to allow of an animistic residuum. The next sentence re-establishes the latent human image with a new and positively restrictive force: the sun becomes a king assuming his state with ceremonial display, and a supplementary restrictive personification gives reinforcement:

> The shifting clouds
> Assembled gay, a richly gorgeous train,
> In all their pomp attend his setting throne.

This picture is completed by a three-fold non-restrictive object-personification:

> Air, earth, and ocean smile immense.

But hereupon we begin to perceive that idle decoration is the sum of Thomson's intention; for he continues:

> And now,
> As if his weary chariot sought the bowers
> Of Amphitrite and her tending nymphs,
> (So Grecian fable sung)—

the whole sequence thus far being from walking to fattening to sitting on a setting throne—no! say rather, playing Apollo on a weary chariot!—and, by this declension, to sea-bathing and, we surmise, drowning. For, momentarily regaining rotundity,

> he dips his orb;
> Now half-immersed; and now a golden curve
> Gives one bright glance, then total disappears.

A consummation unlamented. Observe the retreat from restrictive to non-restrictive in "he dips his *orb*," and the desperate snatch at a final non-restrictive compromise in the curious

> now a golden curve
> Gives one bright glance,

where the swimmer's head is depersonified to a geometrical shape, but a shape still human enough to cast a dazzling look of farewell. This exercise of decorative ingenuity will sufficiently illustrate the fluctuations that are possible between the restrictive and non-restrictive in object-personification. And now, with a clearer notion of the varieties of personification, we may revert to more general considerations.

THE AFFILIATIONS and ramifications of personification are so numerous and far-flung, even in literary expression alone, and apart from connections with other arts, that if we were to list them we should not soon have done. Personification is inseparably involved with myth, with fable, with allegory, satire, the morality play, the masque, the comedy of humours, the type "character." The personifying impulse is in fact a radical tendency of the human psyche in all stages of culture; it is embedded in the very roots of language itself; it is basic to every impulse towards dramatic representation. To condemn it is not merely to impugn the value of many of the most important literary forms, to which it is ancillary or essential, but to be guilty of the folly of King Canute. Yet depreciation of it, depreciation both general and particular, continues along various lines to this day.

It has, for example, been disparaged on moral or ethical grounds. In a famous passage which is probably the *locus classicus* of critical commentary in this field, Ruskin has written as follows:

It is to be noted that personification is, in some sort, the reverse of symbolism, and is far less noble. Symbolism is the setting forth of a great truth by an imperfect and inferior sign (as, for instance, of the hope of the resurrection by the form of the phoenix); and it is almost always employed by men in their most serious moods of faith, rarely in recreation. Men who use symbolism forcibly are almost always true believers in what they symbolize. But Personification is the bestowing of a human or living form upon an abstract idea: it is, in most cases, a mere recreation of the fancy, and is apt to disturb the belief in the reality of the thing personified. Thus symbolism constituted the entire system of the Mosaic dispensation: it occurs in every word of Christ's teaching; it attaches perpetual mystery to the last and most solemn act of His life. But I do not recollect a single instance of personification in any of His words. And as we watch, thenceforward, the history of the Church, we shall find the declension of its faith exactly marked by the abandonment of symbolism, and the profuse employment of personification,—even to such extent that the virtues came, at last, to be confused with the saints . . .[7]

Thus Ruskin, although he admits that in the earlier phases of the Renaissance the fashion has been loftily used. This passage has more than once of late been cited with whole-hearted or modified approval; but nowhere have I seen it examined with any attention.

Now, certainly, in so far as the utterance contrasts personification with symbolism, it is an egregious piece of special pleading. Upon what principle could one prove personification "far less noble" than symbolism? How can it be determined, *a priori*, that the bestowing of a human or living form upon an abstract idea is "less noble" than the setting forth of a great truth by an imperfect and inferior sign? Is it not manifest that Ruskin's opposition lies solely between a *great* truth and an idea presumably minuscule? Which, of course, is logically irrelevant. Unhappily, symbolism is potentially, and has ever been actually, as prompt to serve in the promulgation of any diabolical doctrine, for example Nazism, as of the highest truths. It is equally obsequious to the barber, the pander, and the pawnbroker. It readily provokes scorn of the good and every mischievous prejudice. It has no morals apart from those of its employer. And, on the other side, personification is equally neutral; nor is its sincerity, or the lack of that quality, inherent in its constitution, but in the use to which it is put. And that use may be of the loftiest kind. Ruskin might have bethought him that not merely in Renaissance art, but in the general conception of man-

[7] *Stones of Venice*, Vol. II, ch. 8 (The Ducal Palace), section LV.

kind, God Himself is a personification—*Him* self, without impiety I say.

How, moreover, can this distinction in kind be ultimately sustained? When Fra Angelico shows us God the Father, he is personifying an idea; but is he not, at the same time, setting forth a great truth by an imperfect and inferior sign? Is not Botticelli's Truth, in the allegorical painting, "The Calumny of Apelles," a noble or exalted representation of the ideal, if yet inferior in the sense of more restricted; nevertheless, in fact both a symbol and a personification? (And for whom, we ask incidentally, would the representation disturb belief in the reality of the idea personified?) In truth, symbol and personification are not opposites. The two terms are not even commensurate, for the one includes and transcends the other. Symbol is a term which easily contains personification and much else: a personification is but one among many kinds of symbol.

Recently, however, Ruskin's distinction between symbol and personification has been taken up by C. S. Lewis, in his valuable book, *The Allegory of Love,* and subtly elaborated in a somewhat different direction, allegory taking the place of simple personification in his discussion. "On the one hand," he writes,

you can start with an immaterial fact, such as the passions which you actually experience, and can then invent *visibilia* to express them. If you are hesitating between an angry retort and a soft answer, you can express your state of mind by inventing a person called *Ira* with a torch and letting her contend with another invented person called *Patientia*. This is allegory . . . But there is another way of using the equivalence [between the immaterial and the material], which is almost the opposite of allegory, and which I would call sacramentalism or symbolism. If our passions, being immaterial, can be copied by material inventions, then it is possible that our material world in its turn is the copy of an invisible world. As the god Amor and his figurative garden are to the actual passions of men, so perhaps we ourselves and our 'real' world are to something else. The attempt to read that something else through its sensible imitations, to see the archetype in the copy, is what I mean by symbolism or sacramentalism . . . The difference between the two can hardly be exaggerated. The allegorist leaves the given—his own passions—to talk of that which is confessedly less real, which is a fiction. The symbolist leaves the given to find that which is more real. To put the difference in another way, for the symbolist it is we who are the allegory . . . Symbolism is a mode of thought, but allegory is a mode of expression. It belongs to the form of poetry, more than to its content.[8]

Now it is impossible not to feel at once in this analysis the edge of a very keen intelligence, or to deny to the distinction here emphasized a large measure of plausibility. On general grounds, it is much to be desired that a distinction so clear-cut should if possible be adopted. Yet I think that before we give ourselves to it wholly, we should try what weight it will bear.

For myself, I confess I am troubled at being asked to start by agreeing that the passions which I actually experience are immaterial facts in comparison to the allegorical figures I may invent to represent them. I find it hard not rather to regard the figures as idealizations of my states of mind, idealizations which may have a general pertinency and validity for all men who may be suffering the like emotions under whatever particular circumstances. I incline to regard these idealizations as in the nature of archetypes or archetypal images, of which my own and other men's experiences offer particular illustration. In the sense in which the Platonist can maintain that the ideal is more real than the world of phenomena, it is surely possible for the allegorist to claim that what he is seeking to portray is precisely that ideal world. And the firmer the hold which this visionary world takes upon his imagination, the more deeply rooted, pure, and satisfying will be the reflected images. In what sense, then, does he differ from Lewis' symbolist, who "leaves the given to find that which is more real"?

If, moreover, we consent to the proposition that "Symbolism is a mode of thought, but allegory is a mode of expression," it still has to be pointed out that a mode of thought is not operative in art until it has found utterance in a valid mode of artistic expression. If this be true, symbolism and allegory cannot thus be contrasted as opposites. The true opposite of allegory is naturalism, these two modes being at the extremes of the scale of expression. Symbolism, as a mode of thought, may therefore employ either extreme at will. The symbolist who is sufficiently convinced that we are the allegorical representatives, the "personifications" and "abstractions" of the world of reality, may give himself over to the task of depicting the natural world, secure in the conviction that the more faithfully he portrays this world, the closer he will come to the

[8] *The Allegory of Love* (1936), pp. 44–48.

ultimate verities. Indeed, naturalism, consistently pushed towards meaningful ends, aspires to symbolism. And it is no accident, in turn, that the Symbolist Movement, so called, has been so deeply enmeshed in sense impression.

On the other hand, the symbolist may with equal propriety make use of allegory as a mode of expression. His choice of this mode or that will ultimately be determined, or at least profoundly affected, by the measure of his metaphysical assurance or religious faith. Granted sufficient confidence in the validity of his idealistic vision of reality, he may resort to allegory as the readiest means of conveying his positive affirmations, or, conversely, to satire as the negative expression of the same beliefs. Naturalism, on the contrary, is the mode of a symbolist who is uncertain about the ultimate significance of his symbols; sure only—or at worst merely hopeful—that they have a meaning, that they are veritable symbols. The truth, he feels, is latent in the phenomena, but inextricable.

Inherent in symbol is the idea of exchange, of one thing put for another. To employ it successfully, one must be familiar with its exchange value. This is at once the source of its weakness and of its strength. For the initiate, it can be shorthand for a whole con- geries of conceptual meanings. Allusion to a Joseph, a Daniel, or a Babbitt may convey a wealth of significance. But to the uniniti- ated it means nothing. Of what effect is the Christian symbol mentioned with such approval by Ruskin, of the phoenix to figure the hope of resurrection, if we have no previous acquaintance with that intention? Or of a fish to suggest the Messiah? And it will be admitted that a symbol of which *no one* knows the meaning is of no more use than a hieroglyphic inscription without the Rosetta Stone.

The symbolist, therefore, who makes use of naturalism is faced with a serious dilemma. Although regarding all mankind as in- voluntary personifications or symbols of reality, he yet, of course, is limited to particular examples. The instances, taken together, constitute a sort of symbolic shorthand which neither he nor any- one else can translate into any other terms. By the very definition of his chosen method, all he can do is to describe what has been observed (*tranche de vie*). In so far as his figures are genuinely symbolic, they must be abstractly significant: that is, they are par- ticulars standing for a general. They are types—but typical of what? In sober truth and strict logic, not typical at all. The total, infinite sum of such particulars would indeed together make an image, or type, of the phenomenal world. But the individual cases, by themselves, illustrate only the generalization—if indeed even this—that if in every contributory detail this particular configuration of phenomena could be duplicated, the result would be identical: an affirmation of little use or significance. A is all A's—but there is only one A.

How comes it then that we can be continually speaking with assurance of this or that figure in a naturalistic novel or play as a "typical" character? Is it not in every case because we ourselves, instinctively turning allegorists or personifiers, reduce these figures to embodiments of one or two predominant traits, or qualities; so that, as they pass current from mind to mind, they have no more three-dimensional actuality than what attaches to a personified abstraction—which is exactly what they have become: eponymous personified abstractions. But it is we who have created the symbol out of the original uniqueness and complexity; and, be it well observed, the symbol does not stand for that original figure, but for a class the members of which, in common with the original, all prominently exhibit some characteristic trait. When we call someone a Shylock, we think of the exacting of the pound of flesh, not of those qualities of racial and paternal pride and bitterness which make of Shakespeare's creation a terrible and pathetic human individual; his use as symbol is restricted to the bare outline of an idea.

Almost automatically, therefore, and quite involuntarily, we find ourselves back in the world of idealized abstractions, where the mind is more at home, and where alone, perhaps, the multiplicity of experience can be brought to terms and made endurable. For we are so constituted that we have to make generals of our particulars or be drowned in the flood of phenomena.

If, then, we have to make eponymous personified abstractions out of naturalistic characters before they can become symbolic, the question arises: what advantage is served by leaving to such haphazard and roundabout means the achieving of a necessary end? For if the character is subtly and complexly portrayed, there is a likelihood that our secondary operations upon it will not coincide to produce an image identical or closely similar to that in the minds of others. Your Hamlet may not be mine; and if we are referring to him as a kind of character, as a "Hamlet," we must first sit down to definitions. As symbol, he is unsatisfactory: he will not easily circulate as ready currency because his value is too disputable. The simpler characters, flat, two-dimensional, are more serviceable, because already closer to personified abstractions. All that they lack is the label itself; which anyone may easily supply who knows their story; or which may even be suggested by a descriptive, Dickensian name.

Art has many legitimate uses for counters which are minted with a recognizable face value. The bestowing of a self-explanatory label is a device of great efficiency and economy. It obviates the inconvenient necessity of an initial reading to discover significance. It anticipates and prevents doubt of intention. It makes for a clarity of statement more precise than can be achieved by undenominated symbols. It advances upon and occupies the positions of an argumentative or expositional statement or series of propositions with a suddenness never approached by naturalistic methods, and clinches these with the force of logic—witness *Everyman*. Where the artist's meaning, in the sense of intellectual idea, is clear and unambiguous, and where also the focus of his attention is beyond the world of physical phenomena, he will instinctively employ the device of named abstractions in allegorical configuration. The religious and moral convictions of the Middle Ages made allegory, therefore, a natural mode of artistic utterance, and the ethical and intellectual convictions of the Age of Locke were to do the same for the simpler configurations of personified abstraction. An artist sure of what he wishes to say about the nature of the ordered, ideal world will not wait for chance and our own random inclinations to lead us to his meaning. Like Spenser, he will seek his goal by a more immediate and certain route. Rather than rely on our clumsy, hit-or-miss abstractions from phenomenal representation, he will invent his own personifications, give them appropriate and transparent names, and set them in motion to express his doctrine. For allegory is the most forthright method that we know, of conveying an ethical message in dramatic representational form.

Partly for that reason the method has latterly been unpopular—though there are signs of change in the air. Of the two extremes, explicit statement ("moral") and implication ("meaning"—our cur-

rent fashionable name for "moral"), the Scylla and Charybdis between which the artist is always trying to steer, one seems a greater
peril in one age, the other in another. Oppressed with the riddle of
the world, yet afraid to be called naïve, the modern author shuns
the first risk, of forthright statement, preferring intentional, and he
hopes sophisticated, obscurity. His readers may even read more
meaning into his work than he himself is able to see. If not, who
can say that that is not the reader's fault? Are we not already
blessed with seven types of ambiguity? and who knows how many
more remain to be disclosed?

Thus it is argued to-day that explicit statement is a relatively inferior and immature form of expression. Allen Tate has given positive and vigorous voice to this point of view in the following
passage:

The kind of poetry that is primarily allegorical . . . because its primary
direction is towards that oversimplification of life which is the mark
of the scientific will . . . is a one-sided poetry, ignoring the whole
vision of experience . . . When the preponderance of meanings receives
from the author himself the seal of his explicit approval, in face of
the immense complication of our experience, then the work . . . is
written in the interest of social, moral, and religious ideas apart from
which it has neither existence nor significance. And it is aesthetic
creation at a low level of intensity . . . the characters, images, symbols,
ideas, are simple, and invite restatement in a paraphrase that exhausts
their meaning; they stand, not in themselves, but merely for something else. The *Faerie Queene* belongs to this class of allegory . . . The
narrative lacks inner necessity; it is pure illustration.[9]

Although the clarity of this statement excites admiration, its
judgements raise a fundamental question. When it is said that a
work of art has inner necessity, what in reality is the nature of the
claim? Is it that the content of the work is literally the complex expression of antecedent and concomitant pressures of time and
space, cause and effect and event, differing in no respect from
actuality in the phenomenal world? If so, art and life are indistinguishable, and *The Faerie Queene* has as much "inner necessity"
as anything else, being like all else the involuntary resultant of universal forces. But clearly, this is not the critic's meaning: we have
pushed his "inner necessity" too far when we equate it with physical actuality. It is, then, an imitation of such actuality. Such inner

[9] *Reactionary Essays* (1936), pp. 89–91.

necessity as it can claim is the author's own contribution, the result of his shaping intention. It reflects a selection from various
possibilities in accordance with his total purpose. It is therefore inevitably his reading of existence. Now, in what sense is all this not
equally true of Spenser's allegory? It comes to this: that Tate is
here expressing merely his personal inability to share in Spenser's
kind of vision, preferring complications of a more naturalistic
order. But why "a low level of intensity"? Has Tate read accu-
rately the temperature of Spenser's imagination? Or shall we say
that a documentary transcript from the diffuse phenomenal world,
in Zola or Dreiser, is by its mere nature more "intense" than the
simplicity of allegory? Is the play of haphazard circumstance necessarily more "intense" than the thrust or pull of two equal and
opposite forces—say, duty and desire?

On the contrary, it is possible to hold that allegory is a more advanced form of intellectual and artistic expression than naturalism.
Just as on the physical level it requires a concentration of will and
effort to drive a road through the jungle, so in the world of the
mind, it requires a greater intellectual and imaginative effort to
divine or perceive order within the chaotic multiplicity of consciousness, and to represent that ideality with power and beauty,
than to reproduce, even with high fidelity, our chaotic impressions
and responses to the phenomenal world. Every such act is a recla-
mation, a little fiat in the divine image, and is entitled, if any aspect
of our mental life has such a right, to be called mature. And this
is Spenser's achievement. His subject, as Janet Spens very properly
reminds us, is "the apprehension, description and organization of
the inner world." [10] Being Elizabethan, he "tends to utter his more
intense emotions through the imagery of human figures," having
inherited the medieval view of reality as "a personal God fully reflected in miniature in man and faintly and partially in the different elements of the physical universe." [11] With man in a position
of such pivotal importance, Spenser's primary concern is, as Miss
Spens well says, "not so much with the sensuous fact as with the
mental translation of the fact—with the use which the soul's faculty
makes of the impact and stir of the physical sensation . . . He
cared more for the artificial than for nature, because in the artifact

[10] *Spenser's Faerie Queene* (1934), p. 52.
[11] *Ibid.*, pp. 55, 56.

the sensuous element is more visibly held in solution by the concept." [12]

An analogy may help to throw this question of relative sophistication between allegory and naturalism into clearer focus. Ruskin noted with disapproval the fact that as the hour of the Renaissance grew later, the tendency to personification increased, until the abstract virtues tended to become confused with the saints; so that, in the later litanies, we actually "find St. Faith, St. Hope, St. Charity, and St. Chastity, invoked immediately after St. Clara and St. Bridget." [13] Now, there are two ways of interpreting these data. We may take them, as Ruskin does, as an indication of the decline of faith. Or we may infer a gradually increasing awareness, a sharpening sense, purifying itself from association with particular persons and acts, of the loveliness and beauty of the abstract idea of these moral virtues—a sense which finally elevated them to a reality for the spiritual life no less vivid and vital than that of the human beings who in the historic or legendary past had aspired to exemplify similar virtues in their own lives. It may be thought a loftier, a more adult procedure, to sanctify the pure idea of a virtue than to sanctify a virtuous man or woman. This tendency may be taken as an index of increasing spirituality, if not in the Church, then in the minds of men.

Opportunely, C.S. Lewis' discussion of the beginnings of monotheism provides us with a second analogy. At first, he reminds us, we find a polytheistic universe, in which claims and counterclaims are made for various divinities, rivals in power and worship. The more popular divinities gradually assume the attributes of the lesser, and the hierarchy simplifies towards the point where relatively few gods stand as the presiding genii of particular areas of activity. The goal was never quite reached of a perfectly consistent and non-conflicting hierarchy, but the tendency in that direction was not arrested. Polytheism led inevitably to further simplification and to unification. Monotheism was the natural issue.

The best minds [says Lewis] embrace monotheism. What is to be done with the gods of the popular religion? The answer—or at least that form of the answer which concerns us most—was given by the Stoics. 'Deus pertinens per naturam cuiusque rei, per terras Ceres, per maria

---

[12] *Ibid.*, p. 70.
[13] *Stones of Venice*, Vol. II, ch. 8, section LV.

Neptunus, alii per alia, poterunt intelligi.' [Cicero, *De natura deorum*]
—where the very construction *Deus poterunt* hits off the corresponding
state of mind to a nicety. The gods are to be aspects, manifestations,
temporary or partial embodiments of the single power. They are, in
fact, personifications of the abstracted attributes of the One.[14]

In this way, the older gods are, so to put it, spiritualized into the
virtues and powers of God Himself. The advance in point of intellectual and spiritual maturity is in no need of demonstration.

Now, between these instances of progress and the point at issue
there is a manifest parallel. Just as, in the person of saint and pagan
god, we find the imperfect and mixed embodiment of an abstract
quality which we are enabled, by increasing intellectual and moral
growth, to isolate and conceive in its pure essentiality, so likewise,
in the naturalistic depiction of the finite individual, we find the potential symbol which, first by instinctive simplification and then by
deliberate refinement, we may transform to a pure distillation, an
abstract of the essential quality or idea. Such will be the personified abstraction, constituting the entity to be interwoven in narrative or dramatic context with other kindred entities, and forming
with these the full-blown allegory. The intellectual and imaginative achievement of such a transformation is an affirmation of maturity, not immaturity. Hence a recent writer, in a highly provocative comparison of Elizabethan dramatic conventions with the
hampering restraints of modern realistic drama, can roundly declare that the Elizabethan mind "had not been warped by the
naïve incredulity of scientific naturalism." [15]

So LATELY as 1924, in a study sympathetic in the main to the
eighteenth century, Thomas Quayle comes into collision with the
abstractions of the neo-classical poets. He speaks of the prevalence
of abstraction as a "contagion" and a "mania" in that school.[16] The
personified abstractions, he says (p. 164), are "faint and faded
relics" of medieval allegory. In this attitude, he is obviously at one
with Wordsworth in the famous Preface of 1800. Wordsworth,
we remember well, professes to reject these figures on the ground
that they "do not make any natural or regular part of [the] lan-

[14] *Allegory of Love*, p. 57.
[15] S. L. Bethell, *Shakespeare and the Popular Dramatic Tradition* (1944), p. 87.
[16] *Poetic Diction*, pp. 139, 146.

guage of men": he wishes "to keep the Reader in the company of flesh and blood."

The discussion in the foregoing pages will have served to remind us that we cannot so cavalierly dispose of the matter. We realize that there are losses as well as gains in the abandonment of this mode of expression—losses especially in clarity of aim, in precision and economy of statement. We have seen that any general attack is likely to involve itself in contradiction and inconsistency.

But, again, Quayle is not innocent of the assumption that the presence or absence of personification is determined by the depth and intensity of the poet's emotion—and this in inverse ratio. Thus, on the positive side, he finds that Johnson as a rule was saved from the danger of indulging in such figures "by the depth of feeling with which he unfolds the individual examples chosen to enforce his moral lessons." [17] In some of Young's evocations he finds "a tinge of personal emotion which invests these shadowy figures with something of a true lyrical effect."[18]

It was implied at the start that the bulk of historical evidence lies in the opposite direction. The proof of a lack of personal emotion cannot justly or safely be deduced from the hostile response of a later day; nor is such a lack in the least suggested by the presence of a liking so widespread that it can be called the "mania" of an age. On the contrary, when we listen to explicit statements on the subject by men of that time, we find, as we ought logically to expect, a very different sort of language. Goldsmith, for example—or whoever wrote his fifteenth essay—enumerates the devices of poetry that "serve to animate the whole, and distinguish the glowing effusions of real inspiration from the cold efforts of mere science"; and of these resources he puts "above all, the enchanting use of the prosopopoeia, which is a kind of magic, by which the poet gives life and motion to every inanimate part of nature." [19]

The crucial question thus inescapably obtrudes itself, and we can no longer avoid it. Why did the eighteenth century derive such extreme satisfaction from a device which the nineteenth and twentieth centuries have joined to execrate as frigid and lifeless?

[17] *Ibid.*, p. 140.
[18] *Ibid.*, p. 138.
[19] Goldsmith, *Works* (Globe ed.), p. 328.

Fully to answer this query would require a better history of the last three hundred years in Western Europe than has yet been written. As may be inferred from Whitehead's masterly survey, the explanation has some of its roots in the development of mathematics. Mathematics, defined by Whitehead as "thought moving in the sphere of complete abstraction from any particular instance of what it is talking about," [20] made breath-taking progress in the seventeenth and early eighteenth centuries; and its impulses were felt at many levels less rarefied than the purely abstract. On one level, it impelled towards classification. "Classification," as Whitehead writes without any thought of literary applications, "is a halfway house between the immediate concreteness of the individual thing and the complete abstraction of mathematical notions." [21] But halfway to complete mathematical abstraction is no mean distance in Everyman's Progress. Small wonder that he stopped long for rest and refreshment at this comfortable caravanserai, whose pavilions and gardens were thickly strewn with allegorical personifications, like the Groves of Blarney (of which Professor Lowes lately reminded us) with their classical statues tastefully disposed about the pleasaunce—

> Bold Neptune, Plutarch, and Nicodemus,
> All standing naked in the open air.

Mathematics, as Whitehead makes clear, "supplied the background of imaginative thought with which the men of science approached the observation of nature." [22] So Kepler could apply the laws of periodicity to planetary motion, Newton to sound, Huyghens to light. How these in their turn affected and were reflected in the poets—Thomson, Akenside, and their school—has very recently been exhibited by Marjorie Nicolson.[23]

All these discoveries and revelations in the realm of physical laws of course encouraged and exemplified generalization on top of generalization, exciting the men of the eighteenth century with the heady vision of a supremely ordered universe, where

> All are but parts of one stupendous whole
> Whose body Nature is, and God the soul.

[20] Alfred N. Whitehead, *Science and the Modern World* (1925), p. 32.
[21] *Ibid.*, p. 43.
[22] *Ibid.*, p. 46.
[23] *Newton Demands the Muse* (1946).

"Bliss was it in that dawn to be alive!" But, unfortunately for men's peace of mind, the growing increment of generalization was not ultimately a one-way traffic towards simpler and purer abstraction. There was a counter-effect. "Nothing," Whitehead memorably declares, "is more impressive than the fact that as mathematics withdrew increasingly into the upper regions of ever greater extremes of abstract thought, it returned back to earth with a corresponding growth of importance for the analysis of concrete fact." [24] New generalizations made possible new concrete discoveries, and these in turn exploded the old generalizations. The current of generalization was clogged with the mass of particulars, which continued to collect until they stopped the flow. Thus particulars came to be all that had immediacy and meaning. Preoccupation with individual experience became the rule and the egocentricity of the last century and a half bears witness to our all but universal inability to reach any compelling generalizations. The flower in the crannied wall became the symbol of our helplessness, a symbol repeated in an infinite variety of shapes and contexts to illustrate the same negative conclusion. With all man's intellectual and emotional life re-oriented towards this fundamental predicament, the abstractions of the eighteenth century had lost their meaning. The wheel had come round again to the primitive many; the one had receded into the intense inane. The primrose of the rock was faithful in a sense, Sir Galahad was pure; but fidelity and purity no longer had any purchase on the imagination. To speak at large, the Ice-man was a more endemic figure in this climate.

Looking back once more, we can see that the Romantic ideal was that poetry should in some way rectify this state of affairs. In poetry, the imaginative faculty was to reconcile the general with the concrete, to harmonize and even identify the idea with the image. Wordsworth's statement of the use and purpose of poetry was, in fact, perfectly in accord with Dr. Johnson's: to tell truth agreeably. "Poetry," said Johnson, "is the art of uniting pleasure with truth, by calling imagination to the help of reason." [25] "Its object," wrote Wordsworth, "is truth, not individual and local, but general, and operative." But it is a question whether the means employed by the Romantics and later poets were not better

[24] *Science and the Modern World*, p. 48.
[25] *Lives*, I.170.

suited to convey truth individual and local than general; and
whether, if they had been surer of the general truth they wished
to convey, they would have rested content with representations of
it so idiosyncratic. When Wordsworth's idiot boy, Johnny, "burrs,
and laughs aloud," the poet appears to most readers to be conveying truth individual and local. When Thomson, in the *Castle of
Indolence*, writes

> The sleepless Gout here counts the crowing cock,

he equally appears to be expressing a general and operative truth.
When Goldsmith writes, in *The Traveller*,

> Hence Ostentation here with tawdry art
> Pants for the vulgar praise which fools impart,

he is reducing to felicitous statement no very confined range of
social experience. If we would judge truly the value of this device
of personification, we must judge it by its successes, not by a dis-
mal parade of its failures. No accumulation of languid and lamentable examples from the flaccid fancy of third-, fourth-, and fifth-
rate versifiers should be allowed to discount the merit of a single
triumph in the hands of a genuine poet, if we are to learn what is
possible in this kind, and this kind alone. At its best, it can, in fact,
provide a very special sort of delight. Is there any other resource
at the disposal of the poet so perfectly calculated to unite the general with the particular, the abstract with the concrete? It opens
views of the widest conceptual horizons, and at the same time
brings them into close and familiar neighbourhood. It lends
strangeness to the conventional; it brings the dead to life. As of
everything else in the domain of human expression, Shakespeare
is the greatest, most inexhaustible master of it, as every page of his
work stands ready to testify: "Liberty plucks Justice by the nose,"
"Time hath . . . a wallet at his back Wherein he puts alms for
oblivion."

There is nothing inherently unpoetic about abstraction in itself,
as will always be demonstrated afresh whenever a great poet employs it. As a touchstone of this truth, need one mention the last
twenty-five lines of *The Dunciad*, where concept follows concept
into the night of sense,

> And universal Darkness buries All.

Now, the course of eighteenth-century poetry suggests that the maximum intensity of satisfaction in generalization was reached somewhere about the middle of the century. By that date the positive influence of scientific thought was strongly operative with the least amount of its undermining negative influence. It is important to understand how at this maximum point the device of personification played a vital—and vitalizing—role. Although the age might derive excitement and pleasure from the new revelations of science, men were temperamentally no more "scientific" then than at other times: they needed to humanize their abstractions and generalizations. And this they managed, as Goldsmith emphasized in the passage quoted, through the mechanism of personifying. Generalization was of the utmost importance to them: it was one of the chief ways in which man transcended his private experience and became adult. They would not have exchanged it for any merely private vision of happiness. To generalize was, in fact, to be civilized, and in poetry, no matter how intensely one might feel, it was not decent to autobiographize. Hence the crucial importance and intense satisfaction found in personified abstraction. The device enabled one to particularize in socially, intellectually, and aesthetically acceptable forms. The *mores* of the time demanded that they keep their private concerns in the background; their intellectual preoccupations demanded that they should raise these interests to the level of generalization; and personification allowed them to recapture the most valuable part of the immediacy of personal statement. It allowed them to make the best of both worlds, the public and the private, to be at the same time general and specific, abstract and concrete. Thus they first translated personal experience to decorous generalization; and then, without surrendering the general, re-individualized it by means of personification. By this combination of opposites they gained access to a kind of aesthetic tension hardly present where the particular alone finds explicit statement.

Returning now for a closer inspection of Johnson's elegy on the death of Levet, we can perceive more clearly the functions of this abstract-concrete mode of expression. Johnson's problem, as we saw at the commencement, is two-fold: to express a personal grief, and to celebrate the merit of the departed. There is nothing out of the common order in the death of an old man; and where the life has been useful and fulfilled, lamentation is unseemly. This thought does not lessen the vacuum of personal loss, however; and that sense is itself a testimony to the merit of a good man. It is right, therefore, that grief should find utterance. The conflict can only be resolved by reflecting that, if one cannot ask the public to pity and share one's private grief, that grief may with justice be regarded as part of the general condition: *Sunt lacrimae rerum, et mentem mortalia tangunt.* There is no impropriety in voicing such an idea; and, seen thus in wide perspective, our private woe gains in humility, and wisdom, and dignity. Nearly a third of a century earlier, Johnson had given memorable expression, in *The Vanity of Human Wishes*, to the "doom of man," and had written:

> Year chases Year, Decay pursues Decay,
> Still drops some Joy from with'ring Life away.

It is with the weight of half a lifetime's somber meditation, therefore, and with a perceptible reverberation from that earlier statement, that he opens his elegy:

> Condemn'd to Hope's delusive mine,
> As on we toil from day to day,
> By sudden blasts, or slow decline,
> Our social comforts drop away.

The opening metaphor has been censured—unjustly, in my opinion. The idea is still that of the vanity of human wishes: "*delusive mine*" because the ore which we hopefully extract never yields the expected return; *condemn'd*, because while life endures we cannot escape from this futile labor. It is a pregnant image of the "doom of man" . . . The last line of the stanza is one of the two glimpses Johnson allows us into his personal deprivation. Or suddenly or slowly, he says, "our social comforts drop away"; and within this decorum we may hear, if we care to listen, the footfalls of a lonely old man in an empty room. Half a century later, a poet similarly oppressed with the tears of things would cry, "I fall upon the thorns of life! I bleed!" At least Johnson escaped the distress of surviving into a world which admired that exclamation, though his comment upon it would have been worth hearing. "Dear Sir," he had expostulated to Boswell on a lesser occasion, "I hoped you had got rid of all this hypocrisy of misery." [26]

[26] *Letters,* 715.

His own declaration, with its personal implications, provides the transition from the opening generalization to the second and principal subject: the just appreciation of a humble man's simple merit, before God and his fellowmen:

> Well tried through many a varying year,
> See Levet to the grave descend.

Johnson does not say, "My comfortable companion upon whom I have long depended, and my valued friend." He says:

> Officious, innocent, sincere,
> Of every friendless name the friend—

and we can acknowledge the sense of proportion which rendered praise for the repeated Samaritan gifts of friendly aid in quarters destitute of friendliness, instead of commemorating personal ties where friendship was abundant. Yet Johnson loved Levet; and he tells us he is not forgetting him, in the personified abstraction that opens the next stanza:

> Yet still he fills Affection's eye,
> Obscurely wise, and coarsely kind.

He continues with a series of abstract-personifications, some restrictive, some non-restrictive, which with the utmost economy— as anyone may see who tries to paraphrase—place in the broadest possible view the scope and nature of Levet's charitable life:

> Nor, letter'd Arrogance, deny
> Thy praise to Merit unrefin'd.

> When fainting Nature call'd for aid,
> And hovering Death prepar'd the blow,
> His vigorous remedy display'd
> The power of Art without the show.

> In Misery's darkest caverns known,
> His useful care was ever nigh,
> Where hopeless Anguish pour'd his groan,
> And lonely Want retir'd to die.

> No summons mock'd by chill Delay,
> No petty gain disdain'd by Pride,
> The modest wants of every day
> The toil of every day supplied.

His Virtues walk'd their narrow round,
Nor made a pause, nor left a void;
And sure the Eternal Master found
The single talent well employ'd.

The two final stanzas need not be quoted. It is regrettable that they fall steeply off in power; and noteworthy that they do so in the degree to which they descend from abstract statement to the biographical particulars of Levet's latter days, to his age, and to the manner of his unexpected death. These were matters of record which meant much to Johnson, personally troubled as he was by fears of his own impending final illness and death; but he was unable to give them wider significance. Thus the stanzas serve to point the moral of what we have been considering.

So far, indeed, as concerns the personal or autobiographical element in neo-classical poetry, there is a genuine relation to the music of that age. The poets had invented, and at their best and most characteristic moments used with great distinction, a form of statement in which the unstated private meaning and emotion permeates the general statement which constitutes the explicit content, in much the same manner as that, say, in which the quintessential poignancy of Mozart's private emotional meaning eventually makes itself felt through the impersonal statement and decorous surface emotion of his instrumental compositions. Both poets and musicians have made it their business to keep that element out of sight, as the poets and musicians of the next age were to make it their main affair to parade it; but it can be sensed after long familiarity with the idiom.

We of to-day are the heirs of conflicting ideals. We are ensnared in the egocentricity of the past century and a half. Yet we also feel an affinity with the eighteenth century and are coming to acknowledge more and more readily an admiration for its characteristic virtues. Naturalism is pretty clearly at present on the way out and Romantic egoism has at least fewer admirers. There is, on the other hand, a cry to-day among certain of our younger critics, of a need for a new "mythology." The lack of any such compelling imaginative system, or set of controlling images, is suggested as a root cause of our contemporary malaise. The contention is that great literature, in particular, is impossible without "a ruling mythology that makes intelligible and unitive the whole of that experience from which particular fables spring and from which they, in turn, take their meaning." [27] Not only epic but even great lyric poetry can be based solely upon "adequate and explicit" myth, in this view. Yet we find, reassuringly, that if myth, understood in this very broad sense, is indispensable, it is also inescapable. The misfortune of the eighteenth century is held to be that, under the impact of seventeenth-century thought, the *good* old Christian mythology broke down, and the *bad* new mythology of Newtonian science took its place. Comparative mythology is a fascinating field, but for abundant reasons we must not venture upon it now. We may, however, attend briefly to the causal sequence here asserted. Eighteenth-century poetry, as such critics view it, was at its best no more than elegant or severe or vituperative; on its characteristic level, was prosaic; was never genuinely serious, nor "grand." *Ex hypothesi*, its shortcomings are accounted for by its underlying mythology. Hence the Newtonian mythology was thin and impoverished. Now we are still existing under that dispensation, as revised and brought up to date by a succession of brilliant editors, of whom the latest is Einstein. On this hypothesis, how are we to account for the enormous fluctuations, in artistic tone and temper and achievement, which have occurred in the last two hundred and fifty years? That the impact of science upon literature has been profound has been already fully acknowledged. But it is to be remarked that in so far as neo-classicism, taken by these recent critics as the baleful reflection of the scientific myth, encouraged generalization and abstract-personification, it was at one with the medieval and Renaissance impulse toward allegorizing, which reached its zenith when the Christian "mythology" was most strongly dominant. It was not neo-classicism, in truth, which exemplified the break-up of the older unifying concepts. Rather, neo-classicism is the last historical effort to stave off the collapse of those sustaining postulates which for centuries had given dignity and importance to mankind. That much eighteenth-century poetry is thin is doubtless true. That "it means no more than it intends to mean," as Mr. Schorer has it, is potentially as great a compliment as it was intended to be disparaging. It invites the retort that poetry ever since has been intending to mean more than it means. The great virtue of neo-classical poetry at its

[27] Mark Shorer, *William Blake* (1946), p. 29.

best is that it intends to mean a great deal: it intends to mean that human life is significant according as it corresponds to ultimate ideas of order and value which are not beyond the power of man to apprehend in the largest sense. And it strives to give clear and appropriate expression to this meaning. To say this is to say that it often intends to mean more than it—not *means*, but *says*. Thus, when the poet writes

> Condemn'd to Hope's delusive mine,
> As on we toil . . .
> Our social comforts drop away,

he feels it unnecessary, in order to be understood as a man speaking to men, to cry,

> I fall upon the thorns of life! I bleed!,

or even, But O,—

> But O the difference to me!

Whether we shall ever regain a view of the world so comprehensive and assured as to enable us to state common experience in general terms, ridding us of our ego-rooted private dread of uttering a platitude, is yet to be learned. If such a time arrives, we shall unquestionably find that again we shall need, and freely employ, those ideational fictions, personifications, which spring from, and give visible form to, and implement the structure of abstract thought. Indeed, Janet Spens has suggested that we are already evolving a new mythology. "We think," she declares, "that we are dealing with scientific fact when we talk of mind, matter, silence, vacuum, but in truth we are creating entities, which are quite as much personifications as any of the figures in eighteenth-century poetry." [28] And as these abstracts impinge upon our imaginations, we shall discover as well that they carry emotional overtones along with their intellectual content; and we shall the better understand how it was that in the eighteenth century, as in earlier days, the personified abstraction wielded so potent, and so satisfying, an appeal.

[28] *Spenser's Faerie Queen*, p. 62.

On a Special Decorum in Gray's Elegy

WHEN Chesterfield expatiated to his son on the ideal of decorum, it was not an artificial or narrow code of drawing-room manners he was expounding but an ideal of conduct transcending rules and permeating the whole habit of man's moral being. It is to be sensed in every particular of a man's demeanor, whatever the circumstances. It is the noble ideal of Cicero, and Cicero is its most eloquent expositor. "The right and prudent use of reason and speech," Cicero declared, "the doing of everything considerately, the finding out of truth and the defending it, looks well in any man. . . . And so whatsoever is just is also graceful; and whatsoever is unjust or dishonest is likewise misbeseeming. . . . Wherefore the decorum I here speak of appears likewise in all other virtues. . . . There is in all virtue somewhat that is graceful, and only separable from virtue by imagination. As the gracefulness and beauty of the body cannot well be separated from health, so it is with the gracefulness here in question. It is a decorum that is in a manner so confused with virtue that it is incorporated with it. . . . But the special decorum, as dependent upon the general, is a quality so congruous to Nature that moderation and temperance appear in it with the very image of a generous soul. This we may judge to be the decorum which the poets observe" (from Cicero's *De Officiis*, in L'Estrange's translation).

In critical discussion today there is much about the Augustan proprieties of style and diction among the several genres. The rules, since they were so clearly formulated, were not likely to be ignored. But the niceties of which Cicero was here speaking are of a subtler kind, closer to instinct than to rule. In the decades of Gray's maturity, a period of shifting values, while Chesterfield was preaching the Ciceronian decorum as the preventer of social discord, the creator, adorner, and strengthener of friendship, there were many others who were openly challenging the classical precepts, if not flouting them. In literary activity there were many others, among whom we recognize Gray himself, who were quietly undermining the established ways. In poetry, Gray was interested in more various subject-matter, and in a more individual and even personal style and diction. In asserting that "the language of the age is never the language of poetry," he is applauding the contributions of lively individual invention, not antiquarian revival. He praises Shakespeare and Milton for being "great creators" of words, and declares that none have been "more licentious" in diction than Dryden and Pope. In his own poetry, Gray went much too far in this direction to satisfy Dr. Johnson, whose conservative taste memorably balked at his innovations. "Honied spring" and "many-twinkling feet" from a scholar!

In the face of Gray's willingness to drive literary expression "beyond common apprehension," it is worth while to mark the boundaries of decorum against which he goes to extraordinary lengths not to transgress, even when the nature of his personal involvement would seem to be forcing him to the trespass. I wish to focus attention briefly on a special decorum in the *Elegy* in which "moderation and temperance" display themselves "with the very image of a generous soul." I refer to the decorum of Gray's handling of the poem's inescapable egocentricity. This aspect of the *Elegy* exhibits, I think, a grace far beyond the reach of art.

Gray has designed the structure so that the climax of the poem consists in the concluding epitaph. Assuming for the nonce that the "me" of the opening stanza and the "he" of the epitaph refer to the same person, and that person the poet, the immediate, crucial difficulty is how to devise a memorial in the form of inscriptional verses for oneself that shall be perfectly serious and emotionally sincere; that shall be neither objectionably self-abasing nor apparently self-satisfied; neither too cold and impersonal to communicate emotion nor too revealing of private emotion or self-commiseration. Gray's solution of this extremely delicate problem

—supposing our reading of it to be accurate—is worth scrutiny. But we must be very sure we understand the epitaph's literal meaning. Its felicity, objectively taken alone, is so great that its three stanzas have been memorized by countless readers; yet I doubt that even by these it has always been correctly understood. The first line is not infrequently read as a complete statement in itself:

> Here rests his head upon the lap of Earth.

Tam cari capitis? The head, we would say, of a youth unknown. But, to the contrary, *rests* is of course a transitive verb here, of which *head* is the object, not the subject: It is not a mere *Hic jacet.* A more willing submission is implied: not simply *lies* but *lays to rest.* Here in Earth's lap a youth lays his head to rest. The third and fourth lines that follow indicate two favors the youth enjoyed while he lived. In spite of his humble birth, the fruits of the intellectual life were not denied him. The *And* that precedes *Melancholy* in the fourth line proves that She too was welcomed as a blessing. She was Milton's "*divinest* Melancholy, Whose saintly visage is too bright To hit the sense of human sight": She is the coryphaea of Music, Philosophy, Melpomene, Divinity, and Wisdom.

"Large was his bounty, and his soul sincere" at first sounds rather too smug. But immediately we learn what it implies: that, having a soul capable of commiseration and mutual responsive sympathy, he denied nothing to these appeals and therefore gave himself entirely to each genuine human claim, and received equal payment of reciprocal devotion. Could Life offer any higher good? "He gave to Mis'ry all he had, a tear,/He gain'd from Heav'n ('twas all he wish'd) a friend." It is of course not meant that he was content with a single friend, any more than that his charitable impulses were exhausted by a single object of pity; but that he had experienced true friendship, as he had shared in another's woes. As Blake would one day restate the underlying thought:

> Man is Love
> As God is Love: every kindness to another is a little Death
> In the Divine Image, nor can Man exist but by Brotherhood.

This youth lived, the epitaph declares, in loving-kindness and in the life of the mind. Neither his faults nor his virtues require to be

further enumerated here. Leave them undisturbed to await their
desert in the fullness of time from the justice and mercy of the
Heavenly Father.

On due consideration, we have taken the Epitaph to be autobiographical. But it is introduced by a descriptive sketch of the
anonymous "youth" from the mouth of a conjectural ancient vil-
lager lacking personal acquaintance, who knew his subject only
from detached observation of his outward habit. Such a one, "some
hoary-headed swain," may haply recall how the young man would
hurry out to meet the rising sun, would laze away the noontide,
and wander about muttering to himself and moping melancholy-
mad, careless of appearances and woebegone. Before any one
knew he was ill, he was dead. The stone will tell you more. . . .
He *was* dead? The death is only hypothetical, and the swain too
is imaginary. Set in such a frame, the sketch itself seems only a
fancy-piece.

But on this point we can bring to bear collateral evidence. There
is another sketch written by Gray, and not much earlier, which
tends to show, or to confirm, the essential psychological truth of
this one. Comparison is revealing, for one has details that the other
lacks, and the lights in the two pictures are different. In the *Elegy*,
we read as follows:

> There at the foot of yonder nodding beech
> That wreathes its old fantastic roots so high,
> His listless length at noontide would he stretch,
> And pore upon the brook that babbles by.

The companion sketch occurs in an ode at first entitled "Noontide," later altered to "Ode on the Spring." There we find:

> Where'er the oak's thick branches stretch
> A broader browner shade;
> Where'er the rude and moss-grown beech
> O'er-canopies the glade,
> Beside some water's rushy brink
> With me the Muse shall sit, and think
> (At ease reclin'd in rustic state). . . .

The hoary-headed swain of the *Elegy* could have no idea of what
the poet was thinking when "now smiling as in scorn . . . now
drooping, woeful wan"; but in the other sketch we are told what
it was:

and think
How vain the ardour of the Crowd,
How low, how little are the Proud,
How indigent the Great!

But that would be it, of course! The Elegist had already shared these thoughts with us. They have formed the substance of his poem: "the madding crowd's ignoble strife," "Nor you, ye Proud," and "Nor Grandeur hear with a disdainful smile." The preoccupations of each are alike: only the tone of self-mockery is closer to the surface in the *Ode*, autobiographically rounding in an ironic turning of the tables at the end, where the insects retort:

Poor moralist! and what art thou?
A solitary fly! ...
On hasty wings thy youth is flown;
Thy sun is set, thy spring is gone.—
We frolick, while 'tis May.

But there is no doubt that the same sitter is observed in both sketches: the poet himself.

But the first sketch was written before Gray knew that his friend Richard West, to whom he sent it, was already dead. The second, in the *Elegy*, seems to have been begun a couple of months *after* the news reached him. In imagination, he identified West's death with his own: they were of an age, and West had died at twenty-six.

In the whole *Elegy* there is only one occurrence of the first-personal pronoun as from the poet's own mouth. It closes the first stanza:

And leaves the world to darkness and to *me*.

But at line 93, after the eight poignant lines on the need of every one to be sustained at death by some fond being, to bid him good-bye and to shed tears at parting—a need which Gray, absent and unknowing, was unable to fill when West lay dying—at line 93 occurs for the first time the *second*-personal pronoun:

For *thee*, who mindful of th'unhonour'd Dead
Dost in these lines their artless tale relate.

For nearly ninety lines the poet had, as it were, disembodied himself, diffusing his identity in generalized, impersonal statement.

What he wishes to say after that point is intensely personal, of a nature so private as to be almost incommunicable without breach of decorum. Virtually, it is an autobiographical obituary, occupying a full third of the poem's length. And we now can see how he contrives it. He has so long ceased to mention himself that we have been projecting into his lines our own identity, so that it is *our* voice which has been speaking our own train of thought all this while. It seems, therefore, perfectly natural to be addressing another as "thee." This transference is surely one of the subtlest effects in our literature. For now, we join the poet in addressing himself in the second person, continuing the identification as we imagine "some kindred spirit" inquiring about *us*:

> For *thee*, . .
> If chance, by lonely contemplation led,
> Some kindred Spirit shall inquire *thy* fate.

The supposed answer is further insulated from the man, Gray, by being attributed to an imaginary stranger, unknown both to him and to us, so that we are not roused from our meditative imagining, nor divided from the poet. When, finally, the summary epitaph comes, it is still further removed from reach of Gray's apparent personal responsibility by being read on a headstone, unauthored, possessed of lapidary detachment and finality. Let this stand as a sufficient example of Ciceronian Decorum, that "duty, wherein bashfulness (pudor) and a certain gracefulness of life, temperance, modesty, the composure of all perturbations of the mind, and moderation" appear in so excellent a kind "that it is inseparable from virtue; for whatsoever is decent is likewise honest, and whatsoever is honest is becoming."

The Pre-Romantic or Post-Augustan Mode

THE TOPIC that confronts us is one that carries doubt in its very face. "Pray," asks Christian, "who are your Kindred, if a man may be so bold?" "Almost the whole Town," answers By-ends; "and in particular, my Lord Turnabout, my Lord Time-server, my Lord Fair-speech. . . . Also Mr. Smooth-man, Mr. Facing-bothways, Mr. Any-thing; and the Parson of our Parish, Mr. Two-tongues, was my Mothers own Brother by my Father's side: And to tell you the truth, I am become a Gentleman of good Quality, yet my Great Grandfather was but a Water-man, looking one way, and rowing another: and I got most of my estate by the same occupation."

Our critical terminology is notoriously loose, and I am not too envy-ridden that it has fallen to my colleagues on either side—more timely-happy than myself—to clarify the meaning of the terms *Augustan* and *Romantic*. I, at least, can take their meanings for granted, in so far as they stand conventionally for opposite attitudes and aims.[1]

But, if "Romantic" can and does bear as many meanings as Mr. Lovejoy has taught us to acknowledge, what dubious significance may lurk in the term "pre-Romantic"! "Pre-" in the sense of anticipating, of early, of premature? "Pre-" as preparative, as leading to, as germ-laden, as exhibiting the incipient stages of a disease about to become rampant and epidemic? Or "pre-" merely in a chronological sense, as occurring, whatever its nature, in the period before Romanticism burst forth, when, presumably, all those im-

[1] This was originally the middle term of a symposium discussing the poetic modes, from the Augustan to the Romantic.

plicated meanings of the term, like a swarm of bees, clustered most thickly, or were most fully realized? Obviously, we are in a measure precluded from adopting either of the two first senses until the main term has been satisfactorily defined.

Similarly, the term "post-Augustan" gives us pause. Accepting the general implications of Augustanism just now so magisterially displayed,[2] what should we presume to be the content of a "post-Augustan" era? Is it the fag-end of the day, "as after sunset fadeth in the west"? Is it a sequel imitative, or reactive, standing in some effective or consequential relation? or, again, is it merely a phenomenon casually subsequent in time? Unless the last, the answer here must emerge from further inquiry: it cannot be definitively foreseen.

A causal connection, if assumed to exist in either direction, is a severe curb on free discussion. These given terms of reference deny us any ground of our own, any independent room. Our space and our building have meaning only as they look before and after. We are assigned in advance to either a vestibule or a lean-to, without opportunity for a side-long glance. What is still more unwelcome, we know not which it is—only that the space is the same, whatever it be called. Augustan and Romantic are opposites, we have been taught: yet, apparently, "post-Augustan" is interchangeable with "pre-Romantic," for they cover the same plot of literary ground. The choice of terms depends on our discovering whether we are coming or going, and which is which. Unless perhaps an interrogation point was omitted in the title, which might then have been intended to force a verdict: "Post-Augustan *or* pre-Romantic?"— or should we now add, "Post-Augustan *and/or* pre-Romantic?"

In this dilemma, it may be wiser for a time to abandon altogether the terms in question, and seek for an independent name among the materials within our boundaries. Simply, then, who are the major voices in poetry, the bulk of whose effort falls inside the period we wish, with their help, to define? Let us answer: Edward Young, Johnson, Collins, Gray, the younger Wartons, Akenside, Smart, Shenstone, Macpherson, Goldsmith, Churchill, Chatterton, Cowper, Burns, with, at the one end, Thomson, and, at the other,

---

[2] "Augustan poetry at its best was the last stand of a classic mode of laughter against forces that were working for a sublime inflation of ideas and a luxury of sorry feeling." W. K. Wimsatt, Jr., "The Augustan Mode," *ELH*, XX (1953), 14.

Crabbe and Blake. Merely to call the roll is to advertise the difficulty of finding common denominators for talents so divergent in aim, so various in style, so unequal in attainment. If we search among them for an eponym, several names drop at once from candidacy. No one is likely to plead for Akensidian, Smartian, Shenstonian, Macphersonian, Chattertonian, Blakean as the normative modes. Akenside might perhaps be a typical figure—if we could ever remember by the end of the paragraph what he had been saying! Smart's pious rhapsodizing (at its best approaching the insane, as George Sherburn has dryly remarked) is too special to be representative, either in style or in content. Shenstone achieves his masterpiece in the neo-Spenserian mode, and does nothing else in verse but what others do better. Macpherson writes cadenced prose, loosely regularized by an insistent three-stress rhythm ("The wind and the rain are past: calm is the noon of day. The clouds are divided in heaven") so obsessive that one is almost upset by his occasional departures from it. Quite a number of younger spirits abandoned their minds to imitation in that mode, but all regained their composure before committing more than a nuisance. Next, Chatterton is neo-Tudor, and inimitable, and apart: a dark star. And then Blake, who neither belonged to a school nor established one—unless in the 20th century. And lastly, to the foregoing we may as well add Burns, who, though himself the culmination of an impressive tradition, moves into the main current of English poetic traffic only to be lost in it, indistinguishable from the crowd.

None of these, I think, will serve adequately as eponym for the Age. No more, perhaps, will some with greater claims to be called representative figures. And first, the greatest name of all, which has lent itself to the Age more often than any other. We shall not have to deliberate long before deciding that the epithet *Johnsonian* will hardly do to characterize the poetic mode of his era. For one reason, of course, Johnson's work in poetry was almost all done before 1750, and does not typify at all the bulk of poetic achievement in the second half of the century. For another, although Johnson was a true poet, his major poems are too conventional to set a fashion, and too few to dominate the conventions within which he writes. That is to say, other poets writing in the classical tradition are not deflected by Johnson away from Pope or Dryden. He found the established norm quite congenial, and his innovations within it (if we can call them such) are below the conscious level. But his finest work in couplets displays a density of emotional statement closer, one may almost feel, to the Jacobean than to the Augustan poetic habit. There is a weight of content in his characteristic passages that Dryden would have worked out by expansion, and Pope by simplification. Observe, writes Johnson,

> How nations sink, by darling schemes oppress'd,
> When vengeance listens to the fool's request.
> Fate wings with ev'ry wish th'afflictive dart,
> Each gift of nature, and each grace of art:
> With *fatal* heat impetuous courage glows,
> With *fatal* sweetness elocution flows:—
> Impeachment stops the speaker's pow'rful breath,
> And restless fire precipitates on death.

This is poetry for reading, not for hearing. If we reversed the first couplet, thus—

> When vengeance listens to the fool's request,
> [See] nations sink, by darling schemes oppress'd—

the logic of cause and effect would become clearer, though at the sacrifice of rhetorical point. Yet we should still have to excogitate that the vengeance here meant is a nemesis lying ironically in wait to trip each of us by means of his most cherished desire, granting it only to destroy us; to appreciate how whole nations, involved in their unwise leaders' darling schemes, have collapsed in ruin, frightful demonstrations of the vanity of human wishes. *Vengeance, listens, fool's,* and *request* must all be drawn out in their particular senses before the meaning of that line is clear. And an equal compactness, withholding the facilitating connective elements, is evident in the couplet that immediately succeeds:

> Fate wings with ev'ry wish th'afflictive dart,
> Each gift of nature, and each grace of art.

Here, the syntax is at first baffling: it is not apparent that the object of the verb intervenes between three parallel prepositional phrases, so that what the poet is saying it this: Our every desire, our every personal endowment, whether a natural gift or an acquired and cultivated skill, is employed by fate to feather the arrows of affliction by which we ourselves are brought down.

Such lines as these exhibit pressures that are surely Johnson's own. Whether it could be claimed that they reflect also the characteristic perplexities of the age, I doubt. I doubt equally whether the larger structures of Johnson's thought—such passages as the famous address to the young scholar, where the six parallel couplets, like sequent combers, drive grandly forward to break at last on that inexorable negative ("should thy soul indulge . . . Should Reason guide . . . Should no false Kindness . . . Should tempting Novelty . . . Should Beauty . . . Should no Disease . . . :

> *Yet hope not* life from grief or danger free,
> *Nor* think the doom of man revers'd for thee")—

I doubt, I say, whether such massively insistent and sustained rhetorical statement can be found elsewhere in the poetry of that day or later. This, then, is the Johnsonian mode, or part of it—and not the mode of the Age. On the other hand, there are doubtless sufficient echoes of the Augustan equilibrium. Compare the restrictive balance of Johnson's

> See nations slowly wise and meanly just
> To buried merit raise the tardy bust

with Pope's

> A Being darkly wise, and rudely great.

Or, in another key, Johnson's

> What are acres? What are houses?
> Only dirt, or wet or dry.

Collins, to continue, will not provide us with a paradigm. "A solitary song-bird," asserted Swinburne, "among many pipers and pianists." Surely not that; but probably few of his generation would have chosen him their spokesman. Johnson, as we know, who thought of him kindly and took some trouble over him, disapproved both of his choice of subject and his manner in poetry. Loving the supernatural, Collins, he thought, went "in quest of mistaken beauties" of allegorical description and neglected "sentiment," which latter we may take to refer to the products of rational observation. He also found Collins' style objectionable: his diction labored and injudicious and unmusical, his phrasing wilfully perverse.

There is a deeper meaning than the one intended, in Johnson's
phrase for Collins: "a literary adventurer." All his short life as a
poet—it ended before he was thirty—Collins was looking for a
sustaining subject, and hero-worshipping. Always hoping to graduate, he never truly left school. He continued to think of himself
as an "admiring youth" under tutelage, and to look to others for
the right sentiments and the proper attitudes. Anyone who glances
at the *Odes* in their first edition must be struck by the collegiate
air of the book—its combination of brashness and timidity, so
smacking of insecurity mixed with vaulting ambition. From the
title-page with its Pindaric motto to the last couplet of the concluding *Passions* ode, the reliance on Authority is all-pervasive.
For example, in the opening ode (to Pity) *"Pella's* Bard" is glossed
thus: *"Euripides,* of whom *Aristotle* pronounces, on a Comparison
of him with *Sophocles,* That he was the greater Master of the
tender Passions, ἦν τραγικώτερος." Collins calls upon "Her, whose
Lovelorn Woe" etc., explaining in a note: "The ἄηδων, or Night-
ingale, for which *Sophocles* seems to have entertain'd a peculiar
Fondness." And, concluding the Ode for Music, entitled *The
Passions,* he addresses Music in a paragraph which, considering
Handel's achievement and reputation by that date, betrays an
abject flight from experience:

> 'Tis said, and I believe the Tale,
> Thy humblest *Reed* could more prevail,
> Had more of strength, diviner Rage,
> Than all which charms this laggard Age . . .
> O bid our vain Endeavours cease,
> Revive the just Designs of *Greece,*
> Return in all thy simple State!

Now this is either the cant of the Schools, sheer learned humbug,
or stony insensibility. Since we cannot but assume the poet's familiarity with Handel, whom his friends the Wartons greatly
admired, it is charitable to attribute this passage to youthful bigotry.
It is an example of Collins' failure to escape from the library. He
saw, not Nature only, but Art and Life as well, through the
spectacles of books. Genius he certainly was, but his inspiration
was usually vicarious. His Pegasus sprang from a desk, seldom
from a ground of values independently possessed. Therefore,
description was safer than sentiment. "His greatest fault"—again

Johnson has the right word—"was irresolution." Although he sub-
scribed to the Wartons' youthful manifesto that poetry should be
rescued from "the fashion of moralizing" and restored to "its right
channel" of imaginative invention, the poets whom he most admired
—Sophocles, Pindar, Spenser, Shakespeare, Milton—were not afraid
of substantial sentiment; and the three young Wykehamists were
ready to settle for less extreme objectives than they at first declared.
Even Collins, the most daring of the triumvirate, could write
couplets like the following:

> Each rising Art by slow Gradation moves,
> Toil builds on Toil, and Age on Age improves,

and like

> O blest in all that Genius gives to charm,
> Whose Morals mend us, and whose Passions warm!

The poet in Joseph Warton died also in his twenties, to be
succeeded by the moderate critic, as would probably have been
Collins' case, to judge by the projects reported. Although, at
twenty, in their own conceit mad for trackless wastes and assorted
grisliness, or for tiger-hunts in Georgia with virtuous Indian Swains,
they managed to resist these impulses; and the Warton brothers
pretty well tired out their Miltonic muses by one or two trips to
the charnel-house in a Chippendale chair. Thomas's muse was
sturdier than his brother's; but it can hardly be claimed, interesting
as they are, that either of them was able to develop a style of his
own. They were imitators, not creators; and whatever is best in
their verses mirrors Milton.

The poetry of Gray, on the contrary, reflects a multitude, but
mirrors none. Gray, George Sherburn has said, "typifies the transitional poet who loved tradition yet courted novelty." We should
wish to qualify this pronouncement, which says a great deal in little
space. Gray loved tradition*s*: he was a connoisseur of them. No
one had a more discerning eye, a more discriminating ear, a keener
relish for what was essential in a tradition. It might be the sublime
pomp of the Pindaric ode—what quickened and brought it to
fruition, what lingered after it down the centuries; it might be the
majesty of Milton's achievement, gathering into itself what was
great in Greek, Roman, Italian, and English poetry; it might be

the tragic terror of northern traditions, Scandinavian or British. In whatever direction, he probed for the quintessential, delighting to *report*—to bring home—the special virtues of each kind. Therefore, the object of his search was novelty only indirectly: not novelty for its own sake, but rather, excellence far-sought and far-brought: the distillation of a wide and deep learning in the retort of a refined, sensitive intelligence. The lines of his odes glow and glitter with this distillation. He did not so much court novelty as encounter it by chance in the combining of earlier proprieties. If Gray typifies the transitional poet, he exalts the class to a status above that of the established schools. He did not realize his ideal, but where are his competitors in kind?

Over Goldsmith's pleasant, but for the most part unimportant verse, we need not linger. Easier by far than Johnson's, at its most serious it aims at a kindred goal, and it is appropriate that Johnson should have rounded off the conclusion of "The Traveller" with his own couplets. Their noticeably more involuted complexity lends the needed climactic weight without disturbing the tone. In "The Deserted Village," less ambitious but more felicitous, Goldsmith hits a mean of formal familiarity, of comfortable precision, of politeness in the truest sense, that in verse perfectly answers Johnson's commendation of Addison's prose as a model of the middle style. That it can be equalled elsewhere in the century is doubtful; but that it was elsewhere even attempted may also be doubted. Pope is much too self-conscious for this; Crabbe is not by any means self-conscious enough. Cowper, who can be at once familiar and polite in short metres or in prose letters, is prone in his couplets to be too shrill and insistent; while the blank verse of "The Task" puts in rather for Thomsonian laurels. Yet Cowper's variety and range, of matter and manner, light, or satiric, or Miltonic, his lively and articulate interest in, and sensitive reflection of, so many of the topics of his time, religious, political, social, or literary, might make him a strong contender for the most typical figure, without his ever establishing a mode.

If we have now run through our list without finding any one to set up as the inclusive exemplar of his age in poetry, it becomes apparent that we shall have to reinstate them all as partial representatives, each characteristic in greater or less degree, and in his own fashion. But perhaps, fascinated by the diversity of the procession, we may be charged with being guilty of a half-hearted effort to find the underlying community.

That elements of such a community exist I scarcely doubt. Josephine Miles, in an extraordinarily original and interesting analysis of the common language of poets in the 1740's—among whom more than half of our list appear—has even found it possible to construct an ideal poetic sentence for the lot. They would unite in saying,

> Rise, fair day, before the eyes and soul of man,

and therein, according to Miss Miles, "would combine generally and gently the abstract and the visual in [their] moral imperative. This was [their] major vocabulary, the fair day, in its natural and airy setting; the eye, soul, hand, heart of man in youth and power; above, heaven and God. It was a world viewed, felt, and considered, and its great poetizing power was to bring more and more of what it considered and felt into view." [3]

The elements of Miss Miles's sentence are based in every part on demonstrable evidence. These were the words—the nouns, the adjective, and the verb—most commonly used by the poets of the mid-century, according to statistical count. The verb in its imperative or invocatory form we have all noted: the constant tendency to apostrophize and implore, until we are prompted to borrow Goldsmith's unconscious parody of the habit:

> O!—But let Exclamation cease!

or fretfully to coin an impromptu etymology for the name, *Ode*. We could all, with a little thought, make a brief table of tricks and topics favorite among poets of the period. It would include heads like: Country Pleasures, Times of the Day, Seasons of the Year; Abstractions—Fancy, Solitude, Sleep, Death—inviting description, evoking feeling, tempting the moral comment. As John Dyer put it:

> Thus is nature's vesture wrought,
> To instruct our wand'ring thought;
> Thus she dresses green and gay,
> To disperse our cares away.

[3] Josephine Miles, *The Primary Language of Poetry in the 1740's and the 1840's,* University of California Publications in English, XIX, 2 (1950), 222.

To some of us, one of the most interesting questions is the relative power of the abstract and general to excite emotional vibrations, and the way in which the process works. This is a problem both too large and too limiting for present discussion. Personification has attracted some attention of late;[4] but it is clear that abstraction maintains its purchase on the feelings far beyond the limits of allegorical suggestion. Ian Jack has recently shown how much "grandeur of generality" Johnson gains by his special, "generic," use of the definite article[5] (and the indefinite may be added):

> Dart the quick taunt, and edge the piercing gibe

or

> Against your fame with fondness hate combines,
> The rival batters, and the lover mines.

And compare

> New sorrow rises as the day returns,
> A sister sickens, or a daughter mourns.

Close examination of what I shall denominate "the abstractive correlative" might carry us a long way toward understanding the basic appeals of eighteenth-century poetry.

An amusing if minor manifestation of this affective side of generalizing technique is the special little thrill of delight evoked by the deft use of a philosophic or scientific term in a context where one would not have expected it. A very familiar instance is Cowper's

> O for a lodge in some vast wilderness,
> Some boundless *contiguity* of shade!

Goldsmith loves the same word and uses it in both his major poems, once thus:

> To scape the pressure of contiguous pride.

Another example from Goldsmith's "The Traveller" is this:

> And love's and friendship's finely pointed dart
> Fall blunted from each *indurated* heart.

---

[4] See particularly, Earl R. Wasserman, "The Inherent Values of Eighteenth-Century Personification," *PMLA*, LXV (1950), 435–463.
[5] Ian Jack, *Augustan Satire* (1952), pp. 142 f.

Again, Goldsmith's

> With daring aims *irregularly* great.

Or Thomson's notorious

> And *ventilated* states renew their bloom.

Or Matthew Green's engaging

> *Tarantulated* by a tune

and his

> The *consanguinity* of sound.

Somewhat antiseptic is Cowper's

> The stable yields a stercoraceous heap. . . .

But we must beware of emulating Little Jack Horner.

The delightful shock of abstract vs. concrete issues with an almost seventeenth-century air from Smart's "quick peculiar quince"; and, in general—and not forgetting Pope's "Die of a rose in aromatic pain"—this habit may have significant affiliations with the previous century. Certainly, no one ever understood its musical possibilities better than Sir Thomas Browne. Perhaps, then, on one side, this trait is affined to the impulse to recover the Past, the same force that caused poets to break out in a rash of Allegro-Penserosiads and Spenseriantics.

Goldsmith's "daring aims irregularly great" may stand to remind us of a far-reaching inclination, backed by explicit theory, to set much store by the beauty of irregularity. The aesthetic implications of this impulse in landscape, in architecture, in literature, for the shift from classicism toward the romantic position, have been sufficiently outlined by Lovejoy, who quotes, among much other evidence, Gilpin's remark: "Regularity and exactness excite no pleasure in the imagination unless they are made use of to contrast with something of an opposite kind." [6]

Approval of irregularity might favor the arrival of sublimity, and lead eventually to an Ode on Intimations of Immortality; but it did not by any means relieve this generation of the duty of

[6] A. O. Lovejoy, *Essays in the History of Ideas* (1948), p. 158 ("The First Gothic Revival and the Return to Nature," an essay first published in *MLN* [1932], pp. 414–446).

propriety of language in the kind of writing attempted. This was still a matter of the utmost importance. It accounts among other things for the difference in style between Gray's Odes and his *Elegy.* "The style of elegy," wrote Shenstone, "should imitate the voice and language of grief; or if a metaphor of dress be more agreeable, it should be simple and diffuse, and flowing as a mourner's veil." [7]

Miss Miles has indicated that the flow of the poetic current was more and more toward the visible and sensory, away from the abstract and moral, as the century progressed. If this be so, what we have noticed as arresting abstraction is perhaps an atavistic streak in the temper of the time. But it cannot be merely vestigial in its import if, as we are suggesting, its antiquarian aura links it at some points to that Revival of the Past in terms of which some sturdy critics have mainly read the Romantic Movement.

To be reminded of Browne is to remind ourselves that a stylistic device like the one singled out here may be just as much at home in prose as in poetry. And, in general, I suppose it may fairly be contended that what is typical in the age under survey is as clearly visible in its prose as in the work of its poets—possibly more clearly. This is to suggest that what we discover here is a community of matter—or a common view of things—rather than a primary community of manner. What the poets were looking for was not so much a fresh poetical rhetoric that could be prescriptively established—a dominating, authoritative idiom to supplant the Augustan —as a set of fresh topics to stimulate poetic invention and feeling. Their sensibilities were in the main similarly aligned to the new appeals. But they were generally agreed that they did not want to repudiate the heritage of the recent past: only, they did not want to be confined by it. They wished to extend their range of feeling and utterance; and, in their effort to do so, manner tended to become a little less controlling than heretofore. They were inclined to allow more scope for the development of a heterogeneous poetic utterance. As to style, they came to prefer eclectic habits, to scatter their allegiances. We shall hardly succeed, therefore, in isolating any widely typical post-Augustan or pre-Romantic Mode

[7] William Shenstone, *Works* (1768 ed.), I, 20 ("A Prefatory Essay on Elegy").

in Poetry. For it is this very *uncommittedness* which defines the period at which we have been glancing.

In one of its most important roles, the term *Mode* has musical significance. As we know, the medieval, ecclesiastical modes began, around the turn of the sixteenth to seventeenth century, to prove inadequate to bear the new pressures for musical expression, secular and harmonic. The old diatonic patterns came to seem more and more unwieldy and inflexible, and were gradually loosened by the introduction of more frequent chromaticism, the modern major-minor harmonic coloring eventually supplanting the earlier modality. But the Elizabethan composers were fascinated by the contrast, and delighted in heightening the colors in a crowded interplay of opposed systems. They were close enough to the old to know it in their bones; and they were not as yet so much surrendering its values as renewing their sense of them by experimentally challenging and then reasserting them. The challenge was not hostile, but affectionate. Consequently, one finds in their music a characteristically nostalgic and disturbing beauty—at the hour of farewell, as it were, a premonition of homesickness. Much of the tonal iridescence of these composers comes from their impaired but not severed allegiance to the Modes.

Something of the same kind of interest attaches to the poetry of the mid-eighteenth century. Probably we should acknowledge as a rule that there is always more of the previous age in each succeeding period than in our anxiety to sharpen distinctions we are usually ready to admit. More of the Augustan in the next era, more of the post-Augustan (to call it so) in the Romantic. The period under present scrutiny is, at any rate, too close to the triumphs of Dryden and Pope to be able to forget them, and it is generally well-mannered and decorous—over-decorous, some would say. But it is also discontented, restless, uncommitted, unwilling to stay, yet undetermined to go. These opposing tensions give it a waywardness, an unpredictability, that are continually engaging one's surprised attention. Its variety is as hard to fix as the changes of the natural scene which so beguiled it; and if driven into a corner, we should have to declare that its historic function is to unmodify. Its mode, so to say, is prismatic. It is the time, in short, wherein are to be found coexisting Thomson's spaciousness, Johnson's massiveness, Collins' incorporeality, the Wartons' bi-partisanship, Gray's eclecticism, Young's commiseration, Akenside's reasonableness, Smart's enthusiasm, Shenstone's placidity, Macpherson's rant, Churchill's unmannerliness, Goldsmith's amenity, Chatterton's atavism—rootless in Time as Collins in Space—Cowper's humanity, Burns's pride and passion, Crabbe's sobriety, Blake's extravagance. Each of these qualities finds its own expression in a verbal idiom conditioned in part by outer, but more and more by inner, leading. As Polonius would have it, "For the Law of Writ, and the Liberty, these are the only men."

A Sense of the Past:
The Percy Correspondence

"WHATEVER withdraws us from the power of our senses," Johnson memorably declares; "whatever makes the past, the distant, or the future predominate over the present, advances us in the dignity of thinking beings." The ages of civilized men, activated by the spark of divine discontent, might be roughly characterized, I suppose, by their typical preference of a road of escape from the life of the senses. Times of restless energy and physical self-confidence, like the sixteenth and nineteenth centuries, will pursue the distant and unexplored; times suddenly and forcibly aware of undeveloped possibilities in scientific advance or natural resources will look to the future, like the late seventeenth or early twentieth centuries; times complacently assured and expectant of progress along predictable lines, like the eighteenth century, will give special thought to the past. The body of writing that typifies its period will express these characteristic emphases.

But, of course, every age makes its own response to each of these concepts, though not with equal investments of imagination and emotion; and herein, too, their differences are revealed. Obviously, the most complex and meaningful of the three, richest in substance and most varied with light and shadow, is the sense of the past. An age's idea of the past and consequent attitude, being conditioned by its own immediate history, its temperamental bias and selective lenses, by the degree of authority or novelty, extent and availability, of its knowledge, are by no means always easy to isolate and analyze. We can say with some confidence, with the simplifying aid of distance, that the medieval attitude was by and large undifferentiating, uncritical, trusting, filial; that that of the seventeenth century was challenging and skeptical; that the past tended to make the Elizabethans melancholy, to put them into an *ubi sunt* train of thought. With increased secularization had come less docility in accepting the wastes and ravages of Time. We can say that the attitude of the Augustan Age toward that part of the past which it attended was familiar and friendly, standardizing, seeking its own chosen norms in antiquity, and finding confirmation of its own values. And that the early nineteenth century, on the contrary, sought another past, full of strangeness, difference, and of mysterious, because distant, beauty. And we can say that, thanks to multiple approaches to parts hitherto obscure, and thanks to the powers of mass reproduction by press, phonograph, and camera, and to all the other aids in comparative analysis, the attitude of the twentieth century toward the past has become more complicated, more eclectic, more synthetic, more divisive and contradictory, more specialized, more theory-ridden—in short, more Humpty-Dumpty—than ever before in the world's history.

Fortunately, our present field of survey is only a narrow sliver in the suggested panorama, being confined to the English literary world mainly of the third quarter of the eighteenth century—to that " 'batable Land" known variously as "post-Augustan," "pre-Romantic," or whatever the particular ax may be sharpening toward: the "Age of Johnson," the Antiquarian Decades, the Heyday of Amateur Scholarship and of the pre-episcopal Percy.

The events of the century that led into the Augustan Age had churned up established patterns and raised important issues on several fronts, political, economic, religious; and inevitably heightened an Englishman's awareness of nationality and the kind of values which as an Englishman he represented, instinctively and deliberately—and foreigners were concurring in his praise. Just as in our own century external events have deepened our sense of nationality, by challenging a way of life that had been largely taken for granted and sending us in quest of our radical inheritance, so the jostling of the seventeenth century had produced in the sequel a society more concerned to identify a community of ideas, standards, purposes. The Augustans brought about a purposeful crystallizing of ideals. Though it was not to last, it achieved a precarious stability in a changing world and, in the hands of men of genius, a sharpness of definition and a brilliance that left an afterglow to succeeding generations. Although its seeds had been growing in English soil for generations, it was not indigenous but naturalized, and eventually, hybridized. It is probable that the very perfection and clarity of its formulation quickened its transience. Further effort in that direction would be imitative and secondary. Adventure and discovery lay elsewhere. Perhaps in native traditions, which by comparison were unexplored and relatively obscure.

Physical records, ruined abbeys and castles, historic monuments, the churches themselves in which worship was continued, were a constant reminder, half venerated, half despised, of the native roots, and a provocation to curious investigation. "To abstract the mind from all local emotion," pronounces Johnson in odd but useful phrase, "would be impossible if it were endeavoured, and would be foolish if it were possible." Topographical antiquities obtrude themselves upon everyone's notice and naturally solicit attention and study before literary records are exhumed from out-of-the-way corners of college and family libraries and dusted off for closer inspection. By a combination of factors hardly subject to close definition, the time had now ripened to a point where interest in national antiquities was becoming so powerful and multifarious as to collect the impulsive force of a popular movement.

Antiquarianism is too narrow a term to cover so sweeping and many-faceted a tide of historical curiosity. County histories like Nichols' and Plot's, the *Encyclopaedia Britannica*, the British Museum, the *Biographica Britannica*, topographical poems by the score, Hume's and Robertson's and Hailes's histories, editions of Shakespeare, *Observations* on Spenser, Strawberry Hill, Macpherson's Ossian, Chatterton's Rowley, *Letters on Chivalry and Romance*, *Poems by Mr. Gray, Caractacus:* all in their several ways give voice to the conviction expressed by Thomas Warton on a blank leaf of Dugdale's *Monasticon:*

> Not harsh nor barren are the winding ways
> Of hoar antiquity, but strewn with flowers.

Moreover, it is quite plain that in the middle decades of the century the literary frontier lay backward in time. This is the meaning of the manifestos of Collins and the Wartons and of their experiments and Gray's. Poetry of the Imagination was now to supplant poetry of Reason; and the imagination of that generation fastened itself like a lamprey on the past. Poetry is far more bound by tradition than is literary prose. Prose was free to occupy itself in creative ways in the Novel, there to find, in the immediate and contemporary, abundant problems of technique and discovery. Poetry was far more inhibited and conscious of its high lineage, and therefore imitative and obedient to received doctrine. Where was the excitement in writing poetry unless one could surpass Pope in his own kind? But to turn backward was a liberating experience. Perusing earlier figures and forms, one discovered a poetic literature by no means bound by the familiar rules but yet disclosing lawless excellences that gained the more upon one as one grew more familiar with their modes. Here was adventure: here the fancy leapt across the barriers of centuries to meet the mind of an earlier "maker" in the fresh excitement of uncurbed inspiration. Or so at least it seemed; and one brought back from such expeditions all sorts of rare trophies and novel ideas for experiments of one's own. It was like being given a lyre with other strings—not merely to hear, but to blow, the horns of elfland, though faintly. And one returned, like Thomas Rhymer, to see familiar things with new eyes: "In yonder grave a Druid lies"—in fact, James Thomson, author of the *Seasons*. Or again:

> By fairy hands their knell is rung,
> By forms unseen their dirge is sung;
> There Honour comes, a *pilgrim grey*,
> To bless the turf that wraps their clay;
> And Freedom shall awhile repair
> To dwell, a *weeping hermit*, there.

This is the climate we enter in the best of the Percy Correspondence.[1] This is the intellectual and sentimental temper of the generation with which he came to maturity and planned his literary career. It is not accidental that in the decade of the fifties, when

---

[1] *The Percy Letters*, six volumes, David Nichol Smith and Cleanth Brooks, General Editors (Louisiana State University Press and Yale University Press, 1944–1961).

Rousseau startled Europe by his denunciation of civilized arts and sciences, Percy conceived the scheme of publishing in translation characteristic specimens of the primitive poetry of various nations, from Chinese to Icelandic, including Hebrew (the Song of Solomon in a fresh translation with notes), Spanish (ballads on Moorish subjects), British (bardic performances, when he could find someone who knew enough of old Welsh to provide dependable translations), and adding "Arabic Poetry, Greenland Poetry, Lapland Poetry, North-American, Peruvian, &c. &c. &c." He had varied the classical diet of Oxford by acquiring a modestly competent knowledge of Spanish; his Chinese he got mainly from du Halde's French. His Chinese examples were the earliest to see publication (in 1761 and 1762); but the Chinese fad of the fifties was already widespread, with ramifications in gardening, architecture, furniture, ceramics, literature, and ballet.

The sixties were Percy's golden decade. They saw the appearance of the bulk of his literary accomplishment, including the first two editions of the *Reliques of Ancient English Poetry*, the Runic pieces, the translation (published 1770) out of Mallet's *Histoire du Dannemarc* (*Northern Antiquities*), *Hau Kiou Choaan*, Solomon's Song, the Northumberland Household Book, as well as the inauguration of works which by mere hard luck plus a scholarly pride in thoroughness never reached publication: Buckingham's Works; an annotated edition of the Queen Anne periodical essays; a painstaking edition of the Earl of Surrey's poetry. It was in this same decade that most of Percy's correspondences originated: they are the direct outgrowth of his literary activities, and, on his side, tend to wither when his episcopal duties displace the preoccupations of the antiquary. Wilmarth Lewis has shown how Horace Walpole chose his main correspondents each for a special interest, somewhat as a symphonic composer might call upon various instruments for their resources and timbre, in order to realize to the full the work he was creating. In similar fashion, Percy seems to have picked his men in the first place for what they could contribute to his scheme of life. In his country living at Easton Mauduit in Northamptonshire, he had leisure to follow his interests but found the great libraries inconveniently distant for more than occasional use. It was almost as important to him that his correspondents should be strategically placed as that they should share his special interests. He needed a man in Cambridge, and found him early in Richard Farmer, who was to become the genial Master of Emmanuel College. He needed a man in Oxford, and soon managed to enlist the useful if easy-going Tom Warton. He needed a man in Edinburgh, and got into touch with the bibliophile George Paton (who showered him with rarities) and with Sir David Dalrymple, Lord Hailes. He needed various help in London, and eventually Edmond Malone became an indispensable support, George Steevens having proved unmanageable. For a time there was also Astle of the British Museum, and Capell; and there were others. Percy writes to Warton, in January, 1763: "By one means or other I have access to all the curious Libraries about town, except one, and that is the Library of *Sion College* . . . Could you introduce me to the knowledge of any Gentleman, who has access to that Library, whom I could now and then trouble so far, as to procure it to be consulted for me . . . if it was not a gentleman of the antiquarian turn, who had besides a large portion of candour, he would be disgusted at the frivolous commissions I should sometimes charge him with." In Wales, the problem was not libraries but informed authority, and there Evan Evans came to supply his needs. Thus it happens that the several correspondences in this series of Percy Letters have each a separate local anchorage in some center of learning and together outline the topography of contemporary intellectual life.

In most ways, Farmer was a perfect man for Percy's purposes. Seven years Percy's junior, and therefore not needing to be treated with deference or formality, already learned in his twenties when the friendship began, but without any strong urge to publish for fame; loving learning for its own sake and glad to put his own at the disposal of others in minute enquiry, with academic leisure (of the old scholarly sort where vocation and avocation were indistinguishable) to slake his curiosity at length: Farmer was the recipient of a steady stream of detailed scholarly queries and requests to borrow or buy bibliographical plums. The informality of the connection is signified in a remark of Percy's, in 1763: "I ask your pardon for the constant trouble I give you; many times (I am sensible,) when you have not leisure; but why don't you in those cases throw off some part of the load upon that idle fellow

Blakeway? He has no pupil-drudgery to call him off from the more
noble pursuit of ascertaining the Dates, and settling the readings of
half-penny ballads." Incidentally, the freedom with which scarce
books were borrowed—and kept indefinitely—from collections public or private is breath-taking. For example: among a parcel of
titles requested of Farmer, Percy throws in without comment or
apology, "All your old quarto copies of Shakespeare." The priceless Bannatyne MS (then more priceless because yet unedited),
lent from the Advocates' Library which had only just acquired it,
was in Percy's hands, at his home, for over two years. He gave it
back reluctantly. Through Warton, he borrowed a copy of Surrey's *Æneis* from Warren, with whom he was not personally
acquainted, and returned it seven years later. To all Percy's queries
Farmer seems to have been diligent in reply, and one receives the
impression that in point of tangible services rendered, Percy was
left far behind. The file of letters between the two men is sadly
one-sided and incomplete. To fifty letters from Percy there are
only five from Farmer—but luckily containing a very vivid note
of the young man's first impression of Johnson, who came to visit
him in Cambridge in 1765; and the series, for an unexplained
reason, breaks off two decades and more before Farmer's death.
The latter's style is breezy and offhand, if not especially witty.
He and Steevens would obviously have been more congenial companions. With Farmer, Percy's style is more informal than usual,
but he always sticks to his last and never cuts a caper. It is interesting that he writes, in 1767: "My Friend Mr. Steevens is [so]
perfectly enamored with your Essay [on Shakespeare's learning],
that You must give me leave to bring you two acquainted: He is
absolutely a Prince of Antiquaries and of Scholars: Very Active
and intelligent: Most communicative of what he knows and un-
wearied in promoting the Researches of others: with a large Fortune; and most liberal mind; and most generous Heart; you will
be delighted with him, when once you know him personally: and
he perfectly languishes for your Acquaintance." The few letters
from Steevens to Percy now known to us show that Steevens under-
estimated Percy's touchy self-esteem—or didn't care—and indulged
too freely his spirit of teasing mischief in searching out and rubbing

the sensitive places. It is symptomatic that in the end it was Steevens who became Farmer's literary executor, and that Percy fell back on the steady Malone as the man he could trust.

The correspondence with Malone, indeed, is the most interesting and varied of the series. This is entirely owing to Malone. Soon after the letters of Malone began, Percy went to Ireland as Bishop of Dromore, and Malone became in due course the most faithful and solid link with Percy's old life and the Literary Club. Percy's letters come more and more to be beggars for news and mere annotation on the items already reported. The handicaps of distance from that world, of the paucity of epistolary matter in his present way of life, and of failing eyesight, make the later letters of Percy rather unrewarding. But, however thin the return, Malone, at the source of supply, keeps up a stream of informative, entertaining, gossipy letters—a boon to his aging but still curious friend, and enlightening to readers of today. We learn of Malone's persistent and effective efforts to keep the Club alive in its period of doldrums; of his collecting subscriptions for Johnson's and Goldsmith's monuments; and of his performance of frequent favors and commissions on Percy's behalf. These letters show the great editor in a most attractive light. However uninspired, Malone was genuinely full of the milk of human kindness; and the fidelity he shows as an editor, his staying power, is equally displayed in his bearing toward his friends; in the steadying influence he exerted over Boswell, the patient support and ungrudging expenditure of time and counsel necessary to bring Boswell's cargo into harbor at last, as Geoffrey Scott revealed; and here, again, in his understanding awareness and generous easing of Percy's human hunger in the contracting circle of his worldly existence.

The correspondence with Warton and with Lord Hailes has less to interest the ordinary reader, valuable and revealing though it is in particular ways. The relations of Percy and these men were quite different from that with Farmer, for Percy was relatively obscure when the acquaintance with them began, and they were already prominent figures. Warton, though about the same age, was the Oxford Professor of Poetry, and well known for his original poems and his Observations on Spenser. Percy is therefore concerned at the start to prove it worth Warton's while to correspond with him. His letters are fuller of critical observations than usual, and Warton, at least for the first year or so, is more often on the receiving end than otherwise, and properly grateful for correction and information; reasonably prompt, also, though usually brief, in acknowledgment. Many letters on both sides are lost, but there is a more even numerical division than usual in what survive. Neither writer is personal, nor cultivates the other's acquaintance on personal grounds. They shared each other's interest in chivalric romances, Spanish especially, and in the light that these and early popular verse could throw on poets of stature like Chaucer and Spenser. "I rejoice," writes Warton in 1762, "at your Collection of the Romances referred to in Don Quixote. It will be a most valuable, and a most proper, Illustration . . . I thank you for thinking me qualified to complete Chaucer's Squiers Tale. The Subject is so much in my own Way, that I do assure you I should like to try my hand at it. You are certainly right in thinking that the Public ought to have their Attention called to Poetry in new forms; to Poetry endued with new Manners and new Images."

With Sir David Dalrymple, Lord Hailes, Percy's relations were again deferential, and largely confined to the subject of Scottish antiquities, on which Hailes was then probably the leading authority. He was of the utmost value to Percy in the preparation of the *Reliques*. Besides assisting in questions of local and historical fact and points of language, he transmitted for the collection a full score of pieces admitted by Percy, including some of the very brightest gems of British balladry, "Edward," "Sir Patrick Spens," and "Lord Thomas and Fair Annet." This correspondence, again, is regrettably one-sided. Only five of Lord Hailes' letters have been saved. There are forty-nine of Percy's.

George Paton, another of Percy's Scottish correspondents, was a man the like of whom is seldom seen in these days of professionalized scholarship. Loving learning for its own and auld Scotia's sake, he pursued it purely as a hobby, with selfless unconcern for his own fame. It was an escape from his drab and in every sense unrewarding Customhouse job, and he enjoyed nothing so much as the incessant botheration of minute inquiries with which he was besieged by his wide circle of distinguished and obliged correspondents. The only sort of reputation he really cared about was the kind that travels from mouth to mouth; and this kind he acquired in full and growing measure by knowing more than any-

one else about Scottish topographical and bibliographical antiquities. His scanty education had been very greatly enriched by a
youth spent in his father's and grandfather's bookshop; and by the
same means he began to acquire his own extraordinarily fine library.
Not only did he delight in answering difficult questions but, though
hampered all his life by lack of money, he continually embarrassed
his lucky correspondents with valuable gifts and loans of rare
books, offered with the most amiable and disinterested liberality.

In this kind of embarrassment Percy somewhat uneasily rested
throughout the course of their correspondence. He was always
protesting and insisting on his desire to pay or make some substantial return; but he seldom succeeded. He sent the second and
third editions of the *Reliques* when they appeared; but the *Northumberland Household Book*, which he himself had edited for the
Duke in 1770, and which Paton really coveted, remained out of
reach. Apparently His Grace kept all the copies in his own hands,
and Percy was reluctant to beg one for his friend. Meanwhile, he
kept using Paton for his purchasing agent in Edinburgh; and it
was through Paton that he got the loan of the Bannatyne MS extended for an unconscionable time. One of the interesting appen-
dices of the sixth volume contains extracts from the minutes of the
Advocates about this famous collection, which Percy received for a
six-months' period in the late Spring of 1773 and returned after a
succession of delays at the end of July 1775. It was the Curators,
it now appears from a letter here first printed, who were responsible for negligently uniting as one compilation the two unrelated
MSS which Lord Hyndford had given to the Library, attributing
both collections to Bannatyne, and binding the first part of Bannatyne along with the separate and smaller collection as Bannatyne
Volume I, and the rest as Volume II, dividing by mere equality of
bulk. The mistake was later forgotten, and it became the source
of much scholarly puzzlement.

Another matter hitherto the subject of debate, is cleared up by
the editor of the sixth volume, A. F. Falconer, to the credit of
Percy. Hans Hecht, editor of David Herd's MSS of Scottish songs,
in 1904 accused Percy of soliciting the privilege of correcting
Herd's materials for an enlarged edition, and then, after long delay
during which he held the MSS, returning them finally untouched.
According to Professor Falconer, the initial impulse came from

the other direction, and Percy found himself more involved than he had bargained for. But the matter might be open to another interpretation. After the question of his interest was once raised, he certainly seems to have invited himself in. What appealed to him was the possibility of handling the fragments creatively, "which might give occasion to very beautiful Songs, if supplied and filled up, in the manner that old broken fragments of antique Statues have been repaired and compleated by modern Masters. I think I could fill up the breaches of some of them myself." His proposal is something in the nature of a *quid pro quo*. If Herd will give him leave to "fill up the deficiencies" of his fragments and publish the reconstructions in a "Volume or Two More of old English and Scottish Poems in the Manner of my Reliques," which he intends to publish in "3 or 4 years," he in return will then allow Herd to reprint from his future publication "such of them as suit his subject and plan." And, in the meantime, Percy will furnish Herd with some unpublished Scots songs and poems that he formerly transcribed from the Maitland MS in Cambridge, which, if eked out with additions from Bannatyne, would be enough to make a second volume straight off. That is, the studio restorations, when and if they materialize, might supply Herd with a third volume, if he cared to leave his materials indefinitely in cold storage on the chance that he might wish to make use of the *rifacimenti*. They would, however, by then recently have been published, which would rather take off the bloom. Still, Percy's reputation as an expert restorer was high in this decade, and he might fairly count on enhancing the value of the projected volume.

On human grounds alone, far the most interesting volume in the series is the fifth, the correspondence with Evan Evans, that splenetic, not to say half-crazy, but profound and devoted student of Welsh antiquities. Evans was a Character in the fullest sense. Dogged by poverty, ill-health, and misfortunes contrived in good part by himself, he never managed to set his life on an even keel for long at a time. Like a hibernating animal, he seems habitually to have relapsed during the winter months into a state of semi-torpor (aided by the bottle), incapable of exertion, even epistolary. Thus, he writes on Dec. 6, 1761: "I have been very much out of order this winter by reason of a violent headach . . . it is with great reluctancy as well as pain that I read or write anything that re-

quires any the least attention. Upon this account I must beg you
. . . to excuse me till summer, when I am generally free from this
complaint." But in summer worse may befall: one year, it is a
sudden attack of pleurisy that strikes him down on the road. In
another, it is a severe fit of the stone and gravel. In another,
he is thrown by his horse and dragged by a leg caught in
the stirrup for 200 yards, with serious attendant injury. "Had
it not been for this dismall accident I should be in a condition to
pay the money I owe you, the next quarter payment, but as things
now stand, I must beg of you not to be uneasy till I can get over
this unfortunate and expensive affair." Percy's role is to offer sympathy and encouraging solicitude for the progress of his studies,
augmented by news of Johnson's equal anxiety for their successful prosecution; the loan of a cravat and five guineas at their only
recorded meeting; and finally, spiritual counsel inoffensively prof-
fered and (surprisingly) in that spirit received. "There is our
friend Mr. Johnson," writes Percy, "for seven years of his Life,
so steadily restrained his appetite, that during that time he never
admitted a single drop of any fermented Liquor within his Lips:
and he is now a great example of temperance and sobriety." Percy
is ready to try to find an English curacy for Evans at the latter's
request; but thereupon Evans decides that he would do better to
remain in Wales. Percy's fund of curiosity, meanwhile, about the
British bards never flags, and he keeps prodding Evans to satisfy
it, by putting questions about prosody, dates, styles, subjects, and
by throwing off hypothetical analogies as bait for further comment.
By and large, we see Percy at his most attractive and amiable in
these letters.

Percy was, on the whole, an unusually fortunate man. In spite
of the early death of an only son and the slow drawing down of
blinds in his latter years as his vision departed, he had an ample
share of life's comforts and satisfactions. He lived in a congenial
time; was in harmonious relations with a very large circle of
friendly acquaintances who shared his interests and paid him regard; had, until past fifty, ample leisure to follow his favorite
studies; and never met any serious set-back in his steady rise to
literary celebrity and success in the Church. By the end of the
century to which he belonged, he knew himself in the eyes of a
younger generation something of an institution, a fixed point of

reference through the *Reliques*, one to whom they referred with confidence, and even veneration—witness Robert Anderson, Scott, and Wordsworth in their several testimonies—and with considerable pride when they received his favorable notice.

Yet the man is enigmatic; he does not come clear in one's mind. His letters seldom or never reveal his private thought; he never drops his guard; one never feels that one has seen into his deeper nature. It is clear that he is interested in worthwhile things, that his attitudes are laudable and sound, that he is neither furtive nor hypocritical. He is capable of white lies, but his worst positive fault is a quick temper and a tendency to cherish grudges; but these are usually kept in leash. We know that he and Johnson irritated each other—and why not?—to the point of a minor explosion, which Boswell too officiously set to rights; and that he quarrelled irrevocably with Capell (who had little use for anyone); and that possibly he and Farmer parted over a disputed monetary obligation. We know that he was thin-skinned, could not bear to be twitted or corrected. We gather that he was fortunate in a jewel of a wife, who made his guests welcome and comfortable—including Johnson and Mrs. Williams over a two-months' stay, winning Johnson's high praises—and who made a good mother, all in an agreeable, self-effacing but adequate way. We do not *know* that she was self-effacing; we feel sure that she was neither obtrusive nor intrusive. She passed all tests blameless. But, except in his polished and decorous little song to her, we never hear them speaking to each other: she might as well be by the Indian Ganges' side, he by the tide of Humber, for all we observe of the companionship, which was real and lasting, we must trust and believe.

Clearly, Percy had something of Boswell's knack, if not his devouring stomach, for meeting the "right" people and making it agreeable to meet again. At the outset of his career, his friend the poet Grainger (incidentally one of his most spirited and outspoken correspondents) significantly prophesied a mitre for him—and not for prowess in Divinity, theological debate, or pulpit oratory. His ascent to a bishopric seems as natural as the rise of a good-sized apple to the top of the barrel. He did this, he did that—and there he was. He altered the spelling of his name from Piercy to Percy in accordance with a flattering hypothesis; when Shenstone, to whom he was to have dedicated the *Reliques*, died during its printing, Percy reversed the order of volumes to bring foremost the Battle of Otterburn, and dedicated the work to the Countess of Northumberland; was appointed tutor to her son; then private secretary and chaplain to the Duke; then Dean of Carlisle; then Bishop of Dromore. It is a significant trait of character that he was an assiduous collector of heads, a devotee of the portrait portfolio. Is there anything much amiss with all this? The answer, of course, is, Not at all; and it is merely captious and carping to hint a fault and hesitate dislike. Nevertheless, we can never really love the man, for all his good qualities, because he always holds us at arm's length, and never confesses his human need of us. Reynolds painted his picture, and he takes his place contentedly in that superb historical gallery, posed and impeccable, forever at the three-quarter view.

Thomas Chatterton

EVERYONE at all familiar with Chatterton's story knows that he was a posthumous child. Yet it is doubtful if the fact has ever been given its due weight as a conditioning factor in not so much his physical as his psychic environment. For consider: Chatterton found his ideal father-substitute in William Canynge, the lavish and loving giver of all good things; he found his own deepest identity in Rowley, fifteenth-century poet and historian, receiver of benefits spiritual and material, which he repaid with testimonial honor and devotion to the giver; he preferred death to the further chances of life on earth before he had completed his seventeenth year. In a profound sense, the past was Chatterton's future. This precocious and irresistible urge backward was the most vital impulse in his short existence. Its abnormality, we may reasonably believe, finds its wellspring in the equal abnormality of his father's death before the child was born. By this simple fact, an indissoluble bond was dramatically established in Chatterton's infant mind between his father, the past, and death. The father belonged wholly to the past by virtue of the fact that he had ceased to draw breath before ever the son drew the first gasp of life. He had never touched the present: there was a breach of continuity between generation and generation.

The past to a very young child is all one time, just as the present is one, distinct from all that lies back of one's own physical awareness. There is then and now. The summer of 1752, when his father died, was as far away from the boy as any other part of the past. His father was buried, like his other forebears, in St. Mary's across the way, a family mansion where you went to live when you were dead. That was home, a palatial residence more fitting than the temporary lodging to which his mother had transferred her little family after his father's death. St. Mary's was a fine place, spacious, full of fascination. Famous people lived in it, invisibly—"The Parlyament of Sprytes" would one day testify to this assurance— and their names were recorded on the monuments there. It would be natural for his father to have an impressive tomb. Very early the boy picked his favorite one, and we know in part what use his imagination was to make of it, his frustrated filial needs swarming about the Canynge memorials in unrestrained, fantastic self-fulfillment. By the time he was able to puzzle out the words on tablet and tomb, his emotional life, as the Canynge legend proves, was too deeply involved here to be dissociated by clearer notions and distinctions of persons. Rather, it took over the historical record and fed upon it, transmuting it by a subtle alchemy of which he alone possessed the secret—bones to coral—into the record of that imaginary fifteenth-century society of whose doings Chatterton later made such breath-taking and startlingly full report.

Other significant hints of the associative and affective power of the child's filial hunger may be collected from the second "Eclogue," where artistic unity has all but collapsed under the pressure of unconscious emotional compulsions. The body of the poem paints with amazing brilliance and speed the pageantry of the Third Crusade. But this bold and assured canvas has been enclosed and divided into panels by a weak and unsuitable cheesecloth frame. The descriptive narration is assigned entire to the "pious Nygelle," who, as we learn at the end, has been awaiting his father's return from some undesignated voyage, and who tags most stanzas with the sentimental prayer:

> Sprytes of the bleste, and everyche Seyncte ydedde,
> Poure owte youre pleasaunce on mie fadres hedde.

The filial reunion is indicated with a helpless, anticlimactic appeal to the reader to imagine it for himself. There is pathos here in plenty, but it lies beyond the margin. The mere abstract idea of a meeting between father and son has served as adequate climax for the starved psyche of the poet, even where it is an irrelevant intrusion.

We have no direct evidence on the point, but it is a safe inference that the memory of the elder Chatterton was not denigrated by his widow. Not herself a strong character, she had married at eighteen a man twice her own age; and therefore even if she feared more than loved him, she must have felt, when left at the age of twenty-one with two babies to provide for—a third had died—that times were better when there was a man at the helm. The hard present and the gloomy prospect would not make for a lighthearted home atmosphere, and all references must have pointed the contrast with the past and have exalted the father's stature in his son's imagination. The neighbors would be commiserating ("So young to be left a widow," etc. "Poor child, he never even saw his father," etc.). To a child's mind the inferences would be inescapable. His father, it was plain, was all-important to his family and to him; his father lived in that golden age, the past; his father was dead; and in that case, surely, death (conceived by child and savage as the obverse of life, but yet a conscious state) must be good. By some such associational train of ideas the child's emotional orientations were set in reverse, and the negatives of others became his psychic positives. There was always, moreover, the splendor of St. Mary's at hand to prove that he was right. For St. Mary's was the visible symbol of the difference between the past and the present . . . Whether or not there are errors in the particulars of our hypothesis, it yields conclusions which accord with all the facts presented by Chatterton's life and work.

It is highly indicative, in the light of his subsequent precocity, that the boy was dismissed from his first school as stupidly impervious to knowledge. His mind at that age was too busy with its own inner activity to submit to be distracted. Absorbed by his teeming fantasies, he was as yet insulated against any realization that the drab symbols of modern print could contain value for him, could provide a bridge to parts of his private world that he had not explored. They were associated instead with things that were repellent or at least indifferent to him. The august personages of his fancy would write and express their thoughts in other terms altogether, just as they had dressed more magnificently and built more grandly and lived more dramatically. But when his eye was caught by the old manuscript in his mother's hands, he saw the connection between that mysterious beauty and his other world.

His mother perceived her opportunity in his interest—it was her one recorded moment of insight—and found him eager to learn the black letter and read big old books. The road was now open; he quickly entered and took possession of his kingdom.

Grotesquely unsuited to Chatterton's needs as was the so-called "education" provided by Colston's Hospital, and incarcerated as his body was by the strict regulations of the place, he found it by no means intolerable, and the seven years he spent there were probably the happiest of his life. Since the school taught nothing but writing and accounting, there was the utmost freedom to pursue the wayward bent of his own intellectual interests; and the very paucity of subject matter for scholastic instruction could not but have left more time for reading, even if sub rosa in school hours. Besides, as his sister was later to report on the authority of his schoolfellows, "he retired to read at the hours allotted for play." The school's attention to penmanship—for the boys were to be put apprentices and in them it would by no means be held "a baseness to write fair"—could only reinforce that interest which bookish adolescents usually take in their own chirography, and perhaps even encourage the experimental practice of different styles of handwriting. In fact, we know that it was to the verse-minded Phillips, his older schoolfellow and subsequently the junior master at Colston's, that Chatterton brought his first imitation of antique writing on parchment. Luckier for him, perhaps, had he been less expert or his senior better informed! The fact of his attempting this mischief, however, shows that the early fantasies were proceeding apace and beginning to insist on tangible expression. His trying it on the one person of his acquaintance whom he genuinely admired may tell much or little about his motives. Doubtless these were mixed; but the words of Falstaff have a grotesque relevance in this connection: "To counterfeit death when a man thereby liveth is to be no counterfeit." Judged by the measure of vital energy expended, the boy's outer existence, we may readily allow, was the counterfeit, his Rowleian existence was "the true and perfect image of life indeed."

During these years his expanding mind was God's theater. He became a *helluo librorum*. He spent his little allowance on the circulating libraries, and borrowed elsewhere. Between his eleventh and twelfth years, his sister said, he catalogued the books he had read to the number of seventy, mostly in history and divinity. He lived with monastic asceticism, refusing meat and drinking only water, "because he had a work in hand, and would not make himself more stupid than God had made him." Medical research has latterly brought us the assurance that serious deficiencies of certain kinds in the diet can produce extreme psychosomatic excitement, and it seems clear that Chatterton deliberately kept himself in such a state by denying his body the nourishment it needed. Of artificial stimulants such as Barrett, for reasons best known to himself, tried to coax him into taking he had no need: he had already discovered a far cheaper and more efficient mode of inebriation. He saw the matter in a different light; but the Church could have given Rowley some useful hints.[1]

Be that as it may, Chatterton discovered the condition in which he could work most effectively, wherein ideas "streamed into his mind, as it were, most divinely." His nerves exacerbated by spare diet and moonlight, he became more and more intoxicated with the past, and before he left Colston's he had acquired a deal of out-of-the-way learning, in local history, architecture, heraldry, chivalry, paleography, and the elder poets of England. He re-created fourteenth-century Bristol in his imagination, seizing on the pageantry, the chivalry, and those picturesque aspects of it which appealed especially to a boy. He became at home in that society, and shared with surprising particularity in its community life. He would walk out into Redcliffe meadows with his schoolboy friend, William Smith, and in a particular spot "would frequently lay himself down, fix his eyes upon the church, and seem as if he were in a kind of extasy or trance." By this time, apparently, or very little later, Rowley and his fellows had acquired their full proportions in his imagination. It was himself at about this period that he was idealizing when, through the mouth of Rowley, now conceived as an old man, he described the youth of Canynge:

> I saw hym eager gaspynge after lyghte.
> In all hys shepen gambols and chyldes plaie . . .
> I kenn'd a perpled lyghte of Wysdom's raie;
> He eate downe learnynge wyth the wastle cake. . . .
> Greete yn hys councel for the daies he bore.

[1] Fifty years later another poet was recovered from hallucinations by Peacock's timely prescription of mutton chops, well seasoned.

> All tongues, all carrols dyd unto hym synge,
> Wondryng at one soe wyse, and yet soe yinge.

There is no doubt that the examples of Macpherson, whose current fortunes put rash ideas into his head, and Percy's *Reliques,* which Meyerstein calls "almost the efficient poetical cause of Rowley" and "a model to anyone who wished to produce antique verse, and appeal to his century at one and the same time," were a most exciting stimulus to Chatterton's budding creative impulses. Ossian he imitated in a number of pieces which he readily acknowledged upon challenge; and "The Bristowe Tragedy" may rightly be regarded, as Meyerstein says, as his attempt to match the *Reliques.* Sooner or later, however, he came upon a book which has never received its due as Rowley's inspiration, and which has perhaps an even better claim than the other two names to be considered a formative influence on the actual poetry, if not the ambition, of Rowley's creator. This was Elizabeth Cooper's *The Muses' Library,* 1737 (reissued with new title pages, 1738, 1741), a work which deserves to be better known. In this chronologically arranged anthology, extending from Edward the Confessor to Samuel Daniel, and in its readable notes of introduction, Chatterton found abundant encouragement, a variety of poetic types, metrical patterns, stylistic models, which he copied now closely, now distantly (see p. 203f.); a notable example of a poet-monk, Alexander Barclay, praised editorially for his eminence and merit as the improver of our language and for his elegancy of manners (whilst Lydgate is disparaged); and in general a poetic tone and temper highly congenial to his own inclinations at this impressionable moment. In spite of the ostensible historic range of the collection, its whole content, after the first thirty pages, is really sixteenth-century verse. By plan and editorial handling the book suggests a homogeneity among the elder poets in which distinctions of style and language are relatively insignificant. An untutored reader would naturally collect the impression from its pages that the differences of a hundred and fifty years were quite negligible, a matter rather of individuals than of times. Thus it came about that a fifteenth-century Rowley could write as if he lived in the full tide of the sixteenth century.

But the present point is that *The Muses' Library,* by and large, in tone and temper, in metrics and subjects, is at the very heart of the Rowleian afflatus. Of no other single work accessible to Chatterton can such an assertion be made. The pieces in the *Reliques* are for the most part much lower than Rowley's emotional and rhetorical pitch, the temporal range scattered and late. Variety of interest is the key to Percy's effort and method. By comparison *The Muses' Library* is naïve in the extreme; but it communicates the strong impact of those brave translunary things that were most congenial to Rowley's genius. His works belong beside it on the shelf. Spenser's influence it is possible to overemphasize: he is too patient, too leisurely, too involved with ideas to accord with Rowley's impetuous, dramatic, essentially unintellectual temper. Dixon is right in saying that Marlowe is Chatterton's nearest spiritual kinsman.[2] But this avatar of that fiery spirit canceled an old debt by learning most of all from the younger Shakespeare. There is hardly a scene in his masterpiece, "Ælla," that does not owe thanks to some similar scene or passage in comedy, history, or tragedy.[3]

It is well known that, to aid him in his composition, Chatterton drew up alphabetical lists of old words, one ancient-modern, the other modern-ancient, mostly compiled from John Kersey's revision of Phillips' dictionary, *The New World of Words* (1706, *sic*), supplemented from Speght's Chaucer glossary and Bailey's later work. These lists were obviously for the purpose of building up his vocabulary, so that he could think and write in his chosen language, just as anyone would acquire the vocabulary of a foreign tongue. Chatterton often lamented that he knew no tongue but his own; yet he might have comforted himself with the thought that in that he was actually bilingual. It is scarcely to the point that Rowley's language, strictly speaking, had no existence elsewhere than in his own mind and work. The same thing may be said, and truly, of Spenser's language, and Burns's and Hopkins'— and even Shakespeare's! Rowley's language is distilled from the poets, and the glossarists, with whom he was intimately conversant; and he uses it with perfect mastery and sensitive awareness of its capabilities.

[2] W. Macneile Dixon, *Chatterton* (1930), p. 13.
[3] *The Two Gentlemen of Verona, Midsummer Night's Dream, The Merchant of Venice, Henry IV, V, VI, Romeo and Juliet, Julius Caesar, Hamlet, Othello, Lear, Macbeth, The Tempest* were all obviously laid under contribution, though Rowley well knew how to subdue them to his own needs.

The water slughornes wythe a swotye cleme
Conteke the dynnynge ayre, and reche the skies . . .
The gule depeyncted oares from the black tyde,
Decorn wyth fonnes rare, doe shemrynge ryse;
Upswalynge doe heie shewe ynne drierie pryde,
Lyche gore-red estells in the eve-merk skyes;
The nome-depeyncted shields, the speres aryse,
Alyche talle roshes on the water side;
Alenge from bark to bark the bryghte sheene flyes;
Sweft-kerv'd delyghtes doe on the water glyde.

What antiquating recipe will turn the eighteenth-century music into such as this? On the contrary, this was Chatterton's genuine voice; this was his native speech; in these cadences his thought moved freely, and in them he was most truly at home. The same falling-off in assurance and inspiration occurs when he leaves them for modern speech as when Burns leaves his Ayrshire idiom for contemporary English.

It is natural to suppose that he did not acquire this mastery all at once, however swiftly. And a careful statistical analysis might very probably show an incidence of favorite words, and a varying range of vocabulary, which, together with particular preoccupations of subject and characteristic variations of spelling, would provide clues to the relative order of composition. He may, of course, have worked his poems over as his growing maturity prompted.[4] We have the two versions of the "Battle of Hastings" to show us how rapid this growth was. It is altogether probable that when he told Barrett he himself had written the first version, he was already deep in the composition of the second, and was confident of its superiority, which he could attribute to the "genuine" Rowley without fear that it would be beneath that level. Similarly, when he told his mother that he had written the "Bristowe Tragedie," the confession was no doubt a private piece of self-criticism, an acknowledgment that Rowley's pinion was for a loftier flight:

[4] He must have done so for "Elinoure and Juga" if, as was claimed by his schoolfellow years later, some form of that piece was in existence as early as 1764. For it is highly unlikely that he would have chosen, as the first piece to exhibit Rowley's powers in public print, an early poem which had been laid aside untouched for four years while the genius proceeded on its impetuous course.

Cannynge & I from common course dyssente;
Wee ryde the stede, botte yeve to hym the reene;
Ne wylle betweene crased molterynge bookes be pente,
Botte soare on hyghe, & yn the sonne-bemes sheene.

A better way than acknowledgment, he soon discovered, was at-
tribution to lesser talents, Iscam, Gorges, or Canynge. Such attribu-
tions were critical judgments much less dangerous than confessing
oneself an imitator; and they saved Rowley's name just as well
for excellence. But, in any case, it is much more probable that so
impatient a spirit usually tried a new flight than that he reverted to
labor with hammer and file on his earlier things. So that we might
put some reliance upon the casual evidences of developmental
change.

   Now, having achieved poetry of such assured authenticity, what
was to be done about it? Here we come face to face with the
crucial dilemma of Chatterton's life. It involves us in questions of
time and place as well as private psychological problems. There is,
of course, no doubt that Chatterton's age felt a strong and steadily
increasing interest in the past. Itself one of the most complacent
of times, its self-confident expectations of further advance were
nourished not only by the current scientific progress but by a
vivid conviction of the distance it had already traveled toward
rational enlightenment out of ignorance and superstition. The
more barbarous the past, the brighter the present. "Let us therefore inspect that obscurity!"

   There was little in this impulse that stemmed from respect or
veneration. The abstract idea of age, to be sure, was impressive
to contemplate; the past was picturesque and romantic, interesting,
even awful; but these were the qualities of distance and depended
on the point of view of the beholder: they were not values which
the past had possessed when it was the present. True value still
lay in standards accepted by today, in "those rules of old discovered not devised" which were still current, and in the universal
laws which were being established by the new science. Since the
value of antiquity was thus for this age almost entirely subjective,
imitations, no matter how genuinely and deeply re-creative, could
earn no higher credit than that of ingenuity or cleverness—*unless*
they were downright successful deceptions. Bring to light genuine

relics, or supposed relics, and fame and fortune might follow. Bring forth excellent imitations and nothing followed but mild applause. Hence the way of the literary transgressor never looked more tempting, nor, indeed, at its commencement more innocent; and we are treated in consequence with that curious parade of hoaxes, from Ossian to Ireland, that is so marked a feature of later eighteenth-century literary history. Hence, likewise, the acrimony of the controversies which accompanied the procession: since, for defenders as well as opponents, values were almost entirely conditional upon the bare fact of antiquity, not upon qualities inherent in the documents themselves.

Now Chatterton, it is clear, wrote his Rowleian poetry not to deceive but in response to the deepest promptings of his being. For him the true had no value beyond the sham; in fact, the sham could not be called so without violence to the truth. His emotional maturity, his finest aesthetic perceptions, his deepest inspiration, lay in Rowley. The question of deception was fundamentally irrelevant: Rowley was genuine. But the only way he could win a fair hearing in that time and that place was through deceit.

Yet, making equally for concealment, one can hardly doubt that there were also at work up until the very end obscure but deep-lying compulsions of a private nature in Chatterton's predicament. Names, in their subconscious implications and operations, are curious things to contemplate. "Though my blood run red," warns Ribold in the ballad,

> "My name must not be said.
> Yea, though thou see me fall,
> My name thou must not call!" . . .
> E'en as she spake the fatal word
> Wounded was he with many a sword.

Now Rowley had this primitive significance for Chatterton. He was a projected embodiment of the child's innermost life, an essential personification, emerging from the earliest years, of the dreams and wishes of his secret being. The idea of the first person singular is vague and of late development in comparison with such third-personal projections of identity. When Chatterton began to write poetry, he was Rowley; only by this imaginary identification could he write with confidence and conviction. Rowley's integrity and actuality, the very continuance of that inspiration, depended on such imaginative faith. Had he acknowledged, upon the challenge of outsiders, that he was merely "pretending," and that Rowley was really himself, himself as defined by his social context and others' ideas of him as well as his own, it is hardly possible that he could have continued his make-believe. Rowley in the charity school daylight would have evaporated, leaving only the absurd mockery of this Bristol apprentice seriously trying to write poetry like a medieval monk. So long as Chatterton continued to write poetry under the Rowleian inspiration, so long, it appears to me, would he be committed to the vital necessity of preserving his secret. Artistic self-preservation depended on his persistence in the Great Lie. To confess was to have done, once and for all. As to morals, therefore, Coleridge, Keats, Rossetti, and every other admirer of the poetry is guilty of complicity with Chatterton.

Indeed, even if he kept his secret, it became every day more doubtful that he would be heard. When Chatterton turned for encouragement to the only persons within reach who had an interest in antiquity, he found them cold to poetry. What Barrett wanted was illustrations for his history of Bristol: only on that basis was he willing to entertain verse. Burgum and Catcott had a still more restricted view. Thus, to private necessity and the general pressures of the age were added peculiar limitations of place; and Chatterton, eager for fame, acceded without question to these conditions of Rowley's survival. So long as he could stave off the demand for the production of the documents themselves, he found it easy to feed these local antiquaries the kind of draff and husks for which they clamored: pedigrees, deeds of gift, architectural notes. Never was there a more willing suspension of disbelief than theirs. There might be a certain amount of fraud somewhere, they saw; but it was preposterous to suppose that the boy should have invented everything. Encouragement was their cue: and when they had won his confidence, he might provide them with the originals which he was holding back, and they could judge for themselves and dispense with his services. But he had his own reasons for remaining indispensable. The few "originals" which he produced, with an almost contemptuous lack of due precaution, seemed to pass well enough; but if he was to be condemned to copying off on parchment all Rowley's works, present and to come, the prospect was gloomy and the chances of detection enormously increased. Before long it became clear to him that these owls would never understand that Rowley's poetry was the Thing, and that he must find other foster fathers if his ambitions were to be realized. He must try elsewhere; and who so likely to listen as Dodsley, the publisher of Percy's *Reliques?* So he wrote Dodsley, offering "Ælla" in a letter of incredible naïveté; and was of course completely ignored. When a second letter, hardly so wise as the first, elicited no response, he turned to Horace Walpole, this time having the sense to enclose specimens of Rowley's wares. Here his success was immediate and overwhelming: this must have been the golden moment of his earthly life. Walpole not only found his communication "very valuable" and his notes "learned," but went on: "Give me leave to ask you where Rowley's poems are to be found. I should not be sorry to print them, or at least a specimen of them, if they have never been printed." At last Chatterton had found his own Canynge, the patron who would open all the doors to fortune and fame; and Rowley would come forth from the most distinguished press in England, that which had but a decade before ushered out the lofty odes of Gray!

The sequel is well known. Further inquiry convinced Walpole that the pieces were spurious. He thereupon recommended to Chatterton to be a diligent attorney's apprentice, and told him "that when he should have made a fortune he might unbend himself with the studies consonant to his inclinations." So, in an instant, all the high hopes were dashed to the ground.

In the first bitterness of disappointment, Chatterton started a poem of hate to Walpole, which is important to us for three reasons: (1) its self-pity contains an overt avowal of his abiding filial need, now frustrated anew by Walpole's refusal to fill the vacancy; (2) it is a tacit acknowledgment of his authorship of Rowley; (3) it expresses a defiant faith in Rowley's ultimate survival.

> Walpole, I thought not I should ever see
> So mean a heart as thine has proved to be.
> Thou who, in luxury nurst, behold'st with scorn

The boy, who friendless, fatherless, forlorn,
Asks thy high favour—thou mayst call me cheat.
Say, didst thou never practise such deceit?
Who wrote Otranto? . . .
                          But I shall live and stand
By Rowley's side, when thou art dead and damned.

The poem was never finished.

The same tide of effort to burst the Bristol dam which carried
the appeals to Dodsley and Walpole seems to have prompted him
to send "Elinoure and Juga" to the newly established *Town and
Country Magazine*. The poem, "Written three hundred Years ago
by T. Rowley, a Secular Priest," was dated "Bristol, May, 1769."
If the date is correct—the poem appeared in the May number of
the magazine—it may be that Chatterton was encouraged to send
it by Walpole's being so completely deceived by his first communications in the preceding March.[5] After the shock of Walpole's
considered negative judgment, Chatterton seems to have tried
nowhere else with Rowley until July of the following year, when
he sent the "Charitie" ballade to the same magazine. The publisher
did not print it that month, and inside the August title page Chatterton would have read: "The Pastoral from Bristol, signed D.D.,
has some share of merit: but the author [sic] will, doubtless,
discover upon another perusal of it, many exceptional passages."
But by the time this number appeared Chatterton was dead.

In the meantime Chatterton had been growing up. He still
believed in Rowley; but it was becoming all too plain that Rowley
could do nothing for him in his present need. To find his account
with his own age he would have to turn to other courses. He would
have to learn another language, less native to him but better understood by the public he had to address. He had already been feeling
out these possibilities for some time. With his negative orientation
toward the present, it was inevitable that he should turn to satire.
This was the obverse of the shield. Everything positive that as yet
he had to say lay in Rowley. The first pieces in modern English

[5] It is surely one of the most wryly comic events of Chatterton's career that
this poem, sent at the age of sixteen but possibly written several years earlier, had
the fortune to be modernized the following month, in the pages of the same
magazine, by a Westminster scholar (Robert Nares), signing "S.W.A., aged 16,"
clearly a boy of forward parts!

to reveal any individuality, therefore, were satirical attacks: "Sly
Dick" and "Apostate Will." It is of some psychological significance
that the first deals with filched treasure, the second with dissem-
bling. It is also no accident that one of the most affective concepts
in all Chatterton's work is that of secret, uphoarded wealth, its
discovery and safeguarding, the miser's chest, the "gouler's"
(usurer's) gold, the treasure chest, the cave or cavern, the casket,
or coffin, the murky wood, the underground well.

Disregarding his journalistic prose, which signifies nothing but
a *cacoethes scribendi,* and the urge to see his own words—any
words of his—in print, we watch him now attempting occasional
verse on various subjects and in various kinds—'prentice work, in
large part empty of emotional content. Amongst it are several
poems addressed to "the fair." In all these his emotional immaturity
is painfully evident. He borrows the attitude of conventional gallantry, or the cynical one of the circle of young apprentices among
whom he was picking up a knowledge of life and manners, and
by overemphasis compensates for extreme youth at every turn.

Churchill's recent satires now provided him with congenial
models for violent personal invective; and he adopted the "patriotic," anti-authoritarian point of view with the same facility that
he had applied to other kinds of journalism. The outcry and noise
and ill manners all suited his exacerbated spirit, and he aped the
conventional attitudes of party with perfect mimicry. But apart
from a pervasive animosity, a general hostility which flared to a
brighter intensity when its fuel was some known personality, he
had no convictions. Clever, even talented, though it was, this sort
of work grew on the topsoil of his mind: it was rootless. Intellectually and emotionally he was a mere child in the political sphere,
as he had been in the amatory one: as yet he was not within possible
reach of any deep and genuine experience in these directions. And
unfortunately he had met no one, man or woman, who could or
would teach him, or with sympathetic understanding advise patience at this crucial period.

But in Rowley he had already grown up. In Rowley he had
achieved a rich and deep experience. Its authenticity was a touchstone which only served to reveal the shallowness of his other at-

titudes.⁶ And what, and who, was Rowley? *Vox et praeterea nihil!*
A bodiless ghost, addressing an audience that except for one solitary
soul had died about the year 1600. To the interests of today, even
to the valid and insistent interests of maturing youth, Rowley was
dead. Already receding into the distance, in face of the hurry and
stress of Chatterton's life in London, he could hardly be resur-
rected. There was nothing in that life to fill his place. Yet he was
Chatterton himself: the embodiment, the articulate record of the
most intense life Chatterton had ever known. The dichotomy was
too poignant to be endured. At last, the poet and his age were of
one opinion. If the age was unable to accept Rowley as Chatterton,
there was yet an opposite way out, satisfactory to all concerned.
On the night of August 24, 1770, Chatterton took it, shut the doors
of the present, and became Rowley forever. The world has been
content to remember him so.

When he decided to go home to the past, Chatterton did not
know what the world might conclude. The chances are that he
thought he and Rowley would both be forgotten. Nothing that
he had written had reached print over his own signature. Nothing
—not even the "African Eclogues"—had been adjudged by that
objectively critical intelligence to be as good as Rowley's poetry,
or good enough, therefore, to deserve his name. And, except for
"Elinoure and Juga," which had caused no perceptible stir of excitement, all Rowley's poetry lay still in manuscript, in the hands
of dolts who did not appreciate it, and with slight chance of being
printed. These facts have a bearing on the question of his persistence in a lie, and his determination to take his secret with him to
the grave. What were the profit of announcing to the world that
he had written what no man regarded, when until now his record
of denial was consistent and literally perfect? Why idly brand
oneself a liar, as the last act of one's life, when nothing was to be

⁶ With strictest accuracy he gauged that impact in his fantastic "will":

> "Rowley . . . my first, chief curse!
> For had I never known the antique lore,
> I ne'er had ventured from my peaceful shore
> To be the wreck of promises and hopes,
> A Boy of Learning, and a Bard of Tropes;
> But happy in my humble sphere had moved,
> Untroubled, unrespected, unbeloved."

gained except obloquy? And if, by a stroke of luck, Rowley should be printed and appreciated, his best chances for survival, and for Chatterton as his discoverer, lay, as experience seemed to prove, in his being taken for a genuine ancient. Why, then, destroy that slender hope?

It is perhaps useless to surmise what Chatterton might have done had he chosen to live; but we may be fairly certain that of Rowley, even under the most favorable circumstances, we should have had little more. The better informed he became, the less confident he would be of his ability to write fifteenth-century English good enough to fool the experts, and concomitantly the harder it would prove to lose himself in his fantasy. But even more important, there were too many interests in the maturing mind which would be pressing for expression, and to which Rowley, with his special handicaps, could not possibly give voice. There is some evidence that Chatterton was trying latterly to widen the Rowleian base and range, and we may perhaps regard the japes and fragments appearing only in the collected remains as tentative experiments toward compromise between Rowley and Chatterton, the past and the present. For this reason, it is probable that the best of Rowley is not the very last, but was done in the long solitary hours of freedom in that first year or so in Lambert's office, in the full flood of the early adolescent tide of hope and belief. Rowley was a true Bristolian and one can hardly believe that he ever visited London, in spite of the date, July 4, 1770, on the "Excellent Ballade of Charitie." It is significant that in sending that lovely poem to the magazine from London, Chatterton marked it as from Bristol.

What he would have done in other kinds is probably still more idle to conjecture. His natural bent was clearly toward drama. But if he was going to write a first-class satirical comedy of manners, with his handicaps in social background and education he had a long, hard road ahead of him. To suppose that he could ever have achieved a first-rate tragedy, with the contemporary influences and examples at work upon him, is to suppose that he could have done more in that age than anyone else was able to do with with whatever advantage. And for great verse satire or a great novel his knowledge of life and reflection upon it would long be insufficient. All in all, he may have rung down the curtain at the climax of the play.

A NOTE ON ELIZABETH COOPER'S *The Muses Library*

This 400-page octave is one of the earliest attempts to give a
historical survey of the elder English poets by exhibiting specimens
of their work in a chronological series. The range is from Edward
the Confessor to Samuel Daniel.

The first piece in the volume, the Confessor's rhymed deed of
gift, was turned by Chatterton to his own uses in Rowley's "translation" of "Turgot's" Account of Bristol. It begins:

> Iche *Edward* Koning,
> Have given of my Forrest the Keeping
> Of the Hundred of *Chelmer* and *Dancing*,
> To *Randolph Peperking* and to his Kyndling:
> With Heorte and Hinde, Doe, and Bocke,
> Hare, and Foxe, Cat and Brocke . . .
> To kepen and to yemen by all her might. . . .

Of this Chatterton has made:

> Iche Edwarde Konynge,
> Yeven Brystoe Castellynge
> Unto the keepynge, Off Leofwynne de Godwynne
> Of Clytoe Kyndlynge; Of Ballarde and Battell
> Le Bartlowe for Cattayle
> Alle that on the watters fiote, To take Brugbote. . . .[7]

From Daniel's *Civil Wars* was drawn the piece that ends *The
Muses Library:* the scene in which Queen Isabel watches from a
window while her husband, Richard II, passes through the street
as Bolingbroke's prisoner. Memories of this and of the parallel
scene in Shakespeare may have contributed more than history to
the content of *The Bristowe Tragedie.*

Langland, Gower, and Chaucer are represented in the *Library*,
the first with a long extract relating to the wedding of False and
Mede (pp. 9–16), and two shorter passages, Gower with the short
tale of the envious man and the miser (pp. 19–22), Chaucer with
the Pardoner's Prologue in a villainous text (pp. 24–29). Lydgate
is belittled in a derogatory paragraph of introduction, and given
but eight lines of his own (p. 30). Occleve's praise of Chaucer
is given, with its phrase, "Mirror of Fructuous Entendement"

---

[7] *The Muses Library*, pp. 1–2. Chatterton, *Works* (1803), III, 271. Meyerstein,
Life of Thomas Chatterton (1930), p. 190 n., notes that Chatterton might have
found the piece in Gibson's Camden (1695), p. 344.

(p. 31), which Chatterton borrowed for the opening stanza of the *Battle of Hastings*, No. 1.[8]

Alexander Barclay, in contrast to Lydgate, gets twelve pages in the anthology, with a complimentary introduction which makes him into a much better model for Rowley than Lydgate could ever have been:

An Author [we are told] of great Eminence, and Merit; tho' not so much as mention'd in any Undertaking of this Nature before. He stiles himself Priest, and Chaplain in the *College* of St. *Mary-Otory*, in the County of *Devon*, and afterwards Monk of Ely. . . . The Reader will, no doubt, observe . . . that he greatly improves the Language. . . . And, in Elegancy of Manners, he seems to have the Advantage of all his Predecessors: as is particularly remarkable, in his Address to Sir *Gyles Alington;* his patron. (pp. 33–34)

In fact, this address has good hints for Rowley's *Epistle to Canynge*. Compare the following:

> My spirit shall reioyce to hear that, in effect,
> My workes ye shall reade, and them mende and correct.
> For, though in rude meter my matter I compile,
> Men shall counte it ornate, when ye it list to reade,
> Your tonge shall it polishe, garnishe, adorne, and file.
>
> (pp. 35–36)

> Enowe of odhers; of mieselfe to write,
> Requyrynge whatt I doe notte nowe possess,
> To you I leave the taske; I kenne your myghte
> Wyll make mie faultes, mie meynte of faultes, be less.
> Ælla wythe thys I sende, and hope that you
> Wylle from ytte cast awaie, whatte lynes maie be untrue.
>
> (*Works* [1803], II, 192–193)

Further hints for the satirical parts of the same epistle may have come from Barclay's lines on the pretender to Latin learning (p. 40). These are to be compared with Chatterton's stanza on Syr John. And Barclay's religious hypocrites sound somewhat like Canynge's audience at his Feast:

---

[8] Against the arguments of Bryant, Thomas Warton long ago pointed out that Chatterton could have seen this passage in *The Muses Library*, "a book likely to be found in a Circulating Library, and to be borrowed by a reader of old poetry." Thomas Warton, *An Enquiry into the Authenticity of the Poems attributed to Thomas Rowley* (1782), p. 110.

The maners rude, vngodly and vilayne,
And asses eares cloaked vnder coules,
Knowing nothing, contemning yet the scooles.

(p. 41)

Compare Chatterton:

The ealdermenne doe sytte arounde,
Ande snoffelle oppe the cheorte steeme.
Lyche asses wylde ynne desarte waste
Swotelye the morneynge ayre doe taste,
Syke keene theie ate . . .
Heie stylle the guestes ha ne to saie,
Butte nodde yer thankes and falle aslape.

(*Works* [1803], II, 123)

The characteristic seasonal openings of Robert Fabian ("When *Saturne*, with his cold, isye Face," etc., p. 45), of Skelton ("In *Autumpne*, when the *sunne* in *vyrgyne*," etc., p. 49), of Surrey ("The soote season that bud, and bloom fourth bringes," etc., p. 57), of John Higgins ("When Sommer sweete, with all her pleasures, past," etc., p. 142) may well have helped to teach Chatterton the trick of these natural descriptive introductions, which he so beautifully employs for his own purposes, as in the *Balade of Charitie* ("In Virgyne the sweltrie sun gan sheen," etc.). Surrey's poem, in fact, turns on the same kind of counterstroke ("And thus I see among these pleasant thynges/Eche care decayes, and yet my sorrow sprynges") as does one of Chatterton's most famous pieces, the Minstrel's song in *Ælla* ("yette, to mie wylle,/Albeytte alle ys fayre, there lackethe somethynge stylle").

There is a good deal in *The Muses Library* of that typical Tudor disillusionment with life, and praise of the middle and low estate which Chatterton for his part never learned but imaginatively adopted in the third *Eclogue* and, in general, as Rowley's personal point of view. There is a very large provision of the rhyme royal rhetoric of the *Mirror for Magistrates* (pp. 89–136, 142–156); generous selections from Harington's *Ariosto* (pp. 298–310) and Fairfax's *Tasso* (pp. 345–363) display the eight-line stanza; while Spenser's Masque of Cupid exhibits a further stanzaic development and shows the possibilities of the Alexandrine (pp. 256–264). Shorter meters are represented, in gnomic, lyric, narrative, and reflective contexts—things from Tottel, *England's Helicon*, and the songsters. Churchyard's lines "on the English Poets," Turberville's kindred piece, and Raleigh's to Spenser on the excellence of the *Faerie Queene*, may all have fused to suggest "Ladgate's" lines to Rowley on the *Songe to Ælla:*

Churchyard: . . . Among the noble *Grekes*,
                   Was *Homere* full of skill:
              And, where that *Ovid* norisht was,
                 The Soyll did florish still
              With letters hie of style:
                 But *Virgill* wan the bayes,
              And past them all for deep engyen . . . (p. 138)
              Piers plowman, was full plaine.
                 And *Chausers* spreet was great:
              Earle *Surry* had a goodly vayne,
                 Lord *Vaux* the marke did beat . . . (p. 140)

Turberville: Should others ydle bee,
                 And waste their Age in vaine,
              That myght perhaps in after Time
                 The Prick and Price attaine? . . .
              Yet one among the moe,
                 Doth beare away the Bell . . . (pp. 198–199)

Raleigh: Above the Reach of all that live,
                 or such as wrote of yore:
              And, thereby will excuse
                 and favour thy good Will:
              Whose *Virtue* cannot be exprest,
                 but by an Angels quill.
              Of me no Lines are lov'd,
                 nor Letters are of Price,
              Of all, which speake our *English* Tongue;
                 but those of thy Device. (p. 271)

Now Chatterton's mischief:

              Amongs the Greeces Homer was
                 A Poett mouche renownde,
              Amongs the Latyns Vyrgilius
                 Was beste of Poets founde . . .

              Ynne Norman tymes, Turgotus and
                 Goode Chaucer dydd excelle,
              Thenn Stowe, the Bryghtstowe Carmelyte,
                 Dydd bare awaie the belle.

Nowe Rowlie ynne these mokie dayes
   Lendes owte hys sheenynge lyghtes,
And Turgotus and Chaucer lyves
   Ynne ev'ry lyne he wrytes.

(*Works* [1803], II, 182–183)

In Elizabeth Cooper's Preface, Chatterton would have read of
Rowley's age:

Writers there were; but Tast, Judgment, and Manner were lost: Their
Works were cloudy as the Times they liv'd in, and, till *Barclay*, and
Skelton, there was scarce a Hope that Knowledge would ever favour
us with a second Dawn. (p. xi)

The volume contains Warner's "pastoral" of Argentile and
Curan, in fourteeners, with an introductory note which Percy
quotes with approving acknowledgment when reprinting the
poem in the *Reliques* (*Library*, pp. 157–168); and Chalkhill's
Anaxus and the Witch Oranda (pp. 322–331), in couplets, but
suggestive of Chatterton's *Romaunte of the Cnyghte*, which he
himself turned into couplets for Catcott's benefit. One of Fairfax's
Eclogues is given for the first time, it is said, in print (pp. 364–376).
From this, as Meyerstein notes (p. 176 n.), Chatterton may have
caught an echo for his first *Eclogue:*

Firste Roberte Neatherde hys sore boesom stroke,
Then fellen on the grounde and thus yspoke.

Compare Fairfax:

Poor Shepherd *Eglon*, full of sad Distress . . .
Crown'd with a Wreath of Heban Branches broke:
Whom good *Alexis* found, and thus bespoke.

Of these eclogues of Fairfax, Chatterton would have read in the
introductory note: "the Learning they contain, is so various, and
extensive, that, according to the Evidence of his Son . . . No Man's
Reading, beside his own, was sufficient to explain his References
effectually" (p. 363).

Harington and the poets of Tottel offer specimens of epigram,
such as Chatterton might intersperse here and there in Rowley's
prose, or like Canynge's lines on Johne a Dalbenie (II [1803], 119).
Breton's *Phillida and Corydon* is likewise included, from which
Chatterton could have caught hints for his pretty pastoral duet in

Ælla ("Tourne thee to thie Shepsterr swayne"). He would see
this again in the *Reliques*. Gascoigne's poem on the Fruits of War
(pp. 173–180) contains some heraldic rhetoric which deserves to
be quoted for the stimulus that it could provide to one of Chatterton's special interests:

> Among the Rest that Paynter had some Skil,
> Who thus in armes did once set out the same,
> A field of *Geules*, and, on a Golden-Hil,
> A stately Towne consumed all with Flame,
> On Cheafe of *Sable* (taken from the dame)
> A sucking Babe (oh) borne to byde Mischaunce!
> Begoarde with Blood, and peerced with a Launce.
>
> On high the Helme, I beare it wel in minde,
> The Wreath was Siluer poudred all with shot,
> About the which (*goutte de sang*) did twinde,
> A roll of *Sable*, black and foule beblot!
> The Crest two hands, which may not be forgot;
> For in the Right, a trenchant Blade did stand;
> And in the Left a fiery burning Brand. (p. 174)

In short, *The Muses Library* is a collection thoroughly congenial
to Rowley's temperament, to judge by his extant work. Moreover,
despite its variety of authors and meters, and the span of ages
covered by it, it makes a surprisingly unified impression as a whole.
Dates are almost never obtruded on the reader's notice; authors'
names are mentioned without emphasis, and no running heads
remind one of name or title; there is not even a table of contents
or a list of authors. Through the many epistles and mutual allusion
among the selections, a sense is created throughout of friendship
and community among the poets. That temporal distinctions have
been blurred in this way—and the bad texts of the earlier selections
contribute to the same effect—is a fact of great significance if, as
I conjecture, Chatterton came upon the book just as he was awak-
ening to the possibility of realizing the Rowley fantasies with
original work.

O! synge untoe mie roundelaie,
O! droppe the brynie teare wythe mee,
Daunce ne moe atte hallie daie,
Lycke a reynynge ryver bee;
Mie love ys dedde,
Gon to hys death-bedde,
Al under the wyllowe tree.

This setting of Chatterton's dirge, for soprano with lute accompaniment, is transcribed from a manuscript of dubious date and uncertain provenance. The lute had already grown old-fashioned in England by Chatterton's time, a fact that may have dictated its use here. It is not known that Chatterton played the lute. Musical talent, however, ran in his family (cf. the three-part composition by his father, printed in the 1803 edition of the Works and in Meyerstein's life of the poet) and he may have invented tunes for his simpler lyrics. (Cf. Thistlewaite's testimony that among other things Chatterton studied music. *Works*, 1803, III, 471.) Not much power of invention seems requisite for the present air; and the accompaniment is not beyond the reach of a novice, one would hazard. If it could be proved that Chatterton did invent the tune, or had a hand in its shaping—a hypothesis in support of which no evidence has been adduced—the piece would be useful in helping to determine how the poet himself stressed the rhythmically ambiguous opening and the teasingly subtle refrain. It is in any case an argument against the customary iambic reading of the first two lines, a practice belied by the later stanzas; and the refrain accents seem well accommodated by the melodic line as here conceived.

Samuel Johnson and James Boswell

THAT a close personal attachment could be established between two men so different as Johnson and Boswell in character and experience would hardly have been predicted. Johnson's early impressions were of poverty and insecurity; Boswell's were of social position and established comfort. Johnson knew, long before he came of age, that success in life for him would depend mainly on his own personal effort and proof of merit. Boswell had reason to expect his way to be cleared by his father's distinction and the inheritance of an estate that had been in the family for generations. Johnson had an unprepossessing and craggy appearance, a reserved and defensive and odd bearing, which fenced him like a moat. Boswell had an outgoing good humor, an eager curiosity and readiness of sympathetic address that made him welcome in nearly any company, and invited friendship from all ages, types, and occupations. Johnson thought the world a place where much was to be endured and little to be enjoyed; Boswell thought it an inexhaustible banquet of varied delights, at which the chief call upon endurance was in keeping the appetite poignant and unjaded. Johnson saw suffering as normal; Boswell saw it as mostly avoidable, given a little judgment and moderate good luck. Johnson was a stern moralist, in precept and practice, and, if forgiving to others, relentless toward himself. Boswell greatly admired moral strength but found it easier to be a man of pleasure. Johnson had a mind of extraordinary vigor, range, and logical resource, as well as a startling breadth of learning and an incomparably ready recollection. Boswell's mind was a weathercock so variable that he had to write down his impressions to convince himself of his own continuity. The staple of Boswell's journals, when they are—as is usual—concerned with his own progress, is the fascinated and indulgent register of his changes of feeling and attitude; Johnson's diaries, sparingly kept and reluctantly written, are full of self-accusation over supposed departures from a charted course or failures to make headway in it. When the two first met, Boswell was a twenty-two-year-old of no personal importance nor even (except in his own eyes) of much promise; Johnson was two and a half times his age, and famous as a poet (*The Vanity of Human Wishes*), moral essayist (the *Rambler*), biographer (*Life of Savage*), novelist (*Rasselas*), lexicographer, and personality. Yet, in spite of all this disparity, which could be illustrated without end, these men were in vital ways ideal counterparts, needing only to be brought into sympathetic contact in order to take up their complementary roles. How the event came about has been memorably recorded by Boswell in his *Life of Johnson* (16 May, 1763).

JOHNSON was born on September 18, 1709, a moment when the literary world now known as the Augustan Age was close to its zenith. The brilliant circle of Queen Anne "Wits" was just entering upon the years of its most characteristic and memorable expression. Johnson himself would one day give a masterly summing up of the achievement of these writers, from the vantage point of one who, sympathetic but unworshiping, had spent his mature working life in a London steeped in the familiar memory of their physical presence. But Johnson was not a native Londoner; he was born in the quiet cathedral town of Lichfield, a small country community where manners and society changed but slowly and where one could tell whether one's neighbor took after a maternal grandparent or a father's cross-grained uncle. Johnson's roots were in the tangled and unstirred compost of this provincial society, and he never, in spite of his love of London, where he felt "the full tide of human existence," denied his anchorage in the place of his birth. The pull of the tide is best felt by one whose anchor does not drag.

Johnson's father, Michael, was a respectable member of the Lichfield community, but his business as bookseller, while it kept him in touch with people of education, seldom put him much above the level of bare subsistence. If his stock did not move rapidly from his shelves, there was the more time for his son to satisfy a desultory but omnivorous curiosity about a wider variety of books than would ordinarily be collected in a private library. Johnson had, besides, the benefit of a reasonably good schooling in the Lichfield and Stourbridge grammar schools; and when he was by some temporary turn of good fortune enabled to enter Pembroke College, Oxford, he came there better prepared than most of his fellows to carry on the classical studies that then formed the main business of a university education. But regularity was by this time decidedly repugnant to him. He flouted the rules and neglected the college exercises; his studies were fitful and self-indulgent, and his amusements idle and troublesome to authority. *Mad, violent,* and *bitter* were the terms he later found to describe his conduct and state of mind at this time. "I was miserably poor, and I thought to fight my way by my literature and my wit; so I disregarded all power and all authority." In that era, if not in ours, a university student could go far along the road of inattention to work, and Johnson was not expelled. But, whether from despondency or from a failure of funds, he left college at the Christmas holidays of his second year and returned home in a state of utmost dejection, entirely unsettled as to his future course. Two years later, and before he had found any regular occupation, his father died, leaving him a meager portion of twenty pounds. Johnson meanwhile had been making, and continued to make, abortive efforts to get established as a schoolteacher and to secure literary work of one kind or another.

While he was still in this nadir of gloomy uncertainty, he married in the summer of 1735 a widow of forty-six with three children, aged ten, eighteen, and nineteen, and a fortune of seven or eight hundred pounds. He was twenty years her junior, nearly penniless, with no settled prospects, and in appearance (according to contemporary testimony) gaunt and rawboned to an unpleasant degree, his face scarred with scrofula that had also permanently affected his eyesight; he was given besides to convulsive twitches and oddities of gesture that made people stare. In spite of these formidable handicaps, Elizabeth Porter had had the inspired perspicacity to discern in him the "most sensible" man she had ever known; and for her, certainly, the risks were vastly greater than for him. It is not surprising that her older son, already eighteen, never forgave his mother for her folly. But at any rate, it is more than probable that by this supreme compliment of trust and belief in his human worth she saved Johnson from despair and even madness. In return, eighteen years after her death, he could confide to his private journal: "My grief for her departure is not abated; and I have less pleasure in any good that befalls me, because she does not partake it."

The years of Johnson's marriage were the most crucial years of his life. Until now, he had scarcely been able to force himself, such was his apathy and inertia, to complete the translation of a travel book to which he was committed, and which was already partly set up in print. He had as yet never made a sustained effort to finish any considerable task. He and his wife were well aware of the universal disapproval of their marriage, among their acquaintances and friends; and Johnson could see that the burden of proving its rightness rested squarely on him. We know next to nothing about the character and personality of Mrs. Johnson. But it is certain that in one way and another, with her at his side, he was gradually enabled to loosen and throw off the fetters that had immobilized his will. His sense of obligation and responsibility, his personal pride, his dignity as a man, his ambition and hope, were kindled by the challenge of her presence, her faith in his powers, her affectionate respect and her justifiable need to have her judgment vindicated, to be made proud of her choice; and these elements together combined to forge in him a determined purpose not to fail. The springs of his creative life began to unlock. One by one, in the ensuing years of marriage, most of the works that were to give him his commanding position in his age appeared or were planned and projected. There is not a particle of evidence, nor anywhere a suggestion, that his wife ever tried to obstruct or deflect a single one of Johnson's more serious purposes, however laborious or time-consuming or careless of quick returns it might be. He once in all sincerity assured his cynical young friend Beauclerk that his marriage was a love match on both sides. Clearly, it also rested on a foundation of mutual respect and understanding. Save possibly from her husband, Elizabeth Johnson has never received her due for the part she played in Johnson's achievement.

The couple's first venture was to try to establish a boarding school, at Edial near Lichfield. They rented a large, solid brick house, and Mrs. Johnson put a good deal of money into furnishing and readying it for use. By the efforts of friends, a few pupils were enrolled from the neighborhood, including David Garrick, soon to be famous, and his younger brother, but advertisement farther afield brought no result, and the total number of scholars never rose above eight. The school languished for about a year and expired.

It would be natural if the Johnsons began to grow restive under the coldly appraising eyes of their Lichfield neighbors, and to feel that less constant scrutiny would be a relief. Years later Johnson wrote that in a small country town "every human being is a spy." The couple commenced to think about the possibilities of London. Johnson had been working on a play, a classical tragedy, that he thought one of the London theater managers might be willing to produce; and in the spring of 1737 he and his pupil Garrick went up to see if they could gain a foothold and find a way of life in the city. Garrick was to study law, and Johnson would find work among the booksellers while he finished his play. Thanks largely to Edward Cave, the founder and proprietor of the *Gentleman's Magazine*, he did glimpse the possibility of a livelihood. Consequently, although the play made little progress, Johnson returned home in the summer with an optimistic report, and toward the end of the year the Johnsons packed up and moved to the decent obscurity of London.

For a long while the going was rocky indeed, but little by little Johnson began to establish himself, to get miscellaneous literary assignments with less of an effort than before, and to win time for more ambitious and independent performances. As early as the spring of 1739, his first important creative work, the poem *London*, brought him significant acclaim and went into four editions within a year. He was given the important and continuing job of writing up for the *Gentleman's Magazine* fictionalized reports—since factual reporting was then virtually illegal—of the parliamentary debates: really a major creative effort on the slenderest factual material, but read by the general public as a truthful record. The *Life of Richard Savage* (1744), the *Drury Lane Prologue* (1747), *Irene* (1749), *The Vanity of Human Wishes* (1749), the *Rambler* (1750–1752), and the Dictionary (1755) followed in due course—

the last, unhappily, appearing three years after his wife's death, to which he poignantly alluded in the immortal last sentence of his Preface. The *Idler* and *Rasselas* followed toward the end of the same decade (1758–1759), while he was engaged on his great edition of Shakespeare. The *Shakespeare* finally appeared in 1765, but meanwhile three things of greatest moment had occurred to affect the course of Johnson's history. The first was the granting of a royal pension in the spring of 1762. The second was his meeting with Boswell, on May 16, 1763. The third was his acquaintance with the Henry Thrales, in 1764 or 1765, who were to make a second home for him during most of the last twenty years of his life, and to whom he was consequently indebted for much comfort and happiness. And we may add a fourth of equal consequence to us: the establishing of the Literary Club—that brilliant constellation of talents—in 1764.

The last two decades of Johnson's life were passed in a blaze of celebrity, but his conversation, rather than any biographical events or literary publications, was the chief agent of his increasing fame. Apart from some political pamphlets, written (albeit with much hard-headed good sense) on the negative side of historical progress, his most important work thereafter was the generalized digest of his trip to the Scottish Highlands and islands with Boswell, and his Prefaces to the poets, now called *Lives*, the ripe fruit of a life spent on letters and literary values and their place in the diapason of man's experience. These were published in 1779 and 1781. Three years later he died, on December 13, 1784.

THE LAST quarter of Johnson's life was lived, we have noted, in the full glare of public attention, and also under the anatomizing lens of Boswell's probing curiosity, which has brought him closer to posterity than any other figure in literary history (save Boswell himself, as we are lately discovering).

The immediacy of Boswell's record introduces a danger not ordinarily to be reckoned with, but a danger that carries within it such opportunities of deeper insight that we willingly run the concomitant risk. There is a pitfall for the unwary in the often noticeable disparity between Johnson's writing and Boswell's record of his talk. To put the matter abruptly, Johnson often talked for immediate victory, but he almost always wrote upon oath.

There is a considered and formal finality about most of his writing that demands an answering sincerity in the reader. His talk, however, is always subject to correction by the spirit of the occasion that evoked it. He cannot, therefore, be quoted indifferently from the written or spoken record, as if both had an equal claim to be accepted as his conviction. For a hundred years, indeed, under the powerful influence of Macaulay's mischievous simplifications, readers were virtually persuaded to ignore Johnson's writing as mere hieroglyphics, and to look for the true Johnson in his conversation. There is enough truth in this position to make it a most pernicious falsehood. Johnson's published writing is, in the main, the unrefracted image of his deepest nature, and should be taken at its face value. It is true that the man Johnson is to be found equally in his talk as in his writing, and that the revelation of character and personality which abides in contradiction and overstatement, in the impulsive expression of prejudice, or thrusting for advantage at the risk of inconsistency, is more evident in Boswell's reports than anywhere else. And of course this is a precious and revealing kind of truth. But, although we recognize, when we consult our own experience, that the conversation of ourselves and our acquaintances is always a distorted and imperfect representation of the truth that is in us—something that requires always to be corrected in the light of fuller knowledge—yet we are here liable to forget this obvious fact, because so full a record as Boswell's of actual conversation, so authentic and so vivid, is unique except in fiction and drama. His record is neither of these, as we know; and reading it as history we are easily misled into granting it an authority and weight in particular utterances that the original participants would be quick to deny if they could. Boswell knew this, and continually does his best to provide the friendly correctives so necessary to a true reading. But again, a school of readers who despised him tried to trim away as much of Boswell as possible in order, as they thought, to do Johnson the service of letting him stand out clear. They were misguided; for Boswell is essential to the right interpretation of his subject. Furthermore, the better we know Boswell and the more we learn about what went into his book and how it took tangible form, the better chance we shall have of reading it with genuine comprehension. Thanks to the all but incredible recoveries, in the last forty years, of the vast bulk of Boswell's journals and collectanea (still to be edited and published in their entirety), we already know more about him and his gathering and treatment of source material than anyone but himself hitherto could have known. The fascinating tale of these recoveries, possibly the most remarkable literary news of our century, has been published in newspapers and magazines everywhere, and will be recalled by every reader. In consequence of it, Boswell has suddenly become a twentieth-century "best seller."

BOSWELL IN person is such a collection of assets and liabilities, of genius and imbecility, kindliness and malice, loyalty and betrayal, boundless vanity and abject humility, high spirits and bottomless depressions, lofty resolutions and headlong plunges, intellectual hunger and sensual debauchery, love of cloud castles and passion for factual truth, that his account is very difficult to cast up. He himself, indeed, found the prospect quite bewildering. "My life," he wrote to his friend Temple, "is one of the most romantic that I believe either you or I really know of; and yet I am a very sensible, good sort of man. What is the meaning of this?"

Boswell came of an ancient and very respectable Scottish family. He boasted that the blood of Robert the Bruce flowed in his veins. There is no reason to doubt his claim, but there might be some question whether he could carry it without spilling; the pride of it, he declared, "was his predominant passion." He was an eldest son, and heir to the estate of Auchinleck in Ayrshire. His father was a judge of the Court of Sessions, a strict and dour but humorous Presbyterian; and the regard in which he was generally held opened doors for Boswell and Johnson when they traveled in the Highlands. The father was steady and self-controlled, and found his son's mercurial temper more than he could usually bear. He was in such dread of some new folly that he bribed Boswell, upon the latter's coming of age, into signing himself into perpetual guardianship—a documentary club to bring Boswell to terms if he became too outrageous. But Lord Auchinleck was ready to be kind, even generously indulgent, if only the son would conform to his wishes—which he could never do—and live the sober, settled kind of life appropriate to a "laird." Boswell admired his father and really wished to please him, but inner compulsions were always overmastering his soberer purposes. Respect it as he might, his father's staid pattern of life was not for him; when he tried it, he sank into speechless gloom, from which he would break out into the wildest extravagance. He longed to be an army officer, for the typical peacetime reasons; but a commission required patronage as well as money; and after nearly a year of unsuccessful solicitation in London, he succumbed to his father's desire that he should go to Holland as Auchinleck himself had done, and study Roman law. After the exhilaration of London, where he had made friends with Johnson and many other notables, Utrecht bored him almost to distraction, but he tried hard to hold himself to a regular course, and for nearly a year was not altogether unsuccessful. Then, however, fortune favored him with his father's permission to depart under most lucky auspices to Berlin—in company with Lord Keith, Earl Marischal of Scotland, friend of Frederick the Great, Voltaire, and Rousseau. He was thus fairly launched upon a career of celebrity chasing. Thereafter his orbit widened; he proceeded to Switzerland, where he "collected" the two notable *philosophes* just mentioned. Then he moved south into Italy, and added the reprobate, libertine, and popular hero, John Wilkes, to his belt; he had first met him in London a year previously. Next, he doubled over to present Rousseau's introduction to the Corsican patriot, Paoli, collecting the materials for his first important literary work, *The Journal of a Tour to Corsica; and Memoirs of Pascal Paoli*, published with *An Account of Corsica*, early in 1768.

In the Preface to this work, Boswell confessed to a hunger for literary fame. The book was at once translated into several foreign tongues, and in the third English edition he was able to announce that his desire had been gratified. He became at once a notable figure, and even succeeded in rousing his countrymen to quite a pitch of enthusiasm for the Corsicans and their heroic leader. After Corsica was ceded to France in the following year and Paoli escaped to England, Paoli's London residence became Boswell's headquarters in town, and the friendship between the two was never broken.

Meanwhile, Boswell had been admitted to the Scottish bar (July 29, 1766), and began a professional practice for which he found less and less time as the years went by. Until his death on May 19, 1795, it is singular, in a life so crammed (as we now realize) with trivial incident, how few important dates occurred, apart from those associated with Johnson. On November 25, 1769, he was married to his cousin, Margaret Montgomerie. In the summer of 1773 he made the extended tour through the north of Scotland with Johnson, of which his memorable record was published late in 1785. The great *Life* was published in May 1791. There were his visits to London, to Oxford, to Ashbourne in Derbyshire to meet Johnson, and to Ireland. There were the births of his children, Veronica, Euphemia, Elizabeth, Alexander, and James. There was his father's death in 1782, and his own succession to the estate of Auchinleck; and the death of his wife, on June 4, 1789—the last a calamity in the wake of which his own life rapidly deteriorated.

THROUGHOUT all these years, however, Boswell was projecting new careers and adventures, pursuing celebrities new and old, vainly scheming to get into parliament, writing political pamphlets, throwing off articles for magazines and newspapers, and above all writing his diaries and journals. The last was felt as an absolute duty, possibly his supreme duty in life. It is hardly too much to say that his existence was one never-ending correspondence course with himself. When he awoke in the morning, he jotted down instructions and admonitions for the day's proceedings. For example, on the day when, unknown to him, he was to meet Johnson for the first time, he wrote to himself before rising:

Send breeches mend by barber's boy. You are now on good plan. Breakfast neat today, toast, rolls, and butter, easily and not too laughable. Then Love's and get money, or first finish journal. Keep plan in mind and be earnest. Keep in this fine frame, and be directed by Temple. At night see Pringle. Go to Piazza and take some negus ere you go; or go cool and take letter and bid him [i.e., Pringle] settle all, but not too fast.

And when he retired at night, it was his custom to report—if possible—to himself in writing, in similar brief fashion, what the day had brought forth, and to tell himself what he thought of his conduct in it. As, for instance:

Received a letter from Mr. Johnson treating you with esteem and kindness; nobly elated by it, and resolved to maintain the dignity of yourself.

                                        (*Private Papers*, VII.60)

Or, again,

You resolved to be yourself, to break free from slavery [to the current mistress]. What strength of mind you have had this winter, to go through so much business and at the same time have so violent a Passion! . . . You wavered and knew not how to determine. You saw yourself gone. . . . Was stunned, but resolved to be firm. To bed quite agitated.

(Private Papers, VII.114–115)

Or, once more,

You was in great vigor of genius, and in the library you dictated *Dorando*. You thought it excellent.

(Private Papers, VII.120 [4/15/1767])

These memoranda were full enough to prompt his memory and provide the basis for an informal regular journal, which he strove to keep up to date. This was written in the first, not as before, in the second, person; it was the completed report which he transmitted to himself—and, as it ultimately turned out, to posterity—of what on each day was done and said, seen and heard and felt, by him, or by others in his presence; and submitted for future examination and comparison with other scenes, past or to come. He could use it for enjoyment, or as source material for the books and essays he would write when time should serve, or as a private manual of instruction. "As a lady," he declared, "adjusts her dress before a mirror, a man adjusts his character by looking at his journal." He came to feel secretly guilty when he failed in his task of journalizing, like one who, instead of decanting and sealing up the elixir of life, betrays his essential being by pouring the precious stuff on the ground, to be forever lost.

Boswell had tentatively begun such a record of his life by the time he was eighteen, and already foresaw what a treasury of experience it could prove to him if he could keep it up. In spite of his consuming egoism and *amour-propre*, he had deep within his nature a haunting sense of his own insufficiency, a desperate need for all the props and supports he could find—for particular advice and general wisdom, for the caveats of friends who knew his besetting weaknesses and for the encouraging example of stronger characters who stood firm against the temptations that he found irresistible. One of the valuable uses of his journals was in the amassing and hoarding of intellectual and spiritual stiffening against the devil and mischance. It was in significant part for his own immediate profit that he went to the trouble of preserving the wisdom and counsel that he extracted from his elders and betters.

The lack of sympathetic rapport between Boswell and his father is an important factor in the shaping of his life and accomplishment. Had Lord Auchinleck, like the father of Charles James Fox, been able to initiate his son into the ways of the world, constituting himself the cynical but sagacious mentor and companion of youth, it is likely that Johnson would have remained to Boswell no more than a celebrated name. This was a role the father was incapable of playing: from every point of view it was unthinkable. Never did a son stand in more constant need of sympathetic and understanding guidance; never was an adolescent more susceptible to influence; never was a boy less able to emulate a father's virtues. The two natures were mutually repellent. "I write to him with warmth," Boswell pathetically complains, "but my letters shock him." But Boswell had to pattern himself on others: he was formed to follow, not to lead. He spent much of his life in pursuit of notable personalities, but he was not a toady, not a sycophant. He had to find, outside, the strength that his own nature lacked. If his father could not accept him, a substitute must somewhere be found. In the long list of his friends and companions, the men of his own age are relatively unimportant. The clergyman, Temple, who was to him like a father-confessor, to whom especially he confided his sensual lapses ("Admonish me, but forgive me"), was the only contemporary who in the long run meant much in his life. His most valued friendships were with those of his father's generation. "I really," he once wrote in his journal, "feel myself happier in the company of those of whom I stand in awe than in any other company. [Such society] composes the uneasy tumult of my spirits, and gives me the pleasure of contemplating something at least comparatively great." This attitude of mind is very forcibly illustrated in his *Tour to Corsica*, in what he has to say about Paoli:

The contemplation of such a character really existing was of more service to me than all I had been able to draw from books, from conversation, or from the exertions of my own mind. . . . It was im-

possible for me . . . to have a little opinion of human nature in him
. . . . I ventured to reason like a libertine, that I might be confirmed
in virtuous principles by so illustrious a preceptor. . . . I took leave
of Paoli with regret and agitation. . . . From having known intimately
so exalted a character, my sentiments of human nature were raised,
while, by a sort of contagion, I felt an honest ardor to distinguish
myself, and be useful, as far as my situation and abilities would allow.

When Boswell came up to London in 1762, he came as fully
determined to see Johnson as he was to visit St. Paul's or any other
public monument. He was already familiar with his writings, and
knew from the *Rambler* that here was a man from whom his own
nature could draw the sustenance for which it hungered. He had
heard from their mutual friend Thomas Sheridan, and others,
wonderful things of his talk, and he was impatient to experience
such wisdom and wit. The wit would be an additional delight and
give zest to the discourse, but it was the wisdom, and more especially the moral instruction, that Boswell most wanted.

Boswell's mode of existence from day to day, during the spring
in which he first saw his polestar, has latterly become the notorious
object of sniggering allusion, and it may at first seem paradoxical
that so libidinous a puppy should be so keen for virtue. The paradox is superficial. These are opposite but equally valid demonstrations of Boswell's radical insecurity. In both directions he is trying,
somewhat feverishly, to assure himself of his manhood, to become
a force whose positive impact on his world will be beyond dispute.
Either way he aggrandizes his stature in his own eyes. The testimony of the pulses is the easiest and most immediate kind of re-
assurance, and the level on which Boswell was willing to acquire
it proves how desperate was his need to be reassured. But, again,
he was bright enough to see that such a course in the long run
did not tend to develop the sort of character to which the world
paid tribute. He was a sensualist from weakness, not from principle: fundamentally he was religiously moral, and this was the
side of his nature that Johnson was to love and nourish. Boswell
wished above all things to acquire a character to win the respect
of those whom he himself most admired. In Johnson he very soon
discovered a talisman, from whose presence he could not but feel
that moral strength emanated. After surviving the shock of their
first meeting, which for less resilient—that is, more crystallized—
natures than his would have been the last, Boswell continued to

seek him out, and at the fourth meeting made explicit acknowledgment of his purpose:

Finding him in a placid humor, and wishing to avail myself of the
opportunity which I fortunately had of consulting a sage, to hear
whose wisdom, I conceived . . . , men filled with a noble enthusiasm for intellectual improvement would gladly have resorted from
distant lands, I opened my mind to him ingenuously, and gave him a
little sketch of my life, to which he was pleased to listen with great
attention. . . . Being at all times a curious examiner of the human
mind, and pleased with an undisguised display of what had passed in
it, he called to me with warmth, "Give me your hand; I have taken a
liking to you." [And after their subsequent conversation, which Boswell reports:] "Sir I am glad we have met. I hope we shall pass many
evenings and mornings, too, together." We finished a couple of bot-
tles of port, and sat till between one and two in the morning.

(*Life,* I.404, 410)

Not two months from that date, Johnson was traveling all the way
to Harwich to see his new young friend off to Holland. Why?
Among the motives leading to so benevolent a gesture, we may be
sure that on Johnson's part there was, as well as a spontaneous
response to good nature and to the flattery of youth's sincere deference to age, a recognition of Boswell's human need for strengthening and support, a sense that he himself had something to give
that Boswell sorely lacked. Boswell interrupts his narrative of the
interview quoted above to introduce a paragraph of more general
comment:

I appeal to every impartial reader whether this faithful detail of his
frankness, complacency, and kindness to a young man, a stranger and a
Scotchman, does not refute the unjust opinion of the harshness of his
general demeanor. His occasional reproofs of folly, impudence, or
impiety, and even the sudden sallies of his constitutional irritability
of temper, which have been preserved for the poignancy of their wit,
have produced that opinion among those who have not considered that
such instances . . . were, in fact, scattered through a long series of
years: years, in which his time was chiefly spent in instructing and
delighting mankind by his writings and conversation, in acts of piety
to God, and good will to men.

There is no reason to presume that Johnson was in the least
mistaken in his general estimate of Boswell's worth. It has been
variously suggested that their relation subsisted on a big-and-little-

brother basis; that Johnson tolerated Boswell because he fed him unbounded adulation, and Johnson could browbeat and bully him without protest; that Johnson cherished the lesser man in order to ensure that his biography should be written with a proper stock of materials and with due recording of Johnson's conversational prowess; and that Johnson kept Boswell about for a priming device, to develop the situations and ask the questions that would set him off to most effect in company. The truth is that Johnson never developed any kind of dependency on Boswell, and that Boswell's dependency on Johnson was a valid tribute which did them both honor. Boswell was no "slave" and no "idolater," as Macaulay would have him. He came—whatever Macaulay might suppose —with the laudable desire to be improved, and he venerated his mentor and frequented his society—though by no means so assiduously as is generally supposed—because Johnson seldom disappointed his hopes of improvement. Johnson, for his part, took Boswell as he found him, enjoyed his good humor, was engaged by his busy curiosity, and was moved to reminiscence, to ripe reflection, to critical comment, to witty retort, by his flow of questions and observations. Johnson responded with instinctive sympathy to his filial need, and was glad, from the almost inexhaustible stores of his own knowledge of men, his wide learning, his profound and humane wisdom, to give and go on giving so long as he was asked. He would have been grateful to anyone who would sit with him and by converse keep the black dog outside. Boswell not only performed this service but gave him the additional satisfaction of knowing that he was doing active good. Soon after their acquaintance began, Boswell wrote to another friend, "The conversation of that great and good man has formed me to manly virtue, and kindled in my mind a generous ardor which I trust shall never be extinguished." And, however he might fail in performance, the flame never did go out. Perhaps no greater service can be rendered by one human being to another than the all but involuntary service here exemplified. It was the kind of benefit so memorably praised by Thoreau, "not a partial and transitory act, but a constant superfluity," which came from Johnson like warmth from the sun. Johnson's whole life and all that he wrote were, in Heaven's eye, in the service of moral purpose; but he was not a reformer: he did not think to cure the world's stomach-ache by warning it against eating green apples. The apple, he thought, had been eaten already, and there was little enough to be done about it but endure the pain with as little whining as possible.

BOSWELL's total debt to Johnson was in the long run incalculably great. What in the eyes of posterity he might have amounted to, had they never come together, is an interesting question and one to which, even today, more than a century and a half after his death, only tentative answers can be given. So much fresh knowledge about him has come to light in our own time, and is still being disclosed, that we cannot yet assess all the evidence. It may fairly be said that a number of his important writings are still in manuscript, though we need not suppose that what is unprinted will be different in kind from what we already have, or that his personal or literary reputation will be much altered by what is yet to come. There is no doubt that the new discoveries have occurred at a historical moment more favorable to their tolerant reception than he could ever have expected. His wife, who execrated his journalizing, predicted that it would leave him "emboweled" to posterity. But the possibility did not greatly disturb him, who confessed to a strange feeling of not really wanting anything about himself to be concealed. The temper of the present age is so accustomed and friendly to the clinical revelation of intimate detail, in both historical and imaginary biography—the novel—that Boswell's frank self-disclosure is generally accepted with tolerant amusement rather than consternation or disgust. In a curious way, with the upsurge of psychological investigation and the subsiding of Christianity, the old Christian truisms about the beast in man have again become *news,* and all genuine confirmation of the animal side of human nature is welcomed with eager curiosity and even delight.

The nineteenth century, when it thought about Boswell apart from Johnson—which it seldom did—was inclined to regard him as a zany. It admired his two masterpieces, but it gave him little credit for them and was content to seek no farther. It now seems probable that the verdict of the twentieth century will do him justice as a writer. The present age is ready to acknowledge that a man who has written a work universally regarded not only as the greatest of its species, but also as possessing unique originality, must himself have had genius; and, proceeding from that assumption, it will analyze and explore the character and quality of his art. The current popular excitement about Boswell is, however, too much affected by the prevailing breezes to be acceptable as an objective judgment. The unstudied achievement of the *London Journal*, published in 1950, seems, it is true, to display an innate sense of narrative art beyond what we could have inferred from the works earlier known, but except in single episodes it is a question how much is due to artistic control and how much to favoring circumstance or to Boswell's besetting desire to live in such a way that his life would make a good story. His power of invention and his shaping hand operate on events themselves and not primarily on the literary product. His imagination and creative energy are often responsible for the living narrative that he records. But the structure of life is inevitably episodic, and Boswell seldom labored at the realization of a larger unity than life was ready to offer. The great arches of character development and fulfillment, the slow elaboration of purpose and act and result, he neither planned nor often attempted, in life or in art. He preferred the given framework of journey or biographical fact. His best achievements have a unity for which he is only indirectly responsible. The *London Journal*, the *Corsica* episode, the account of his visits to Voltaire and Rousseau, the *Tour to the Hebrides*, and the *Life of Johnson* have the kind of coherency and completeness that sufficed him: a unity comprised of chronological sequences or scenes, beginning and ending at fixed moments of historical time and connected by a personal identity.

In our present view, Boswell's miscellaneous writing—his letters, his periodical essays, his pamphlets with a political purpose, his magazine articles written to persuade or impress, his *jeux d'esprit* in verse or prose—will not in sum total set him high in the ranks of literature. His journals, *apart* from the record they contain of Johnson's conversation and deportment, will certainly give him a leading place among the diarists of all time, not so much on literary as on psychological grounds. But because they do contain the Johnson record, they possess a high degree of literary importance. They are the indispensable preliminary sketches of the most remarkable parts of Boswell's two great literary achievements.

We may say, then, that without Johnson, Boswell's literary accomplishment would have given him at best a second- or third-rate place in the annals of eighteenth-century literature. Johnson gave him the subject matter and the impulse for his two master-pieces, and without Johnson he did not—it may be unfair to say, *could* not—achieve the front rank. The effect of Johnson's per-sonality on Boswell's was galvanic. Johnson aroused Boswell to such a pitch of admiration and absorbed attention that the unusual combination of faculties composing his latent genius was rendered incandescent.

Boswell, we have said, with his adolescent capacity for hero worship, was predisposed to imitation. The need to imitate made it natural for him to project himself imaginatively into another personality and catch instinctively the tone of voice, turn of phrase, physical mannerisms, the characteristic habit and attitude of the object of his attention and admiration. This native faculty of mimicry facilitated and cooperated with a gift of memory for certain kinds of experience—a gift rare if not unique, and amount-ing almost to total recall. We can readily see how all these ele-ments of Boswell's personality would come into play in their greatest intensity in Johnson's presence, to subserve the ends of biography through conversation.

It is, then, the conversations in the *Tour* and the *Life* that give these works their unique distinction. It is because Johnson was a *great* talker that Boswell wished to preserve as much of his talk as possible, and went to the enormous, wearying effort of writing it down. And it is mainly because Johnson's conversation was so truly valuable that the books which preserve so much of it are themselves not merely interesting and curious, but great and memorable.

ALL THE characteristic features of Boswell's genius at work with spontaneous and happy art upon congenial material are displayed in possibly the most famous and brilliant scene in the *Life*, the account of Johnson's first meeting with John Wilkes at the dinner of the brothers Dilly, in May 1776. There was hardly a man of note in England whom Johnson more abominated than Wilkes. Wilkes was a notorious offender against the values Johnson most prized. He was a libertine in private life, a member of the Medmen-ham Abbey brotherhood, who turned the forms of religion into Rabelaisian license; and for his obscene verses on Woman he had been duly reprobated in the House of Lords. He was a rabble-rouser, who had done his utmost to weaken the King's authority by his cool and calculated ridicule and defiance of a House of Commons subservient to the Crown. The kind of liberty that was meant by those who cried "Wilkes and Liberty" was in Johnson's mind nothing more than license. And of such patriotism he declared that it was the last refuge of a scoundrel. He had directed his most pungent political tract, *The False Alarm*, specifically against Wilkes and his claim to be readmitted to parliament. "It will not be easily found," he had written, "why, among the innumerable wrongs of which a great part of mankind are hourly complaining, the whole care of the public should be transferred to Mr. Wilkes and the freeholders of Middlesex, who might all sink into nonexistence, without any other effect, than that there would be room made for a new rabble, and a new retailer of sedition and obscenity." Wilkes, besides, had fled the country for several years and had been outlawed for failure to reappear to answer the charges against him; had eventually surrendered and been sentenced to twelve months in jail. Persons rioting in his behalf had lost their lives.

Boswell, being familiar with the whole history of the violent and mutual hostility between Johnson and Wilkes, conceived, as he declares, an "irresistible wish" to bring them together. He opens his narrative with deliberation, conscious that it was "a very curious incident" and willing to take due credit for his part in it—which was in fact that of its only begetter. No one else would have dreamed of it, much less tried to bring it to pass. "How to manage it," he admits, "was a nice and difficult matter." He first overcomes the objections of his host, Edward Dilly, to including Johnson when Wilkes is to be among the dinner guests; he does this by offering to take full responsibility. But to persuade Johnson even to enter a room with Wilkes will, he realizes, be a feat in itself. In a sentence that reveals in successive steps, and with ironic understatement, the complexity of his own attitude toward Johnson, he confides in the reader: "Notwithstanding the high veneration which I entertained for Dr. Johnson, I was sensible that he was sometimes a little actuated by the spirit of contradiction, and by means of that I hoped I should gain my point." With perfect knowledge and practiced skill he proceeds to draw out Leviathan with an hook, and the monster is unaware that he is caught. "I therefore," says Boswell, "while we were sitting quietly by ourselves at his house in an evening, took occasion to open my plan thus: 'Mr. Dilly, sir, sends his respectful compliments to you, and would be happy if you would do him the honor to dine with him on Wednesday next along with me, as I must soon go to Scotland.' JOHNSON: 'Sir, I am obliged to Mr. Dilly. I will wait upon him—' BOSWELL: 'Provided, sir, I suppose, that the company which he is to have, is agreeable to you.' JOHNSON: 'What do you mean, sir? What do you take me for? Do you think I am so ignorant of the world, . . . that I am to prescribe to a gentleman what company he is to have at his table?'" There might be people very obnoxious at that table, hints Boswell, whipping the water into foam. "Well, sir, and what then?" Johnson exclaims, ". . . as if I could not meet any company whatever, occasionally." "Pray forgive me, sir," replies Boswell meekly, "I meant well. But you shall meet whoever comes, for me." "*Thus I secured him.*" The inimitable page that follows exhibits Boswell disposing with equal mastery of an unforeseen obstacle that arises on the very evening, half an hour before the dinner, from Johnson's forgetfully having ordered dinner at home with Mrs. Williams, Johnson's blind lodger. It is filled with vivid pictorial and dramatic detail: Boswell's consternation to find the Doctor covered with dust and "buffeting his books"; his vehement entreaties, first to Johnson, then to Mrs. Williams. "'Yes, sir,' said she, pretty peevishly, 'Dr. Johnson is to dine at home.' . . . She gradually softened to my solicitations, . . . I flew back to him, still in dust, . . . he roared, 'Frank, a clean shirt,' and was very soon dressed. When I had him fairly seated in a hackney coach with me, I exulted as much as a fortune hunter who has got an heiress into a post chaise with him to set out for Gretna Green." The sequel is in every respect worthy of this wonderful prologue, and must be read entire. The drama is superb, the persons display their essential selves, the conversation is witty, mischievously anecdotical, and classic. While Boswell keeps himself "snug and silent," watching what may ensue, Wilkes and Johnson join in good-natured fun at the expense of Boswell and the Scotch, and one of Johnson's best-known mots is elicited. (The dinner, we should recall, took place in the second year of our American Revolution.) "Amidst some patriotic groans, . . ."

writes Boswell, "somebody said, 'Poor old England is lost.'
JOHNSON: 'Sir, it is not so much to be lamented that old England
is lost, as that the Scotch have found it.'" There is nothing in the
pages of the comic dramatists, and nothing in the greatest masters
of the social novel, that surpasses this scene in conveying the
sense of living and breathing reality. And it is all true; for a
brief while, by virtue of Boswell's unparalleled talent, we are
transported through time and space and rendered actually present
in an eighteenth-century London dining-room, No. 22 the Poultry,
Wednesday, May 15, 1776. Boswell's dual accomplishment on this
occasion, as creative dramatist and ideal recorder, constitutes a
double charge on our gratitude which we can never sufficiently
acknowledge.

AND NOW, if it has become evident that Johnson was all-important in fructifying Boswell's latent genius, making possible the
full realization of his potentialities as an author, it is proper to
ask in return what Boswell did for his "venerable friend" and mentor. The first and most immediate service is inferential. Evidence
in the *Life* points to many hours of solace gained from agreeable
companionship by one who dreaded to be left alone. "When we
had left Mr. Scott's, he said, 'Will you go home with me?' 'Sir,'
said I, 'it is late; but I'll go with you for three minutes.' JOHNSON:
'Or *four*.'" (It was during this unpremeditated call that Johnson
defied Boswell to take down in shorthand a passage of prose. "It
was found that I had it very imperfectly," Boswell ruefully confesses—thereby disposing of the common misconception that he
took down the great conversations at the time. He did nothing of
the sort; *he remembered them*.) Johnson's occasional outbursts of
impatience at Boswell's perpetual questioning are often recalled
("I will not be baited with *what*, and *why*; why is a cow's tail
long? why is a fox's tail bushy?")—and recalled to the exclusion
of his expressions of pleasure in Boswell's society. But there can
be no doubt of his fondness; his letters carry—together with plenty
of admonition and reproof—abundant demonstration of his unforced love. "My dear Boswell," he ends a letter of 1777, "do
not neglect to write to me; for your kindness is one of the pleasures of my life which I should be sorry to lose." And again, "I
set a very high value upon your friendship, and count your kind-

ness as one of the chief felicities of my life." This sort of thing could be multiplied. But when he felt that Boswell was trying to tease or force such expressions out of him, he could be very forthright: "You always seem to call for tenderness. Know then, that in the first month of the present year [he is writing on January 24, 1778] I very highly esteem and very cordially love you. I hope to tell you this at the beginning of every year as long as we live; and why should we trouble ourselves to tell or hear it oftener?"

Besides the alleviation of loneliness, Johnson owed to Boswell a variety of new acquaintances and new experiences. Wilkes is a signal example of the former; and the trip to the Hebrides is the most outstanding instance of the latter. It was the greatest *adventure* of his life—and indeed to take to the road in rough and wild country, subject to every vicissitude of bad lodging, food, and transportation, sometimes on horseback and sometimes tossed about on a high sea in an open boat, is no slight undertaking for a city dweller at any age, let alone one in his sixties, lethargic from corpulence and ill health. But Johnson's intrepid spirit was evident in his having anticipated even the probability that he would be called upon to defend himself against physical attack: he had brought north with him two pistols with sufficient powder and ball. He never ceased to look back on this expedition with satisfaction keener than that aroused by any other of his journeys, whether to Wales or Paris with the Thrales, or to any of the nearer places he visited. Three years later, he could write Boswell: "The expedition to the Hebrides was the most pleasant journey that I ever made. Such an effort annually would give the world a little diversification." And again, two years before the end: "Shall we ever have another frolic like our journey to the Hebrides?" Could they have contrived the ways and means, he and Boswell would certainly have gone on other frolics; they discoursed with avidity of a trip through the Baltic to visit Catherine of Russia, and even of going to see the Great Wall of China! "He talked," writes Boswell, "with an uncommon animation of traveling into distant countries; that the mind was enlarged by it, and that an acquisition of dignity of character was derived from it."

Certain it is that without Boswell Johnson would never have been brought to make this journey to the Hebrides. And thus it came about that in addition to the pleasure of it, Johnson owed

to Boswell the inspiration for one of his most characteristic and
entertaining works, his *Journey to the Western Islands of Scotland*,
a book full of alert curiosity, of attention to natural and social
phenomena, informative and wisely reflective, and rising to the
memorable eloquence of the passage on the ancient Christian settlement of Iona.

Whatever withdraws us from the power of our senses, whatever
makes the past, the distant, or the future predominate over the present,
advances us in the dignity of thinking beings. Far from me and from
my friends be such frigid philosophy as may conduct us indifferent
and unmoved over any ground which has been dignified by wisdom,
bravery, or virtue. That man is little to be envied whose patriotism
would not gain force upon the plain of Marathon or whose piety
would not grow warmer among the ruins of Iona!

Before such dignity of utterance, Scott's famous lines, "Breathes
there a man with soul so dead," sound like the noisy declamation
of a jingo. Had Boswell been nothing more to Johnson than the
indirect instigator of this one work, he would still have been greatly
useful.

But of course he did much more: he wrote his own incomparable
account of the journey, in which Johnson himself holds the center
of attention and proves a more absorbing object of contemplation
than anything the Highlands could show. Here for the first time
the complementary talents of the two men are seen in complete
and harmonious fusion; and here for the first time emerges to
full view the three-dimensional, solid, and indestructible figure
of Johnson, taking up, at once and forever, his indisputable place
as the friend and companion of the generations to come.

BOSWELL preserves and manages to convey with incomparable
vividness the very habit of Johnson's conversation: its pursuit of
underlying principles, its characteristic thrust toward the positions
that command the area of debate, and its sinewy athletic challenge.
We can see the man matching the play of ideas with a similar
expenditure of physical force, using far more lung power than
the occasion requires, and blowing out his breath in gusts after
making a good point, like the picture of Boreas on an old map.
This violence and muscularity is central in Johnson's nature: he
was not a temperate man. He could be rigidly abstemious, as Bos-

well tells us, but not moderate. Moderation lies in an equipoise between opposite tensions: it is the classical ideal of virtue, to be so perfectly balanced that one is effortlessly at rest. Johnson, on the contrary, needed always to be proving his strength; effort and living were for him synonymous terms. "To strive with difficulties and to conquer them," he once wrote, "is the highest human felicity; the next is, to strive, and deserve to conquer; but he whose life has passed without a contest, and who can boast neither success nor merit, can survey himself only as a useless filler of existence; and if he is content with his own character, must owe his satisfaction to insensibility." This conviction, radically Christian, but also felt in the blood, that life on earth is no place for rest, that we are here to fight for the good, permeates every aspect of Johnson's being. It is this that lends a dark and terrifying weight of guilt to his paradoxically inveterate habits of indolence and procrastination, causing him to load his private meditations with an urgency of self-condemnation that to some readers is merely ludicrous. In him, sloth contained more of disease than of vice; but by temperament and conviction he found himself incapable of distinguishing in his own case. His heart and his mind were united to the end in proclaiming, "I will be conquered: I will not capitulate." Knowing the fathomless subtlety of self-love, could one ever safely feel exonerated from blame? At what point was one freed from the moral imperative of "dogged" effort?

Certainly, Johnson was most essentially himself in combat with ideas. From his earliest years he displayed an unwillingness to take things on trust, to fall into step at command. What in the young is frequently called—and no doubt often is—sheer obstinacy, may develop in the mature man, given judgment, into strength of character, a habit of resistance to adventitious pressures. Young or old, Johnson was all his life temperamentally disposed to gainsay. In his youth, he told Boswell, he always chose the wrong side of a debate. And in later years, well knowing how interwoven are truth and falsehood, he would allow himself, in the heat of contest, to try how much of lesser or immediate truth could be found in the opposite camp. "A man," he once wrote, "heated in talk, and eager of victory, takes advantage of the mistakes or ignorance of his adversary, lays hold of concessions to which he knows he has no right, and urges proofs likely to prevail on his opponent, though he knows himself that they have no force." Once, hearing that a man with whom he had carried on a long argument had afterwards expressed elsewhere his thankfulness because Johnson had convinced him "that an opinion which he had embraced as a settled truth was no better than a vulgar error: 'Nay,' said Johnson, 'do not let him be thankful, for he was right, and I was wrong.'"

This negative habit was strikingly evident in a trick he had of commencing or summarizing a position with "No," before any of his hearers had signified an intention to contradict. "No, sir, he was irresistible." It was as if he were merely opening the door on a debate that had already been proceeding in the closed chamber of his own thoughts. And, indeed, conversation was for him but the audible part of a perpetual discussion, the ultimate goal of which was the discovery and defense of truth, not by guess, not by instinct, intuition, nor even by revelation (unless all else failed), but by rational means. Essentially, Johnson was dedicated to reclaiming as much as possible of human life from the rush-lights and snares of irrationality and the "dangerous prevalence of imagination." In this incessant dialogue, he was, ideally, the devoted antagonist of falsehood and obfuscation. He feared the enemy, because he saw that the possibility of defeat was always imminent, from within or from without, whether from man's natural though corrupt love of the lie, as Bacon said, or from mere human liability to error. Therefore he entered every contest with a determination to win. At times, when he felt himself hard pressed, he was blustering and overbearing and willing to settle for the shadow, not the substance, of victory. Not to give ground in battle was essential. At the worst, to be exercising the mental faculties in a rational, discursive way was preferable to any sort of capitulation. On a wider ground, surrender in solitude to reverie, to uncontrolled imagination, to the "chasing of airy good," was abjectly to give away advantage. Johnson hated to be alone with his thoughts because the surrender to vacancy was then so much harder to resist. He dreaded the mild insanity of sleepless nights; they were a frightening reminder of how thin was the partition between the rational and irrational. So he clung to his companions far into the small hours, in the hope of wearying himself into slumber when retirement could no longer be postponed.

The aggressive habit of his mind continued to the very end of his life. It is indicative that his last work, the *Lives of the Poets,* is his most unconstrained, most athletic and vigorous, most various and self-assured expression of his views on literature and the literary life. Not for nothing had he spent a great part of the last quarter-century in conversational debate, constantly exercising his intellectual muscle in that arena of impromptu challenge and defense against all comers. However it might be with the heavy body, there was evident no lethargy of the mind.

Nor was there any wavering or unsteadiness in his estimates of the great figures on whom he pronounces. It is very striking how he refuses to be seduced by his own enthusiasms or prejudices. Shakespeare, Dryden, and Pope were probably his best-loved authors. Yet, although he praises them all magnificently, his praise always discriminates: he tells where their special excellences lie, and, without abating any of the force of his admiration, turns his level judgment on their weaknesses, whether of character or of achievement, in order to reach a verdict that shall be dispassionate and just. His discussion of Shakespeare's and Dryden's faults of neglect or carelessness, and of Pope's affectation and self-deception in life as in letters, is a model for all hero-worshiping critics, showing the true height of praise that can offset shortcomings so considerable and so clearly discerned. And on the contrary, in the face of his antipathy to Milton the man and the republican, his noble, whole-hearted tribute to Milton's towering grandeur is unshaded by the least hint of grudging reservation or disparagement. His judgment and his magnanimity are perfectly matched, and there is no trace of meanness anywhere, either in blame or praise. The critic himself is great, and without awe or false humility or pride salutes the greatness of the poet.

It has been customary to regard Johnson as the epitome of conservatism, as the last of the great Augustans, or rather, as a belated Augustan, the final bulwark to be borne down by the flood of the new Romanticism. Conservative he doubtless was, in politics, in religion, in literature, in precept, and, at least by intention, in practice. But we must be careful not to take his conservatism too simply, as a mere desire to preserve the *status quo,* a dislike of change. Principles apart, a temperament so dynamic as Johnson's could not be apathetic. His nature was passionate, and he held his principles passionately. "Everything about his character and manners," wrote Boswell, "was forcible and violent." When we call him conservative, we must think of a strenuous conservatism. But conservatism, of course, like any other attitude, becomes strenuous not while it is dominant and taken for granted but when it is confronting serious challenge. Johnson's age, however tamely some observers would picture it, was only superficially stable. The generally placid surface which we see from afar belies the truth that the actual state of affairs is just simmering to a boil. Everywhere accepted values were being undermined; the common core of agreement was dissolving. On the Continent the ferment of ideas was leading directly to the French Revolution. In England the Industrial Revolution had already begun, and the whole social pattern was being more and more rapidly altered by its impact. Around these great cycles of change were revolving many epicycles, religious, artistic, and literary. The forces at work were far too powerful to be successfully opposed; and, as always, the battle line was not clearly drawn on any wide front. Things gave way piecemeal, here and there, and bit by bit; and most of Johnson's generation display traits both new and old, both forward-looking and retrospective. The past itself becomes an avenue to the future: to cast an eye down its long vistas is to be lured away from the familiar present.

Johnson himself exhibits some of the complexities of his day. Anticlassical by temperament, he declared that there was always open an appeal from critical theory to nature, which in his case meant that he refused ultimately to be bound by any formal rule. For him there is only one final authority, and that is not literary, it is divine. Nevertheless, on a lower level he took his stand, by and large, in opposition to the powerfully disintegrating tendencies of his day. And since these tendencies have not even yet spent themselves, but bear us forward upon the same current, he seems perhaps to speak to us over a great distance. It requires of us some effort of will and sympathetic imagination to recover his critical position.

THE BASIS of it, clearly, is religious. It rests squarely upon the radically democratic assumption, uncongenial to the prepossessions of our time, that we are all moral beings with a common stake in the working out on earth of our personal salvation. Democratic, because under the infinite overarching heaven our differences, comparatively, are insignificant. Democratic, because we all face the same impartial, inescapable examination:

> *There* is no shuffling; there the action lies
> In his true nature, and we ourselves compelled,
> Even to the teeth and forehead of our faults,
> To give in evidence.

In this view, the grounds of agreement are compelling and far-reaching. The human predicament remains fundamentally the same in all times and places. Man's nature has not been, in the measurable past, and in the measurable future is unlikely to be, significantly modified by either science or philosophy.

Some truths, Johnson believed, are too important to be new. The most important truths have been known for a very long time. They require always to be restated. And because, as he says, of themselves "they raise no unaccustomed emotion in the mind," one of the paramount uses of literature is to restate them in fresh and varied ways, so that they may be vividly and meaningfully re-experienced. "Men more frequently require to be reminded than informed." The literary ideal, therefore, would be to convey the most important sentiments in the most effective manner to the widest possible audience. The pleasure of novelty, absent from the great and familiar verities, is restored to them by the felicity, or convincing power, with which they are presented—"what oft was thought, but ne'er so well expressed." It is this power for which Johnson especially admired Milton: his ability to give a different appearance to known truths, "with pregnancy and vigor of mind peculiar to himself. Whoever considers the few radical positions which the Scriptures afforded him will wonder by what energetic operation he expanded them to such extent and ramified them to so much variety."

The same ideal makes it natural to set a high value on generalization, the depersonalizing of experience, the distilling of particular instances into a statement comprehending the class as a whole. Johnson and his older contemporaries responded with a keen delight to "the grandeur of generality"—an emotion peculiarly antipathetic or, rather, all but unknown, to the modern sensibility.

Yet, upon occasion, Johnson himself manages to combine generality with intensely personal statement, in an amalgam of which he alone had the secret, and which carries a lofty dignity about it that defies familiar approach, as if he were in intimate converse with the Spirit of History. The Preface to the Dictionary contains striking examples of such writing. Thus:

But these [i.e., his first ideal intentions] were the dreams of a poet doomed at last to wake a lexicographer. I soon found that it is too late to look for instruments, when the work calls for execution, and that whatever abilities I had brought to my task, with those I must finally perform it. To deliberate whenever I doubted, to inquire whenever I was ignorant, would have protracted the undertaking without end and, perhaps, without much improvement; for I did not find by my first experiments, that what I had not of my own was easily to be obtained; I saw that one inquiry only gave occasion to another, that book referred to book, that to search was not always to find, and to find was not always to be informed; and that thus to pursue perfection was, like the first inhabitants of Arcadia, to chase the sun, which, when they had reached the hill where he seemed to rest, was still beheld at the same distance from them.

I then contracted my design, determining to confide in myself, and no longer to solicit auxiliaries which produced more encumbrance than assistance; by this I obtained at least one advantage, that I set limits to my work, which would in time be ended, though not completed.

Characteristically, Johnson aimed at generalized statement in his writing, and approved, in his critical comment on the work of others, that which was inattentive to the disguises of local customs and manners, and particular instances. "Great thoughts," he declares, "are always general, and consist in positions not limited by exceptions, and in descriptions not descending to minuteness." And in obedience to this prescription, he will describe the downfall of a beautiful girl in the abstract manner that follows:

> What care, what rules your heedless charms shall save,
> Each nymph your rival, and each youth your slave?
> Against your fame with fondness hate combines,
> The rival batters, and the lover mines.
> With distant voice neglected Virtue calls,
> Less heard and less, the faint remonstrance falls. . . .

In crowd at once, where none the pass defend,
The harmless Freedom, and the private Friend. . . .
Now beauty falls betrayed, despised, distressed,
And hissing Infamy proclaims the rest.

Johnson's ideal had already begun to be displaced in his own lifetime by a greater liking for the individual instance, picturesquely or vividly described; by an increasing distrust of the grand generalization, consequent upon the weakening of religious conviction and the fragmentation of agreement as to the purpose and destiny of man. Sensibility was increasingly cultivated as a virtue in and of itself; and the verbal celebration of fine feeling was audible between inarticulate sobs and floods of tears. Self-consciousness and egocentricity became more and more the order of the day, and feelings came to be prized rather for their claims to the distinction of rarity than for their purchase on another heart.

To an age prone to believe that salvation lies in the perfection of a "space ship," and that human perfectibility proceeds in a one-to-one ratio with the multiplication of "gadgets" that increase a man's accessibility to conflicting claims on his attention, Johnson offers a loud and tonic, "Why, no, sir!" If we will consent to listen to him, he will offer us, instead of panaceas applied from without, a variety of arguments and his personal example to convince us that we might profit by self-scrutiny. He will assure us that luck is not the measure of success, and that if success comes without being paid for in advance by unremitting effort, we shall either lose it, or be destroyed by it, or earn the right to keep it by paying off the debt. He will urge us to clear our minds of cant. He will warn us that we cannot ultimately evade the responsibility for our own acts and will enjoin us therefore to give the best that is in us. He will teach us that the cost of such a discharge of responsibility is nothing less than all we have, that the battle is incessant, and that our effort is of supreme importance. He will show us the sense of self-fulfillment and exhilaration that comes of acquitting oneself as best one can in the never-ending combat for the true and the good. "The certainty," he will tell us, "that life cannot be long, and the probability that it will be much shorter than nature allows, ought to awaken every man to the active prosecution of whatever he is desirous to perform. It is true that no diligence can ascertain success; death may intercept the swiftest career; but he who is cut off in the execution of an honest undertaking, has at least the honor of falling in his rank, and has fought the battle, though he missed the victory." Johnson, in a word, can add a cubit to our human stature, and make us proud that we belong to the same order of being.

Johnson's Shakespeare

WHEN Johnson undertook to make an English dictionary, he had already fixed upon one of the chief instruments by means of which he would prosecute his design. This was Shakespeare, from whose use of the language—a use neither erudite nor special nor obsequious to social prejudice high or low—the enduring diction of the common intercourse of life could in Johnson's judgement be amply illustrated. He had been reading Shakespeare since his earliest years and had of late returned to him with the critical eye of an intending editor. He had surveyed Shakespeare's range of vocabulary and of ideas; he had estimated the kinds and the causes of obscurity in his work and had calculated the most promising ways of elucidating his text and his meaning. Johnson's *Miscellaneous Observations on the Tragedy of Macbeth*, put forth in 1745 in the wake of Sir Thomas Hanmer's sumptuous edition printed at Oxford, is a doctoral demonstration of the right use of an editor's skills: clarification of obscurities in the text; historical illustration; emendation of corrupt readings. The deadly page or so in which by way of conclusion Johnson urbanely, almost casually, puts his critical finger on the weaknesses of Hanmer's edition, while at the same time impudently confessing that he has read no more of it than this single play, confirms our impression of latent power. His words fall unerringly from the top of Olympus:

surely the weapons of criticism ought not to be blunted against an editor, who can imagine that he is restoring poetry, while he is amusing himself with alterations like these. . . . Such harmless industry may, surely, be forgiven, if it cannot be praised. . . . There is no distinction made between the antient reading, and the innovations of the editor; there is no reason given for any of the alterations which are made; the emendations of former cricks are adopted without any acknowledgment, and few of the difficulties are removed which have hitherto embarrassed the readers of Shakespeare.

By this masterly exercise, Johnson invited attention to his own pretensions, and he appended to the pamphlet specific proposals for a ten-volume edition in a small format, with two specimen pages containing Macbeth's soliloquy, "To be thus is nothing, But to be safely thus," etc.

Tonson's threat of a suit against Johnson's printer-to-be, Edward Cave, was enough to stifle further proceeding in the edition proposed. Disappointed in his immediate purpose, Johnson turned his concern with Shakespeare to present account by going through the plays and collecting on index slips thousands of passages illustrative of Shakespeare's use of specific words. When sorted alphabetically and disposed, as subsequently they would be, according to gradations in the sense, these verbal citations amounted to a relatively complete Shakespeare Glossary. Besides their forthcoming employment in the *Dictionary*, where they were to become the backbone of illustrative usage, they made Johnson the unproclaimed but greatest living authority on Shakespeare's diction. They also provided him with an invaluable and ready tool for explication whenever it should prove possible to resume the reluctantly abandoned editorial project. They included an ampler body of Shakespearian quotation than is finally found in the *Dictionary* and for reasons of common sense ought to have been —and presumably were—preserved against need.

In short, it is sufficiently obvious that, long before Johnson began regular work on his edition of Shakespeare, he had in fact already completed a very important and onerous part of such an editor's business. One may assert that the *Dictionary*, among its many treasures, contains in a diffused and unheralded state its author's first major work of Shakespearian scholarship. Consciousness of this achievement enabled him to turn readily and with self-confidence to the preparation of the edition, when finally the *Dictionary* was off his hands.

In the intervening decade, his interest had not slept. During these years, thanks to Garrick's expanding prestige and in particular to his good offices on behalf of *Irene*, Johnson's connection with the London stage became very close. His acquaintance with Green Room society was current and undeniably fascinating to him, and theatrical questions were of course habitual topics of his conversation. His mind being so constituted as to press always toward principles and general truths, dramatic theory in one aspect or another was inevitably much in his thoughts. Some of that thinking, as Professor Sherbo has pointed out, is reflected in the miscellaneous writing of the *Dictionary* years.[1] Everyone knows the Prologue for Garrick's opening of Drury Lane in 1747: a thumbnail sketch of the course of English drama, beginning with "immortal Shakespeare." There is also a good deal of related, scattered, periodical writing. Various essays appear in the *Rambler* and the *Adventurer* on the drama and the drama's rules, on kinds of plays, their properties and their effects. Johnson's obiter dicta on these subjects often foreshadow, now faintly, now very distinctly, positions which he would assert with finality in the next decade.

Charlotte Lennox's collection of the novels and histories on which Shakespeare founded his plays was perhaps prompted, and certainly encouraged, by Johnson. It supplied him with a welcome occasion to expatiate upon the poet while at the same time doing a signal service to a friend. The work, *Shakespear Illustrated*, was published in three volumes in 1753 and 1754. To recommend it, Johnson wrote, over Mrs. Lennox's signature, a beautifully turned Dedication to the Earl of Orrery. In this, he declared that little of Shakespeare's genius is to be discovered in his plots, and proceeded with a lofty tribute to that skill in characterization wherein the poet is supreme, recapitulating the praise of Dryden and Pope, reducing to prose the hyperbole of his own Prologue, and anticipating the noble phrases on Shakespeare's truth to nature that were to constitute the most memorable paragraphs in the Preface of 1765. "His chief skill," Johnson writes in Mrs. Lennox's name, "was in human actions, passions, and habits, . . . his works may be considered as a map of life . . . and he that has read Shakespeare with attention, will perhaps find little new in the crouded world. . . . His heroes are men . . . and his reputation is therefore safe, till human nature shall be changed."

[1] Arthur Sherbo, *Samuel Johnson, Editor of Shakespeare* (1956), ch. 1.

The most substantial testimony, however, to Johnson's lively and continuing concern is to be found in his *Proposals* for a new edition of the plays. The *Proposals* were published on June 8, 1756. It will be worth an effort to try to fix the calendar of significant dates for this edition as precisely as we can, for Boswell's paragraph about Johnson's "indolence" in its pursuit has colored most of what is generally circulated about the matter. Most of the contemporary allusions have been conveniently gathered by Professor Sherbo,[2] and these can be further sifted as evidence of progress.

We know that Johnson agreed to prepare the eight-volume work for publication within eighteen months. The terms of his contract stipulate that "the work shall be published on or before Christmas 1757," and the agreement was signed on June 2, 1756. In fact, he was engaging to proceed at an average rate of two months per volume, allowing an extension of two months for final corrections, for writing a preface, and for enfolding stray notes and latecomers in an appendix, if that should be required. It is at present a current fashion of literary scholars—for today we are all Shakespearians— to edit one or another of the plays for a pocket series, one play to a volume, with individual introduction and notes. It may be doubted that a single such editor, with all modern mechanical advantages, has responsibly engaged to deliver one play in the time within which Johnson undertook to deliver five; and it is not easy for us to credit that he was serious in this commitment. But he was a practical man in business calculations; if he did not think it extravagant to enter upon such a task with these conditions, it could only be because he believed that he had already performed the essential preparatory work.

The *Proposals* amply demonstrate that he had an enlightened notion of what was entailed and likewise just views of his own qualifications. To explain by the light of historical knowledge; to rely upon the earliest texts and to produce collateral readings; to restrain conjecture: these are the sound principles which he announces. Nowhere does he speak with greater personal assurance than when he declares: "With regard to obsolete or peculiar diction, the editor may perhaps claim some degree of confidence, having had more motives to consider the whole extent of our

[2] *Ibid.*, pp. 8–10. See also *Life*, I.496 n. 3.

language than any other man from its first formation." Boswell, with the skepticism of hindsight, but also tacitly acknowledging the arrogance of Johnson's confident expectation, says that in the *Proposals* "he shewed that he perfectly well knew what a variety of research such an undertaking required." [3] We too must believe that he understood the extent and difficulty of what he had promised. "No other authour," wrote Johnson of his poet,

ever gave up his works to fortune and time with so little care: no books could be left in hands so likely to injure them, as plays frequently acted, yet continued in manuscript: no other transcribers were likely to be so little qualified for their task as those who copied for the stage, at a time when the lower ranks of the people were universally illiterate. . . .

His edition, Johnson must have believed, would rest on a solid foundation of work already behind him, and accordingly the timetable could be fast. As we read the scanty evidence, there seems little doubt that he made a remarkable and strenuous effort to meet his commitment, and that in fact he all but succeeded. In reading the signs, we must take much more seriously his own words than what others said or guessed about his rate of advance. At the start, he could not wait for the collection of further variant readings from earlier editions not yet seen. These, he doubtless hoped and expected, would offer themselves as he proceeded, assisted by copies lent from public and private libraries and by friendly informants; better readings would be easier to introduce on the proof-pages than would augmented annotation. For the present need, his text, tentatively regulated, could be set up from any convenient predecessor and further corrected when better lights should be afforded. He was already thoroughly familiar with Warburton's edition of 1747, the volumes of which he had heavily annotated; and he may at first have chosen to set his text from this one. But when subsequently a new edition of Theobald's Shakespeare came to hand, he adopted it for many of the plays. He had promised in any case to take in the valuable notes of earlier editors. But his own annotation necessitated reprinting so much of Warburton's commentary that neither he nor his compositor could

[3] *Life,* I.319.

dispense with the edition of 1747. Textually, the choice between Theobald and Warburton at this point was immaterial, both texts being based on Theobald's earlier edition of 1740 and therefore often alike.[4]

We conceive, then, that Johnson took a play as printed by Theobald or Warburton or both and worked through it again with an eye to obvious stumbling blocks, collating, where difficulties appeared, primarily with the First Folio and such quartos as were within reach; altering textual minutiae as he saw fit, mainly by the light of common—or rather, Johnsonian—sense; chiefly careful to explain obscure words or verbal uses and not passing over difficulties of interpretation without attempting to clarify them by notes of his own or of former editors. As he proceeded, he tagged the text and tallied his comments with numbers from 1 to 9 successively repeated to the play's end and thus readied his mixed copy for the printer, allowing for necessary improvements in the revises. Should none appear, he knew that as it stood his new edition would be an advance in accuracy and in clarification of Shakespeare's meaning over Warburton, Hanmer, Theobald, Pope, and Rowe.

His progress was such that inside of a year the plays, one by one, were being set in type. On June 21, 1757 he wrote to Thomas Warton, "I am printing my new edition of Shakespeare." [5] Whether the order of plays was fixed at the beginning we do not know. It is, however, unlikely that he tackled them in the order in which they finally appeared. As we do know, years earlier he had editorially examined and annotated *Macbeth* for the *Miscellaneous Observations* of 1745, and he may already have been working on the projected edition before it was blocked.[6] Indeed, the very choice of a particular play for a specimen would suggest as much. But, as anyone would be likely to do, he now probably followed his inclination and convenience and took up the plays in no preconceived order, perhaps more than one at a time. When

[4] See A. M. Eastman, "The Texts from which Johnson Printed his *Shakespeare*," *JEGP*, XLIX (1950), 182–191; A. Cuming, "A Copy of Shakespeare's Works which Formerly Belonged to Dr. Johnson," *RES*, III (1927), 208–212; G. B. Evans, "The Text of Johnson's *Shakespeare* (1765)," *PQ*, XXVIII (1949), 425–428.

[5] *Life*, I.322.

[6] Professor Sherbo calls attention to a score of notes, scattered among all volumes of the 1765 edition, that seem to bear hints of editorial work undertaken previous to 1745. See *Shakespeare Quarterly*, IX (Autumn 1958), 426–428.

he was satisfied that in a given play there was little more for him to explain, he would ask the printer for proofs. For an exactly contemporary parallel the procedure of Edward Capell may be cited. Capell's edition of Shakespeare was published in 1767, and in his preliminaries he refuses to animadvert on Johnson's edition because, he declares, his own "was finish'd, within a play or two, and printed too in great part, before that appear'd: the first sheet of this work (being the first of volume 2) went to the press in September 1760: and this volume was follow'd by volumes 8, 4, 9, 1, 6, and 7; the last of which was printed off in August 1765" [7]

By whatever method he proceeded, Johnson had done enough so that when the contract date approached, he could write without qualification to Burney, on December 24, 1757, "I shall publish about March." [8] He knew that he must allow time for writing a preface, and he probably already anticipated adding an appendix of additional notes. But he could not have written with such assurance without having calculated how long it would take him to complete the edition at the rate he was going. In the same letter, he purposes to send for Burney's use more copies of his *Proposals* and extra receipt forms for the use of subscribers.

Percy had visited Johnson in London a month or so earlier than the date of this letter and had received from him the same confident assurance that he expected to publish before Easter. Percy reported this, hinting simultaneously his own private doubts, in a letter to Shenstone of November 24, 1757.[9] But Johnson alone knew what was done and what remained to be done, and on March 8, 1758 he wrote again to Burney, presumably forgetting the single sentence dropped casually and without circumstance in his previous letter about his expectations. He now expresses himself more fully on the subject, acknowledging the receipt of Burney's draft for subscriptions collected and enclosing more receipt forms and additional copies of the *Proposals*. "I am ashamed," he writes, "to tell you that my Shakspeare will not be out so soon as I promised my subscribers; but I did not promise them more than I promised myself. It will, however, be published before summer." [10] If "be-

[7] Edward Capell, *Shakespeare* (1767), I.18–19 n.
[8] *Life*, I.323.
[9] Hans Hecht, *Thomas Percy und William Shenstone* (1909), p. 4.
[10] *Life*, I.327.

fore summer" means by the beginning of summer—that is, according to Johnson's *Dictionary* definition, by June 21—this confident statement signifies that Johnson believed that the next two and one-half months were enough to enable him to write his preface and tend to anything else that still remained undone. It must mean also that by this time he had corrected page proof—necessarily including footnotes—of the bulk of the plays, and that what was left to do was mainly the printer's job. In connection with the *Proposals*, he adds that they, "I think, do not profess more than I have hitherto performed. I have printed many of the plays, and have hitherto left very few passages unexplained."

At this point, Johnson seems to have been so confident of his imminent freedom that he did not hesitate to launch a new venture, the *Idler*, to begin on April 15, 1758. But perhaps there was a deeper reason. Be that as it may, on April 14, the day before the first number appeared, he writes to Warton to ask for more notes and to thank him for those already received, declaring that "a commentary must arise from the fortuitous discoveries of many men in devious walks of literature. Some of your remarks are on plays already printed: but I purpose to add an appendix of notes, so that nothing comes too late." [11] From this it is certain that the printing had proceeded so far that nothing more could be added for many plays at the due place in the text; but, equally, that this is not true of all. It is also clear that the Appendix is the tool on which Johnson is relying to make good any omissions. On June 1, 1758, he again begs more notes from Warton and writes that Langton is coming to Oxford and "brings some of my plays with him, which he has my permission to shew you." [12]

It is noticeable that Johnson nowhere speaks or writes of *volumes* but only of plays. This is a natural form of reference, if he was proceeding as we have been supposing. But a moment's attention is due to Percy and Burney, both of whom speak of volumes. When Percy writes to Shenstone on November 24, 1757 and again on January 9, 1758, he refers to volumes, but in a self-contradictory way. In the earlier letter he believes that Johnson is not finished with the *second* volume, and in the later, apparently alluding to the same visit, he recalls that Johnson was on the *third*

[11] *Ibid.*, pp. 335 f.
[12] *Ibid.*, pp. 336 f.

volume when he (Percy) was in London. It is not surprising, if plays were what Percy saw, not volumes, that he was confused as to how far along in terms of volumes Johnson actually was. Another explicit reference to volumes comes immediately after the March 8th letter to Burney in the memorandum by Burney of a visit to Gough Square, in Boswell's *Life*.[13] It is here to be duly noted that the date of the visit is undetermined. Burney has written up an amusing anecdote for Boswell's book, quite certainly at a distance of many years—perhaps as much as a quarter of a century after the event described and therefore after Burney had become possessed of his own set of the edition. Under these circumstances, it would be natural for him to have resorted to the published work in order to prompt his memory. He writes that he recalls Johnson's showing him "some volumes of his Shakspeare already printed" and remembers "opening the first volume, at the Merchant of Venice." We need not take the reminiscence *au pied de la lettre*. As late as the spring of 1765 (May 18), Johnson could still offer to show Garrick "such plays as you would see, and they shall be sent." [14] The plays, when Burney saw them, need not have been in the form of volumes. There would be good reason for Johnson to keep them loose until he thought publication was near, but he evidently did now think it was near. A great part but not all had been completed.

Now, however, comes a blank in the record for a full year. On June 26, 1759, the booksellers paid Strahan £150.[15] The round sum suggests that though this payment was substantial, it was only on account and not a full settlement for what had been done to date. We lack a dependable date until December 18, 1761, at which time Strahan received another payment of £119.12.6. In that month, also, his ledger contains his reckoning for printing volumes I–VI, namely 207 sheets at £1.4.0 per sheet, 1000 copies of each, together with costs of £17.9.0 on the same date for extra corrections and alterations on the same. The daily accounts are not

[13] *Ibid.*, pp. 328 ff.
[14] *Letters*, 168.
[15] I owe this and subsequent particulars from Strahan's ledgers to my colleague, Professor Robert D. Harlan, who has studied and transcribed the originals (British Museum, Add. MS. 48802A). His knowledge and liberal counsel have been of great value. Professor Allen T. Hazen's experienced aid, too, has helped to improve my exposition of the bibliographical evidence.

known to have survived nor is the cost of paper included. Paper
the booksellers may have supplied. Whatever the date when Johnson had finished work on the six volumes, there is no reason to
doubt that Strahan had printed off the corrected sheets of all six
before the date when this portion of the edition is entered on the
ledgers.

Besides the evidence already adduced from Johnson's correspondence in 1758, suggesting that by then he was far advanced
toward completion, a previously unnoticed fact tends to confirm
the probability. Although, as the Appendix in the final volume
would show, he had amassed abundant additional notes for all the
plays, he had already introduced a great many by means of
asterisks and obelisks upon the pages where they belonged, interspersing them between the notes numbered numerically. Such a
procedure was not indefinitely expansible: to extend it much
further would have meant drastic reconstituting of the pages. But
it is a natural inference that had the printing not already gone far,
such a bulk of irregular additions would not have been introduced
at all in this fashion. On a careful, if not perfect, count, the figures
for these interpolated notes, by volumes, are as follows: in I, 82
additions; II, 105; III, 39; IV, 132; V, 101; VI, 93. He was still to add
in the Appendix for I, 44; II, 58; III, 36; IV, 32; V, 19; VI, 32. On the
other hand, a noteworthy contrast appears in the last two volumes
of the edition. These volumes, moreover, are separately accounted
for in Strahan's ledgers of October 1765. Here, almost none of
such interpolated additional notes occur: the figures run, for volume VII, only 7; for volume VIII, 11. Yet the tally of additions in
the Appendix is hardly affected thereby: for volume VII, there are
12; for VIII, 45.

Reflecting upon Johnson's confident forecast of 1757–1758, we
cannot suppose that by April 1758 he had done no work on the
plays of the last two volumes. We may infer that they were less
advanced than the rest, and so remained until the others had been
printed off in sheets, certainly not later than the autumn of 1761.
It may be assumed that they were held back for that reason and
not sent to the printer until 1763 or 1764, giving him time to
include the notes he then had in hand in a regular series without
supernumerary interruptions. The additional notes that came in
after the proofs had been returned were presumably sufficient

in number to be roughly commensurate with those forming the Appendix of notes to the six volumes printed long before. In the absence of more factual evidence, we must be content with less than certainty.[16]

Further information on the stages of Johnson's progress is scarce and indecisive. After his positive declaration to Burney in March 1758 that he would publish "before summer," he seems to have made no more predictions. He worked on the unfinished volumes at Twickenham, at Joshua Reynolds's house, in the late weeks of 1763. In the summer of 1764 he stayed with Percy at Easton Mauduit, correcting proofs of *Othello*, the play that stands last in the edition. He continued work until September 1765, writing the Preface in the summer of that year. The edition was at last published on October 10. The size of it was 1000 copies, of which, we have seen, the first six volumes had been in sheets at latest since the end of 1761. The September entry in Strahan's ledger is, for volumes VII and VIII, 79½ sheets at £1.4.0 per sheet, and for extra corrections, alterations, and appendix to these, £19.5.0. There followed immediately a reprinting by Strahan of these two volumes, with five half-sheets recomposed and 3½ sheets added, in the amount of 750 copies. (The other six volumes were simultaneously reprinted by other printers, in the same quantity.) The booksellers made a payment in the following January to Strahan of £114.13.0. He reckoned the sum of their three payments at £384.5.6.

The long delay from the spring of 1758 until autumn of 1765 in the wake of the brave initial achievement has not been explained. Obviously, it could not have arisen from prolonged effort to improve what had already been done on the edition. It is more likely that, having failed to meet his deadline and having overrun it by half a year, Johnson lost his incentive to finish at top speed. He had nearly reached the limit of his main drive, which was explication. No discernible crisis occurred in his life at this moment and, had he proceeded with the same momentum as before, he would certainly have dispatched the work before his mother's death (January 1759), an event which deflected the current of

---

[16] The evidence adduced of inking set-offs in the final signatures of volumes III, VI, and VII may tell us something of printing-house economies but has no bearing on Johnson's progress as editor.

his thought and afflicted him with grief. The likeliest explanation —since guess we must—of his abrupt loss of pace is his unwelcome realization, now that he was about to be released from the congenial task of clarifying the sense, that possibly on the historically illustrative side, and most certainly on the textual, his edition would bear a great deal more work and was far from meeting his own standards. So long as he had had other editorial duties to perform, he could defer this one. Books that others put into his hands he could buffet as stoutly as any, but to ferret them out by his own efforts was an ungrateful waste of time. He wrote to Dr. Birch at the beginning: "I have likewise a further favour to beg. I know you have been long a curious collector of books. If therefore you have any of the contemporaries or ancestors of Shakespeare, it will be of great use to lend me them for a short time; my stock of those authours is yet but curta supellex." [17] But there were limits set by decent pride to this sort of appeal. And generally, when he exhorted his collector friends to "bring in!" they seemed likely to hide their rarer treasures. It was unlucky that the *Proposals* had been so explicit: "The edition now proposed will at least have this advantage over others. It will exhibit all the observable varieties of *all the copies that can be found* [italics added], that, if the reader is not satisfied with the editor's determination, he may have the means of chusing better for himself." After his promise of "a careful collation of the oldest copies," he was naturally reluctant to abandon his work to inevitable censure; but he was equally, and probably more, reluctant to do what was needed, in the face of his heightened awareness of the obstacles to be encountered in pursuit of textual comparison and illustration. I suspect that his predicament is not uncommon with scholars who have completed the congenial part of a long and complicated undertaking. So long as the work remains in one's own hands, one can intend, and even expect, a change of attitude or a burst of energy or other favoring circumstance. The arrival of George Steevens on the scene was unhappily mistimed: five years earlier would have made all the difference, if a light phrase may be pardoned. Even as a latecomer, Steevens proved invaluable, mercurial though he was. But an earlier collaboration might have obviated Johnson's less than

[17] *Letters*, 97.

admirable declaration in the published Preface: "I collated such copies as I could procure, and wished for more"; it was an evasive confession of his failure to discharge an acknowledged obligation. More than mere wishing was requisite from the start.

Whatever the causes of Johnson's delay, however, his conduct in this whole business, with its initial impressive drive and sudden neglect, does not deserve the name of "indolence." Such has been its constant epithet from his day to our own; in fact, this episode has come to stand as the classic example of Johnson's constitutional inertia. Raleigh regarded it as a paradigm of all authors' commitments long deferred in performance. "There is nothing singular or strange," he wrote in a memorable essay, "in this chapter of literary history. The promises of authors are like the vows of lovers; made in moments of careless rapture, and subject, during the long process of fulfillment, to all kinds of unforeseen dangers and difficulties." [18] But our over-familiarity with Johnson's sluggish habits and irregular hours and his consequent self-recrimination have led us to exaggerate his inattention to duty, even in the face of the staggering amount of work he accomplished. For though "unwilling to work," he yet laboured "with vigour" and at breath-taking speed. Most often, his strong sense of moral obligation and responsibility overcame disinclination—more especially when he had bound himself to deliver on a stated day. The *Dictionary* is an astonishing performance even by the calendar alone, and the *Rambler* and *Idler* papers are no mean demonstration of dependability. As already noted, it is at the moment when we lose track of the edition that Johnson was beginning the *Idler*, which for two years thereafter he punctually delivered every week. This new enterprise will hardly serve as proof of "indolence." But it is barely possible that self-reproach over the unfulfilment of the edition prompted him to undertake the weekly responsibility. The faithful discharge of this new engagement might gradually reconcile him to the continual postponement of the earlier obligation. The deadline was dead, beyond resuscitation; henceforth he would obey his inclination.

IT IS TIME now to consider what the edition stood for and what Johnson accomplished in it. The critical position for convenience

[18] Sir Walter Raleigh, *Johnson on Shakespeare* (1908), p. xi.

named Neoclassicism has most certainly not been ignored of late years, but in discussing Johnson it unfortunately cannot be taken for granted. Like Macaulay's schoolboy—if not indeed *from* him— we all learned long ago what the pernicious doctrine was, and we learned then that Johnson was one of its chief proponents and defenders. Later, however, as Johnson drew more and more critical scrutiny, he began to be seen in a clearer light, and it became evident that he did not perfectly fit the conventional definition. But because neoclassicism—*horresco referens*—had fallen from grace and because subsequently Johnson has been rapidly climbing the ladder of critical esteem, it has of late come to seem natural and necessary to push the two as far apart as one dares in order to keep our hero's image shining and untarnished. But now that Johnson's critical position has been redefined and vindicated, it may be time to tack about and ask whether our ideas of neoclassicism may not also be in need of some corrective adjustment. At the moment, it may be more serviceable to literary history to try to see English neoclassicism in a truer perspective—and by truer is meant here more sensitive and recognizant of its living actuality—than to insist too emphatically on Johnson's independence, minimizing his affinities with the school in which he was enrolled at birth and from which he never withdrew his expressed allegiance. It is, at any rate, immediately pertinent to ask how the doctrine affected or influenced Johnson's attitude toward Shakespeare and how it is reflected in the features he chose to emphasize in critical characterization, whether for praise or blame.

Johnson saw Shakespeare primarily as a dramatic *poet* and not first of all as a poet–*playwright*. But he neglected the poems and sonnets and, like others of his century, appears to have paid them scant respect. The moral and ethical values on which he believed literature based its claims of importance to men were so supremely exemplified in the plays that the nondramatic works could, presumably, be ignored without loss of anything essential. It was as a man speaking to men of the ever-recurring conditions and perplexed relations—the universal system—of human life that Shakespeare was finally to be judged. Shakespeare is "the poet of nature," that is, the poet of *human* nature. Human nature, within perceptible limits, is always and everywhere the same. It is the same because, contrary to the rest of the creation, man is born with the faculty of ratiocination and, however widely he may wander from its guidance or abuse it or be confused by it, his conduct as a human being is inevitably referred by himself and his fellows to this common criterion of rationality. Judged by what they think and do and say, Shakespeare's characters are convincingly "true to nature"—so convincingly true that they give us the illusion of reality. He "must have looked upon mankind with perspicacity in the highest degree curious and attentive." To read Shakespeare is to read the book of life. To interpret Shakespeare with full understanding is to increase our knowledge of mankind. Shakespeare's characters are indefinitely expansible, Johnson believes. Each, though an individual, "is commonly a species." This, to a classicist, is the highest conceivable praise. The persons in Shakespeare's plays "are the genuine progeny of common humanity, such as the world will always supply." They "act and speak by the influence of those general passions and principles by which all minds are agitated." The operation of Shakespeare's imagination is characteristically the opposite of prismatic: its light, instead of breaking into the component colors, is like "the wide effulgence of a summer noon." "Great thoughts are always general," and it is general truths that this poet, beyond all others, teaches and illustrates by word and example.

He has won every point, Horace wrote, who has blended the profitable with the agreeable. To teach important truths delightfully is the classical ideal. It is this ideal that Johnson finds so happily exemplified in Shakespeare's work as a whole. Classicism, as practised by the great Romans and by their great followers and imitators, is a critical faith. It therefore has analogies with religion. Like a religious faith, it aspires toward perfect achievement, though it can never quite attain to that state. And like religion, it has a creed that aims to summarize and formulate the essentials of its convictions or beliefs. The effort to normalize leads naturally to codification. Hence, the "rules." Perhaps too much has been made of them by students of neoclassical theory. The gamut of genres and their separateness, consistency within each kind, propriety of language, deference to great precedent: these were matters of significance, magnified by their availability for critical discussion.

But they and their corollaries began with common sense and the observation of nature, and should be reducible to the same. They are the restrictive and, so to say, negative part of the doctrine.

There is a positive side as well. Not one of the major English classicists but believed that the so-called rules could be broken by genius, in obedience to the higher commands of inspiration. Just as the builders of philosophical systems, during the Christian centuries, developed their argument on the level of human reason but abrogated or abjured their logic in the presence of the Divine, so the classical theorists worshiped the genius that spurned the familiar rules and "found a nearer way" to its sublime effects. The inspiration that cannot be rationally accounted for is always exalted to the highest place. In such contexts, discourse tends to gather supernatural overtones. Inspiration is godlike, and Longinus is its prophet. The rules of the road are for earthly travel; Pegasus is for the azure fields of air. The possibility of upward flight, in fact, was so essential an element in this critical world-view that (to adapt Voltaire's phrase) it may fairly be said, had not Longinus existed, it would have been necessary to invent him. Paradoxically, by opening a way—even a royal one—for the sublime, he confirmed the rights of sense and judgement. By placing the highest authority beyond challenge, he referred the rules to their due and defensible service and proper sphere of influence. Just as in the political sphere there must be, according to Johnson, a supreme power in the state, not subject to control or dispute if law and order are to prevail in the ordinary walks of life, so must provision be made in the realm of art for the concept of irresistible authority if "every pelting petty officer" in the shape of a rule is not to contend for superior powers. Thus, the acknowledgment of the reality of the unchallengeable sublime is a safeguard of the rules, and lesser issues may be equally settled, subject to regulative norms and rational judgement.

It is doubtless true that Johnson's view of Shakespeare is conditioned and limited by his neoclassical principles. His prejudices are shared with others of his age. His dislike of overblown language or wordplay in moments emotionally charged or when conveying trivialities is one illustration of his inhibitions with regard to propriety of diction; others are his disapproval of words vulgarized by association, his distaste for "licentious pleasantry" or clowning, and his impatience with Shakespeare's circumlocutory pomp in descriptive narration. More important, his reprobation of hasty conclusions that fail to confirm morality and to apportion due rewards and punishments is vitally significant of his principles.

Yet the last is perhaps less insistent than we might have anticipated. Certain concessions to Shakespeare's dramatic procedures lie deeply embedded in his critical thought. Recent study of Johnson has called attention to the inconsistencies in his critical attitudes as questions of special interest. His well-known defence of Shakespeare's disregard of the unities of time and place has been shown to be not quite so daring as formerly supposed nor as he himself perhaps imagined. Yet it is conclusive. As Wimsatt has happily put the case, "even if he is only kicking an open door, he does this with such ample energy and gusto, such resonance, reverberation of splintering material" that critical carpentry can never restore it.[19] It is another example, to set beside Boswell's familiar one, of Johnson's talent for *pedalogical* demonstration.

Johnson's discussion of "the mingled drama" that Shakespeare's work exemplifies throughout is not so much a defence as an explanation. It is so far-reaching in its implications that, with the other indications of heterodoxy, it leads Wimsatt to declare "that Johnson was an outright dissenter against the neoclassic rules and proprieties." [20] Another recent critic, Matthew Hodgart, would appear to coincide in the main with this view. Wimsatt finds in these manifestations signs that Johnson was struggling, not with entire success, to free himself from the straitjacket of theory: "we confront here some incompleteness of conversion," he writes, "an unresolved tension between the neoclassic conscience and the liberating impulse." [21] Hodgart puts it another way. Holding Johnson to be a confirmed classicist so long as critical theory is being debated and also in the delivery of ex cathedra judgements on particular authors or works, Hodgart nevertheless finds that in the crucial cases, Shakespeare being the crux of cruces, Johnson's sense of reality always defeats his theory.[22] In this view, Shakespeare is the touchstone that serves to prove Johnson's deepest

---

[19] W. K. Wimsatt, Jr., *Samuel Johnson on Shakespeare* (1960), p. xxii.
[20] *Ibid.*, p. xx.
[21] *Ibid.*, p. xxi.
[22] M. J. C. Hodgart, *Samuel Johnson and His Times* (1962), p. 108.

critical convictions—convictions that lie below the level of conscious theory, that he finds difficult to acknowledge in himself,
and that he is therefore at pains to rationalize as best he can. Theory
being found inadequate or contradictory, he resorts to the testimony of immediate experience.

That Shakespeare is such a critical touchstone for Johnson
appears undeniable and is not unrelated to the fact that the critic
wrote some of the finest pages in our literature under this stimulus.
But, bearing in mind what was said earlier of neoclassicism as a
living, working critical faith, one may arrive at the belief that
Johnson's alleged departures from orthodoxy are not the flagrant
impieties they are accused of being. Dick Minim is a caricature of
criticism, not a paradigm of neoclassical theory. The greatest
critics of this school were not the old moles the Romantics persisted in finding them. As suggested above, it would be difficult
to point to an English classicist of eminence, poet or critic, who
did not welcome the advent of the imperious genius able to
triumph over the rules. Provision for exceptions was an integral
part of the system. In accepting Shakespeare as he did, Johnson
was not untrue to the classical ideal. If he seems to concede too
much, he is only demanding for Shakespeare the rights always
claimed for the greatest of the ancients. On the one hand, he is
appealing for the privilege of genius to be judged by achievement
rather than by rule. On the other, he is inviting acknowledgment
of "a faithful mirror of manners and of life" as initial and primary.

He starts, therefore, with the premise that "there is always an
appeal open from [the rules of] criticism to nature." On this is
based his justification of the "mingled drama." It is true to life: it
exhibits "the real state of sublunary nature," and it fulfils the end
of poetry as classically stated, "to instruct by pleasing." It furthers
the ends of both tragedy and comedy possibly more successfully
than can either separately, because it "approaches nearer than
either to the appearance of life" by showing the concatenations,
the mutual involvement of contrary modes of existence. He appeals
to "daily experience" to refute false objections against the "interchange of mingled scenes." Not forgetting "the common satiety
of life" that "sends us all in quest" of novelty, he reminds us that
"upon the whole, all pleasure consists in variety."

His objections to the unities are equally based on an appeal to nature. The specious logic that upholds them in the guise of common sense is undermined and blown away by a deeper common sense. "It is time," Johnson declares,

to tell [the critic], by the authority of Shakespeare, that he assumes, as an unquestionable principle, a position, which, while his breath is forming it into words, his understanding pronounces to be false. It is false, that any representation is mistaken for reality. . . . [If by any spectator it should be,] there is no reason why a mind thus wandering in extasy should count the clock, or why an hour should not be a century in that calenture of the brains that can make the stage a field.

Thereupon, the inspired common sense of what follows:

Time is, of all modes of existence, most obsequious to the imagination; a lapse of years is as easily conceived as a passage of hours. In contemplation we easily contract the time of real actions, and therefore willingly permit it to be contracted when we only see their imitation. . . . Such violations of *rules merely positive* [italics added], become the comprehensive genius of Shakespeare. . . .

In all this and much more, there is, properly understood, nothing radically contradictory to the principles of neoclassicism, which are themselves founded on human nature and the observation of it—"those rules of old" not invented in a closet but "discovered" in life. "Rules merely positive" are later inventions and subject to question.

Least neoclassical, perhaps, is the historical argument introduced by Johnson immediately subsequent to his discussion of the unities. Here, although still appealing to experience, he is insinuating a criterion of relativism into critical judgements, which, pushed to its conclusions, would go far to minimize the likelihood of arriving at permanent standards. "Every man's performances, to be rightly estimated, must be compared with the state of the age in which he lived, and with his own particular opportunities." "The English nation, in the time of Shakespeare, was yet struggling to emerge from barbarity." "The publick was gross and dark." "He that wrote for such an audience was under the necessity of looking round for strange events and fabulous transactions." "Those to whom our authour's labors were exhibited had more skill in pomps or processions than in poetical language." One possible deduction from such reflections is that Shakespeare's native disadvantages ought to be added to the sum of his accomplishments to enhance his value. Another is that in fairness we should measure him by the expectations and standards of his contemporaries and not by our own; it would then follow that standards of absolute excellence are, when viewed in historical perspective, to some extent necessarily unfair, and doubts arise of the possibility of fixing a base upon which to set up valid and stable criteria. Thus, the neoclassic position is undermined. But Johnson does not pursue these negative implications, choosing rather to emphasize the wonder of what Shakespeare actually achieved and using the historical argument to account for deficiencies.

Johnson's deepest convictions are moral rather than aesthetic. In praising Shakespeare as he does, setting him in the highest place, explaining or apologizing for his lapses, extenuating his ethical laxity, is Johnson betrayed into concessions he cannot afford? Do his convictions actually give way before superior power?

In his critical philosophy, it is basic that poetry ought to give moral instruction while giving delight. Is this altogether consonant with his pronouncement that "Shakespeare is above all modern writers the poet of nature"? To Johnson, the statement means that Shakespeare shows in greater measure than anyone else what is generally true about human nature, regardless of time or place. To this extent, therefore, he is held to be a teacher and to fulfil the classical requirement. But there are serious reservations, and we had best examine Johnson's exact words. The crucial paragraph is the following:

His first defect is that to which may be imputed most of the evil in books or in men. He sacrifices virtue to convenience, and is so much more careful to please than to instruct, that he seems to write without any moral purpose. From his writings indeed a system of social duty may be selected, for he that thinks reasonably must think morally; but his precepts and axioms drop casually from him; he makes no just distribution of good or evil, nor is always careful to shew in the virtuous a disapprobation of the wicked; he carries his persons indifferently through right and wrong, and at the close dismisses them without further care, and leaves their examples to operate by chance. This fault the barbarity of his age cannot extenuate; for *it is always a writer's duty to make the world better* [italics added], and justice is a virtue independant on time or place.

The highest instruction, Johnson would maintain, does not stop short with showing what men are; by its ordonnance of events and their agents, it shows in addition what men ought to be. By the expressed or implied judgements upon human character and conduct in the action of a play, the poet teaches morality. When he shows the meaning and consequences for human existence, morally considered, of the truths he reveals, he reflects in his microcosm the moral macrocosm which is God's universe, in which we are all actors. But, Johnson asserts, this meaning Shakespeare does not always exert himself to reveal. And it is not true that, in the final assessment of Shakespeare's genius, for Johnson this shortcoming does not really matter. On the contrary, it is primary, "his first defect," and will always matter profoundly while man faces eternal judgement. In spite of this, however, Shakespeare shows so much more than others about human nature that we can perceive the *ought* even when the poet himself through haste or negligence fails to display the fitting conclusion. When he does fall short, it is not his knowledge of life that is at fault but his will. In his greatest work, art and nature and will combine to enforce irrefutable truth.

THE REPUTATION of Johnson's edition of Shakespeare has fluctuated, as we might expect, with the reputation of the critic himself. Although there were sporadic attacks on it in its own day, such as those of Kenrick and Ritson, and although even Johnson's admirers confessed that in some aspects it was disappointing, the "manly" Preface never lacked praise and in general the edition was rated above its predecessors, as it deserved. The nineteenth-century myopia that beclouded all Johnson's writing—while it excepted his talk as preserved by Boswell—found his *Shakespeare* equally reprehensible with the rest. Knight deemed its influence unquestionably evil; Macaulay proclaimed that "it would be difficult to name a more slovenly, a more worthless edition of any great classic."

Johnson's name began to be rescued from this Slough of Despond in the very first decade of our own century. In 1903, Nichol Smith administered an eloquent corrective to Macaulay's abuse, declaring: "Not only was Johnson's edition the best which had yet appeared; it is still one of the few editions which are indispensable." [23] Raleigh, five years later, struck a brilliant and decisive counterblow against the detractors in his little book, *Johnson on Shakespeare*, and predicted the course of scholarly opinion for the next fifty years.

The twentieth century will treat him more respectfully. The romantic attitude begins to be fatiguing. . . . There is a taint of insincerity . . . from which not even the great romantics are free. They are never in danger from the pitfalls that waylay the plodding critic; but they are always falling upward, as it were, into vacuity. . . . When the inspiration fails them their language is maintained at the same height, and they say more than they feel.[24]

By this time, Johnson's merits and demerits as an editor of Shakespeare are familiar ground. No doubt, he was sadly remiss in the collation of texts, though he knew the importance of this duty in differentiating between the obscurities of corruption and those of mere unfamiliarity of phrase. He knew that the authority of the First Folio was primary and that not all early printings were of equal value. He understood the value of contemporary writings in throwing light on obscurities in his author, but he was not the Elizabethan specialist to exploit this knowledge to full advantage. He did much less in relating the plays to their sources and analogues than he might have done or probably should have done. He was laudably conservative in conjecture—far more so than his own predecessors and contemporaries—and reluctant to alter the text even where he was puzzled by it. He was, moreover, superb at the explication of knotty passages. The chief value of his annotation, a value that continues even today, lay in this ability to wrest whatever sense could be extracted from obscurities not actually corrupt.

Such shortcomings as Johnson exhibits in critical appreciation arise chiefly from his unwillingness to recognize that anything of value could be learned about his author from stage performance or even, perhaps, from reading the plays with a physical theater and theatrical conditions very prominently in mind. Or, to put it as Hodgart has done, he saw the plays as ethical poems, not as the productions of a practical man of the theater. In fact, he thought not only that one learned no more from seeing than from reading,

[23] D. Nichol Smith, *Eighteenth Century Essays on Shakespeare* (1903), p. xxxi.
[24] Raleigh, *Johnson on Shakespeare*, p. xviii.

but that stage performance was actually a handicap and obstruction to understanding Shakespeare. (And perhaps, in view of habitual conditions of dramatic production in his day, Garrick notwithstanding, there was some justification for the prejudice.) New and fruitful approaches in dramatic theory from the brilliant band of critics of our own day have thrown fresh light on drama in general, and directly and indirectly have taught us much about Shakespeare's plays that Johnson neither saw nor imagined, nor certainly could have found acceptable had it entered his mind.[25]

DESPITE ALL legitimate subtractions, Raleigh's prediction that in our century Johnson's reputation would be redeemed has been amply verified. A new difficulty, however, rooted in certain historical facts and considerations, has of late arisen to unsettle opinion. It turns upon two not unrelated questions, the answers to which can significantly affect our whole assessment of the critic's achievement. One is the degree of originality in Johnson's general commentary on the poet, particularly in the Preface. The other is the extent of specific obligation to previous annotators which fell short of honest acknowledgment. The first question, being of a semantic kind and depending to a considerable degree on how originality is conceived and defined, seems less capable of objective solution and can safely be referred to the final historical consensus. The other, however, challenges Johnson's good faith as an editor and bespeaks a brief review of facts and probabilities.[26]

By one of those odd coincidences of literary history, it happened that, about the time when Johnson slackened his pace as an editor, another critic, Benjamin Heath, motivated by the exasperation that Warburton often inspired, went systematically through the edition of 1747, castigating as he went; before his indignation had subsided, he had compiled a book, nearly six hundred pages long, of often shrewd and always biting commentary. Then he, too, laid by his work for some years. Not until the news reached him—presumably late in 1764—that Johnson's edition was actually about to materialize was his concern over Shakespeare and War-

---

[25] For a judicious appreciation of Johnson's contribution to bibliographical criticism bearing on Shakespeare's text, see R. E. Scholes, Shakespeare Quarterly, XI (Spring 1960), 163–171.

[26] These questions are discussed in careful detail by Professor Sherbo in the third and fourth chapters of Samuel Johnson, Editor of Shakespeare.

burton reactivated. It was, he himself declared in his preface, in consequence of this anticipation that he was induced to send his own manuscript to the printer, in order "that the publick might receive about the same time whatever information was ready to be laid before it relative to this subject." Heath's motives are disingenuously represented in this preface. It is clear that he thought his effort too considerable to be consigned to the rubbish-heap but knew that, if Johnson performed his task as thoroughly as one had reason to expect of such a critic, there would be no further need to dust Warburton's frock. It was, therefore, essential to publish first, for the little that was independent of beating and binding a bishop could not make much of a stir. The book, *The Revisal of Shakespeare's Text*, appeared anonymously in February 1765.

Johnson received a copy of Heath's book before he had written his preface or closed his appendix to all further entries. Subsequently, in the Preface, he mordantly characterized the work: its author, he observed, "attacks [Warburton's errors] with gloomy malignity . . . and . . . bites like a viper." But he has selected "some just remarks" from the book for his appendix of additional notes. Obviously, he read Heath with attention. His own commentary, however, was in great part long since in print. It must take its chance. He was not the self-doubter to turn back and revise it now on Heath's account. Nor was he the man to feel an obligation to register coincidence of opinion with Heath in an appendix, any more than to record a difference, should one have occurred.

Coincidences there are, and the explanation is not far to seek. Emendation apart, much of Johnson's explanatory comment owes its existence to Warburton's native footnotes wild, to that critic's truly perverse misunderstanding or wilful misinterpretation of Shakespeare. Johnson often declares that he would not have supposed the meaning of a passage possible to mistake had not Warburton or occasionally Theobald given evidence to the contrary. The wildest warblings would obviously be those most certain of correction. The natural consequence was that Heath, who was stalking the same game, would often be found at Johnson's side— or Johnson at Heath's—in countering Warburton's crazy dodges. Frequent coincidences would hardly be surprising, since often enough the passages in question admit of a common-sense interpretation, which both critics were alert to discover. We need not infer a borrowing in either direction. Supposing, moreover, that in the spring or summer of 1765 Johnson had found an opportunity to bestow a systematic revision on previously printed annotation of all eight volumes for whatever purpose, one would expect consequently to find cancels and irregularities of printing in considerable number. Cancels, indeed, there are—nineteen of them, sixteen of which have been shown by Allen Hazen to have been prepared for the sole purpose of softening the impact of some of his blows upon Bishop Warburton.[27] No cancels have any connection with Heath, unless the latter's sarcasm against Warburton produced an opposite reaction in Johnson.

The Yale edition of *Johnson on Shakespeare* enables every interested reader to obtain immediate access to all Johnson's writing that directly concerns Shakespeare. What one is moved to say, by way of conclusion, about his originality on the subject mainly concerns the great Preface to his edition. It is little more than one might say of the originality of the ideas in Shakespeare's sonnets. In the final reckoning, their novelty is not the thing that matters. If an author's writing abounds, to quote Johnson in a different context, "with images which find a mirror in every mind, and with sentiments to which every bosom returns an echo"; and if, in addition, he succeeds in giving his discourse so living a body that, as we read, we seem to come into possession of the full meaning of these ideas now for the first time, and so felicitous and authoritative a form that we have neither power to better nor wish to change it, we may then credit him with that highest and most difficult originality of all, which subsumes and supersedes earlier statements and compels later ones into its own channel. To this kind of originality, in its best pages, Johnson's Preface attains. It is not to be superseded, and it is indispensable.

[27] Allen T. Hazen, *TLS* (Dec. 24, 1938), p. 820. In a contribution to the *European Magazine*, XXIV (October 1793), 296, William Seward asserts that it was Tonson and Millar who urged Johnson to soften his strictures on Warburton. I owe this reference to Mrs. Elizabeth Lebans of Somerville College.

Walking Stewart

JOHN STEWART "the Traveller" was born in Bond Street, London, in 1748 or 1749.[1] His father was a Scottish linendraper, of whom nothing else is known. In an autobiographical sketch prefixed to one of his books, Stewart declares that he was born "of the most animated and passionate parents"—meaning the phrase as a compliment to them and to himself. Whether there is any relation of cause and effect between their emotional vigor and the fact that as an infant he often "wandered from home" cannot be determined. At the age of six he was sent to a country school; but he contrived his escape by inventing discreditable stories about the institution, in consequence of which his parents removed him from its noxious influence. At ten, he was sent to Harrow. "Here," he says, "I remember an obstinate inattention to school-books, and I was called the blockhead of the class, while I was the first player at every game, and the leader of every enterprise, such as robbing orchards, fighting the town's-people, and riding jackasses to London." [2] Such conduct abridged his stay at Harrow; and at thirteen he was sent to the Charterhouse, where he pursued the same course. "My inattention to school-books was stronger than ever, and I declined every kind of learning except writing what were called Moral Essays or Themes, and these the master declared I performed

---

[1] The *D.N.B.*, perhaps following Rees's *Annual Biography and Obituary* (1823), VII, 101–109, or the Life of Stewart by "a relative" (1822), gives 1749. Stewart himself, in his *Scripture of Reason and Nature*, published in 1813, gives his age at that date as 65.
[2] *Scripture of Reason and Nature* (1813), p. iv.

superior to any boys of the class." [3] But the single talent failed to redeem a multitude of shortcomings, at least in the opinion of the master, who advised Stewart's father to send his son abroad, "as the only chance that remained of his acquiring habits of industry and application." The father was by this time willing to have his son at a wholesome distance. Through George III's favorite, Lord Bute, the Scot who had just become prime minister, a post as writer to the East India Company was secured for the boy, in the year 1763; and thus at the age of fifteen he set sail for Madras.

Arrived on the Eastern verge of the world, Stewart was not long in discovering that there were other evils than those which a schoolmaster might invent for a recalcitrant pupil. He made acquaintance with a system of abuses against which Burke, some twenty years later, was to thunder in the House of Commons. "At the time of his arrival in India," as one account puts it, "extortion, cruelty, and fraud were methodized into a code, and an emulation of eagerness in the pursuit of individual gain, or rather of plunder, distinguished too many of the civil and military servants of the Company." [4] It would be not at all surprising if a boy, introduced at so early an age to such an environment, should succumb without a struggle to the temptation of getting easy and unscrupulous wealth—especially a boy whose conduct hitherto had been far from inspiring confidence in the firmness of his principles. What Stewart did, on the contrary, was to write to the Court of Directors of the Company, pointing out the enormous abuses that flourished under its administration. The Directors were by no means eager for investigation, and of course Stewart's letter was ignored.

The young reformer's protest was not, as it proved, a momentary flash of indignant innocence. For a year or so, while the routine of clerical duties was becoming steadily more distasteful, his moral sense was increasingly outraged by the iniquity of the system of which he was a part, as its manifold ills further revealed themselves to his growing intelligence. He came to understand, however, that he alone could not change so vast a heap of wrong: all that he could do was to sunder his connection with it as soon as possible. Much of the evil, he saw, arose because the English knew so little of the native languages that they could have no sympa-

[3] *Ibid.*
[4] *Annual Biography and Obituary*, VII, 103.

thetic understanding of the people as human beings, and were forced to rely on the misrepresentations of rascally interpreters. He resolved to learn the native tongues and himself become an interpreter of a different sort. In so doing he would be cutting himself free from the office tasks which he despised, and would have an opportunity to alleviate at least a slight amount of human misery. At the same time he would be satisfying a craving, already strong, to travel and know men and manners. The money earned in this way would be honestly got; and when he had saved a moderate sum, he could return to Europe and live on his income. All this was the veriest midsummer madness to his associates. Why did one go out to India if not to get rich? But Stewart was headstrong and obstinate. He addressed a second letter to the Court of Directors, which, says the *Gentleman's Magazine,* "from its juvenile insolence and audacity, is preserved on their records to this day." He set out in this document his considered opinion of their policy, and told them besides "that he was born for nobler pursuits, and higher attainments, than to be a copier of invoices and bills of lading to a company of grocers, haberdashers, and cheesemongers."[5]

He was now eighteen. Looking back, some twenty-five years later, he uttered an indictment of the Company which shows how little he afterward modified his view of its practices:

The employ of the East India Company's servants in that country is an impeachment to the wisdom and virtue of the metropolitan government. The inferior station of servants, called writers, are confined to copying letters and bills of sale in the different offices; when they rise to the office of factors, they are made deputies, paymasters, storekeepers, &c. &c. When senior and junior merchants, they are employed in subordinate settlements to record and execute the councils of interpreters; and when they are called to the government, all the knowledge they possess to execute the important trust is, the character of the different interpreters, estimated according to their abilities of drawing revenue from an exhausted and depopulated country.

Why are not the writers sent to the manufacturing towns to learn the state of the investments, to relieve the poor weaver from an oppression, which destroys industry in its source, and is the cause of all debasement in the quality, and deficiency in the quantity? Why are they not sent into the country to learn the languages, customs, and tempers of the natives—to see how the collection of the revenue is formed—to remove the baneful hand of oppression, which destroys

⁵ *Gentleman's Magazine,* Vol. 92, Pt. I (March 1822), pp. 279–280.

and depopulates the farms? Why are they not appointed collectors?
Is it that this knowledge might impede the interest of the superior
agents, and that the mystery of making Asiatic fortunes might be
exposed? [6]

Stewart bade the East India Company good-bye probably in
1765. And now, for the space of almost forty years, his career becomes a labyrinth hard to trace. It is difficult to distinguish fact
from fable, and impossible to establish a chronological sequence,
in the maze of rumor that marks his progress. Unlike most adven-
turers, Stewart in later life steadily resisted the narrative impulse.
To requests for anecdote and reminiscence he would reply that his
travels had been prosecuted for the philosophical study of man.
His conclusions about racial characteristics were, as—to our loss—
he believed, the valuable part of his experience; and perhaps he
did not wish to weaken those conclusions be associating them with
the doubts that attend travelers' tales of moving accidents and hair-
breadth 'scapes. His acquaintances, therefore, seldom heard him
indulge in personal anecdote; and when he did so, it was always
to enforce some generality by means of apposite illustration. Unfortunately, even apposite illustration is usually omitted from his
books. The extraordinary character of his experiences, however, he
was never disposed to minimize. He could refer to it—and to the
fact that he was not in the role of common men—in terms like the
following:

I must here call the most impressive attention of my readers to the
vast range of my travels throughout various nations, civilized or
savage, from the equator almost to the pole, and entreat of them
seriously to reflect what must have been the exquisite degree of sagacity,
thought, prudence, and wisdom, that enabled me to perform such unparalleled travels, and return to my native country with health, life,
and property unimpaired, and then to put this question to every man's
conscience, whether the philosophical speculations of such a mind,
though contrary to all our mental, educational, and constitutional
habitudes, and even natural instincts, is not deserving of the most
serious examination, before they are condemned to oblivion and
contempt.[7]

From accounts written within a year or so of Stewart's death, it
appears that on leaving the Company's service he struck into the

[6] *Travels over the Most interesting Parts of the Globe, to discover the Source
of Moral Motion* (1790), pp. 219–220.
[7] *Scripture of Reason and Nature*, pp. xxi-xxii.

interior of India with the general purpose of learning the native
dialects. According to the *Gentleman's Magazine*, he "prosecuted
his route over Hindostan, and *walked to Delhi*"; "he traversed the
greater part of the Indian Peninsula." [8] Wandering of this sort must
have consumed at least a couple of years, during which Stewart
acquired a considerable proficiency in the tongues. In an evil hour
his adventurous disposition drew him to Seringapatam, the capital
of the warlike and treacherous Hyder Ali, no friend to the English.
This tyrant, hearing that a European had been so bold as to enter
his city, gave orders for his instant arrest. Stewart, examined upon
his motives, protested that his purpose was merely to see the capital
of Mysore. Hyder Ali replied that he might remain, that in fact
he must remain, that he was to consider himself henceforth a subject. Stewart made the best of a bad situation, and proved himself
useful as an interpreter. He acquired some knowledge of military
tactics, and was raised to command a troop of Hyder Ali's sepoys.
In this capacity, he became a valuable aid. The native officers
hated him because he always saw that his men were paid promptly
and in full; but his division "became distinguished for exact discipline and superior valour." [9] Hyder Ali, himself a Mohammedan
usurper, was embarked upon an aggressive program of self-
aggrandizement; and Stewart had abundant opportunity to display his courage. He seems to have received more than one wound
in this service. In a desperate encounter with the Mahrattas, about
1769, he was severely injured and left untended while others had
the benefit of native surgery. Probably this was just as well for
him. He got a boy to bathe his wounds three or four times a day
with "simple warm water"; "and under this novel system of surgery," according to the historian, "they recovered with a rapidity
not exceeded under the best hospital treatment." [10] His injury on
this occasion may have been the wound in the right arm of which
the *Gentleman's Magazine* speaks. But there is talk of more serious
mischief: we hear of another wound by which the crown of
Stewart's head was indented to a depth of nearly one inch. Whether
the skull was creased to that extent by the groove made by a passing

[8] Apparently, though the fact has not been elsewhere noticed, he got as far
east as the Malay Peninsula. See *Travels*, pp. 233–235.
[9] *Annual Biography and Obituary*, VII, 104.
[10] *Quarterly Review* (October 1817), p. 51, quoting from Colonel Mark Wilks,
Historical Sketches of the South of India, II, 147.

bullet, or stroke of a sword, or whether a bullet penetrated to that depth and desisted from further encroachment, is a point of physiological interest. In either case, the "solidity and compound mass" of the cranium involved cannot but compel admiration.

The seriousness of this injury justified Stewart in appealing to be allowed to leave in order to consult a European surgeon. Characteristically, Hyder Ali granted permission, and then, possibly dreading Stewart's disclosure of military secrets, gave instructions to his escort that he should be murdered on the borders of the kingdom.

Whether [says one authority] Mr. Stewart had received a private notice of his design, or was indebted for its discovery to his own sagacity, he contrived, when on the bank of a river, to lull the vigilance of his guards, and plunging into the stream, swam over to the other side; he was followed by his treacherous attendants, but he successfully eluded their pursuit, and, after encountering many perils, and enduring great hardships, (aggravated by the condition of his wound,) he at length arrived at a British fort, placed himself under the care of an English surgeon, and in the course of a few months was entirely cured.[11]

This mode of departure from Mysore did little to advance Stewart's grand design of acquiring a modest competency. He can have brought away not much of his earnings under Hyder Ali Khan. He had therefore to cast about for an opening which should give employment to his unusual knowledge and talents. Fortune now threw him somehow—presumably he had sought Madras again in fleeing from Mysore—into connection with Mohamed Ali Khan, better known as the Nabob of Arcot.[12] He entered the suite of this monarch, and found favor. Perhaps beginning as interpreter, he was elevated to be the Nabob's private secretary, and "in a short time," we are told, "became his prime minister, in which capacity he was required to superintend the sumptuous revels which dis-

[11] *Annual Biography and Obituary*, VII, 104, perhaps following the account in the Life by a relative. The story in the *Gentleman's Magazine*, Vol. 92, Pt. I (March 1822), pp. 279–280, substitutes Tippoo for his father Hyder Ali in recounting this episode; and attributes Stewart's escape, less romantically, to the intercession of Sir James Sibbald when the latter was settling terms of peace with Tippoo, from Bombay. Tippoo did not succeed to the throne of Mysore till 1783, however, which seems an improbably late date for Stewart's business. Hyder Ali was in all likelihood the monarch whom Stewart served; but certainly a less colorful departure from Seringapatam is possible.

[12] It ought to be mentioned that the account in the *Gentleman's Magazine* places the Hyder Ali episode *after* Stewart's association with the Nabob.

tinguished the court of that sovereign." [13] In this way, Stewart
came to play a part in swelling the vast bulk of the Nabob of
Arcot's debts, by helping to maintain "what they call [the scornful
reference is Burke's] 'the splendour of the Durbar.' " But little of
that splendor seems to have accrued to Stewart. The Nabob was
an old hand at Falstaff's game. Let his ministers come to him for the
funds with which to proceed, and he would cry, "Lay out! lay
out!" By this technique, he soon got himself into debt to Stewart in
a swingeing sum. But the prime minister was not for nothing
named Stewart. Through private economies best known to himself
and doubtless strictly honest, he gradually collected his predetermined £3,000. Upon reaching that goal, he promptly resigned,
and set out in the general direction of England. But he was in no
hurry to arrive. He crossed India once more and passed into Persia.
He strode—not rode—in triumph through Persepolis, and made
acquaintance with other parts of Persia. Before he left the country,
he had "completely mastered" the Persian language. It may have
been then that he pushed up into more inaccessible regions, amongst
the Turcomans, "a nation of Tartars inhabiting the uncultivated
parts of Turkey," whom he expressly says he visited. [14] He came
down and emerged upon the Persian Gulf. Across this body of
water he made assuredly the most uncomfortable passage upon
record.

[While Stewart was] crossing the Persian Gulf, in a vessel manned
exclusively by Mahometans, a violent storm arose, which misfortune
the crew attributed to their having a Giaour on board; a counsel was
held, and it was determined that the new Jonah should be cast over-
board. It was with much difficulty that Mr. Stewart persuaded them
to modify their resolution; it was at length settled that he should be
immured in a hen-coop and suspended from the main-yard until the
storm abated. In this elevated station he remained for some hours, nor
was he released till the storm had entirely subsided. [15]

These hazards surmounted, Stewart proceeded into countries
which our authorities are careful to distinguish as "Abyssinia and
Ethiopia." He "has been present," declares the *Gentleman's Magazine*, "at the latter place [*sic*], at an entertainment of the Natives,

[13] *Annual Biography and Obituary*, VII, 105.
[14] See *Travels*, p. 231. The *Annual Biography and Obituary*, VII, 105, says he
"traversed a great part of Persia and Turkey" on his way home.
[15] *Annual Biography and Obituary*, VII, 105.

who, disregarding sexual distinction, appeared *in statu naturae*." [16]
His impressions of these peoples, it is interesting to note, were not
at all favorable: all that he has to say in print of "these ignorant
and malignant children of Africa" is conveyed in a single sentence:
"All the natives near the sea form nations of pirates; and all the
inland inhabitants nations of robbers, not only of property, but
the more outrageous violence of persons." But in fairness he takes
care to mention that the civilized nations are quite as prone to
this "universal delirium of passion"—the difference being that the
latter have more power to do harm. [17]

Stewart now began to think seriously of getting home. At this
point the account parallels the speed of his desire, borrowing something of the genius of the country through which he was passing:
"He crossed the Desert of Arabia, and arrived at Marseilles"—a
sentence which belongs in the *Arabian Nights*. Once in France, his
speed is moderated; we learn that he walked through the whole
kingdom. Next he crossed the Pyrenees, tramped through Spain
and Portugal, and finally landed in England, about the year 1784.

He invested his Indian savings in the French funds, purchasing
an annuity of £300 per annum. To settle down was far from his
mind:

I then formed a general plan of life and happiness, which was to
travel over all the world, to trace the causes of human misery, and the
causes of human welfare and its perfectuability [sic]; and in prosecut-
ing my extensive travels, and meeting with a perpetual change of laws,
customs, and instincts among various nations, my mind burst the
barrier of local prejudices, mental habitudes, and even instincts; and
I began to reason things in the pure medium of nature, and to discover
the refractions of practice as they influenced or befouled the pure
medium of theory to enjoy actual, and advance it into improvable
good; and this high state of mental sensibility, generated by the perpetual action of thought and reflection on the new scenes of travel,
has produced my new system of Philosophy of Sense and Nature. [18]

In pursuance of his plan, Stewart probably spent the next half-
dozen years in peregrinations about Europe. The only country
which he omitted to see appears to have been Norway. He visited

---

[16] The *D.N.B.*, more discreetly, says he traveled through Ethiopia and Abyssinia, "noting the most curious customs."

[17] *Travels*, pp. 236–239.

[18] *Scripture of Reason and Nature*, pp. vi–vii.

Sweden, and Lapland, and traveled as far east as Russia.[19] Regretfully he gave up the idea of visiting China, as he found "no means to penetrate into this country, all entrance," he says, "being refused to strangers." [20] In the autumn, probably, of 1786, Michael Kelly, the operatic tenor and friend of Mozart, ran across him in Vienna. Stewart had just arrived (on foot) from Calais, having passed through Italy and the Tyrol, and was on his way to Constantinople.[21] It is certain that he spent much time in France, and was in that country at the outbreak of the Revolution. It was then that the young Wordsworth met him, and was much impressed by his conversational eloquence. Of this period he himself writes as follows:

I was residing in Paris in the beginning of the mad revolution, with the highest reputation of a philosopher, and in possession of the confidence of the leaders of all parties, occupied in converting my funded property into national domains, when all on a sudden I perceived the most dreadful symptoms of mob government, and took my departure with the dereliction of all my property, to save my liberty and my life, while the horrid events of the progressive revolution proved the wisdom of my conduct, and the anticipative discernment of a thoughtful, prudent, and experienced mind.[22]

It was at this crucial moment in the history of the world that Stewart came of age as a philosopher, for his first work was published in 1789 or 1790: *Travels over the Most interesting Parts of the Globe, to discover the Source of Moral Motion; communicated to lead Mankind through the Conviction of the Senses to intellectual Existence, and an enlightened State of Nature.* The work opens with an Invocation to Truth and a Dedication to the Child of Nature, who is in fact a projection of Stewart's idea of himself. The body of the book is a series of characterizations of the moral condition of the peoples of the world, unalleviated by a single reference to personal experience. The second volume bears a different title, appropriate to its loose statement and first working out of the author's system: *The Apocalypse of Nature; wherein*

---

[19] It is possible that he also made his first trip to America in this decade.
[20] *Travels*, p. 226.
[21] M. Kelly, *Reminiscences*, 2d ed. (1826), I, 246–248. Kelly's account is amusing and vivid. Stewart made a lively impression on him as "a great oddity," hostile to beefsteak and the English climate, but loving the arts—well-informed, accomplished, and "of a most retentive memory."
[22] *Scripture of Reason and Nature*, pp. xix–xx.

the Source of Moral Motion is discovered, etc. These books were followed in the next year by a two-volume sequel, *The Moral World Displayed,* dated not according to the new French calendar, or any calendar yet known, but thus: "In the Second Year of the Intellectual World, or the Publication of the Apocalypse of Nature." His first work, Stewart declared, had been "hurried to the press with a precipitancy" consonant with "the present conjuncture of events," when the moral world was "agitated and threatened with dreadful storms," and wisdom was called upon to "leave its outward occupations," to form "moral conductors, that may convey the thunderbolt of revolution, to purify, and not destroy the moral elements or associations of mankind." [23] He urged his readers to open his volumes rather

in the rural scenes of solitude, where nature affords a clearer atmosphere for the judgement, than in the literary mist of the cabinet or library, where verbal ideas alone arise and circulate, to perpetuate prejudice, and confound truth. The study of nature should be pursued in the cabinet of nature—groves, forests, lawns, lakes, &c. &c. Here real ideas or things present themselves to contemplation, and the great standard of truth becomes nature's self. [24]

With the new era of sense and nature thus inaugurated, Stewart seems to have felt it safe to extend his investigations into fresh territory. The issue of August 1, 1791, of a newspaper published in Albany, New York, bore the following announcement:

On Thursday last arrived in this city from London, viâ New York, and the same evening set off for Canada, Mr. STEWART, the noted pedestrian—who, we are told, has travelled over the greater part of Europe, Asia, and Africa on foot; and has come to this country for the purpose of completing his travels, by making the tour of the American world. Mr. Stewart is a middle-aged man, about six feet high—and what is particularly remarkable, he is said to eat no animal food, and but one meal a day. [25]

How long Stewart remained in this country is uncertain. To publish, in the fourth year of the era of intellectual existence, [26] his

---

[23] *Travels,* pp. xvi-xvii.

[24] *Ibid.,* p. xxviii.

[25] *Notes and Queries,* 2d Series, VIII (September 24, 1859), 247.

[26] I.e., in 1793. In the same year also appeared *The Book;* and in 1794, *The Tocsin of Britannia, with a novel Plan for a Constitutional Army; The Second Part of the Tocsin of Britannia, or Alarm Bell of Britons, with Plans of National Armament and National Defence, addressed to the British Yeomanry;* and, finally, *Good Sense addressed to the English Nation.*

third work, *The Revolution of Reason*, he must have been back in London. In August 1793, he was seen by an acquaintance entering one of the rooms at Bagnigge Wells, appareled, not in his customary blue coat with a red cape, but "disguised, like a gentleman, in a new white coat and an umbrella in his hand." [27]

He probably made, in the course of the nineties, more than one extended tour in America. He is said to have resorted to the habitual occupation of the British visitor, lecturing, and thus to have eked out a subsistence. In one of his works he speaks of having lived in an American family for the space of two months. He paused to publish a book in New York. It was called *The Revelation of Nature*,[28] and consisted of a poem with notes, together with "The Prophecy of Reason" and institutes of a proposed "Homoousia Society." The *Revelation of Nature* was thought well—or perhaps ill—enough of to be republished forty years later, in Middletown, New Jersey.

Back in England, Stewart fell upon comparatively evil days. The payment of his annuity, during the chaos of affairs in France, hung fire, and for some time he was dependent on the charitable assistance of "a humane and respectable tradesman in the borough of Southwark, who had married his sister" [29]—a debt which he was careful to repay. He applied to the English Government for an appointment as "oriental interpreter"—he is said to have known eight languages—but was rejected; and he settled down with a resigned mind to the condition of poverty. When the peace was established, the French government proposed a settlement with its foreign creditors at a ratio of one for three, which, Stewart writes,

they knew would not be accepted, till a failure in the negotiation of Amiens would enable France to confiscate the whole. My profound thought and reflection on my experience of the French character, national and personal, enabled me to avoid the snare, by accepting the fraudulent payment, by which I preserved a third part of my property; while the great body of creditors lost every farthing of their funds in France, which I had predicted to most of them, and was called an eccentric man.[30]

[27] Joseph Ritson, *Letters* (1833), II, 24.
[28] Doubtfully dated 1796 by the Library of Congress.
[29] *D.N.B.*, from John Taylor's *Records of My Life*, I, 284 ff.
[30] *Scripture of Reason and Nature*, pp. xx-xxi.

About the years 1798–1799, De Quincey, then quite young, had sight of Stewart at Bath.

He frequented the pump-room [writes De Quincey], and I believe all public places—walking up and down, and dispersing his philosophic opinions to the right and the left, like a Grecian philosopher. The first time I saw him was at a concert in the Upper Rooms. . . . I remember that Madame Mara was at that moment singing; and Walking Stewart, who was a true lover of music (as I afterwards came to know), was hanging upon her notes like a bee upon a jessamine flower. His countenance was striking, and expressed the union of benignity with philosophic habits of thought. In such health had his pedestrian exercises preserved him, connected with his abstemious mode of living, that, though he must at that time have been considerably above forty, he did not look older than twenty-eight; at least the face which remained upon my recollection for some years was that of a young man.[31]

Stewart now gravitated westward and was seen in Devonshire about the turn of the century. He crossed to Ireland. At this time he was laboring upon his *Opus Maximum, or a great Essay to reduce the Moral World from Contingency to System.* Passing over to Scotland, he was near shipwreck. With the boat on her beam ends and everyone expecting momentarily to go to the bottom, Stewart was not unmindful of his duty to posterity. He took occasion to entreat the sailors that, if any one of them should escape, he should preserve the precious manuscript of the *Opus Maximum* from destruction. Stewart lived, however, to publish it himself in 1803; in which year he also issued out his *Tocsin of Social Life: addressed to all Nations of the civilized World; in a Discovery of the Laws of Nature relative to human Existence.*[32] In the same year he announced that he was to give a course of lectures on the human mind, the price to be two guineas the series of twelve.

HIS TRAVELING, except for brief jaunts within his own country, was now at last ended. He settled in London, and soon became a familiar figure in its thoroughfares. It was difficult to avoid encountering him, for he habitually frequented "the most noted promenades and resorts of the people," conspicuous in his Armenian

---

[31] De Quincey, *Works*, ed. Masson (1890), III, 103–104.
[32] This work is reviewed in the *Gentleman's Magazine*, Vol. 73, Pt. II (September 1803), pp. 851–852.

dress, which he persisted in wearing until it was threadbare. It has
been suggested that he adopted this costume in order to attract
attention, with a view to the wider dissemination of his philosophical opinions.[33] He was so ubiquitous, indeed, that he became a
legend to the Londoners of his day. An anonymous contemporary
so portrays him:

Who that ever weathered his way over Westminster Bridge has not
seen *Walking Stewart* (his invariable cognomen) sitting in the recess
on the brow of the bridge, spencered up to his throat and down to his
hips with a sort of garment planned, it should seem, to stand *powder*,
as became the habit of a military man; his dingy, dusty inexpressibles
(really *inexpressibles*); his boots, travel-stained, black up to his knees,
—and yet not black neither, but arrant walkers both of them, or their
complexions belied them; his aged, but strongly marked, manly, and
air-refined face, steady as truth; and his large, irregular, dusty hat,
that seemed to be of one mind with the boots? We say, who does not
thus remember *Walking Stewart*, sitting, and leaning on his stick, as
if he had never walked in his life, but had taken his seat on the bridge
at his birth, and had grown old in his sedentary habit? To be sure, this
view of him is rather negatived by as strong a remembrance of him
in the same spencer and accompaniments of hair-powder and dust,
resting on a bench in the Park, with as perfectly an eternal air; nor
will the memory let him keep a quiet, constant seat *here* for ever,—
recalling him, as she is wont, in his shuffling, slow perambulation of the
Strand, or Charing Cross, or Cockspur Street. Where really was he?
You saw him on Westminster Bridge, acting his own monument; you
went into the Park,—he was there, fixed as the gentleman at [West-
minster Bridge]; you met him, however, at Charing Cross, creeping
on like the hour-hand upon a dial, getting rid of his rounds and his
time at once! Indeed, his ubiquity seemed enormous,—and yet not so
enormous as the profundity of his sitting habits. He was a profound
sitter. Could the Pythagorean system be embalmed, what a hen would
now be tenanted by Walking Stewart! Truly, he seemed always to be
going, like a lot at an auction, and yet always at a stand, like a hackney-
coach! Oh! what a walk was his to christen a man by,—a slow, lazy,
scraping, creeping, gazing pace,—a shuffle,—a walk in its dotage, a walk
at a standstill! Yet was he a pleasant man to meet. We remember his
face distinctly, and, allowing a little for its northern hardness, it was
certainly as wise, as kindly, and as handsome a face as ever crowned
the shoulders of a soldier, a scholar, and a gentleman.[34]

[33] See *Annual Biography and Obituary*, VII, 106. A colored print of him in this
characteristic garb was to be seen for some years in the shop windows of London.
De Quincey, *Works*, III, 117.

[34] *London Magazine* (November 1822), quoted in De Quincey, *Works*, III,
119–120.

This impression is confirmed by a similar recollection of De Quincey's:

I met him and shook hands with him under Somerset House. . . . Thence I went, by the very shortest road (*i.e.*, through Moor Street, Soho—for I am learned in many quarters of London), towards a point which necessarily led me through Tottenham Court Road: I stopped nowhere, and walked fast; yet so it was that in Tottenham Court Road I was not overtaken by (*that* was comprehensible), but overtook, Walking Stewart. Certainly, . . . there must have been three Walking Stewarts in London. He seemed nowise surprised at this himself, but explained to me that somewhere or other in the neighbourhood of Tottenham Court Road there was a little theatre, at which there was dancing, and occasionally good singing, between which and a neighbouring coffee-house he sometimes divided his evenings.[35]

Other men associated him more particularly with St. James's Park, "where he sat in trance-like reverie amongst the cows, inhaling their balmy breath and pursuing his philosophic speculations." [36]

H. G. Bohn remembered Stewart when he lived in this locality, near Spring Gardens (St. James's Park); and noticed that he had developed the habit of walking "regularly two miles before breakfast, one out and one in. He started with his coat buttoned up to the neck, and opened it by degrees at established intervals, buttoning up again as he approached home." [37] An explanation of this procedure by Stewart himself makes it seem somewhat more rationally elastic: "I clothed myself," he writes, "at all times very warm, which, by buttoning and unbuttoning, I could accommodate to the sudden change of climate and season, and preserved thereby that equilibre of the secretions and excrements on which health and life depends." [38] The deeper principles which underlie this statement must await fuller consideration.

When De Quincey came up to London in 1807 or 1808, he made a point of seeking Stewart out. From motives of delicacy, he did not inquire for him at his lodgings, knowing that he was poor, and wishing not to put him to any embarrasment; but he found

[35] De Quincey, *Works*, III, 107.

[36] *Ibid.*, p. 108; *Gentleman's Magazine*, Vol. 73, Pt. II (September 1803), pp. 851–852. This park, as more than one pleasant old mezzotint attests, was a customary station for milkmaids with their cows. You bought your drink by the glass, and could have it, warm and fresh, from the cow of your own choosing— unless you preferred to make your selection according to the faces of the maids.

[37] Lowndes, *Manual*, ed. Bohn, V, 2515.

[38] *Scripture of Reason and Nature*, p. ix.

him at a favorite coffee house in Piccadilly. Stewart affably invited
him to his rooms in Sherrard Street, Golden Square, and there De
Quincey continued to visit him, seeing much of him during the
next four or five years. He was so struck with Stewart's mind that
he made notes of their conversations on various topics. He found
him generous, sympathetic, and unselfish, and quite the finest
natural talker he had ever met. "Walking Stewart," he says, "was,
in conversation, the most eloquent man—limiting the meaning to
the eloquence of nature, unsustained by any range of illustration
from books—that I have ever known." [39] From a man who knew
the circle of Coleridge, Wordsworth, Lamb, and Hazlitt, such
testimony is extraordinary. And other witnesses are equally emphatic.[40]

De Quincey was impressed, too, with Stewart's veracity: such,
he found, was his noble reverence for truth that, "to have won a
universal interest with the public, he would not have deviated, by
one hair's breadth, from the severe facts of a case." [41] One general
observation, distilled from all the sufferings and dangers of his
adventurous life, De Quincey never forgot: it was that in all
Stewart's experience among uncivilized and barbarous peoples he
had never met a savage who would attack a defenseless man provided the stranger could make him understand that he was throwing himself upon the native's hospitality and forbearance.[42] So far
as his own private history was concerned, Stewart went to the
length of declaring, "upon the veracity of a man of nature," that
he could not remember having had a single personal quarrel with
any individual during his forty years' wandering. "I considered an
angry man," he declares, "in a state of disease, and whenever I
observed its symptoms, I guarded my mind from the contagion as
I would my person from a putrid fever." [43]

He must have started with a magnificent physical endowment.
But he laid a great part of his lifelong vigorous health to the credit
of his physical and moral regimen. In various parts of his works he
sets down his convictions about the proper diet for man.

[39] De Quincey, *Work*, III, 96.
[40] *Annual Biography and Obituary*, VII, and *Gentleman's Magazine*, Vol. 73,
Pt. II (September 1803).
[41] De Quincey, *Works*, III, 95.
[42] *Ibid.*, pp. 95, 115.
[43] *Scripture of Reason and Nature*, p. viii.

I have observed [he says] amongst nations, whose aliment is vegetables and water, that disease and medicine are equally unknown, while those, whose aliment is flesh and fermented liquor, are constantly afflicted with disease, and medicine more dangerous than disease itself, and not only those guilty of excess, but others, who lead lives of temperance.[44]

He therefore has no doubt that the vegetable diet is man's only congenial food, a doctrine confirmed by humanitarian considerations as well; and believes that fermented liquors are "absolutely heterogeneous" to the human system.[45] In his travels he had tried to adapt his diet to the nature of the country through which he was passing.

In travelling, if my body was wet, and must continue any time in that state, I abstained from all nourishment till it was dry, and always escaped the usual disorders of cold, rheumatism, and fever. When I was in the frigid Zone, I lived upon a nutritious aliment, and eat much butter with beans, peas, and other pulse. In the torrid Zone I diminished the nutritious quality of my food, and eat but little butter, and even then found it necessary to eat spices to absorb the humours, whose redundancy are [sic] caused by heat, and are noxious in hot climates. In cold climates nature seems to demand that redundancy, as necessary to strength and health.[46]

He "paid much attention to the quantity as well as quality of [his] food, allowing full time for its digestion." [47] The only hint of physical ailment during his entire life is his assertion that he was for a time afflicted by "a muscular debility contracted by the pernicious use of tobacco in smoking"; but this he rectified by strict temperance and hygienic methods of his own devising. "In lodging," he writes, "I took care to preserve the purity of the air in the daytime, by a small aperture in the top sash of a window, so as to avoid all draught or current, which is dangerous; and at night I slept in an inner chamber, with a window open in the front room." [48] Much of this sounds like common sense today; but anyone familiar with the ordinary living habits of the eighteenth century will recognize the rarity of this brand of common sense at that time.

[44] *Apocalypse of Nature*, pp. 170–171.
[45] In *The Moral World Displayed*, I, 40 ff., he develops these ideas with warmth.
[46] *Apocalypse*, pp. 173–174.
[47] *Scripture of Reason and Nature*, p. ix.
[48] *Ibid.*, p. x.

Stewart gives a somewhat startling account of his moral regimen, in the more limited sense of the term:

In my moral relations, I found it necessary to happiness to withdraw
myself from all family connexions, and to live independent of the
caprices and follies of my species: this exposed me in some measure to
the danger of venereal indulgences, which are necessary to health in
youth, but not in age. I took care, however, to use a strong lotion of
coarse soap, quite hot, boiled in a pint of water, immediately after
coition, and thus escaped from all disease. Arrived at the age of sixty,
I left off all intercourse with the sex, considering the discharge of
semen at that age as the discharge of vitality, in both the energy of
the mind and body. I still indulge in female dalliance, without injury
to their sex, and without danger to my own constitution; and such is
my economy of moral and physical pleasure, that, according to the
poet, I taste the honey without wounding the flower.[49]
I observed [he says further] that the six senses were distinguished by
the character of noxious and innocent; that the first three, of thinking,
seeing, and hearing, were the innocent; and the last three, feeling,
tasting, and smelling, the noxious. I pursued happiness, or systematic
pleasurable sensation, in the cultivation of the first class, and the
abstinence or control of the latter.[50]

Stewart cultivated his physical welfare with such notable success that he became a byword in the insurance offices. He used to
take a sardonic pleasure "in presenting himself annually to establish his continued existence"—to the amused annoyance of the
directors, who protested that he had already lived twenty years
too long.[51]

At some date between 1810 and 1814 Stewart's affairs suddenly
burgeoned into affluence. His long-outstanding claims upon the
Nabob of Arcot were at last acknowledged as valid by the East
India Company, the Nabob's sponsor. In satisfaction of Stewart's
claims, the Company paid him a lump sum of from £10,000 to
£15,000.[52] Sudden wealth did not turn Stewart's head; but he now
found it possible to put his philosophical theories into fuller operation. He invested his money in new life annuities which brought
him £900 or more a year, a sum which was adequate to all his

---

[49] *Ibid.*, pp. x-xi.
[50] *Ibid.*, pp. xii-xiii.
[51] De Quincey, *Works*, III, 98.
[52] The *Gentleman's Magazine* says £15,000; the *Annual Biography and Obituary*
gives £10,000; De Quincey believes it was £14,000; while Taylor says £16,000.
The *D.N.B.* adopts the smallest of these figures.

wishes. Loving to be "in the full tide of human existence," he moved to more elegant quarters in Cockspur Street. His new apartments he fitted up in the way best calculated to favor the cultivation of the innocent senses. He hung his rooms round with a multitude of mirrors, pictures after the Chinese taste, and transparencies of landscapes; and he installed an organ of satisfying amplitude, which was supplemented from time to time with other musical instruments. Then he flooded everything with the blaze of candelabra. The effect was declared overwhelming. "The reflection of light from all quarters," says one witness, "and the multiplicity of objects reflected by the mirrors, gave a brilliancy to the whole scene, scarcely to be imagined." [53] Not for nothing had Stewart been Master of Ceremonies to the Nabob of Arcot. He now indulged his hospitable inclinations to the full. He engaged professional musicians and gave frequent concerts. He provided excellent dinners (neither vegetarian nor wineless, presumably, for they were remembered with lively pleasure) to select friends, Charles Colton, Thomas Clio Rickman the disciple of Paine, John Taylor the publicist, and Robert Owen. With such as these he held philosophical conversation during the meal, but insisted on lecturing to them before the wine was removed. He himself, like Oliver Goldsmith before him, partook very sparingly of the sumptuous provision laid before his guests. In time, finding he made little headway with his indoctrinations, he substituted soirées to which he invited both sexes, providing both music and whist for entertainment, and diffusing among a large and brilliant company "cheerfulness and a spirit of frank communication." [54]

But Stewart was under no illusions concerning the light in which he was regarded. He knew that the majority of his guests looked upon him merely as an agreeable eccentric, and he lamented his failure to propagate his theories. To most persons, he writes,

my philosophy in the analogical part was totally unintelligible; and it was not till after many years of controversy that they left off laughing when I spoke of the transmutation of matter passing through the agent mode of man into the patiency of all sensitive nature, to retribute good or evil in an immensurate ratio of multiplication of interest in extent and duration throughout the whole organism of the universe.

[53] *Annual Biography and Obituary*, VII, 108.
[54] *Ibid*.

They smiled at the cultivation of my sense of sight in the furniture of my apartments, and called them a baby-house, when they were calculated to effect the end of cheerfulness by lights, mirrors, and transparent blinds, to guard against the melancholy which philosophic reflection, if not managed with economy, is apt to produce. . . .[55]

In my little Epicurean heaven of apartments, . . . I have seen men of the world smiling at the baby simplicity of the Man of Nature; and, in the midst of the most enrapturing melodies, or philosophic converse, turn towards each other in groups, and converse with great zeal on the pulling down of an old house, the quarrels of the parish, or the triumph of political factions. Great Integer of Nature, how civilized refinement, in its powerful habitudes, denaturalizes man, and will not permit him to study, or to walk, or act in the single and peaceful paths of nature!!! to perform the great function of manhood, the enjoyment of modal or predicamental good, identified with the material and improvable good of all nature.[56]

But he did not cease his efforts to open men's minds to the true philosophy. As the years went by, one work followed another from his pen. It would be tedious to list the titles, though some of them—as *The Roll of A Tennis Ball through the Moral World*—are not devoid of appeal.[57] Most of these books are printed in the smaller sizes, to make them conveniently portable. All of them, doubtless, were printed at the author's own expense.

Stewart came to feel more and more strongly that the world was not yet ready for his message, nor would be for generations to come; and latterly he became convinced that in the present state of moral being it was better that his books should be neglected of the multitude. But what might happen to them in the meantime, before their date matured, worried him considerably, and he gave it a good deal of thought.

A notion [says De Quincey] obstinately haunted his mind, that all the kings and rulers of the earth would confederate in every age against his works, and would hunt them out for extermination as keenly as Herod did the innocents of Bethlehem. On this consideration, fearing that they might be intercepted by the long arms of these wicked princes before they could reach that remote Stewartian man or his precursor to whom they were mainly addressed, he recommended to all those who might be impressed with a sense of their importance

---

[55] One is reminded of Dr. Johnson's friend, Edwards, who had tried in his time to be a philosopher, but "cheerfulness was always breaking in."

[56] *Scripture of Reason and Nature*, pp. xv-xvi, xviii-xix.

[57] There is a fairly complete list in Lowndes's *Manual*, V, 2515-2516.

to bury a copy or copies of each work, properly secured from damp,
&c., at a depth of seven or eight feet below the surface of the earth,
and on their death-beds to communicate the knowledge of this fact
to some confidential friends, who, in their turn, were to send down
the tradition to some discreet persons of the next generation; and thus,
if the truth was not to be dispersed for many ages, yet the knowledge
that here and there the truth lay buried on this and that continent, in
secret spots on Mount Caucasus, in the sands of Biledulgerid, and in
hiding-places amongst the forests of America, and was to rise again
in some distant age, and to vegetate and fructify for the universal
benefit of man,—this knowledge at least was to be whispered down
from generation to generation; and, in defiance of a myriad of kings
crusading against him, Walking Stewart was to stretch out the influence
of his writings through a long series of λαμπαδηφόροι to that child of
nature whom he saw dimly through a vista of many centuries. If this
were madness, it seemed to me a somewhat sublime madness: and I
assured him of my co-operation against the kings, promising that I
would bury the "Harp of Apollo" in my own orchard in Grasmere at
the foot of Mount Fairfield, that I would bury the "Apocalypse of
Nature" in one of the coves of Helvellyn, and several other works in
several other places best known to myself. He accepted my offer with
gratitude; but he then made known to me that he relied on my assistance for a still more important service—which was this: in the lapse of
that vast number of ages that would probably intervene between the
present period and the period at which his works would have reached
their destination, he feared that the English language might itself have
mouldered away. "No!" I said, "*that* was not probable: considering
its extensive diffusion, and that it was now transplanted into all the
continents of our planet, I would back the English language against
any other on earth." His own persuasion, however, was, that the Latin
was destined to survive all other languages; it was to be the eternal as
well as the universal language; and his desire was that I should translate
his works, or some part of them, into that language. This I promised;
and I seriously designed at some leisure hour to translate into Latin a
selection of passages which should embody an abstract of his philosophy.[58]

There is no doubt that Stewart's works would have gained in
dignity and effectiveness from such a treatment as De Quincey
proposed. They are written in a style which can safely be called
vile; they are endlessly repetitious and almost completely lacking
in coherence of parts. They end anywhere and begin again and
again. In the *Sophiometer*, for example, the reader will discover no
fewer than twelve repetitions of "The End." The first occurs on

[58] De Quincey, *Works*, III, 112–113.

page 112. A "Conclusion" follows immediately; but the last "The End" comes at the foot of page 324. Beyond that point, the text runs on for twenty-four *unnumbered* pages. Amusingly enough, on the actual last page the type runs to the very bottom, leaving no room on which to print "The End." Another aspect of the book is noteworthy. It commences in fine large type with much lead between the lines. On page 110 the lines close up. Then the type size is reduced; and toward the end it becomes really minute. These changes have no correspondence with the divisions of the argument: they merely signify a finer thread of verbosity.

Neverthless, it is our duty to find out if we can what the man was trying so desperately to express. Roughly sketched, his system can be pictured somewhat as follows.

The universe is altogether composed of eternal and indestructible matter. All matter is one infinite whole, a "Great Integer," which, if you will, may be called Nature. It is, however, incessantly combining and recombining into forms, or "modes." When portions of it combine into the mode of man, it becomes active, or "agent"; in all other forms it is passive, or "patient." Only while it is a portion of man's mental life, we gather, has it any directive power; at all other times, or in all other forms, it has merely receptive potency. Into the final causes or cause which may have set the whole in motion, it is idle to inquire: speculation on this subject only leads to the construction of metaphysical phantasmagoria, such as God, the soul, etc., which have no correspondence with anything that man can actually know. It is because man has devoted so large a part of his thinking to the asinine pursuit of metaphysical questions that he has proceeded so short a distance on the road to "perfectuability."

We must not make the mistake of thinking that a certain portion of agent matter remains constant in an individual man until his dissolution. The fact is far otherwise: there is a perpetual interchange of material atoms between man and all surrounding matter from moment to moment. In Stewart's view, in fact, the individual human body is the most wraithlike identity imaginable: it is perpetually dissolving and recombining with a speed that is terrifyingly swift. A man at any single instant is not the same man he was at the instant before: he has given off a portion of himself in the interim, and taken unto himself at the same time an equivalent part of the circumambient atoms. This is a fact which is demonstrated to conviction by what we observe of the physical processes in the human body.

It follows from this community of matter that the interests of the whole material universe are intimately the interests of every individual man. This is the basic truth of morality. It concerns man tremendously to act always in such a way as to further material well-being in its largest sense. The standard of well-being is the preponderance of pleasurable sensation over pain. Since all matter not at the moment incorporated into the agent mode of man is simply the passive register of sensation, the power of the agent to cause pleasure or pain upon the rest of the universe is incalculably great, and man's moral responsibility, in consequence, is literally infinite. But he must perceive that this responsibility is no abstract duty: rather, the most practical self-interest. For, his identity being truly co-terminous in space and time with the universe itself, he is really—if he could only see it—the causer of his own future happiness or misery. "I am the slayer and the slain"— but in a less metaphysical sense than the poet intends. Alexander stopping a bunghole groans under the pain inflicted upon the sentient universe by Alexander the tyrant.

This is not the Pythagorean notion of metempsychosis. That the soul of our grandam may haply inhabit a bird, Walking Stewart, like Malvolio, would have been prompt to deny: not because he thought nobly of the soul, but because he did not believe in the soul's existence. He scoffed at the idea of the perpetuation of the individual consciousness after death. But he vehemently denied that his theory was thereby invalidated. The sentient atoms do not need to know that they were once Alexander in order to feel the pain. They do not need to know anything; they have no intellectual consciousness: they merely suffer.

Morality, therefore, in Stewart's view, has been hitherto restricted to an absurdly limited scope. It is not simply the science of man's conduct considered with reference to his duty to himself and his fellow man. True morality takes in infinitely wider vistas: it is referable to all being, and must be established on the broadest of bases.

But to determine a morality which has reference to so vast a

scale demands a profound judgement and the most delicate calculation. It is not only that one must determine the relative weight of
conflicting goods. Nor does it involve only the clash between immediate private and ultimate public good. Good itself does not
remain constant, and no absolute standard of good can be established. For the universe is in a constant state of flux, and what is a
good today may be an evil tomorrow. Good is so only with reference to a particular set of conditions. All virtue, therefore, is relative. And if this is true of private and social morality, so also is it
of politics and economics.

No one can hope, amongst the dubious probabilities on this side
and on that, to do more than calculate the approximate good. And
even this is beyond the powers of all save the Child of Nature, who
will be sympathetically attuned to the vast sentient world, and
will thus be able to form his decisions upon a scale of reference
broader than the restricted interests of most men or groups. Such
a child of nature will be uncontaminated by all the falsifying influences of civilization, our vicious social habits, our silly conventions, our religious superstitions, the blind system of education
whereby we stuff the memory and suppress the reason, the prejudices of family, of class, and even of race. He will not look for
reward to the consolations of a Christian or a pagan heaven, but he
will find his adequate satisfaction in the joy that follows from the
sublime contemplation of his unity with the whole sentient universe, as he feels his happiness in all things and all men through
eternity.

Such is the bare skeleton of Stewart's philosophy. De Quincey
is not far wrong when he calls it "a sort of rude and unscientific
Spinosism." To be sure, Spinoza's philosophy without God is
Hamlet without Hamlet; but if we consent to call God matter, the
comparison may stand. It is only in his last work that Stewart
seems to be conscious of any such affiliation, and the fact is perhaps indicative of his learning about Spinoza late in life. Probably
he had been started in this direction by what he may have picked
up in youth of Eastern philosophy; but the turn which Indian
mysticism took in his handling was toward the opposite pole, of
utilitarianism. The closest recognizable affiliation with other philosophical thought, however, is Stewart's patent relation to Bolingbroke, as that sage's system is presented in Pope's *Essay on Man*.

Stewart quotes Bolingbroke frequently, almost always in Pope's words. The familiar couplet,

> All matter, motion, rightly understood,
> Proves true self-interest universal good,

Stewart calls "the most important idea that ever came from the mind of man"; but he adds that Bolingbroke uttered it "without any meaning," because he had no conception of the immortality of matter. The idea of the couplet, as Stewart understands it, is the very motto of his whole philosophy, and again and again he recurs to its demonstration. If he can once drive home to his readers this truth in its literal, not figurative, signification, they must, he feels, grant all the rest of his system, for it all leans upon this. But the proof of it depends on a conviction of the material (and moral) identity of man and nature, and to repeated demonstrations of this vital hypothesis he devotes a major effort.[59]

If space permitted, an entertaining florilegium could be assembled of Stewart's more whimsical notions and mannerisms, and of that sublime egotism which makes him exalt himself, "the only man of nature who ever appeared in the world," above Dr. Johnson, David Hume, Shakespeare, Socrates, and even, I fear, Christ himself. He had an inveterate proclivity to *last words*, and is always breaking off to invoke mankind as if from the moment before his dissolution. One of his favorite notions is that the bayonet or pike is the natural weapon of Englishmen, and that ten thousand Britons armed with this weapon and solidified, as it were, by a sympathetic union of spirit, would be victorious against millions. The pike should be called "the paraclete of the world," for its power, "depending on its connexion with moral energy of free men, would subject the physical to the moral force, and harmonize man with the universal machine of nature, in its appetency to augment system, or good, and diminish contingency, in time and futurity." [60] He is fond of inventing names of this sort, and envisions various moral tools for the better calculation of practical and universal good: for example, the *Sophiometer*, the *Panoscope*. He insists that thought is the sixth sense, and defends this notion throughout his later work. He adds a codicil to his *Moral Will*

[59] See, e.g., *Apocalypse*, pp. 210–214; *Book of Intellectual Life*, pp. 60–64.
[60] *Sophiometer*, p. 229.

and Testament, bequeathing to mankind the benefits of earth
bathing or a "warm mud-bath," which is an infallible panacea
that makes other medicine unnecessary.[61]

WHAT MAKES Stewart's system interesting is that it is an image,
surprisingly free from literary influences, of the floating ideas of
his time. I say this, though he loudly cries his originality in every
book he writes. In fact, his writing throws odd lights on the moving
currents that coursed confusedly and obscurely through contemporary life. His works give us an almost unique opportunity to
sense the atmosphere of popular thought in the turbulent years
1790–1818, as it condensed in a robust but untrained intelligence.
    We can see in this mind's offensive violence against formal reli-
gion, in his reference to an "oven-baked god," the effects of that
wave of skepticism which swept through Europe after the religious
fervor of the preceding age had spent itself—that wave which
lifted Hume, Voltaire, and the Encyclopedists upon its crest and
undermined the bases of traditional authority, to make possible
the French Revolution. We can discern the concurrent inability of
the century to live in this rarefied air of intellectual doubt, and the
instinctive effort to compensate itself for what it had forgone, by
constructing in other terms a religion of nature which turns out at
the last to demand an equal, if not greater, amount of faith. We
can follow the emphasis on sensibility, and watch the course of
the favorite notions which cluster about the name of Rousseau—
ideas of the state of nature and the natural man, as these doctrines
come to be worn into habitual use by the popular mind. We can
discern the subsequent union of sentimentality and the humanitarian impulse. In Stewart's work this spirit inveighs against the
evils of slavery, of the custom of duelling, of the favorite English
sport, hunting; and the last antipathy in turn passes easily into
vegetarianism as a humane article of belief. We can watch the
early growth of the utilitarian movement in Stewart's maxim, "To
effectuate the highest possible good with the least possible evil,"
as a flexible standard of conduct—a principle which naturally followed upon the skepticism that shook the rigid moral code of

[61] See, e.g., his "tariff of pain and pleasure," in *Moral World Displayed*, I, 206
ff.; and also his words on the "tyrannicide," in *Sophiometer*, pp. 108–110.

religion. We can see the romantic faith in man's rational powers as adequate to lead him with splendid swiftness to a state of perfection. And we can follow in the change of attitude visible in Stewart's works toward the French Revolution that growing doubt of the immediacy of the millennium when men saw the actual issue of magnificent ideas working themselves out in the violence of the mass mind. It is symptomatic of this change that in Stewart's first work he exalts the absolute freedom of the press as the chief instrument of man's welfare, but that in his last work he advocates such freedom in Latin only:

I exhort, in these last words of a child of nature, the Sovereign Congress of the civilized world to declare the press absolutely free in the Latin language only, while the native languages shall be subject to law. . . .

I can now say with truth and reason, O nature, great integer of self, let thy eternal fellow part dissolve in peace, for mine eyes have seen thy salvation; and I now promulgate, in the Latin tongue, this momentous instruction of the true Copernican moral system of universal good in theory and practice, to tranquillize the ocean of sensitive life into which my particles are every moment transmuting from a mode to a world or universe, where good and evil will be retributed in the ratio of the diameter of half a pound of brain to the whole brain of the universe; because as every particle, like the waves of water, must feel the whole agitation of the wave it is recombined in, so the consciousness of animal life makes every human particle feel all the action of the organic system it is changed into; and thus one body of man becomes every moment all the bodies of sensitive life throughout the organism of the universe. What can resist the progress of this momentous truth of universal and eternal interest, if the harmony of practical order can be preserved from the ignorance of the mob and the lettered idiotism of talent, wit, and literature, mistaking the formation of human character to be through volition and not intellectual power, beginning with the higher and not the lower classes of society, whose poverty disposes them to confusion, change, and revolution?[62]

Before we dismiss Stewart as a harmless lunatic, it may be useful to pay brief attention to a few of his notions which seem not so typical of his own as, possibly, of a later day.

It is not merely that the general notion of the relativity of moral standards has been appropriated by our own time with such em-

[62] *Book of Intellectual Life*, pp. 176, 178.

phasis as to make it seem a characteristically modern idea.[63] This denial of abstract good results for Stewart in some interesting corollaries. It leads him, for instance, to anticipate the doctrine, advocated by certain modern physicians, of benevolent murder. As he puts it:

in this case, partial seeming evil is general good, and must be also partial good, if the individual is a fraction of the whole of existence. It may be a general and partial good that I may die to save a wise man or a wise nation; but it would be both a partial and general ill, for an individual to agonize through a long life of disease and torment, from which no good can arise to the whole, the species, or the part.[64]

Oddly enough, his relativistic theories lead him to a position of doubt with regard to Newtonian physics. "Real order," he says,

or fixation, or a determined ratio of motion does not exist; and this truth is an induction from the eternal motion of matter in the increase and decrease of all bodies.

The ratio of falling bodies, which Sir Isaac Newton was supposed to have calculated with accuracy, must be false in the abstract, and a deviation is caused by the incremental or excremental motion of the earth, which diminishes or augments attraction, though the human intellect cannot mark so imperceptible a difference or derangement from universal order.[65]

Again, in his disapprobation of science, Stewart strikes a note which, while it sets up Rousseauian overtones, is vibrating perceptibly today. Science, he declares, "has erected a Tower of Babel to look into the skies and discover the relation of the planets, before sense had laid the great foundation of self-knowledge." The nations of the past

all rose and set in science, without ever approaching sense; and if we contemplate with wisdom the present awful crisis of the political world, there is every reason to fear, that modern nations, who have carried science to its acme, will follow their example; and while they have discovered all the relations of science, live in a total ignorance of sense, to discover man and his relations to the moral world of sen-

---

[63] See, e.g., Havelock Ellis, *The Dance of Life*, a work more representative of the popular temper than professional philosophical works on ethics. For a characteristic statement, in Stewart, of the doctrine of flexibility of moral good, see *Revolution of Reason*, pp. 191–200.

[64] *Revolution of Reason*, p. 122.

[65] *Moral World Displayed*, I, 11–12.

sate good. His food is used to poison instead of nourish; his clothes and lodging, to produce disease instead of comfort; his moral institutions, to produce the misery instead of the happiness of domestic life; and his policy, to check the progress of reason, and all human perfectuability (forcing man to sip in torture, the last dregs of life, without the virtue of fortitude to dissolve it).[66]

He therefore proposes "that the study of the sciences be universally suspended over the whole globe—that the human mind, freed from the blandishments of the Syrens of science and arts, might be able to return to its home, or invert all the force of its faculties upon self." [67]

In his feeling that modern education was conducted on a wrong principle, tending not to liberate the mind, but rather to suppress individual intellectual initiative and perpetuate inherited prejudice, Stewart once more strikes a modern note. Children's minds, he says, under this discipline become mere sacks of information. The society which he desiderates can only be produced by abandoning such methods, and he is voluble on his own educational ideals. In certain ways these foreshadow "progressive" notions in vogue at present. The great end is to teach *how* to think and not *what* to think; and in the earlier years play should be used as the chief method of instruction. Reading and writing should be taught as a sport, "while the tuition of thought and skill, to conduct means to their ends, should accommodate the sports and games to the growing capacity of the juvenile mind." [68]

In his denunciation of the acquisitive society, Stewart, at least in his earlier works, is almost as outspoken as are certain contemporary critics. Industry he calls "the arch fiend," "the dreadful enemy to truth and happiness." In all competitive societies, he declares,

the poor have been ever left a prey to the rich; who, in proportion to the sympathy they possess, have rendered them happy or miserable. Laws, if properly established, would no doubt procure them relief;

[66] *Sophiometer*, pp. 13–16. Stewart appears here to be using the term "science" in a broad significance; yet the opposition to "sense" suggests a somewhat restricted interpretation. "Sense," as he uses it, ought to include "science" in the wider meaning.
[67] *Apocalypse*, pp. 154–155.
[68] For exposition of these ideas, see especially *Scripture of Reason and Nature*, pp. 95–106, and *Book of Intellectual Life*, pp. 84–89.

but the rich, who make them, wish for no alteration; and nothing but extreme necessity, brought about by insurrection, can compel the rich to such an operation.[69]

But the question has even wider issues, and in a noteworthy passage Stewart pursues it as follows:

Let us examine the present effects of industry amongst mankind. The English are by far the most industrious nation upon the globe; but what is the consequence? Nationally, they are the most powerful and the richest people; every individual wears upon his back the value of five days labour; inhabits a house, whose rent is equal to the daily value of four days labour; his daily food equals the value of three days labour; and these calculations are formed upon an average of the whole; so that the support of a subject of England may require twelve days labour. We will suppose his own superior industry to equal four days labour of a stranger, and his skill or product of his ingenuity is exported and procures him the value of eight days labour from foreign countries. What is ultimately its utility or effect upon his happiness?

The poor man, upon whom the unequal division of labour falls, must be reduced thereby to a piece of mechanism, or mere animal state of existence.—His life must be spent in the alternate occupations of toil and sleep, which must deprive his essence of all consciousness, and depress him to a very low state upon the scale of existence, if bodily health should render him absent from pain, but sickness must render it miserable and deplorable.

Let us now inquire, whether the misery of the poor promotes the happiness of the rich. They escape from bodily toil, which leaves them in such a vacuum of indolence, that the body loses all its vigour and health, the foundation of happiness. The mind, to avoid stagnation, creates various factitious desires and wants, pursuing them with an energy, that agitates, and not undulates the current of life. Castles are occupied by themselves and families, where forms of etiquette and proud ceremony turn their pompous habitations into gloomy prisons, and where the elastic balmy air of the atmosphere is forbid entrance to purify the morbid air of the drawing-room, exhausted with the heat of candles and fire, infected with the respiration of unhealthy and numerous companies, and which turns their inhabitants into spectres in appearance, and invalids in substance. The mind participates of the debility of the body; and memory, to avoid the tedium of inactive life, fills itself with all the rubbish of ancient and modern history, courts domestic anecdotes, which overwhelm the faculties of judgement, and reduce the mind to the same state of unconsciousness with excessive labour, and is evinced by that easy behaviour, and thoughtless loquacity of the rich and great, which seem to indicate no vacuum

[69] *Apocalypse*, p. 262.

in life, but is, at the same time, a sure proof of want of judgement, sensibility, and consciousness, without which rational existence can have no excellence over animal, and the mind can possess no powers to expand into intellectual existence.

Industry, therefore, seems a necessary evil, or relative good, according to the present system, as it gives power and riches to nations; but the morality of nature regards all excessive occupation, as an enemy to human happiness, and demands a medium of repose and labour to enable the mind to expand into consciousness, by contemplation of its self, and to invigorate the corporeal faculties, to procure the perfection of essence, a sound mind in a sound body.[70]

Stewart declares that only that society is entitled to the name Society which guarantees to its every member "food, lodging, and clothing, with or without labour, according to [his] condition," and that all societies that have not this condition, whatever their political form, deserve only the name "human aggregation." [71]

As it is with competitive individuals, so it is with competitive nations.

In the present commercial and political system of the world, nations, like individuals, place welfare in the destruction of competitors, and millions are plunged into the abyss of misery, that one may obtain an abundance which promises joy in its progress, till increasing to redundancy, it produces evil; and I am conscientiously convinced, that all degrees above or below the line of competency in national power, or individual property, are affected by a parallel ratio of evil. This point of competency should be the great object of human study.[72]

Contemplation of the state of the world under the evils of the competitive system leads Stewart to forecast a league of nations. The enormities of modern destructive warfare will, he believes, "render national confederacy as necessary to the safety of mankind, as domestic government" to individual nations.[73] Were it not for the narrowly selfish principles according to which present society conducts itself, collective wisdom in the deliberations of national councils must ere this have forced "the boundaries of error beyond the circle of national interest, and [have extended] confederacy to involve the limits of the whole quarter of the globe,

[70] Ibid., pp. 179–183.
[71] Book of Intellectual Life, pp. 73–74. He believes that Britain alone, through its Poor Laws, guarantees this right.
[72] Moral World Displayed, II, 35–36.
[73] Apocalypse, p. 200.

and progressively to the globe itself, which would certainly be the progress of association, if founded upon the principles of truth and reason." [74]

So he wrote in his first book; and in his last he set down words which, in the light of subsequent history, are peculiarly arresting:

In that quarter of the globe called Asia, the progress of intellectual power has been so perpetually disturbed by wars, bad government, and famine, that man has had no leisure for study or reflection; and all the energies of mind have been employed to feed the body, and preserve mere animal life: and this great mass of animal power, without a spark of intellectual life, or knowledge of self and nature, is preparing an enormous mass of physical force, when subjected by Russia, to give the united empire of the world to that power. [75]

This was his warning, if the nations of Europe should not with sufficient rapidity develop "essential intellect," the knowledge of self and nature, as distinguished from "technical intellect," or the knowledge of arts and sciences.

It would be easy to prolong the citation of interesting and characteristic passages from Stewart's writings. But his books, though scarce and unlikely ever to be reprinted, may still be perused in the great public libraries; and our own account of him must be now concluded.

In the year 1821 Stewart's health at last began to fail. He left London on a visit to Margate, thinking that the sea air might do him good. But he received no benefit. He came back to London, where his health steadily declined. January 1822, saw him seriously unwell; and, on the morning of February 20, he was found dead in his rooms in Northumberland Street. He had habitually carried poison, in case he should at any time wish to end his life. An empty laudanum bottle was found in his room; but it was not ascertained that he had committed suicide.

It seems appropriate to close this study of an all but forgotten man with the eloquent tribute of the genius who alone has preserved Stewart from oblivion, and who alone has done justice to his personality and character:

He was a man of genius, but not a man of talents; at least his genius was out of all proportion to his talents, and wanted an organ, as it

[74] *Travels*, p. xlvii.
[75] *Book of Intellectual Life*, p. 207.

were, for manifesting itself, so that his most original thoughts were delivered in a crude state, imperfect, obscure, half-developed, and not productible to a popular audience. . . . He was a disproportioned intellect, and so far a monster: and he must be added to the long list of original-minded men who have been looked down upon with pity and contempt by common-place men of talent, whose powers of mind, though a thousand times inferior, were yet more manageable, more self-interpreted, and ran in channels better suited to common uses and common understandings. . . . Actually, therefore, he will be lost and forgotten. Potentially, he was a great man. . . . He was no madman; or, if he was, then I say it is so far desirable to be a madman. . . . On the whole, Walking Stewart was a sublime visionary. He had seen and suffered much amongst men; yet not too much, or so as to dull the genial tone of his sympathy with the sufferings of others. . . . His mind, like a shell taken from the sea, still echoed and murmured to the multitudinous sounds and forms amongst which his former years had been passed. The many nations amongst whom he had walked, "passing like night" (as the Ancient Mariner describes himself) "from land to land,"—the black men, and the white men, and the "dusk-faces with white silken turbants wreathed,"—were present for ever, and haunted his inner eye with imagery of the noblest kind, and with moving pageantries, in the midst of silence. . . . His mind was a mirror of the sentient universe—the whole mighty vision that had fleeted before his eyes in this world: the armies of Hyder Ali and his son Tippoo, with oriental and barbaric pageantry; the civic grandeur of England; the great deserts of Asia and America; the vast capitals of Europe; London, with its eternal agitations, the ceaseless ebb and flow of its "mighty heart"; Paris, shaken by the fierce torments of revolutionary convulsions; the silence of Lapland; and the solitary forests of Canada; with the swarming life of the torrid zone; together with innumerable recollections of individual joy and sorrow that he had participated by sympathy;—lay like a map beneath him, as if eternally co-present to his view, so that, in the contemplation of the prodigious whole, he had no leisure to separate the parts, or occupy his mind with details. . . . Ignorant of philosophy in its forms and terminology, he was, by capacity of profound reverie, a true philosopher . . . and . . . he was, as a man, the most comprehensively benign, the most largely in sympathy with human nature, of any whom I have yet known.[76]

[76] Rearranged sentences from De Quincey's two essays on Stewart, in the order of the following references: Works, III, 117, 102, 103, 115, 99, 115-116, 101.

Strange Relations:
The Author and His Audience

I F WE ponder the matter, we are likely to conclude that literary
art, had it not already arisen, could hardly have got started in a
world where printing was an available medium. Literature is so
deeply rooted in the oral, beneath the written, stratum that, when
we write, our traditional choices of phrase are conditioned by the
primordial instinct. The signs are in the language itself: we "speak
the tongue that Shakespeare spake," "It is well *said* by a noted
writer." [1] Literature is so naturally, so fundamentally, an affair of
telling, as opposed to *recording*, that the traces are omnipresent:

> But first I pray yow, of your curteisye,
> That ye n'arette it nat my vileynye,
> Thogh that I pleynly *speke* in this mateere,
> To *telle* yow hir wordes and hir cheere,
> Ne thogh I *speke* hir wordes properly . . .
> Whoso shal *telle* a *tale* after a man,
> He moot reherce as ny as evere he kan
> Everich a word. [2]

Or, in the nineteenth century, at random,

> To know the change and feel it,
> When there is none to heal it,
> Nor numbèd sense to steel it,
> Was never *said* in rhyme. [3]

---

[1] Lord Kames [Henry Home], *Elements of Criticism*, XVIII, 2.
[2] Geoffrey Chaucer, "General Prologue," *Canterbury Tales*, lines 725–733.
[3] John Keats, "In a Drear-nighted December" (early printed version), lines 21–24.

If this seem a trivial point, it is important to correct the impression. For the relation of author and public, actual or imagined, expressed or implied, is of profound significance to literary causes and effects, a universally pervasive concern of the subtlest psychological complexity and abiding perplexity. The gradual detachment, through print, of the writer from a present and familiar audience is one of the most far-reaching influences of modern times in our Western civilization; and its special problems emerge with crucial insistence for the first time in the eighteenth century. Not that the question was simple, even before the invention of printing: but it was different.

Chaucer's example is useful at the outset. He was the gifted inheritor of an *oral* tradition a millennium old, but sophisticated by careful study of the Romans and improved by genius for its own immediate purposes. How subtle an instrument it became in his hands is only of late coming to be recognized, critically discussed and disputed, in the light—or shadow—of subsequent experimentation with narrative techniques. Tales like those of the Wife of Bath, the Merchant, or the Nun's Priest, in which characters speaking in their individual ways are presented by other characters with their own personal bias, who in turn are quoted by a narrator who is the posed and highlighted self-portrait of the poet who, himself visible and audible, projects these inventions with histrionic skill upon the senses of a present audience: such tales are a study in mental refraction sufficiently complex. But the overriding fact in this complexity is the original rapport between Chaucer and his hearers. Many of these were his personal friends and most of them he probably knew by sight. He wrote with their outlook in mind, with the conditions of a personal oral delivery in mind. This familiarity, abetted at need by tone of voice, by a look, and ever checked by the involuntary, spontaneous response of attention intimately observed, made for him the effective ambit of creative possibility beyond which he did not need, or perhaps wish, to venture. That he must have thought of being read in other places and later times does not affect his creative technique in the least. Human nature changes at a geological rate, and, if Virgil and Ovid can speak to *us*, shall we not be understood by those that come after? *The Hous of Fame* and the epilogue to *Troilus and Criseyde* are a sufficient commentary on that question as it concerned Chaucer. The present point is how very manifest are the influences of the *social conditions* within which he works, how enormous their benefits, how confidently he seizes advantages made available by them, how sensitively he perceives the opportunities and limitations of these quasi-personal relations, so that we vicariously seem to know him better than we know our next-door neighbor.

Thus much space has been accorded to Chaucer because he can stand as the ideal paradigm of a kind of relationship between poet and audience that existed for centuries. Nor, of course, though printing would eventually transform it, did the situation change immediately or suddenly with the invention of printing. In the sphere with which we are at the moment concerned, the effect on contemporary thought and practice was slight. Poems circulated in manuscript copies, primarily among friends and acquaintances, and were doubtless read aloud to small interested groups, in upper-class society. Ambitious and aspiring works were written with such an audience in view. Lyrics and private effusions were written for private presentation or to be sung; sometimes for particular occasions. Poets had no other kind of publication in mind, and hardly envisaged any other kind of reader. Why should anything so personal be printed? Publication by print came in time to be recognized as a safeguard against corruption by miscopying, and as a kind of insurance against loss; but was not resorted to by the author himself without apology and at least the pretense of his having been driven to publishing in self-protection, for the integrity of his work. Not financial protection; for what mercenary reward worth considering could a poet hope for or expect? A *dedicated* work might attract a present, large or small, but publication had nothing to do with such a gift. When Queen Elizabeth ordered Burleigh to reward Spenser with £100, he protested, "What! all this for a song?" Spenser, at any rate, anticipated no commercial profit from the *sale* of his work, nor in fact was there any system or convention to ensure payment. His audience was an enlightened circle of connoisseurs. *A fortiori*, Shakespeare's sonnets were not matter for a printer, and doubtless were issued without the author's knowledge or consent. As for the plays—and as for drama generally —they were made for living performance and subject to continual alteration according to changing circumstances and current theatrical need. Publication was simply irrelevant. Drama was an *oral* art. Play *printing* was an art of embalming. Time enough, after a playwright's death, to think of collecting and printing his works. While he lived, they were worth more to him on the stage than on the shelf. On the shelf, in fact, they might be a palpable disadvantage, profitable only to thieves.

Shakespeare and his fellow playwrights always had a cross-section of their total contemporary—if not potential—audience in full and present view, just as Chaucer had had. They could study their reactions and cut the cloth to suit the emergent taste. They could show them their own image, analyze their form and body, and interpret them to themselves. The gamut was wider than Chaucer's, more democratic, but the connection between author and audience was close and capable of accurate tuning all along the scale. There need be little uncertainty in the dramatist's mind as to whether his work was reverberating with the intended resonance.

Poetry and drama flourished in the Elizabethan age without asking help from printing, and apart from poetry and drama imaginative literature as yet was small in amount and of slight importance. Printing was not only inessential to the life of poetry but even a rude encroachment upon its aristocratic preserves and oral traditions. By and large, printing was still an irresponsible upstart and intruder, regarded with jealous suspicion by literary society and by the State. The number of presses was arbitrarily limited and their output restricted in various ways under both Tudors and Stuarts. The medium continued to be relatively unrespectable in the world of *belles lettres* for at least a hundred years longer—a fact that can be detected in the reluctance of authors, so late as past the mid-eighteenth century, to admit their names to the title pages of their published work. For women, of course, the indecency lasted for still another century.

Certainly until after the Civil Wars literature was the leisured accomplishment of amateurs—authors without a professional compulsion, not writing for a livelihood, and under no sort of commitment to the press. The war spawned a great deal of controversial publication, both political and religious, but not yet literary. This ephemeral writing, however, as it became more frequent, also began to develop habits of greater regularity, so that by means of journals and periodicals a new kind of outlet for literary expression appeared, to be exploited in the next age. What appeared in these media of belletristic writing, like essays, tales, brief biographies, may be considered the first generation of literature conceived and conditioned by its commercial purpose and mode of existence. As such, it constitutes a turning point of vast consequence in the relations between author and audience. From this moment onwards, gradually but increasingly, there develops a race of authors who write to an indefinite body of readers, personally undifferentiated and unknown; who accept this separation as a primary condition of their creative activity and address their public invisibly, through the curtain, opaque and impersonal, of print: writers to whom in due course, as J. W. Saunders puts it, "print became the normal, and in time entirely respectable, medium of communication with any audience, and prose the normal language of professional literary expression." [4] The questions raised by this altered relationship, the variety of ways in which a solution has been attempted, are intertwined with most of the significant literary problems that have arisen in the last two and a half centuries, and have never been more troublesome and disturbing than they are today.

CHANGES so profound did not proceed at an equal pace in all branches of literature. Poetry, though it had in the end to accept and live with the new conditions of dissemination, could afford to be more resistant to these influences. Especially in its higher reaches, it had a very ancient and well-understood tradition that sustained its patrician estate and kept it conservative in hereditary surroundings, and aloof from the chaffering world of prose. Its appeal was to a culture and a kind of audience long familiar. So long as it could find a means of support free of commercial conditions, it was relatively secure. It did not have to modify its address or recognize an altered relationship on account of publication in print.

The reading public of Milton, Cowley, Waller, Dryden, Prior —and even, to a degree, thanks to the unique confluence of genius and character, of Pope himself—was probably roughly commen-

---

[4] John Whiteside Saunders, *The Profession of English Letters* (1964), p. 93.

surate with their social world as a whole. We have only to read over the list of subscribers to Prior's great folio of 1718, *Poems on Several Occasions*—the title page does not carry its author's name —to see that this is true. Dedicatory letters frequently confirm the fact. We must, however, recognize that subscription publication was in itself a sign of change, and a necessary concession to the weakening of aristocratic obligations under the old system of support. But lofty poetry was, as Saunders has remarked, "indispensable to Augustanism." It occupies the status of "the civilising literary art par excellence." [5] It is at once the proof, and the measure, of high value in that cultural ideal, and this of course is why it was of such importance that Pope or another should crown the age with an epic—just as, upholding the classical values later in the century, Reynolds and his followers aspired to paint "heroic" subjects in the grand manner of Michelangelo: epics of the sister art.

But, on a less exalted plane, it is worth contemplating briefly the advantages which so distinguished an artist as Prior could derive from his sympathetic and intimate rapport with that select audience of his. The differences of Church and State between them were far less considerable to his art than the community of education, the common circle of acquaintance at the university and in town, the same reading, a shared vocabulary, similar experiences, *like* amusements and games, a kindred range of allusion, clichés, tricks of phrase, speech cadences on a common tonic. Such a community knows all the byways and shortcuts of conversational interchange as well as a schoolboy knows his physical surroundings; and an art that can employ this intimacy of reference can convey abundant meaning, on subjects proper to it, with the greatest verbal economy. The artist—say Prior—knows that six-sevenths of his poetic substance can be safely lodged, and to better effect, in his reader's imagination if only he select the right seventh to show. It is an art wherein, to change the figure, the harmonics are more important than the fundamental notes. But, continuing the musical analogy, we know that you cannot elicit the same timbre from every sort of instrument. Prior is an exquisite composer for the instrument he knows best—his own public. He is as

[5] *Ibid.*, p. 114.

sensitive to its overtones as Chopin to those of the piano. His most
refined effects are calculated for it alone, and indeed are things
unattemptable and inconceivable elsewhere:

>   She, first of all the Town, was told,
>   Where newest INDIA Things were sold:
>   So in a Morning, without Bodice,
>   Slipt sometimes out to Mrs. THODY's;
>   To cheapen Tea, to buy a Screen:
>   What else cou'd so much Virtue mean?
>   For to prevent the least Reproach,
>   BETTY went with Her in the Coach.
>
>   But when no very great Affair
>   Excited her peculiar Care;
>   She without fail was wak'd at Ten;
>   Drank Chocolate, then slept again:
>   At Twelve She rose: with much ado
>   Her Cloaths were huddl'd on by Two:
>   Then; Does my Lady Dine at home?
>   Yes sure;—but is the Colonel come?
>   Next, how to spend the Afternoon,
>   And not come Home again too soon;
>   The Change, the City, or the Play,
>   As each was proper for the Day;
>   A Turn in Summer to HYDE-PARK,
>   When it grew tolerably Dark.[6]

Prior was almost the last considerable poet with opportunities of
this kind to prompt and condition his art.

At the higher reaches the problem is not acute. There are time-
honored ways of beginning—which is the chief embarrassment,
as Johnson observes in his first *Rambler* paper. The hieratic robes
are in themselves a cloak, and the god-inspired poet is not supposed
to appear in the glare of day. He is rather to be heard than seen,
whether he invoke the Muses or an honored name:

>   Descend, ye Nine! descend and sing![7]

or

>   Awake, my St. John! leave all meaner things
>   To low ambition, and the pride of Kings.[8]

---

[6] Matthew Prior, *Hans Carvel*, lines 21–42.
[7] Alexander Pope, *Ode for Musick, on St. Cecilia's Day*, line 1.
[8] Alexander Pope, *An Essay on Man*, I, lines 1–2.

But, as patronage ebbed and the tide of print rose, the serious poet faced a serious problem. If he knew how to address a "fit audience though few," that audience would hardly support him. If he was to live, he had to find place and preferment. For a brief time, this was not too difficult for literary merit to do. The great Whig and Tory statesmen made it their business to look out for most of the abler writers in the days of Anne. The posts these writers found were supposed to leave them leisure to write; but on the other hand there were conditions and consequences. Their status as poets necessarily became more amateur, while they devoted time and energy to political activity, whether in office or by the pen. Prose was here far more effective than poetry, and for these men prose became a duty. Indeed, the obligations of office could almost remove them from the sphere of *belles lettres*. Steele became more interested in politics than letters. Addison managed to evolve a compromise reasonably suited to his gifts. Swift never laid claim to being a literary man: published anonymously or not at all, and certainly always from unmercenary and unprofessional motives. Prior was an able but reluctant diplomatist who would have preferred a life of poetry. Gay never found a satisfactory solution, and for all his gifts and occasional successes, remained a frustrated poet.

Of all the Augustans of Anne's and the first George's day, Pope was the only avowed, lifelong, wholly dedicated poet. There was never, among his varied interests, any question of the primacy of poetry:

> This subtle Thief of life, this paltry Time,
> What will it leave me, if it snatch my rhyme?
> If ev'ry wheel of that unweary'd Mill,
> That turn'd ten thousand verses, now stands still?[9]

Goldsmith might look back with nostalgia to the days "when the great Somers was at the helm" as the golden age of patronage, but it was only relatively so, and in fact Pope derived none but indirect benefits from the current posture of affairs. Poetry was not a dependable calling, even so early; and it very much concerns us to study the means Pope devised to make it approximately so for himself, in the face of his special handicaps of ill health and a

[9] Alexander Pope, *The Second Epistle of the Second Book of Horace*, lines 76–79.

religion whereby he was "deny'd all posts of profit and of trust."

Initially, of course, we grant him modest means, determination, self-command, and the genius to win recognition early in life. Next, since patronage did not seek him out, he compelled a kind of dispersed and shared patronage by subscription. By his subscribers he was at once sustained and supplied with a primary audience that constituted a surrogate for that earlier traditional, aural-oral relation and a partial escape from the facelessness of an anonymous public. Next, he singled out from the larger body of his supporting audience various particular friends in order to address them by name in his Horatian imitations, and of these moral essays, epistles, or satires he made a more and more personal thing, turning the discourse into some semblance of dialogue, and sprinkling the text with familiar allusion to contemporaries. To these, in spite of their intimate, conversational tone, he gave such extreme finish that they derogate very little from his claim to be regarded as a poet of the very highest order. But, at the same time, they rescued him from the frustrating sense of bardic isolation, from the fate ironically hit off in the epistle already quoted:

> Go, lofty Poet! and in such a crowd,
> Sing thy sonorous verse—but not aloud!—[10]

a fate altogether likely in a patronless world of print, *sans* visible audience.

A further move in the same direction of projecting the image of a select Augustan community within which he lived and fraternized, was to contrive the publication of his literary correspondence. This was tantamount to a prose translation of the verse epistles— more informal, with the added charm of apparent actuality: a kind of eavesdropping on the best company. What a revelation! and how reassuring to any doubters of Pope's assumed rights of superiority, as adumbrated in his scornful verses:

> Ask you what Provocation I have had?
> The strong Antipathy of Good to Bad.
> When Truth or Virtue an Affront endures,
> Th'Affront is mine, my friend, and should be yours . . .
> Yes, I am proud; I must be proud to see
> Men not afraid of God, afraid of me . . .[11]

[10] *Ibid.*, lines 108–109.
[11] Alexander Pope, *Epilogue to the Satires*, Dialogue II, lines 197–200, 208–209.

In these ways, and by such means, Pope was in actual fact creating his chosen audience in his own ideal image, recovering from the alien world of the press something—indeed much—of the feeling of an exalted society where choice spirits met face to face, shared the same principles, of truth, honor, integrity, love of country, loyalty, hatred of the base, scorn of the mean: intelligent, beauty-loving, witty, but candid, trustworthy, and arcadian in rural delights. We cannot say but that this was Pope's honest idea of his truest self, and these are the values he promulgates in poem after poem. Moreover, since he is continually addressing a named company in the first person, we, who would uphold the same ideals, have no difficulty in identifying ourselves with that good society, and are uplifted together. While Envy howls, and Flattery sickens, the curtain of black print dissolves, the illusion of union is complete, we are gathered into the artifice of eternity:

Truth guards the poet, sanctifies the line,
And makes immortal, Verse as mean [No, Mr. Pope! as *noble*] as
[thine.][12]

While we read, the spell holds; and, while the spell lasts, we believe.

THIS SYMPATHETIC rapport with a known, or at least clearly envisaged, audience was what every man of letters needed to establish, in order to be convincing and successful as a "creative" writer. But the path to it through printed prose was still uncharted. It is obvious from this distance—but the solution was instinctive—that the way to get in to a public personally unknown was to knock at the front door in person. Written correspondence was normal between friends, useful between strangers, communicable to a third party. All personal letters were in greater or less degree unavoidably autobiographical, and might naturally flow into narrative, with comment on the action at will. Ideally, autobiography was an extended letter to a friend. Point of view was in effect automatic, and one started with an identified audience. These are enormous initial advantages.

Letter writing between friends was clearly congenial to great numbers of English in the eighteenth century—so congenial that

[12] *Ibid.*, lines 246–247.

probably four-fifths of the best letters in English carry that super-scription as to place and time. Circumstances so favorable are by no means to be taken for granted. People lived far enough apart for letters to be wanted and needed, in a dearth of easier, more immediate ways of communication. Town dwellers do not write to one another, except to invite, accept, and thank. In the country, where obligations (accompaniments of real property) kept you more or less immobile and isolated, letters were a sensible enrich-ment of the day, able to change its entire complexion, and when you were the recipient you paid as happily for a good long letter as for a ticket to theater, concert, or ball in town. The pleasure was mutual, and with these incitements letter writing rose to the level of superb art—a genre of the utmost variety, flexibility, and felicity of expression. The capabilities of English prose have hardly elsewhere, in its whole range, been so inventively and thoroughly, if casually, explored. Cicero and his fellows, in this art if nowhere else, would have to give place. Only to *name* stars of the first magnitude—Chesterfield, Lady Mary, Gray, Walpole, Cowper—is to be convinced of this truth.

In the simplest verbal interchange we have, at the least, the Auto-crat's complexity of persons, to be elaborated as we please. For ex-ample, there are the "real" Gray, the "real" Walpole, Gray's Gray, Walpole's Walpole, Gray's Walpole, and Walpole's Gray. There are also Gray's Walpole's Gray, and Walpole's Gray's Walpole. In this colloquy, the main dialogue proceeds at the second remove, between Gray's Gray and Walpole's Walpole, but prompted by "moi-mêmes" who have unavowed investments in the venture, and prodded and nudged by the others at unspecified moments, some-times quite insistently. All these are potentially operative forces on a level of conscious awareness. As for the materials of such inter-change, they are as limitless as the purposes prompting their selec-tion: narrative, descriptive, expository, opinionative. Johnson told Mrs. Thrale that to write when one had nothing to tell was "the great epistolick art," [13] and Cowper demonstrated this art in its utmost perfection, not once but often. Every such letter is a dra-matic monologue.

[13] *The Letters of Samuel Johnson*, ed. R. W. Chapman (1952), II, 228 (October 27, 1777).

We must now try to translate the actual relationships adumbrated in the paradigm suggested, into a not-so-brave *new* world, that of imaginative prose—prose fiction—in the medium of print. It is not surprising that this particular genre should preempt our discussion henceforward. It is at once the most significant product of the changes taking place in that literary world, the most revealing and problematic from a critical point of view, and the most portentous, historically considered. Moreover, especially at the outset, the novel was interrelated with most other reputable forms of literary prose and grew away from them in a haphazard, unpremeditated fashion—not by arbitrary definition or plan. As Saunders says, "The joy of the novel, *then*, was the same as the joy of the biography, but salted to taste by the ancillary joys associated with essays, real-life letters, true travel stories, histories and other forms. The novel is not a thing apart, but a form of literature which derives inevitably from, and remains integrally interconnected with, the host of the other prose forms in this age of prose." [14]

We must consider what happens when an unknown X and Y are substituted for the known relations of the paradigmatic original. Let X be the author and Y the reading public, each unknown to the other. Then X's X at once develops a range of possibilities previously denied. (1) X's genuine autobiography; (2) assumption of alien identity, even to shift of sex; (3) fictitious events; (4) opinions on these corresponding to the author's real views; (5) opinions opposite to the author's true ideas and values; (6) a mixture of these options in varying proportions. The reading public must guess the character and intentions of the primary X; and since the public, Y, is a multiple, Y^n, there will be a variety of guesses. But, if the work is a success, Y will guess in the general direction X has predetermined for it. But why? how?

There, of course, lies the heart of the problem: how to establish an understanding, a mutual give-and-take, reciprocity of emotional, intellectual, moral response with a person or persons never seen? The old assurance from proximity has been taken away at a difficult time: just when the literary profession, as profession, is beginning to walk by itself, and when imaginative prose is trying its powers in many new directions. A solid, tangible public would

[14] Saunders, *Profession of English Letters*, pp. 104–105.

have been fortifying at such a moment. How can an insecure author with a bantling be at home with a Cheshire Cat?

While she was still looking at the place where it had been, it suddenly appeared again. "By-the-bye, what became of the baby?" said the Cat. "I'd nearly forgotten to ask." "It turned into a pig," Alice answered very quietly . . . "I thought it would," said the Cat, and vanished again.

[After she had gone some way] Alice looked up, and there was the Cat again, sitting on a branch of a tree. "Did you say pig, or fig?" said the Cat. "I said pig," replied Alice; "and I wish you wouldn't keep appearing and vanishing so suddenly: you make one quite giddy." "All right," said the Cat; and this time it vanished quite slowly, beginning with the end of the tail, and ending with the grin, which remained some time after the rest of it had gone.[15]

In such circumstances, an act of faith is the first requisite. If the author believes hard enough that the audience is truly there, he may from time to time see it materialize. But he must not look for guidance from it—can only expect hindsight. Knocking at the front door in person is not so easy to do but is part of that act of faith. Since Y doesn't live anywhere in particular, X must trust that he has come to the right lodging, where he or his simulacrum will find a sympathetic welcome. He knocks, and with an asking face presents his credentials in the form of a printed book telling his story. Suppose it begins: "I was born in the year 1632, in the city of York, of a good family, though not of that country, my father being a foreigner of Bremen, named Kreutznaer, who settled first at Hull." [16] Y is in his library and does not appear at the door. He glances at the book briefly, sees that it is packed with arresting circumstance which holds one's attention and generates confidence in its veracity. He sends out a few coins to the waiting figure at the door, bids him leave his testimonials and come back another day, after his case has been considered as it may deserve. Whether the author, in whatever guise, will ever find his way back, or learn Y's opinion, is doubtful. Does it matter? Yes!

"But I don't want to go among mad people," Alice remarked. "Oh, you can't help that," said the Cat: "we're all mad here. I'm mad. You're

[15] *Alice in Wonderland*, ch. VI.
[16] Daniel Defoe, *Robinson Crusoe*.

mad." "How do you know I'm mad?" said Alice. "You must be," said the Cat, "or you wouldn't have come here."[17]

There are two realities, the author and the reader. But they never confront each other in person. The whole transaction takes place in the world of "Als ob." It is not a *terra firma*, not at all reassuring to a family man with responsibilities. There must be a way to get closer to the reader. Is it by implying more than appears on the surface of the writing? Is there a promise of a compact, a more intimate relation by signs behind the back, or over the head, of the narrator? Can he be made to speak more than he realizes, so that a secret recognition may be exchanged between real author and reader? Watt calls attention[18] to the following passage in *Crusoe*, where the hero is salvaging anything useful he can bring ashore from the wrecked ship:

I smiled to myself at the sight of this money; O drug! I exclaimed, what art thou good for? . . . e'en remain where thou art, and go to the bottom, as a creature whose life is not worth saving. However, upon second thoughts, I took it away.

Is it an ironic signal from Defoe to the reader? We shall never know. Defoe's inexpressive countenance gives no second sign. Either he does not see the opening or he refuses to follow it up, and our perplexity increases fiftyfold with other impersonations, most notably with Moll Flanders. When this author has fused himself with the imagined person, the process is so remarkably thorough that he seems to have nothing still unexpressed on that subject: to have nothing left over that he wishes to communicate privately. He is content to be measured in the dimensions of his characters, whatsoever obliquities, inconsistencies, or limitations they may display. As an author, he is for the newer generation of running, or bustling, reader—a *public* without privacies—and why should he want a closer relation than what he already enjoyed?

If Defoe is often puzzling because he seems too straightforward to be trusted, Swift is so for the opposite reason. He is for the reader of today, who of course accepts nothing at face value. The world of print was made to order for Swift: it offers him personal

[17] *Alice in Wonderland*, ch. VI.
[18] Ian Watt, *The Rise of the Novel (1964)*, p. 119.

anonymity, self-concealment, the means of directing his fire from a selected ambush against any object he may choose. His disguises are innumerable, and in each he discloses only so much of himself as he pleases to reveal. His own point of view is almost never overt, and is usually at the extreme distance from that of his mouthpiece. He is nearly as great a master of matter-of-fact narrative as Defoe, but he uses it for setting springes and gins. Consider the first paragraph of *Lilliput* as a suitable opening for a book of wonders. Thus, in part:

> Soon after my return from Leyden [where I studied physic for two years and seven months], I was recommended . . . to be surgeon to the Swallow, Captain Abraham Pannell, commander, with whom I continued three years and a half . . . When I came back I resolved to settle in London . . . I took part of a small house in the Old Jewry; and being advised to alter my condition, I married Mrs Mary Burton, second daughter to Mr Edmund Burton, hosier, in Newgate Street, with whom I received four hundred pounds for a portion.[19]

Swift will always entrap the reader if he can, and delight in the trick. But the reader whom he cannot fool is the one he is really after, *quasi alter ego*. Such a one is his true and private audience. If he can find one such in a thousand readers, he may be pleased; but even so he will not openly acknowledge him, essential to Swift's sufficiency though he be. Irony is the instrument, a sort of Geiger counter, by which he finds out his proper reader. But, though the signals are mutually reciprocated, they generate no warmth. Nor do they always reach conviction. Gulliver's fourth book is a stumbling block for any who feel themselves sealed of the tribe. How much confidence does he inspire in us that we have read him as he meant?

Of the two authors touched upon, neither, it appears, satisfactorily solved the problem of an author's relations through the opacity of print with an audience of readers. If the authors are content, the reader is not. His side of the connection is left uncertain and incomplete. Defoe's X is crystal clear and solid but what of Y's, the reader's, Defoe? The last-named takes so little independent room in the picture that, for purposes of the book's contribution to any society, X and Defoe may as well be lumped together. Swift's X, on the contrary, though solid enough to be

[19] *Gulliver's Travels*, pt. I, ch. I, 2nd paragraph.

taken over without change as the reader's X, is so obviously a distortion of the author's meaning that the reader must attempt to resolve the anamorphosis by seeking for Swift himself. But the range of possible inference left open to Y in this element of the equation is too wide to be reduced to comfortable assurance. At the end of the book Swift is still to seek.

It may be possible to establish a closer solidarity between author and reader by means of correspondence, or by adopting the techniques of epistolary interchange. This experiment is tried by Richardson, and then exploited by him with overwhelming success. It drastically modifies, and even transforms, several factors in the configuration. First and foremost, it circumvents the Cheshire Cat. By identifying, characterizing, and fixing an audience of named individuals *within* the story itself, Richardson evades, or avoids, the vagueness of address that so constricts and formalizes the ordinary autobiographer. He writes to particular people, whose friendly concern may be assumed; who naturally condition what he says and the way he says it. He can count on a response, which itself provides one of the elements of narrative continuity and keeps alive expectation. It relieves the relentless fixation on the first person, develops secondary foci of interest, removes the embarrassment of an appearance of total recall or the subterfuge of an impossibly detailed journal. It provides unforeseen opportunities for reconsideration, in the light of developing events and differing points of view. It makes easy openings for explication and discussion and for the expression of fresh insights.

Moreover, it alters the whole time scheme with vivid benefits. The temporal range is moved forward into the immediate past, with the excitement of recent events, merging into the passing hour and anxiety for the imminent future. There is little occasion for summoning up a cold past. Emotion, therefore, not recollected in tranquillity, but as reflected in the present pulse rate, is the element in which the communicated thoughts now live. It animates the writer, the recipient of the letter, and inevitably the new reader at whatever distance. Distance, in fact, of time and place is nonexistent while we read, and we move unconsciously into position as the recipient of Clarissa's letters, to which we react with corresponding sentiments.

This is a triumphant annihilation of the barrier between writer

and reader. It is, in fact—with the reservation soon to be made—
the ideal to which novelists normally aspire—or at least until
recently did aspire. To live vicariously another life with such
psychological intensity that for a certain time our own is subsumed
in the other: this, whatever critical pundits may say, is the goal
of a novel reader in his essentiality. This is the way of children
with story books; this is the experience that the readers of novels
in the eighteenth century sought and cherished: this is the characteristic joy of prose fiction, its promise, its potency, and its
danger. At the time when first-rate novels could be counted on
the fingers of one hand, what was it that readers of all classes, from
the servant maid to the top levels of sophisticated culture, were
seeking from them? Not objects of critical disquisition but vehicles
of vicarious experience. We have a perfect opportunity to test the
assertion by the voluntary testimony offered to Richardson by
Fielding in the letter written after reading the fifth volume of
Clarissa. After praising the consistency and naturalness of characterization, Fielding continues:

Shall I tell you? Can I tell you what I think of the latter part of your
Volume? Let the Overflowings of a Heart which you have filled
brimfull speak for me.
   When Clarissa returns to her Lodgings at St Clairs the Alarm begins,
and here my Heart begins *its* Narrative. I am Shocked; my Terrors
[? rise], and I have the utmost Apprehensions for the poor betrayed
Creature.—But when I see her enter with the Letter in her Hand, and
after some natural Effects of Despair, clasping her Arms about the
Knees of the Villain, call him her Dear Lovelace, desirous and yet
unable to implore his Protection or rather his mercy; I then melt into
Compassion, and find what is called an Effeminate Relief for my
Terror. to continue to the End of the Scene. When I read the next
Letter I am Thunderstruck; nor can many Lines explain what I feel
from Two.
   . . . The Circumstance of the Fragments is Great and Terrible; but
her Letter to Lovelace is beyond any thing I have ever read. God forbid that the Man who reads this with dry Eyes should be alone with
my Daughter when she hath no Assistance within Call. Here my
Terror ends and my Grief begins which the Cause of all my Tumultuous Passions soon changes into Raptures of Admiration and Aston-
ishment by a Behaviour the most Elevated I can possibly conceive, and
what is at the same time most Gentle and most natural . . . During
the Continuance of this Vol. my Compassion is often moved; but I
think my Admiration more. If I had rec'd no Hint or Information of

what is to succeed I should perceive you paving the way to load our admiration of your Heroine to the Highest Pitch, as you have before with wonderfull Art prepared us for both Terror and Compassion on her Account. This last seems to come from the Head. Here then I will end: for I assure you nothing but my Heart can force me to say Half of what I think of the Book.[20]

That, we can hardly doubt, is the way the novel ought to be read, and it is a sincere tribute on a first reading when the work was new.

It is to be observed that what has been said of the reader's intimate involvement with Richardson's heroine relates to that precisely. The epistolary form unites us to the characters, not to the author. Clarissa may be a bond of association between us and him, may elevate him in our estimation and arouse our admiration of his genius. Otherwise, it does not bring us to a personal intimacy. That Richardson felt this separation from his audience might be inferred from the great amount of his own writing around and about the novel. He was unwilling to leave it to speak for itself but had to be discussing it with all and sundry, in his own person.

Now, this was an aspect of an author's relation to his public that Fielding was disposed to take upon himself as his immediate concern. He had a great deal to say about his greatest novel, about the forms of fiction, about the conduct of the narrative, about self-appointed critics, about the character and actions of his invented persons, about the conduct of life itself; and he chose to incorporate all this in the body of the novel, in introductory essays, in running comment, and in the witty, wry, ironic manner in which he reported events. He gives us so much of himself that in effect he becomes, not a character in the book, but the Master of Ceremonies, and much the most interesting person in it, if at the same time apart from it. We feel that we know him better, and more intimately, on his own chosen terms, than anyone else to whom we are introduced. Without this personal voice at all times in our ears, the book would be a vastly different sort of thing. This is why he could not have written it, like the other novels so far mentioned, in the first person as a character; and this is why the cinema version, excellent though it be, and faithful up to a point, is so compara-

[20] Quoted by E. L. McAdam, Jr., in *Yale Review*, 2nd ser., XXXVIII (1948), 304–305.

tively thin and unsatisfying to the reader of *Tom Jones,* and so entirely different in effect. This is why, though *Robinson Crusoe* might be turned into a movie without much loss—perhaps with perceptible gain—Fielding's novel is in fact untranslatable. The kinship of Fielding and Chaucer has been noted before. It is a truth that Fielding has returned in very characteristic fashion to a close semblance—in spite of prose and print—of the early oral techniques of the great narrative poet. The point need not be labored. Both authors are conspicuously present on all occasions, as ironic observers and commentators, and as essential parts of the scene and total effect. It is an amusing coincidence, a pretty parallel, that the figure in which Fielding presents himself as author, as he opens his novel, is that of mine host, or "master of a public ordinary," who offers a bill of fare under the general heading of Human Nature, with chapter titles for particular items, in the antique descriptive manner—as it were a General Prologue with hints of dietary variety in store.

Fielding's solution brings him and the reader into close relationship, and in his hands is so successful as to serve as a model for a great part of the novel writing of the next century. But it is retrograde from the advance in psychological realism achieved by Richardson's epistolary method. What it gains in propinquity of author and reader, it loses in distance between author and characters. Author and reader remain together outside the story and can only guess at thoughts and motivations by the outward signs. To be sure, Fielding presumes upon his appointed distance not infrequently; but his typical stance will be seen on almost any page. Thus, for example:

It surprises us, and so perhaps it may the reader, that the lieutenant, a worthy and good man, should have applied his chief care rather to secure the offender than to preserve the life of the wounded person. We mention this observation, not with any view of pretending to account for so odd a behaviour . . . it is our business to relate facts as they are . . .[21]

The problem, then, is how to fuse the two halves and yet keep them distinct. How can the author identify himself with his characters so closely as to express their thoughts and emotions as

[21] *Tom Jones,* bk. VII, ch. 12. Cf. *Troilus and Criseyde,* bk. III, lines 575 ff., and I, lines 492 ff.

they arise, and yet remain free to comment at will on these matters in a comfortable companionship with the reader? How be in the action and out of it at the same time? How be at once first and third person, at once actor and explicator?

This is the paradoxical problem to which Sterne finds a paradoxical solution. "Writing," declares Tristram

when properly managed (as you may be sure I think mine is), is but a different name for conversation. As no one, who knows what he is about, in good company would venture to talk all;—so no author, who understands the just boundaries of decorum and good-breeding, would presume to think all. The truest respect which you can pay to the reader's understanding, is to halve this matter amicably, and leave him something to imagine in his turn, as well as yourself.

For my own part, I am eternally paying him compliments of this kind, and do all that lies in my power to keep his imagination as busy as my own.[22]

As a description of Sterne's actual practice in *Tristram Shandy*, this is not at all bad. He goes a stride beyond Richardson along the road of psychological immediacy. Instead of enabling the reader to examine subsequently a series of letters exchanged between persons writing to one another in an imagined present, he adopts the personally immediate address of Fielding to *his* audience, as the author engaged in writing the book. But, since he is writing in the autobiographical mode, he is at the same time the book's nominal hero and the nexus of action. As author, he addresses an immediate audience, and therefore in an immediate present (as one would in a letter). But, as character, he cannot speak to an audience that has no existence within that fictional ambience. He is thus forced to bring his readers inside the book's action and make them part of the proceedings. He can do this only by assuming the contemporaneity of their mutual communications, so that each participant is a part of the other's present. The book therefore reverts in effect to the original condition of oral discourse, and becomes a conversational interchange between speaker and hearer, Sterne's X and Y; which is to say, between Sterne's Tristram and Sterne's image of ourselves as party to the unfolding of his anecdotes. The style has all the apparent ease and inconsequentiality of the most casual, unpremeditated talk. Since the time of conversa-

---

[22] *Tristram Shandy*, bk. II, ch. 2.

tion is always current time, is now, the relevant past is drawn into it as an integral component of present consciousness. We are by degrees—in the disconnected fashion in which odd bits of information about our acquaintances are usually acquired—informed of what transpired in Tristram's earlier history and that of his family. But we are not allowed to sit like passive buckets while Tristram fills the void. Sterne's is no idle boast: he *is* "eternally paying us compliments" of his attention, whether he addresses us as "Sir," "Madam," "My Lord," "your Reverences," "my dear friend and companion," or as "my fellow-labourers and associates in this great harvest of our learning now ripening before our eyes." He continually includes us in his "We"; he is always asking us questions and soliciting our views on the point at issue; guessing our thoughts; and even putting the words into our mouths from time to time. For example:

My uncle Toby Shandy, madam, was a gentleman . . . [of] a most extreme and unparalleled modesty of nature:—though I correct the word nature, for this reason, that I may not prejudge a point which must shortly come to a hearing; and that is, whether this modesty of his was natural or acquired.—Whichever way my uncle Toby came by it, it was nevertheless modesty in the truest sense of it; and that is, madam, not in regard to words . . . but to things;—and this kind of modesty so possessed him . . . as almost to equal, if such a thing could be, even the modesty of a woman,—that female nicety, madam, and inward cleanliness of mind and fancy, in your sex, which makes you so much the awe of ours.

You will imagine, madam, that my uncle Toby had contracted all this from this very source;—that he had spent a great part of his time in converse with your sex; and that, from a thorough knowledge of you, and the force of imitation which such fair examples render irresistible,—he had acquired this amiable turn of mind.

I wish I could say so . . . no, he got it, madam, by a blow.—A blow!— Yes, madam, it was owing to a blow from a stone, broke off by a ball from the parapet of a horn-work at the siege of Namur, which struck full upon my uncle Toby's groin.—Which way could that affect it?— The story of that, madam, is long and interesting;—but it would be running my history all upon heaps to give it you here.—[23]

Beyond this degree of involvement of the reader in the conduct of the narrative it seems hardly possible to go. If the primary object

---

[23] *Ibid.*, bk. I, ch. 21.

be to bring the author and unknown reader into the closest working relation, this seems to be the *ne plus ultra*.

But the sacrifices resulting from Sterne's method are equally
conspicuous. At a stroke, it reduces the plot, or story content, to
a level of second-rate interest. Progressive though the digressions
may be, narrative suspense and expectation are done away with,
except for brief episodes: no one ever read *Tristram Shandy*
through to find how it comes out. And, if the sequence of events
is given over for a continuous present, the development of character is also surrendered. The interest in the character of the
"hero" is all of a piece throughout, and really slight; while the
most memorable parts of the book are third-personal episodes that
do not much benefit from the novelties of Sterne's method but
conform to the old-fashioned continuities of character description,
action, scene and dialogue.

After Sterne's *succès fou* with the first two volumes, he did of
course become personally acquainted with the cream of his reading
public and doubtless joined in abundance of good talk. But all this
social experience had little perceptible effect on the artistic method,
which proceeded up hill and down dale as inspiration drove or
flagged. Since time present galloped faster than time past, he was,
as he humorously pointed out, losing ground all the while in the
recounting his own life story, and might go on with it as long as
breath continued. But the fictitious collocation of author and
audience remained as before.

THE NOVEL writers of the eighteenth century did not, to my
knowledge, discover any other kinds of author/reader relationship
than those exemplified by the five great masters so far considered.
The autobiographical novel in the first person continued to find
favor, since it offered infinite variety in the choice of protagonist,
with consequent identification of the reader and hero, to whatsoever degree. *The Vicar of Wakefield*, autobiographical in form, is
original in displaying a refined and sympathetic irony from its
memorable opening to the concluding paragraph. The amiable
complacency of the Vicar, who must be supposed to possess full
knowledge of all the subsequent events of the tale before he begins
telling—a tale that offers little justification for his optimistic views

of life—is conveyed with a delicacy inimitable and sweet. We love the author who can approach us in a semblance so irresistibly appealing: we feel close to him by virtue of the affectionate gratitude he inspires.

It will hardly be argued that the exploitation of eccentric protagonists, human (as John Buncle), animal or inanimate (as Pompey the Little or Chrysal), taught much about either life or novelistic techniques. The novelty of the angle of vision offers no unusual illumination, nor any unfamiliar relation of author and audience.

The novel à clé, or scandalous romance, dependent on private information shared by author and reader, is analogous to the satiric tradition in that it is to be, as it were, translated. While it puts writer and reader in a closet together with the door closed, this intimacy is not truly productive of a mutual sympathy. Once the reader is possessed of the key, he takes little interest in matters (if any exist) aside from the main affair—or in the author himself—and discards the book like a sucked orange.

The moral fable and the Eastern Tale, both much practiced and favored in our period, can be illustrated with masterpieces, notably Johnson's; but they have designs on the reader of a kind different from those with which we are here mainly concerned, and must be put by. The author/reader relationship generated by the apologue is analogous to pulpit and congregation, a benevolent condescension and a willing submission. They are extended *exempla* in an undelivered sermon.

The further exploitation of the epistolary method produced occasional triumphs, like *Humphry Clinker* and *Evelina*, but I think no new insights. The novels that followed the central road of third-personal narrative, like *The Spiritual Quixote*, did not rise to the level of their great "prose-epical" prototype, entertaining though they often are. Of most examples of the picaresque style much the same can be said. The pursuit of Sterne's eccentric path proved a blind alley to his immediate imitators and successors. We remember Johnson's pronouncement: "Nothing odd will do long. Tristram Shandy did not last." [24] This was doubtless true—and undisputed by Boswell—at the time it was spoken. But the oddity of the book was the least permanent thing about it.

[24] *Boswell's Life of Johnson*, II, 449 (March 20, 1776).

A GENERATION of novel readers trained on the prefaces of Henry James does not need to be reminded that the paramount technical problem which has exercised the ingenuity of novelists for the last century has been how to obliterate the reader's consciousness of the author during the reading of his book, so that the work can pass directly into vicarious experience without any apparent intermediary. This was very far from being Sterne's object. Although he couched his fiction in first-personal terms, he meant the subterfuge to be transparent. The events of Tristram's personal history may be fanciful, but the whimsical cast of his mind is virtually indistinguishable from that of his author, and what he has to say about life and the techniques of composition is identical with what Sterne himself professed. In this respect, therefore, he was moving rather up- than down-stream, as the subsequent history of the novel—unless for three-quarters of a century we have been in a confounding backwater—seems to show. What Sterne did positively and memorably demonstrate, however, was the unsuspectedly small part rational order played in human affairs: how inevitably imperfect and fallible were the efforts of verbal communication and how comically mistaken was the assumption of mutual understanding in any the most common interchange of ideas. The exploration of unreason was a disturbingly fruitful line of development for the future of the novel. Once this conception had thoroughly permeated the vulgar consciousness, all that was called for was the indefatigable erection of monuments to our insignificance.

Sterne's other major innovation, the overt injection of the reader into the texture of his design, was, like his self-portraiture, against the current. As the novel has grown to maturity, it has gained in self-assurance as the dominant art form. With the growth of the fiction-reading public to unimagined size, it has become evident that the competent practitioner need never worry about finding readers. Consequently, he has ceased to be preoccupied with the problem of public relations, and has retreated further and further into the cave of his privacy, whence from time to time issue sibylline utterances which the eager seeker after esoteric experience may interpret as he likes. Far from admitting his responsibility to convey any personal convictions, the modern novelist flatters

himself with their concealment, and denies to the reader the right
to impute to *him* any moral or other statement that his characters
may express or imply. The veil of print has finally thickened to
inviolability, and the separation of author and reader is as total
as the former can contrive to make it.

Oddly enough, the reader, formerly the object of the author's
solicitude, does not resent this reversal of responsibility but reveres
it. So the present-day reader pursues the novelist into his secret
lair in search of wisdom, confident that inaccessibility is the seal of
wisdom. In this he resembles my Father Shandy:

> As the dialogue was of Erasmus, my father . . . read it over and over
> again, with great application, studying every word and every syllable
> of it through and through in its most strict and literal interpretation.—
> He could still make nothing of it, that way. Mayhap there is more meant
> than is said in it, quoth my father.—Learned men, brother Toby, don't
> write dialogues upon long noses for nothing.—I'll study the mystic and
> the allegoric sense.—Here is some room to turn a man's self in,
> brother.[25]

The reader is not easily balked, these days. Saul Bellow recently
expressed his impatience with the tendency of contemporary society to deify, or at least to hallow, the artist. "We look to the
artist," he is reported as saying to a campus audience, "to transmit
new modes of conduct, to supply ideas, clues, hints; to provide a
form of life. We have made artists a privileged class, a breed of
holy men who have replaced the lives of the saints. Artists are
more envied than millionaires, they are beyond authority, for them
the rules are waived." [26] It is to be noted parenthetically that this
deification usually results from word-of-mouth fame, not word of
critics: a subvariety of oral tradition.

Thus the whirligig of time brings in his revenges. From having
been a pursuer after a valid relation with his audience, the author
has become the pursued, and for the same reason. The ancient
need for a personal bond between author and audience still exerts
its force. The satisfactions of a relation through the medium of
print are not sufficient. We still want the closer connection: the
face, the living voice, the charisma of a physical presence that we

---

[25] *Tristram Shandy*, bk. III, ch. 37.

[26] Report of a lecture at Stanford University, in the *San Francisco Chronicle*
(*San Francisco Sunday Examiner and Chronicle*), May 15, 1966, "This World"
Supplement, p. 41.

can touch. Why does a successful author attract the crowds when he goes on the University Circuit as lecturer? Why does every announcement of a new novel in the Sunday supplement have to be accompanied with a photograph of the author thereof? What is the audience motivation in the publishers' Meet-the-Author parties? Why are TV interviews with authors so much in demand? —"I found his book interesting. What is he really like?" The book will not tell. But also, disregarding financial profit, is there not still a felt need on the author's part to come face to face with his embodied audience, to gauge their attitudes and qualities, like a dramatist's wish to see and hear the response to his play? McLuhan quotes John O'Hara's words in *The New York Times Book Review*, November 27, 1955:

You know your reader is captive inside those covers, but as novelist you have to imagine the satisfaction he's getting. Now, in the theater —well, I used to drop in during both productions of *Pal Joey* and watch, not imagine, the people enjoy it.[27]

It appears, then, that the problems latent in the medium of the printed word have not yet been worked out to the mutual satisfaction of author and audience. The difficulties with which the eighteenth-century novelists wrestled are still with us. The deprivation they encountered was serious. It was a loss of a vital, meaningful, and responsible connection mutually acknowledged. With the changed conditions of the world of print, time-honored and traditional values had been alienated almost without anyone's fully realizing what was taking place. The gulf stream, as it were, had shifted outward and the climate would be different thereafter.

The vital and meaningful aspects of the old relation are visible in every worth-while personal association. What they contributed to literature is evident in the best of our earlier poetry and drama, and very visible in the private letters of the century upon which we have come to confer. The responsibility to which we allude is primarily moral. The menace to it implicit in the separation was never better expressed than by Johnson, in his fourth *Rambler* essay, which excites the indignant protest of today's graduate students, who invariably misread it. "If the world," he declares,

[27] Quoted in Marshall McLuhan, *Understanding Media* (paperback ed., 1965), p. 53.

be promiscuously described, I cannot see of what use it can be to read the account; or why it may not be as safe to turn the eye immediately upon mankind, as upon a mirror which shows all that presents itself without discrimination . . . Many writers, for the sake of following nature, so mingle good and bad qualities in their principal personages, that they are both equally conspicuous; and as we accompany them through their adventures with delight, and are led by degrees to interest ourselves in their favour, we lose the abhorrence of their faults . . . To this fatal error all those will contribute, who confound the colours of right and wrong . . . In narratives where *historical* veracity has no place, I cannot discover why there should not be exhibited the most perfect *idea* of virtue; of virtue not angelical, nor above probability, for what we cannot credit we shall never imitate, but the highest and purest that humanity can reach, which . . . may, by conquering some calamities, and enduring others, teach us what we may hope, and what we can perform. Vice, for vice is necessary to be shewn, should always disgust . . . Wherever it appears, it should raise hatred. [He has already suggested a reason that was more adequate, though not more apt, in his own time than today: "These books are written chiefly to the young, the ignorant, and the idle, to whom they serve as lectures of conduct, and introductions into life. They are the entertainment of minds unfurnished with ideas . . . not fixed by principles . . . not informed by experiences . . ." He concludes:] There are thousands of readers of romances willing to be thought wicked, if they may be allowed to be wits. It is therefore to be steadily inculcated, that virtue is the highest *proof* of understanding, and the only *solid* basis of greatness; and that vice is the natural consequence of *narrow* thoughts, that it begins in mistake, and ends in ignominy.

If we have travelled far, it is along the road that Johnson foresaw. What he reprobates, Stendhal adopts as a definition of the genre.[28] As Wayne Booth, condemning Céline's best-known work in his admirable *Rhetoric of Fiction*, comments:

inside views can build sympathy even for the most vicious character . . . it is hardly surprising that works in which this effect [impersonal narration] is used have often led to moral confusion . . . too often for us to dismiss moral questions as irrelevant to technique . . . Caught in the trap of a suffering consciousness, we are led to succumb morally as well as visually . . . we cannot excuse [Céline] for writing a book which, if taken seriously by the reader, must corrupt him . . . Taken seriously, the book would make life itself meaningless except as a series of self-centred forays into the lives of others.[29]

[28] Cf. Stendhal, *Le Rouge et le Noir*, epigraph to pt. I, ch. 13: "Un roman: c'est un miroir qu'on promène le long d'un chemin." (Saint-Réal.)
[29] Wayne Booth, *The Rhetoric of Fiction* (1961), pp. 378–384.

The contemporary abrogation of moral responsibility on the part of the author, in favor of novel excitations of 'reader participation', is one of the results of the separation and consequent mutual privacy of the acts of writing for print alone and of solitary reading. It is difficult to believe that an art which by this kind of enablement has so far outpaced the currently accepted mores of a permissive society can go much further in the same direction. We may rather hope and expect, in the light of such abundant evidence of unquenchable need to break through the barriers of print, that there will come a fresh effort toward the re-establishment—inside the literary forms themselves, and not for mere cabinet exhibition —of a mutually candid, cordial, and honorably responsible relationship between the author and his chosen audience.

Printing as an Index of Taste

"PRINTING," says D. B. Updike, "always reflects the tendencies of its period in forms of art and aims in life . . . we unconsciously govern our printing by the kind of life we approve." When one puts books side by side, century against century, nothing seems more evident than that the physical contrasts are full of significance, the artifacts emblematic each of its time and place. Yet, consulting the index of so comprehensive a cultural history as B. Sprague Allen's *Tides in English Taste*, one finds there references to Dress, Furniture, Gardens, Grottoes, Hermitages, and so on; but never once to Printing, which is so obviously not only the conveyor of information but also in itself a valid form of artistic expression, and in one way or another related, or tangential, to most of the arts of modern life in the West. Between general histories of printing on the one hand and detailed accounts of presses, printers, and foundries on the other, one might be led to conclude that little has been done in the study of printing as a sociological record, or as a manifestation of artistic standards within the broader context of periods of culture. The paucity of such investigations may perhaps justify, as it has prompted, the observations which follow.

In its finest essence, a book may truly be "the precious life-blood of a master-spirit, embalmed and treasured up on purpose to a life beyond life"; but, physically, it is the collaborative product of many minds and many hands: hands trained to habitual skills and set in traditional ways, and minds predisposed by knowledge, judgment, and taste. Although few books can have been so unlucky as that unique first printing of Goldsmith's *The Traveller*, set up from the fair copy exactly as it left the author's hand—the pages neatly stacked in reverse order—yet, that any book at all, fitted together by a collaboration inevitably so dispersed, should achieve a unity of effect is in itself something of a wonder. In its combination of many crafts, all essential but so loosely yoked and unsimultaneous, it is rather like a building of the age when printing from movable type was first invented. But although the multiform influences that go into the making of a book may often pull in different directions, we must not forget the weight of tradition operative in the particular society for which the book is created—a weight national in its scope and character, and in typography requiring an obedience that Stanley Morison has called "almost absolute." "Type design," as Morison says, "moves at the pace of the most conservative reader." For that reason, type design will occupy us less in this inquiry than the selection and ordering of these movable symbols.

A moment ago we referred to the analogous character of architecture as an art dependent on collaborative effort. There are other similarities. Without insisting too strongly on the three-dimensional qualities and potentialities of printing, we may properly remind ourselves that they exist. For, as Morison again remarks, printing is properly a department of engraving. Its derivation, despite the powerful influence of manuscript characters on its development, has not been in a straight line from handwriting. Roman inscriptions have made indelible contribution to the character of our uppercase letters, and the influence of epigraphy upon title pages has been recurrent and conspicuous to the present day. In the eighteenth century, engraved titles are not at all uncommon. The variety and ornateness of letter thus made possible were a constant invitation to elegant display. In company with vignettes, engraved letters made a more homogeneous effect. Throughout the century, music books were frequently engraved; and the lavish use of engraved illustrations on nearly every page of such a *de luxe* production as Pine's *Horace*, 1733–1737, suggested and justified engraving the letterpress as well. Engraving early taught the way to open, shaded, and ornamental letters, to be pursued to such extravagant lengths with the technical advances of the nineteenth

QVINTI

HORATII FLACCI

OPERA.

VOL. II.

LONDINI

AENEIS TABVLIS INCIDIT

IOHANNES PINE

M DCC XXXVII.

Figure 1.   Title page of John Pine's engraved
Horace (1737), Volume II.

century. Hints of these developments appear in such inconspicuous places as the engraved title page of Thomas Ewing's little Dublin edition of Shakespeare, 1771, with its rococo and not unattractive frame, And while Baskerville's Italic letter shows clear traces of his beginnings as a writing master, his Roman letter perpetually reminds us that he was also a lapidary.

BOOKS IN the aggregate compose a library, and a library is an important architectural feature of a house. Whether a man reads his books is for him to choose; but will he nill he, the fact of his library faces him every day as part of his domestic environment. Like the other physical appointments of an hereditary house, its books together are a relatively permanent feature. The current possessor may augment or diminish an inherited library, or leave it alone, but he cannot be unaware of it. He may think of it as part of the furniture of a room but it is really more indigenous than that. It is a three-dimensional way of decorating his walls and is thus a kind of sculpture, with some of the values of high relief. The other architectural features of the room are properly designed to present its ornamental values in a harmonious interplay.

The eighteenth century fully appreciated the beauty of fine binding and took care that it should be lasting. Books were regularly bought unbound, for here personal taste could find expression, and in the library books could thus be given the desired appearance as sculpturesque details in an overall effect. Because they were durable, this was a kind of slowly evolved sculpture, in which the generations could quite naturally collaborate. In an ancestral house, there would be many old books; and thus size naturally became a function not merely of temporary preference but of inheritance as well, with an appeal comparable to that of old paintings and antique sculpture. Ancient folios were impressive in a library, and perhaps few but actual scholars properly valued the old books that were small.

But sculptural and architectonic values inhere also in the individual books, and not merely in respect to the structure of ideas or their stylistic properties. Even in a physical sense, books can be classical or romantic, though like most utilitarian artifacts they are the imperfect reconciliation of conflicting prerogatives. Ideally, perhaps, every book ought to be physically expressive of its content.

But the difficulties of earlier type founding would alone have thwarted such an aim; and it is doubtful that, except in an undefined way, it ever exerted more than an indirect influence.

In fact, when we think of the fluctuations of taste and fashion in eighteenth-century England, it seems remarkable how seldom we find them consciously reflected in bookmaking. The oriental interest, for example, which affected so many of the applied arts as well as literature—architecture, furniture, pottery, textiles, gardening—appears to have left no mark on the designing of books. It would have been easy to introduce Eastern motives into their decoration, in arabesque ornaments or otherwise. *The Prince of Abissinia* (now *Rasselas*) might have exhaled an aura of specious distance; *The Citizen of the World* might have emphasized its imaginative detachment with a physically piquant charm; *Oriental Eclogues* might have been decked out with exotic trimmings quite as appropriately as Garrick's four-poster bed! Probably Bentley's rococo designs for Gray's poems, 1753, take us as far in this direction as the age was able to go (see Fig. 2).

Or, to consider another strong impulse: the interest in the Past. Is it not paradoxical that Walpole, who spent close to £100,000 on giving architectural substance to his Gothic fancies and wrote a Gothic novel besides, was invariably classical in his style of printing and never seems to have thought of purchasing for his own press a single letter of Gothic or Old English type? In this distaste he agreed with his generation, which was quite insensitive to the visual appeal or antiquarian suggestion of black letter, using it only for practical purposes. Occasionally, at the beginning and end of the century, two or three words on a title page might be set off by it. At the beginning, this was simply for emphasis, a survival of earlier typographic habits; at the end of the century, it was clearly used for atmosphere and romantic suggestion. In 1765, it is not on the title page (though it occurs elsewhere) of Percy's *Reliques*, a Dodsley publication; but in the early nineties, the Egertons and Joseph Johnson used it on Ritson's titles for *Ancient Songs*, *Ancient Popular Poetry*, and *Robin Hood*. Generally, throughout the central years it was shunned in literary connections, perhaps because its strongest associations at that time were discordant or vulgar. Black-letter ballads, for example, were a low form of verse. Although the Caslons included all sizes of

O D E

On the Death of a Favourite CAT,

Drowned in a Tub of Gold Fishes.

WAS on a lofty vafe's fide,
Where China's gayeft art had dy'd
   The azure flowers, that blow;
Demureft of the tabby kind,
The penfive Selima reclin'd,
   Gazed on the lake below.

Her confcious tail her joy declar'd;
The fair round face, the fnowy beard,
   The velvet of her paws,
Her coat, that with the tortoife vies,
Her ears of jet, and emerald eyes,
   She faw; and purr'd applaufe.

Still

Figure 2. Page from *Designs by Mr. R. Bentley for Six Poems by Mr. T. Gray* (1753). Greatly reduced in reproduction.

black letter in their books of type specimens, Philip Luckombe writes, in 1770: "At present Black Letter is so far abolished [i.e., in English use], that it is seldom used in any work than what belongs to Law, and more particularly to Statute Law. It is therefore possible that Black Letter, in time, may become altogether unregarded. . . . Several Printing Houses are without [it], and yet well provided with every other good, and more useful, Materials . . . [It] is," he concedes, "sometimes used instead of printing in Red, what is designed to be made more conspicuous than common." Obviously, Luckombe sees no artistic values in it; and it is certain that there are few typographical evidences of the Gothic impulse at the time. Inconceivable then would have been Stanley Morison's recent praise of black letter as "in design more homogeneous, more picturesque, more lively" than "the grey round roman we use."

THE QUESTION of size in books has psychological implications not to be instantly resolved, which interplay with obvious practical considerations. When we have allowed for convenience at one end of the scale and conspicuous display at the other, there still remains a wide range of possible choices. But here, as elsewhere, powerful traditions come into play, and there is never a single reason for a preference. It seems clear that the eighteenth century had a notion of correct relations between subject matter and physical size. Even as there was one style and vocabulary appropriate to epic and another to satire, so, they may have felt, there ought generally to be an apparent correspondence of size to substance. This was a particular among the abundant questions of style and taste, dress and decorum; and, as such, had immediate connections also with the body and face of type. The rules of proportion should be visible here as in architecture; and Luckombe confidently pronounces that a Dedication is to be set in letter two sizes larger than the body of the work; a Preface in Roman one size larger than the letter of the main body; the Contents in Italic of the same size as the body; the Index in letter two sizes smaller than that of the body; with other rules for the running title, and so on into minuter details.

There is, of course, no absolute decree about the size, and obviously many books were, for various reasons, reprinted in different sizes. Johnson reminds us that a cheap edition of Pope's *Iliad* clandestinely imported from Holland compelled Lintot "to contract his folio at once into a duodecimo, and lose the advantage of an intermediate gradation." Richardson gave Hervey practical reasons for preferring octavo to duodecimo for a reprint of the *Contemplations on a Flower-Garden,* which had first appeared in quarto: "Small Print is dearer than large: Your Book wants Bulk, and it would be thinner, I think, in a smaller Type."

It is reasonably certain that, as the reading public swelled to take in lower social levels, the size of books tended generally likewise to descend, resulting at the end of the century in the publication—disregarding issues *de luxe*—of far fewer folios and quartos than at the commencement, and of many more octavos and duodecimos. When Boswell talked of printing the *Life* in folio, Malone told him he "might as well throw it into the Thames, for a folio would not now be read." Yet tradition and public expectation were not so suddenly overturned but that size remained a much more prominent factor than it has since become—although even today we have our traditions in these matters.

One of the proprieties that kept its hold throughout the century was that of printing separate poems with any claim to serious notice in quarto; or even, if before 1750, and especially if dedicated to someone noteworthy, in folio. Interesting in this connection is the fact that Goldsmith's only works to be printed in his lifetime in a size above duodecimo or (but rarely) octavo were *The Traveller, The Deserted Village,* and *Threnodia Augustalis.* Did Goldsmith have a personal antipathy to larger books, or was this by chance? Shenstone wrote amusingly to Lady Luxborough, June 1, 1748: "I am always in Hopes that whenever an Author is either a tall or even middle-size Man, he will never print a Book but in Folio, octavo, or duodecimo; & on the other Hand, when he is short & squat, I collect that his partiality to a Figure of that kind, will induce him, to my great discomfort, to publish in Quarto." We might here observe that Smart, who wrote an Ode to a lady apologizing for his being a little man, in which he calls himself an "amorous dwarf," printed all of his poems in quarto except the first, which was a folio! But whatever the personal preferences, the reams of now forgotten poetry that issued, decade after decade, in all the dignity of Caslon's heavily leaded English Roman, in quarto pamphlet form, impress one, as perhaps nothing else can do, with a sense of the honor in which poetry in that age was held among the general reading public.

In contrast, that puny Hercules, the Novel, struggling for a place in the sun, could make few pretensions to honorable estate, although Fielding tried hard to find it an ancient pedigree. Self-respecting people whose education had carried them into ancient authors had little regard for books that served only for pastime. One might at most find room for a large and handsome edition of a favorite classic, like the Tonsons' *Don Quixote*, enriched with three-score full-page illustrations. *Current* fiction was different, and must be content to be inconspicuous. Its readers were probably stealing from duties the time they gave to it, or had other sufficient reasons for not advertising their occupation. "Here, my dear Lucy, hide these books," cries Lydia Languish: "put 'The Innocent Adultery' into 'The Whole Duty of Man' . . . cram Ovid behind the bolster —there—put 'The Man of Feeling' into your pocket!" Obviously, it was inevitable that novels should be published in duodecimo, more especially because of the class of reader that could be anticipated for them. Lady Mary Wortley Montagu, who became an inveterate novel reader, has at least to justify, while she admits, her predilection to her daughter; but few would have acknowledged the vice so openly. Leonora, Addison's literary lady, had similar tastes but she compounded for the offense by displaying (on her higher shelves) "all the Classick Authors in wood" and "a set of Elzevirs by the same hand."

We notice besides that Leonora, though having other objects to accommodate in her library, pays due heed to the sizes of her books, which are ranked from large to small, with porcelain and china jars, tea dishes, and bric-à-brac disposed so as to provide the architectural dividers between the folios and quartos, the quartos and octavos. The reputable John Clarke, drawing up a careful list of books to form the nucleus of a worth-while library, a list filling nearly a hundred pages of his *Essay upon Study* (1731), pays the same deference to size, proceeding from folios to twelves, sub-dividing by categories of knowledge, and interspersing critical remarks. He gives short shrift to lighter reading. Even of the English poets—apart from their translations of the classics—few are admitted: Spenser, Milton, Buckingham, Cowley, Waller, Addison. About Milton he has serious reservations. As for Plays and Romances,

Plate I. "Spring," by William Kent, for Thomson's *The Seasons* (1730), quarto. Slightly reduced in reproduction.

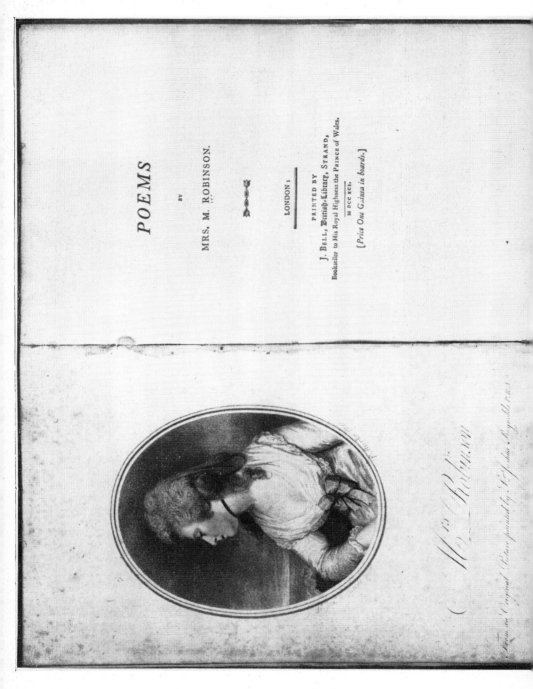

Plate II. Frontispiece and title page of Mrs. M. Robinson, *Poems* (1791), printed by John Bell. Greatly reduced in reproduction.

Plate III. "Amelia Struck by Lightning," by Sir William Hamilton, for Bensley's edition *de luxe* of Thomson's *The Seasons* (1797), "Summer," ll.118 ff. Greatly reduced in reproduction.

NIGHT

THE

THIRD,

NARCISSA.

Plate IV. Page of Edward Young, *Night Thoughts* (1797), Night
III, illustrated by William Blake. Greatly reduced in reproduction.

they are, he declares, "generally very indiscreetly and foolishly writ, in a way proper to recommend Vanity and Wickedness, rather than discredit them; have a strong Tendency to corrupt and debauch the Mind with silly mischievous Notions of Love and Honour, and other Things relating to the Conduct of Life . . . [They] should be very sparingly and warily meddled with, especially by young People. I know but two *Romances* I can heartily recommend, *The History of Don Quixot*, and the *Adventures of Telemachus*." In this connection we recall Johnson's reservations about such reading in the fourth *Rambler*. But, in keeping with the sense for size to which we are attending, it is noteworthy that when, in the 1740's, auction sales of important libraries began to be regularized in the London book world, the catalogues were arranged and the sales proceeded in accordance with these same physical categories—a method which became traditional.

As the century runs, single *plays* are printed almost invariably in octavo. The reason, simple or complex, is by no means obvious, since in the seventeenth century with equal regularity plays were printed in quarto. The change in convention comes quite punctually at the opening of the new century, if we except a few authors who had been established in an earlier decade. It seems to have evoked no comment at the time: as if a new class of play readers had suddenly appeared, unmindful of custom but equally expectant of consistency. Such abrupt fractures of convention are baffling and fascinating. No apparent cause, either political, social, or economic, will account easily for this one. Perhaps the universal consciousness of a secular anniversary begets at such times the frame of mind expressed by Dryden in his *Secular Masque:*

> 'Tis well an old age is out,
> And time to begin a new.

The century mark, with its psychological overtones, may not be so artificial a division as some rational historians would insist.

PICTURE WRITING, no doubt, far antedates the alphabet, and letters are a conventionalized surrogate for a more lively form of graphic communication. The later divergence of the arts of writing and pictorial illustration need not blot from our minds their radical relation. As in the Platonic myth of the sexes, the impulse to re-unite, or at least to reaffirm the primitive kinship, has been both spontaneous and ineradicable throughout the history of the Book. The ways in which this impulse has expressed itself are highly characteristic and, from the historical and sociological points of view, inevitably comprise one of the most important branches of bibliographical inquiry, broadly conceived.

There is a valid distinction between the primarily expository or diagrammatic illustration and the primarily decorative—though of course beauty is always useful and utility seldom aesthetically barren. And in decoration there is a distinction between the abstract and the representational. This distinction, in the sense intended, suggests a separation of typographic from pictorial ornament. Even here, however, the difference is not absolute, for typography has never entirely lost its pictorial appeals. At its most conventional, it still *illustrates* its meaning, both by the aesthetic values of its characters and by the ornamental suggestion of natural objects. Varieties of type face, modulations of page color and inking, interplay of upper and lower case, the use of printers' flowers, are all of them means to the same end of illustration. Thereafter, more obviously, come engravings on wood or metal, of emblems, factotums, head- and tail-pieces, vignettes, calligraphic inventions; and lastly, full pictorial illustration. So far as engraving could carry them at that time, all these resources were of course available to the eighteenth-century printers. But their use was by no means consistent; and to follow their various applications as the decades pass is to become possessed of valuable but commonly neglected testimony to the spirit of the Age.

The uses of roman and italic, as Luckombe shows, were in the middle years not rigidly settled but yet fairly static. It is to be wished, he remarks, "that the intermixing Roman and Italic may be brought to straighter limits, and the latter be used for such purposes as it was designed for; viz. for varying the different Parts . . . —for passages which differ from the language of the Text—for literal citations from Scripture—for words, terms, or expressions which . . . authors would have [to be] regarded as more nervous; and by which they intend to convey to the reader either instructing, satyrizing, admiring, or other hints and remarks." In recommending a reduction of their intermixture (for a characteristic example see the Preface to *Pamela*, Fig. 3), he follows the visible current toward typographic simplicity and consistency. He reveals also

how elastic the relations between author and printer could be in determining the appearance of a work. Gentlemen being gentlemen, he thinks it better if they keep their fingers out of the printer's pie—"especially," he says, "if the Author should chance to be a humourous Gentleman . . . for then a Compositor is obliged to conform to the fancy of his Author, and sometimes to huddle his work up in such a manner as is no Credit either to him or his Master; whereas the Gentleman that leaves the gracing of his work to the judgment of the Printer, seldom finds room to be dissatisfied upon that score. By the Laws of Printing," he continues, "a Compositor should abide by his Copy, and not vary from it. . . . But this good law is now

PREFACE

BY THE

EDITOR.

 F to Divert *and* Entertain, *and at the same time to* Inftruct, *and* Improve *the Minds of the* YOUTH *of* both Sexes:

I F to inculcate Religion *and* Morality *in so easy and agreeable a manner, as shall render them equally* delightful *and* profitable *to the* younger Clafs *of Readers, as well as worthy of the Attention of Perfons of* maturer *Years and Underftandings :*

A 3   I F

Figure 3. Richardson's rhetorical typography, Preface to *Pamela* (1740). Slightly reduced in reproduction.

looked upon as obsolete, and most Authors expect the Printer to spell, point, and digest their Copy, that it may be intelligible and significant to the Reader." Such a policy gives a large autonomy to the compositor, and seems clearly to indicate that, though a mid-eighteenth-century author could, and might wish to, involve himself with the details of style and pointing, he need not regard it as a duty, because the printer was ready to accept it as his own responsibility.

Standing additional guard against improprieties was that still more important officer, the Corrector, who went over the copy both before and after it was set in type, and who might often prove a large factor in the prosperity of the printing house: "for it is a maxim with Booksellers," says Luckombe, "to give the first edition of a work to be done by such Printers whom they know to be either able Correctors themselves, or that employ fit persons, [who] though not of Universal learning know the fundamentals of every Art and Science that may fall under their examination. . . . [The Corrector] often finds occasion to alter and to mend things . . . either wrong or else ill digested."

We must not invade the niceties of eighteenth-century pointing at present. But the single question of capitalization is not only perplexed but is of considerable literary importance, and has significant implications for style and meaning, especially in poetry. These we may not entirely neglect.

It seems clear that authors might have as much or as little to do with the matter as they chose. Where an author's practice varied from publication to publication, it is natural to assume that he took little personal interest in capitalization, or else that he was not equally concerned with all editions of his work. Prior's 1718 folio, for example, shows an idiosyncratic and subjective attitude, capitalizing nouns, pronouns frequently, occasionally adjectives, setting personal names in caps-and-small-caps, with an additional refinement of italicizing place names. Such a procedure results in a greatly restricted use of italics, and makes for a homogeneous yet vivid, even dramatic, page. But these practices are not found in later editions of Prior. Pope capitalizes judiciously and subjectively —but not according to any clear rule: and his practice is not respected after his death. Gay avoids capitals in 1720 and in his *Fables*, 1728; but *The Beggar's Opera*, of the latter year, as a rule capitalizes nouns. Young's *Universal Passion*, in its second edition, 8vo 1728, avoids unnecessary capitals but, to even matters, indulges in a rhetorically rib-nudging, eyebrow-raising, winking-and-blinking use of italics to a degree seldom seen. For example (Satire III, p. 47):

Not all on *books* their Criticifm wafte;

The genius of a *difh* fome juftly tafte,

And *eat* their way to *fame*; with anxious thought

The *falmon* is refus'd, the *turbot* bought.

Impatient art rebukes the fun's delay,

And bids *december* yield the fruits of *may*.

Figure 4.   Edward Young, *Love of Fame, The Universal
Passion* (1728).

Neither Tonson nor his printer can be accountable for this intimate
appeal to the reader: only the author himself could be so officious.

Again, Thomson's *Seasons*, which were published by different
booksellers, show conflicting evidence. Some copies of the octavo
edition of 1730–called 2d edition, B-type, by J. E. Wells–are
comprised of separately printed parts. Millar, who printed *Spring*,
follows conventions different from Millan's, who printed the other
parts: Millan uses italics in proper naming and important personifications, while Millar sets proper names, personifications, and
emphatic words in small capitals, uses no italics, and avoids sub-
stantive capitalization. In the editions of 1744 (Millar, 8vo) and
1746 (Millar, 12mo), however, nouns are regularly capitalized,
and italics are sometimes employed, as well as small capitals, for
reasons not always self-explanatory.

I have seen no evidence to support Geoffrey Tillotson's hypothesis that in the time of Pope capitalization was even loosely–still
less "rigorously"–dependent upon format.[1] It is clear, however,
that there is a quite abrupt shift of convention just at the midpoint
of the century. Before 1750 poetry was likely to be generously
capitalized; after 1750 it was likely to be given a modern capitalization. There are exceptions on either side of the line but they do
not conceal the fact that 1750 is the Great Divide. And prose seems

[1] Professor Tillotson has subsequently convinced me that, if *format* be understood as referring only to *size*, he is correct in asserting a relation: small sizes
are more generously capitalized than large. This I had not observed.

to have followed roughly the same course. *Pamela* (3d edition) regularly capitalizes the nouns: *Clarissa,* 1748, does not, though its preliminary matter is heavily capitalized. *Tristram Shandy* is capitalized in modern fashion, though one might have expected Sterne to make his nouns strut. In a letter to Baskerville, April 7, 1757, Dodsley writes: "In the specimen from Melmoth I think you have used too many Capitals, which is generally thought to spoil the beauty of printing; but they should never be used to adjectives, verbs, or adverbs."

The rather surprising thing is that so conspicuous and far-reaching a change should have evoked so little contemporary comment. The whole visual effect of a page of type is transformed by it. For us, this entails also a change in psychological response. Men do not ordinarily leave unremarked the swift departure of time-honored custom. Presumably, the generation schooled to capitalize nouns would go on writing in their habitual way. Gray capitalizes all his nouns as a matter of course, in his surviving holographs[2] of the *Elegy*. Personifications, naturally, were no exception to the rule—but neither did they give rise to it. That they became exceptions because of the general proscription of capitals in printing of the latter half of the century is doubtless a natural consequence of their affinity to proper names. Once a typographical shift had occurred, a certain class of images was thrown into high relief, that before had claimed no more notice than what intrinsically was the due of each. Coleridge's taunt, therefore, that Gray's personifications depended upon the printer, had thus become valid in a psychological sense during the decades between the two men, but is critically anachronistic. Historically speaking, it exaggerates psychologically and thereby distorts the figure. To restore the balance, we ought never to capitalize personification in a modernized text.

When it is realized how much more casually capitals were understood in Gray's time, the question begins to be less mystifying. If all nouns could be capitalized at will by an educated writer, then equally no nouns needed to be so, unless for personally compelling reasons. Was it not provincial to capitalize? Latin had no such convention; but grammar and meaning survived without it.

[2] This is true of the Pembroke and Egerton MSS, and presumably of the Eton MS, which I have not seen.

Practically, the rule if absolutely enforced was a handicap to refined rhetorical effects. Little stress was laid on it in school, when even spelling was relatively unimportant and English not a subject of serious study. Perhaps, the age seems to have felt, the problem might as well be tossed back to the printer, who had in a sense invented it by making people conscious of "lower" and "upper case" where, before, speed of writing had determined the shape and size of letters.

There were, to be sure, a few "humourous Gentlemen," as Luckombe would call them, who took a very great interest in the typographical aspects of their work, and whose work for that reason is itself especially interesting. One of these is the denigrated but well-deserving Shakespearean scholar, Edward Capell. Capell's *Prolusions,* published by J. & R. Tonson in 1760, but of which the last page reads, by way of colophon, "From the Press of Dryden Leach, in Crane-court, Fleet-street, Oct. 6th 1759," is a book that shows in every minute particular that there is not a typographical detail in it which has not been considered afresh by the editor in the light of his aesthetic and scholarly purposes, and resolved or justified anew. As printing, it is severe and clean but not at all forbidding. Capell has carried his dislike of unnecessary capitals into the title itself and the running heads. Still more striking is the fact that, except in the play included, the lines of poetry have no initial capitalization. There are other unusual features, of which only one can be mentioned here. As an instance of his "humour" and of the lengths to which he was willing to go in imposing his wishes on printer, publisher, and public: he insisted on dividing words, monosyllables included, just where they fell at the end of a line. In his Introduction, we meet with such oddities as repr-inted, kn-ows, tw-elve, thro-ughout, mi-ght, gr-eater, and Sha-kespeare. Ancient MSS gave a precedent, and even title pages not so ancient. But what advantage was gained is hard to discover. For willfulness we can only set it beside Edward Rowe Mores' classical fervor in beginning his sentences with a lower-case letter, except when they opened a paragraph. To be sure, Ritson was to fly still higher when he set himself to revise the mother tongue in publishing his *Engleish Romanceës,* elegantly printed by Bulmer for the Nicols, "Bookselers to His Majesty in Pel-Mel," 1802.

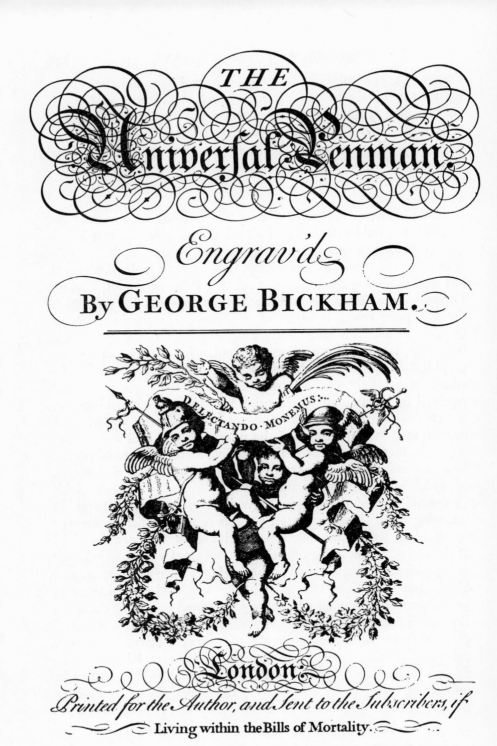

THE

Universal Penman.

Engrav'd

By GEORGE BICKHAM.

DELECTANDO · MONEMUS:

London

Printed for the Author, and Sent to the Subscribers, if
Living within the Bills of Mortality.

Figure 5. Engraved title page of George Bickham, *The Universal Penman* (1743). Greatly reduced in reproduction.

"THE HISTORY of printing," according to Stanley Morison, "is in large measure the history of the title-page." This is because the "preliminaries" of a book, being less strictly regulated by established conventions than the pages of text, allow more freedom of individual expression to the designer.

When we come to them in a chronological study, the prevailing sobriety of the characteristic eighteenth-century title pages is what strikes us first. Gone by Charles II's day are the exuberant or fantastic engraved titles of the seventeenth-century baroque style. Gone, too, by the eighteenth century was that garish typographical splendor beloved of Lamb and humorously referred to by Coleridge when quoting the "fullswoln" title of Heylyn's work on Laud: "I am sensible [he writes] how dimly this magnificent Title shines in the above Reflex Image, shorn of its Beams, the Types of many sizes, and the fulgency of red-lettered Small, Great, Greater and yet Greater Capitals. It is worthy the attention of any Philosopher disposed to favor the Public with The Physiognomy of Title-pages as an appendix to Craniology, Chiromancy and the like Sciences." But now and again Religion, State, Science, or the Fine Arts might still prompt monumental expression, as in Bickham's *Universal Penman* (Fig. 5) and *Musical Entertainer* or Pine's *Horace* (Fig. 1) (of the 1730's), where the engraver's cunning could be splendidly displayed.

A rough-and-ready division of eighteenth-century title pages might be made into two classes, the Inscriptional Tablet and the Handbill. "Printers," Richardson once wrote to Aaron Hill, "have often the Honour of being heard in the Business of Titles"; but obviously the author's wishes have primary rights in deciding what the title page shall contain. Whether it shall be determinative, descriptive, or suggestive; whether to include or omit the writer's name; whether to add a motto, and of what sort: these decisions reveal the author. It was not Bowyer or Lintot who decided for *The Works of Mr. Alexander Pope* (Fig. 6) or picked the long Ciceronian motto. Looking at the matter from the point of view of young Mr. Pope: if a man is to publish his "works" before the age of thirty, and if his name is to go upon the title page, that "Mr." is a significant gesture of self-depreciation. It makes the name less like a signature by third-personalizing it, so to speak; and it modestly announces the author's social status. Milton's

THE
WORKS
OF
Mr. *ALEXANDER POPE.*

CICERO pro ARCH.

*Hæc ſtudia adoleſcentiam alunt, ſeneЄtutem obleЄtant; ſecundas
res ornant, adverſis perfugium & ſolatium præbent; dele-
Єtant domi, non impediunt foris; pernoЄtant nobiſcum, pe-
regrinantur, ruſticantur.*

LONDON:
Printed by W. BOWYER, for BERNARD LINTOT between the *Temple-Gates.* 1717.

Figure 6. Title page of Alexander Pope, *Works* (1717). Greatly
reduced in reproduction.

POEMS

ON

SEVERAL OCCASIONS.

LONDON:

Printed for JACOB TONSON at *Shakespear's-Head* over againſt *Katharine-Street* in the *Strand,* and JOHN BARBER upon *Lambeth-Hill.* MDCCXVIII.

Figure 7.   Title page of Matthew Prior, *Poems on Several Occasions* (1718). Greatly reduced in reproduction.

example may stand for a precedent. Another hypersensitive being, later in the century, was to refine the nuance by a further shade, when he allowed his works to be published as "Poems by Mr. Gray" (not "Mr. Thomas Gray").

But if a man's only "works" are juvenilia—poetical "Trifles," mostly written under the age of five-and-twenty, as Pope calls them in the Preface—perhaps the only decorous thing to do in publishing is to leave the identification to others. One does not put one's name over the park gate. The curious will discover it soon enough. Alternatively, one might decently sign the Dedicatory Letter, and append as vouchers—if one were Prior—a list of some fifteen hundred distinguished subscribers. The "works" could then be informally titled, and one's modesty need moult no feather. We infer, therefore, that neither was it Tonson, but Prior himself, who rejected "Works" in favor of "Poems on Several Occasions" for the sumptuous folio of 1718 (Fig. 7). Or, once more, could anything be more revelatory of the author than the title pages of each of Richardson's books, where certainly there was no rivalry between author and printer (see Fig. 8) for the "honor of being heard in the business of titles!" Yet Richardson was chary of affixing his name to his title pages (except as printer!); and even to the end of the century one is often struck by the fact that works of genuine scholarly importance fail to carry the name of the author.

It hardly needs saying that the finest title pages of the century belong to the inscriptional, not the handbill, kind—though the latter often prove more interesting and amusing. Bad taste is seldom dull to the student but its infinite variety is harder to generalize about. Besides, posterity has an incorrigible streak of idealism, and likes to believe that an age is most truly represented in its excellences. This amiable weakness it is, as one may suspect, to our ultimate interest to indulge and abet.

The title pages of Pope and Prior (Figs. 6, 7) just now under discussion, from Lintot and Tonson respectively, are good examples of refined conservatism that show an awareness of the best seventeenth-century precedents in this kind. The fine double rule that frames the text is traditional. The triangular device on the Pope is restrained in its laureate symbolism, familiar but not stereotyped; the elongated engraving by Cheron on the Prior is tastefully orna-

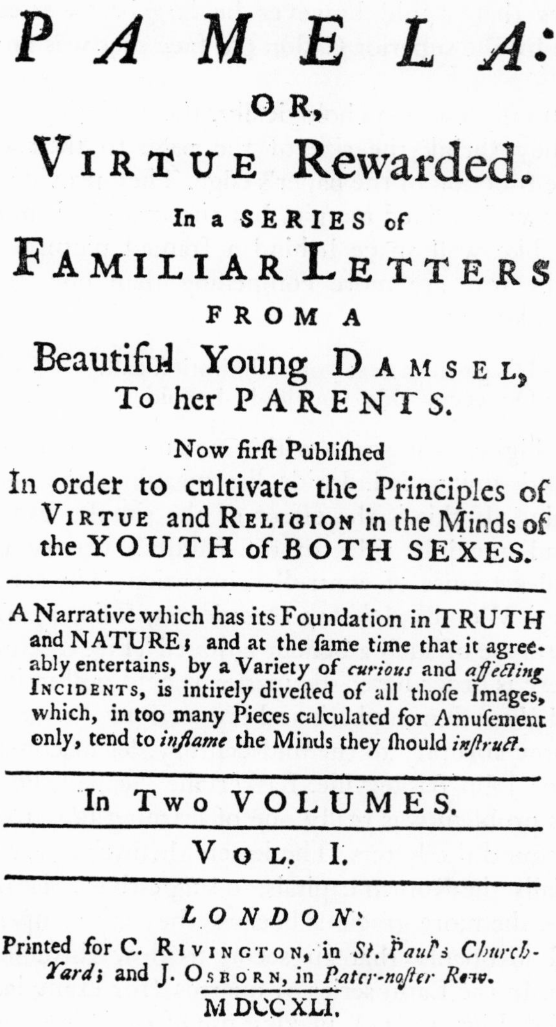

PAMELA:
OR,
VIRTUE Rewarded.

In a SERIES of
FAMILIAR LETTERS
FROM A
Beautiful Young DAMSEL,
To her PARENTS.

Now firſt Publiſhed
In order to cultivate the Principles of
VIRTUE and RELIGION in the Minds of
the YOUTH of BOTH SEXES.

A Narrative which has its Foundation in TRUTH
and NATURE; and at the ſame time that it agreeably entertains, by a Variety of *curious* and *affecting*
INCIDENTS, is intirely diveſted of all thoſe Images,
which, in too many Pieces calculated for Amuſement
only, tend to *inflame* the Minds they ſhould *inſtruct*.

In Two VOLUMES.
VOL. I.

LONDON:
Printed for C. RIVINGTON, in *St. Paul's Church-*
Yard; and J. OSBORN, in *Pater-noſter Row*.
M DCC XLI.

Figure 8. Title page of Samuel Richardson, *Pamela* (1741).

---

mental. The variation of type sizes and characters on both is considered and unobtrusive, except that perhaps Prior's huge folio
page has forced a disproportionately large letter on the word
"Poems." "Works," on the Pope title, looks less pompous in red
than it does in a black-and-white reproduction. These are good

Dutch types that would however be largely superseded in the next decade by the superior Caslon old face that was now about to be cast.

Architecturally and psychologically, the enclosing rules are important. They shrink the size of the page to their own limits, usurping the function of the paper's edge. They provide the uneven lines of type with a fixed margin, but that margin is unrelated and disengaged, like wall space behind a framed picture. *Two* rules bounding the text are more compelling than one, as a couplet surpasses blank verse:

> His gardens next your admiration call:
> On every side you look, behold the wall!

The wall is higher: the space within not merely *de*fined but *con*fined—isolated—uninvaded. Inside lies meaning; the space outside means nothing. If this is the effect of the simpler examples, even the long and ungainly titles of the handbill variety pick up by means of rules a sense of controlled intention. The second edition of Anthony à Wood's *Athenae Oxonienses*, folio, 1721, is a fairly dignified instance of such a benefit enjoyed (Fig. 9). In spite of its fullness, there is order here: the matter is held within its appointed bounds, and given due emphasis and proportion.

Passing now abruptly to the mid-century, let us come at once to the genius of John Baskerville. Baskerville "leaped the fence" and saw that his problem was really one of learning how to manipulate the space around the letters. The letters themselves are very beautiful, especially the Roman capitals, so suggestive of lapidary depth. But they are the more gracious because they are so open in feeling and treated so openly that air seems to flow through them and round them. In the Latin series of quartos (for example, the Virgil and Lucretius, Figs. 10, 11), making use of capitals almost entirely, and varying the type with such restraint that every modulation is distinctly felt, Baskerville distances his letters from one another and disposes their lengths of line with a judgment so nice as to force the surrounding space to collaborate in completing the outlines of half-suggested sculptural forms—graceful monumental urns and pedestals on which inscriptions are cut. These effects seem to establish their existence quite solidly in the open air, in three dimensions rather than two. They quite escape the local restriction of

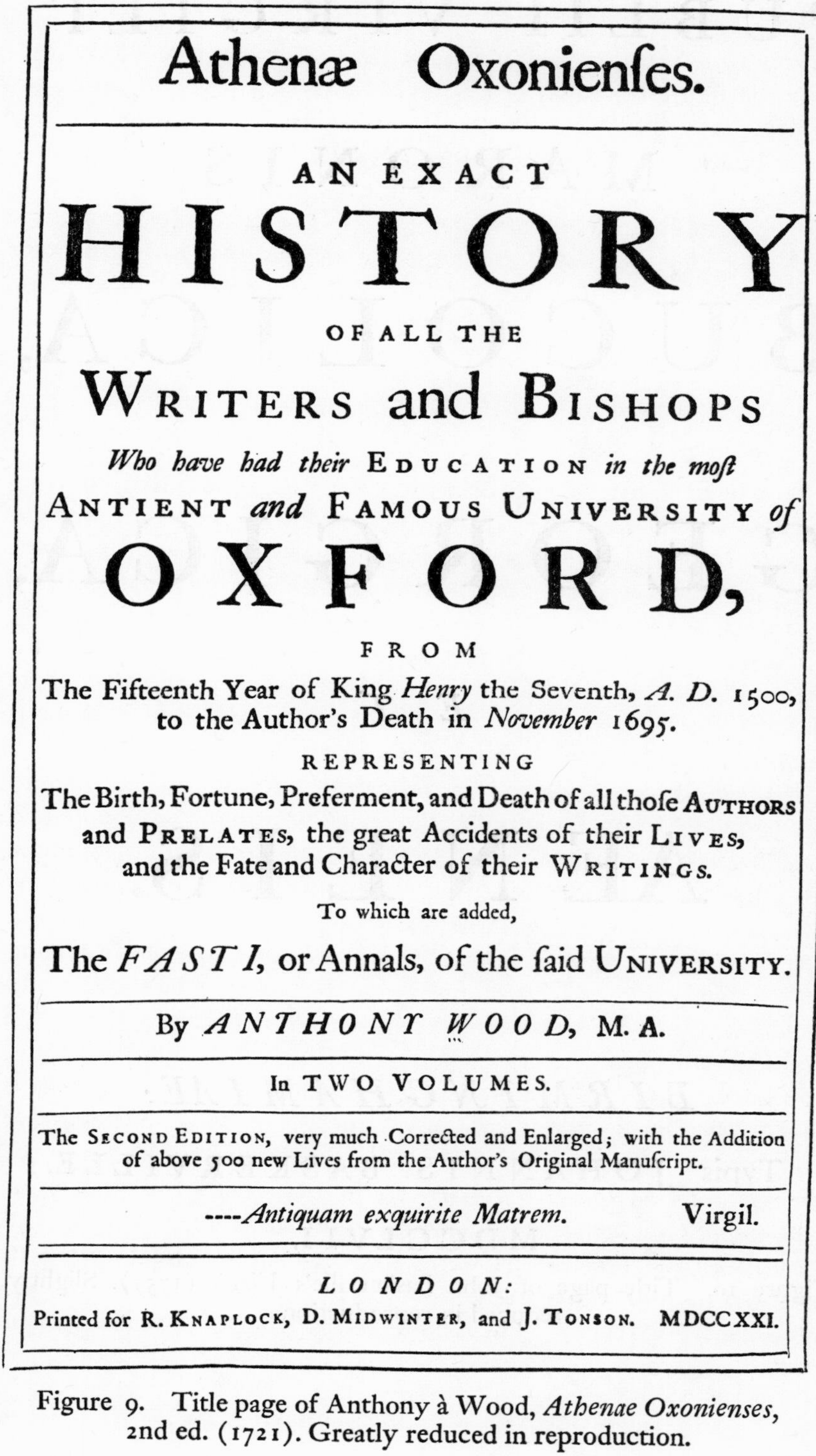

Athenæ Oxonienses.

AN EXACT

HISTORY

OF ALL THE

WRITERS and BISHOPS

Who have had their EDUCATION *in the moſt*

ANTIENT *and* FAMOUS UNIVERSITY *of*

OXFORD,

FROM

The Fifteenth Year of King *Henry* the Seventh, *A. D.* 1500, to the Author's Death in *November* 1695.

REPRESENTING

The Birth, Fortune, Preferment, and Death of all thoſe AUTHORS and PRELATES, the great Accidents of their LIVES, and the Fate and Character of their WRITINGS.

To which are added,

The *FASTI*, or Annals, of the ſaid UNIVERSITY.

By *ANTHONY WOOD*, M.A.

In TWO VOLUMES.

The SECOND EDITION, very much Corrected and Enlarged; with the Addition of above 500 new Lives from the Author's Original Manuſcript.

----*Antiquam exquirite Matrem.* Virgil.

LONDON:

Printed for R. KNAPLOCK, D. MIDWINTER, and J. TONSON. MDCCXXI.

Figure 9. Title page of Anthony à Wood, *Athenae Oxonienses*, 2nd ed. (1721). Greatly reduced in reproduction.

PUBLII VIRGILI

MARONIS

BUCOLICA,

GEORGICA,

ET

AENEIS.

BIRMINGHAMIAE:

Typis JOHANNIS BASKERVILLE.

MDCCLVII.

Figure 10. Title page of John Baskerville's *Virgil* (1757). Slightly
reduced in reproduction.

TITI

LUCRETII CARI

DE

RERUM NATURA

LIBRI SEX.

BIRMINGHAMÆ:

Typis JOHANNIS BASKERVILLE.

MDCCLXXII.

Figure 11. Title page of John Baskerville's *Lucretius* (1772). Slightly
reduced in reproduction.

tablets on a wall and claim kinship with marble colonnades. The historians of typography tell us that Baskerville was a transitional figure between the old face and the new, and that as such his influence was pervasive on all the type designers for half a century to come—on Wilson and Fry, the Martins, Didot, Bodoni, and Figgins. But as a *printer*, in his handling of type, he again seems transitional, in that he reflects something of that new attitude toward the manipulation of spatial design which led from the formal patterns of the Italianate garden, through the open but considered park designing of "Capability" Brown, with its carefully plotted vegetation, judicious architectural ornament, spacious prospects, and gentle contrasts, to the cult of picturesque and untouched nature: a progress from human law to humanized nature to wilderness. I do not mean to press the parallel too closely, which in printing was hardly completed unless in the crude excesses and deformed grotesqueries of nineteenth-century display printing. I would only emphasize that Baskerville's unique genius, in its instinct for the importance of the spatial element therein, was akin to that of the masters of his day in landscape architecture.

Most of his better successors in his own century took heed of Baskerville's teaching, and some of them carried it to an extreme. A good example of workmanlike simplicity in titling is to be seen in Dryden Leach's handling, for J. & R. Tonson, in 1767, of Capell's duodecimo edition of Shakespeare. The general title appears only in the first volume: the later volumes have more economical and even more attractive title pages. Equal refinement is apparent throughout the same editor's *Prolusions*, already discussed. Too many books begin to show a dull subservience to the new conventions in their titles, the pronouns, conjunctions, and prepositions all centered on a separate line apiece down the middle of the page. George Ellis's *Specimens of the Early English Poets*, printed by T. Rickaby in 1790, shows an exaggerated deference for space in its title (Fig. 12) but is, overall, a chastely and beautifully printed book. Its use of black letter on the title page is a sign of the times. A more successful title page, with a charming frontispiece, to a book of poetry that lacks nothing except poetic merit, is John Bell's elegant subscription edition of Perdita Robinson's *Poems* (Plate II). The thick and thin parallel rules are almost a signature of Bell's work, and noteworthy for several reasons. They probably reflect a French influence, and it is remarkable that in England they appear so late. When thin double rules are such a time-honored convention in English printing, it is odd that it seems to have occurred to no one for generations to try the effect of thicker and thinner rules set side by side. Had they done so, they would have discovered that this novel proceeding thrusts forward the space between, making the heavier rule a third dimension by way of shadow to the forward surface. The earliest indisputable evidence I have noticed that this optical illusion had been grasped by any printer occurs in the title page of Fournier's *Manuel Typographique*, 1764 (Fig. 13) where, devising a typographical frame, Fournier suggests a third-dimensional shadow by thickening the rule on the top

S P E C I M E N S

OF THE

Early English Poets.

LONDON, PRINTED FOR EDWARDS, PALL-MALL.
1790.

Figure 12. Title page of George Ellis, *Specimens of the Early English Poets* (1790).

and right inner sides, in contrast to the other two sides, where he uses thin rules. Engraving, of course, had always done what it chose but its lessons, so far as I know, had never been applied in strict typography. But now, if such an effect of a raised surface could be got with straight lines, why not with curved? Why not with letters? Why not open letters with shadows? It appears to have been the French again who led the way, and their ornamental alphabets of the mid-century have the dubious distinction of pioneering in the excesses that disfigured the scene in the following century. But meanwhile, splendid examples of the mildly romantic use of type can be seen in Bensley's sumptuous edition of the *Fables* of Dryden, with Lady Diana Beauclerc's illustrations (Fig. 14); and in Bulmer's *Principal Rivers of Great Britain*, beginning with the *Thames*, 1794–1796, with Farington's colored illustrations, or the *Milton* with Richard Westall's illustrations, 1794–1797, published by Boydell "from the types of W. Martin." These must be nearly the first times that a title page carried the names of publisher, printer, and type cutter, all three. There could be no clearer sign that printing as an art had come of age during this century, and that public appreciation of its refinements could now at last be assumed as a social and economic fact.

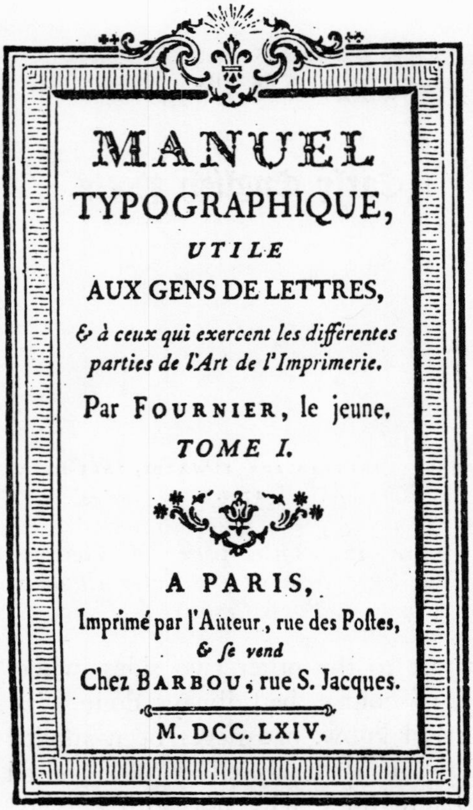
MANUEL
TYPOGRAPHIQUE,
UTILE
AUX GENS DE LETTRES,
& à ceux qui exercent les différentes parties de l'Art de l'Imprimerie.
Par FOURNIER, le jeune.
TOME I.
A PARIS,
Imprimé par l'Auteur, rue des Poſtes,
& ſe vend
Chez BARBOU, rue S. Jacques.
M. DCC. LXIV.

Figure 13. Title page of the younger Fournier, *Manuel Typographique* (1764), Volume I.

THE CONNECTION between landscape gardening and printing is not so forced as might first appear. The association between Nature and Books, from a time when books were handwritten and even antedating Christianity, is sufficiently evident in the very borrowing of our terms. *Liber*, the inner bark of a tree; *paper* from papyrus, *book* from beech, *folio* from folium; then the interchangeable terminology, as *margin*, *border*, *river*, *flowers*. There is even a borrowing in reverse: "sermons in stones, books in the running brooks"; and that archetypical image, the Book of Nature, in which Addison read the message of his famous hymn, and which the eighteenth-century landscapists, like the philosophers and poets, tried so hard to interpret in their fashion. From the days of illuminated manuscripts, the writers and makers of books have felt

THE

FABLES

OF

JOHN DRYDEN,

ORNAMENTED WITH

ENGRAVINGS

FROM THE PENCIL OF

THE RIGHT HON.

LADY DIANA BEAUCLERC.

———————

LONDON.

PRINTED BY T. BENSLEY,

FOR J. EDWARDS, N° 77, AND E. HARDING, N° 98, PALL MALL.

———————

MDCCXCVII.

Figure 14. Title page of T. Bensley's edition of Dryden's *Fables*, with Lady Diana Beauclerc's illustrations (1797). Greatly reduced in reproduction.

the need to "call in the country" to adorn their pages and remind us in the artifact of the natural world around. Head- and tail-pieces, floral initials, twining borders: few book ornaments but suggest natural phenomena, vines, trees, birds, or flowers. The mutual sympathy is charmingly realized in the tastes of the romantic lady recalled previously in her other enthusiasm, Addison's Leonora. "As her reading," wrote the Spectator, "has lain very much among Romances, it has given her a very particular turn of thinking, and discovers it self even in her house, her gardens, and her furniture. Sir Roger has entertained me an hour together with a description of her country-seat, which is situated in a kind of wilderness, about an hundred miles distant from *London,* and looks like a little enchanted Palace. The rocks about her are shaped into artificial grottoes covered with wood-bines and jessamines. The woods are cut into shady walks, twisted into bowers, and filled with cages of Turtles. The springs are made to run among pebbles, and by that means taught to murmur very agreeably. They are likewise collected into a beautiful Lake, that is inhabited by a couple of Swans, and empties itself by a little rivulet which runs through a green meadow, and is known in the family by the name of The purling Stream."

In Leonora's day, few well- or even ill-printed books dispensed with the use of floral engravings on wood or metal for ornamental divisions, an inherited tradition that was now becoming too stereotyped and unimaginative. But occasionally we run across a book, like Thomson's *Orpheus Caledonius,* 1733, where the convention seems to have been given fresh thought, resulting in an individual series of blocks, some signed with the maker's initials (in this case F?rancis H?offman). A few handsomely printed works also carry finely engraved initial capitals, like the Prior folio already inspected. By the middle of the century, however, the conventional cuts were giving way to the use of printers' "flowers," which harmonized better with the lighter types of Caslon, and which that founder had made available in an abundance of extraordinarily attractive examples, eminently serviceable because of their flexibility in inexhaustible combination. They are interchangeable with type and could be so handled by the compositor.

They are descended, in fact, from an ancient and honorable tradition inaugurated by the early Venetian printers, who evolved them from Moorish motives. Caslon was not at all slavish in his

inventions, and his flowers have received memorable praise from
W. A. Dwiggins, who wrote: "Excellent as single spots, the Caslon
flowers multiply their beauties when composed in bands or borders
as ornamentation for letter-press. They then become a true flower-
ing of the letter forms—as though particular groups of words had
been told off for special ornamental duty and had blossomed at
command into intricate, but always typographical patterns." These
are the graceful decorations one frequently finds in the little books
of poetry published by the Dodsleys in the forties, fifties, and
sixties, printed usually, I believe, by Woodfall or John Hughs.
They appear to advantage in Dodsley's *Collection* and in the later
editions of Shenstone's collected poems. Why their vogue was so
brief in England is not easy to guess. They were developed with
enthusiasm and inspiration by Fournier during these same years,
and in his fertile hands became perhaps the most conspicuous
feature of French printing for many years. But in England their
use declined to the vanishing point from about 1770 onward, and
in 1771 Luckombe predicted their disappearance on the simple
ground that they took time to devise and compositors were not
paid extra to work out ways of using them in "floating" combinations. "It is feared," he wrote, "that Head-pieces, Facs, and Tail-
pieces of Flowers will not long continue. . . . But this might be
remedied, were Printers to recompense the Compositor for his
painful application; and then to preserve the substance of his
invention intire, for occasional use." The Caslons display some of
these combinations in their specimen books.

A MORE direct invocation of nature was the use of scenes, engraved usually on copper but now and again—less elegantly—in
"wooden cuts." Few authors would object to an attempt to enhance the appeal of their work by such means; and, of course,
many a book, pedagogical or scientific in aim, absolutely required
it. For example, the system of Comenius, in *Orbis Pictus* and other
manuals thumbed by generations of school children, depended
essentially on pictorial identification.

A class that was perennially felt to invoke the assistance of the
illustrator was the Æsopic Fable—a *genre* so significantly congenial
to the eighteenth-century way of thought, to its typifying, per-

sonifying, generalizing habit, and also so abundant, that it is really curious not to find whole shelves of dissertations on it. Æsop was one of the first authors read by schoolboys learning Latin: a very paradigm of the *utile-dulce,* and in one language or another he continued to be read throughout life. The Oxford University Press in 1698 did not scorn to publish a scholarly edition with texts in Greek, Latin, Hebrew, and Arabic. Who can doubt that early indoctrination by Æsop helped to form Dr. Johnson's lifelong habit of homely animal comparisons, to vivify his discourse? These characteristic *mots* of his are often unhatched fables: they always rest on a misuse of natural faculties, some disturbance of propriety in nature —the egregious cow, the bull out of context, the dog that walks elate.

Æsop in English was likely to appear in a small size, with a cut for each fable. Croxall's version, first appearing in 1722, 8vo, and often reprinted in 12mo, has oval woodcuts in oblong picture frames, crude enough by later standards but now and then suggesting rural scenery with sensitive charm (Fig. 15). But the

Figure 15. Woodcut illustrating Samuel Croxall's *Æsop* (1722), Fable 50, "The Oak and the Reed."

apotheosis of this style of illustration comes in the work of Thomas Bewick, who contributed to editions of the fables of Gay and others in the seventies and eighties, but whose exquisite art was most perfectly set in Bulmer's and Martin's quarto reprints

of Goldsmith, Parnell, and Somerville in the nineties (Fig. 16).
Fables by modern authors were inclined to strive for elegance, and
occasionally succeeded. Edward Moore's *Fables for the Female Sex*,
8vo 1744, with Hayman's pictures engraved by Grignion, Mosley,
and others, has one or two attractive plates; and Dr. Cosens'
Economy of Beauty, a quarto dedicated to the Princess Royal,
Charlotte Augusta, 1777, tries hard to be politely exalted. Wilkie's
Fables, 1768, illustrated by Wale, is less pretentious but not more
successful. Gay's *Fables*, for the most part feebly illustrated, were
reprinted as often as sixty times before the end of the century.

The crowd of French and Dutch illustrators and engravers who
fill the scene up to 1740 give ground in the middle decades to
native artists. Without forgetting Vertue, Kent, Hogarth, and
Hayman, who arrived early, we are not greatly surprised that in
1738, instead of an Englishman, Tonson employed Vanderbank
and Vandergucht for the aristocratic, extra-illustrated quarto *Don
Quixote*. Foreign engravers like Gravelot and Grignion held their
lead beyond the mid-century; but the natives, John Pine and
George Bickham, produced masterly work in the thirties. Fourd-
rinier did the heavily illustrated duodecimo sixth edition of Dryden's *Vergil*, 1730, as he did also Gay's *Fables*, after the designs
of Kent and others; and on the whole one must call them dread-
fully cluttered and ungainly. The little anonymous head-pieces
for the Pastorals and Georgics, in the same Dryden, are far more
appealing. And in general, apart from scientific illustration, like
the hand-colored plates in the *History of Rare Plants* by Cambridge's Professor of Botany, John Martyn, and the same scholar's
uncommonly handsome quarto edition of Vergil's *Bucolicks*
printed by Reily for Thomas Osborne in 1749; or from the great
antiquarian folios on classical architecture (as the works by Chambers, Adams, Soane, Dawkins, and Wood)—apart from such, one
has the impression that most of the best illustration even to the last
decade of the century was not full page, but decorative work on a
small scale. Most (I think) of the illustrating of novels, in the way
of selected scenes, is execrable jobbery—Hayman's *Pamela* pictures
being a charming exception—and this is perhaps equally true of
the cheaper editions of poetry. But after 1780, thanks in part to
the stimulus of the Royal Academy and to Boydell's financial
encouragement, with better masters, better opportunities for learn-

THE TRAVELLER.

Remote, unfriended, melancholy, slow,

Or by the lazy Scheld, or wandering Po;

Or onward, where the rude Carinthian boor

Against the houseless stranger shuts the door;

Or where Campania's plain forsaken lies,

A weary waste, expanding to the skies;

Where-e'er I roam, whatever realms to see,

My heart, untravell'd, fondly turns to thee:

Still to my Brother turns, with ceaseless pain,

And drags at each remove a lengthening chain.

Figure 16.   Thomas Bewick's wood engraving for W. Bulmer's edition
of *Poems by Goldsmith and Parnell* (1795).

ing, the whole scene was rapidly transformed and uplifted. Flax-man was inventing his classical designs for line engravings; that gentle Quaker, Stothard, was creating his sensitive vignettes; John Bell was paying good prices for the best work he could buy, for his engraved titles and frontispieces to popular editions of the poets; Fuseli and Blake were exploring new spiritual and emotional paths; and Bartolozzi was producing competent engravings of first-class painting on the grand scale.

Some favorite works, appearing in their successive dresses decade after decade tell us much about currents of taste, not only in print-ing but also as to changes of attitude toward an author and his subject matter. *Paradise Lost* has been interestingly followed from this point of view by Collins Baker. As he observes, the work of successive artists reveals the conception of Milton's theme chang-ing from the spirit of literal acceptance of biblical revelation to the grandiose and theatrical interpretations of the same scenes by the Royal Academicians like Westall in Bulmer's *de luxe* edition, by Fuseli and Hamilton, by Blake and John Martin. But because of Milton's cosmic and religious subject, his poem is perhaps less revealing of contemporary taste than more mundane and homely classics.

Such a work is Thomson's *Seasons*. In its first collected form, it was a dignified quarto, graced with illustrations by the fashionable Kent (Plate I). These pictured, in their lower halves, faintly Clau-dian landscapes, trees in the foreground on either side, water in the middle distance, hills in the background, human figures near at hand disposed in typical attitudes, with classical buildings be-yond. The skies are filled with allegorical beings in troupes, Zephyr and Flora, Apollo and Boreas, with the signs of the zodiac figured against a bare strip of heaven. Soon after, the separately printed parts, given a general title page, were issued in octavo with a plate apiece, depicting statuesque personifications of the several seasons, after the marbles in the gardens of Versailles. Various redactions of these ideas appeared during the succeeding decades. *The Col-lected Works of Thomson*, in two volumes 8vo, 1763, barren of typographical ornament, contains plates for each season, again after Kent, unacknowledged, and with a plate each for the other major poems, signed by Wale.

But in the final decade of the century, this world is swept away.

The Seasons has become a national, secular monument, on which
is lavished all the splendor of which fine printing is now capable.
The Dedication, to the Queen, is engraved from T. Tomkins'
script, in the round and highly flourished English writing-master's
hand. Bensley's title page (Fig. 17) is a handsome show piece, with
black letter, shaded letter, Roman and Italic letter of many sizes.
The name of the type cutter, Vincent Figgins, appears on it along
with Bensley's, the two engravers', the publisher's, and the illustrators' names. The half- and full-page plates are after paintings
done especially for the work by William Hamilton, R.A., engraved
by Tomkins and another academician, Bartolozzi. Hamilton's paintings are mainly of deep woodland scenery, filled with romantic
and picturesque appreciation, and based on sentimental or melo-
dramatic passages in the poem (Plate III). The cultivated nature
of Shenstone's generation has been left behind. There are no urns
nor spires nor bogus ruins among these woods, and the nymphs
that inhabit here are willowy Regency Beauties, whom satinwood
furniture would more befit than a gnarled root, even if moss-
covered, for a seat. They are closer to Byron than to Fielding. The
type face relies on its own majesty. There are no shifts of type,
except in the running heads; the capitalization is according to
modern conventions. It may be confidently asserted that there is
not a detail in the work, whether in control of paper, ink, letter
press, illustrations, or of style and attitude toward subject matter,
poet, or print, that would have been possible—even conceivable—
when the poem first appeared. To such a degree had the span of a
single lifetime transformed the world of printing.

Bartolozzi and Tomkins were "historical engravers" to Her
Majesty but it is a question whether book illustration for works of
imagination really tried at any time during the century to be other
than immediately contemporary. In the collected edition of Pope,
1751, generously illustrated by a number of artists, Samuel Wale,
picturing Pope's modernization of Chaucer's tale of January and
May, gives us a glimpse of an Italianate garden, with balustrades,
pilasters, ordered cypresses, and a paved rectangular pool. But
what did a medieval garden truly look like? and was Pope's poem
medieval? and was January so much medieval as antique? B.
Sprague Allen holds up to laughter for their Palladian décor the
illustrations in Rowe's and Theobald's editions of Shakespeare. To

THE
SEASONS,

BY

James Thomson.

ILLUSTRATED WITH

ENGRAVINGS

BY

F. BARTOLOZZI, R. A. AND P. W. TOMKINS,

Hiftorical Engravers to Their Majefties;

FROM

ORIGINAL PICTURES

PAINTED FOR THE WORK

BY

W. HAMILTON, R. A.

LONDON:

PRINTED FOR P. W. TOMKINS, NEW BOND-STREET.

THE LETTER-PRESS BY T. BENSLEY.

THE TYPES BY V. FIGGINS.

MDCCXCVII.

Figure 17. Title page of Bensley's edition *de luxe* of Thomson's *The Seasons* (1797). Greatly reduced in reproduction.

be sure, it requires an effort for us to imagine Malcolm and Donalbain lying in chambers designed by Sir William of that ilk, and it is odd to see Macbeth appearing at the witches' cavern in a Ramillies tricorne, wig, and frogged waistcoat. But the problem was not a simple one. The works themselves were little concerned with antiquarian verisimilitude, and Elizabethan attire, which satisfied Shakespeare ("Cut my lace, Charmian"), was equally wide of the mark. Moreover, the illustrators had their eye on contemporary theatrical performances, which set no more store by historical accuracy than Shakespeare himself, and did not hesitate to reconstitute the plays to suit modern taste. If it was better thus to soften their gothicism in living representation, for what class of reader should an artist strive to hammer it home? There were not then two audiences, one of readers and one of playgoers. Those who saw would wish to read, and would bring visual impressions to the reading, not readily to be cancelled out by antiquarian illustrators, if such there had been. Hayman's pictures in Hanmer's edition are thus valuable evidence of contemporary theatrical convention. The point of publishing octavo editions of Shakespeare, with illustrations, was to make a popular playwright still more popular and easily understood. Only gradually, as Antony Sampson interestingly shows in his article, "The Printing of Shakespeare's Plays," do we see the playwright climbing (in print) through the laureate sanction of Pope's handsome quartos, and the more stately accolade of Hanmer's Oxford edition gowned in the types of Dr. Fell, through the annotated editions of the textual editors, scholars addressing scholars with scholarly concern but no concern for surface charm; to the ultimate splendor of the Boydell Shakespeare, 1792–1802—a rise which symbolizes and epitomizes the changing attitude of the reading public toward this author, and his final romantic deification. This last edition was printed by Bulmer at the Shakespeare Press, from Martin's type especially cast for the work, and, as all the world knows, with a series of illustrations designed and engraved by the acknowledged masters of the day. Here at last we do note occasional gestures, token payments, of regard for historical truth and propriety in the appearance of slashed hose and gothic architecture. But stagecraft too had now finally begun to defer to historical criticism; and with few exceptions these

artists, "historical painters" though they were, remained imaginatively tethered to the contemporary theater.

Had Blake been admitted to this company, he would as we know
have refused to be so bound. His designs for *Midsummer Night's
Dream* and *Macbeth* show him the inhabitant of another world.
His treatment, again, of other men's texts, like Blair's *Grave*, and
Young's *Night Thoughts* (Plate IV), not to mention the *Book of
Job* and *Dante*, prove, if proof were needed, that his ideas of book
illustration cannot be traced from any line that we have been pursuing. His own works are in a world that antedates printing; but
neither do they derive from any medieval tradition of illuminated
manuscripts. Had Blake not existed, he could never have been, as
the current fashion would phrase it, extrapolated. The most we
can aver of him is that he chose the most plausible moment at which
to appear. As he stems from no tradition, so he established none,
and his influence on the course of printing is nil. "Typographic
tradition," Stanley Morison has declared, "is the embodiment of
the common-sense of generations." This is a kind of sense to which
Blake never cared to lay claim.